A COMMENTARY

ON

The Epistle of James

BY

GUY N. WOODS

Other Books by the Same Author:

COMMENTARY ON JOHN

A COMMENTARY ON THE EPISTLES OF PETER, JOHN AND JUDE

THE SECOND COMING AND OTHER SERMONS

SERMONS ON SALVATION

HOW TO USE THE GREEK NEW TESTAMENT

QUESTIONS AND ANSWERS—OPEN FORUM

GOSPEL ADVOCATE

P. O. Box 150

Nashville, Tenn. 37202

1991

ISBN 0-89225-012-7
Paperback ISBN 0-89225-444-0

TO
ALL SINCERE STUDENTS OF
THE SACRED WRITINGS

A GENERAL INTRODUCTION

This volume completes the Gospel Advocate Series of Commentaries on the New Testament. It is the authorized and official Commentary on James in this Series.

In this book the scholarly author has maintained and, indeed, raised the high standard of excellence established in his earlier *Commentary on Peter, John and Jude.* The thousands who have read, with pleasure and profit, this volume will be delighted with the Author's *Commentary on the Epistle of James.*

This is a *rare* book, not that it is old or scarce, but in that it is eminently worth a careful reading and mature study. It is a book that will be read and cherished by grateful students hundreds of years from now.

Brotherhood material on James is relatively scarce. This volume will fill a long-felt need. We send it forth with a feeling of great satisfaction, believing that it will help thousands to a better understanding and appreciation of the "Practical Epistle of James."

It is our confident expectation and prediction that this volume will enjoy a wide circulation.

B. C. GOODPASTURE

PREFACE

Since the appearance of "A Commentary on the Epistles of Peter, John and Jude," by this writer, and published by the Gospel Advocate Company, just ten years ago, hundreds of requests have come to us urging the publication of a similar Commentary on the Epistle of James, thus completing the Gospel Advocate Series of Commentaries on the New Testament books. During this period the author of these notes has preached in approximately three hundred and seventy meetings throughout the land, and he can scarcely recall a meeting in which inquiries regarding the production of such a volume were not received. In harmony with its plan to complete its series the Gospel Advocate Company now makes available this final volume. It was produced by invitation of B. C. Goodpasture, Editor of the *Gospel Advocate* and President of the Gospel Advocate Company.

The same general method which characterized "A Commentary on the Epistles of Peter, John and Jude" has been followed in this work. In this, as in that effort, we have followed the usual methods of ascertaining to the best of our ability the mind and meaning of the sacred writer; and have then set it out in simple, unadorned English. The work has been prepared for *the average student* of the Scriptures and not the specialist or cloistered scholar. In writing these notes we have sought always to keep in mind those whose time is limited; who are without access to the sources relied on by scholars; who are sincerely desirous of knowing what is taught in the book of James; who are not acquainted with, or interested in, the *denominational theologians* of the age; and who would not be edified, but merely bewildered, by an array of their various and often false opinions.

The Scripture text followed is that of the American Standard Version. At the close of the commentary will be found an interlinear translation containing the Greek text, a literal translation, and the King James' Version, of the book of James. This is from Berry's Interlinear Greek New Testament, and used by special arrangement with the Zondervan Publishing House, the last known publishers of that work. The student will find this to be a valuable addition to the Commentary. From it he will be able, at a glance, to see the Greek text, a literal English equivalent of each word therein, and the King James' Translation.

We send this work out, conscious of its many imperfections, regretful that we are unable to produce a better Commentary on the Epistle of James, and with the earnest hope and prayer that it will direct all who consult it into a clearer and deeper knowledge of the "Gospel of Common Sense," as the Epistle of James has been aptly styled; and if it shall, in some measure, accomplish this, we shall feel that the tremendous task involved in its production has been fully justified.

GUY N. WOODS

P. O. Box 150
Nashville, TN 37202

CONTENTS

10   CONTENTS

INTRODUCTION
BY WHOM WRITTEN

The General Epistle of James was written by the man whose name it bears: "James, a servant of God and of the Lord Jesus Christ. . . ." (James 1: 1.)   This, however, does not determine his identity fully, inasmuch as there are at least *three* men prominently mentioned in the New Testament named James: (1) James, son of Zebedee and Salome, brother of John and one of the apostles of the Lord (Matt. 4: 21; Mark 1: 19; Luke 5: 10); (2) James the Less, son of Alphaeus, and also an apostle (Matt. 10: 3; Mark 3: 18; Luke 6: 15; Acts 1: 13); (3) James, a brother in the flesh of Christ (Matt. 13: 55; Mark 6: 3; Gal. 1: 18, 19).

Four women were present at the crucifixion who were vitally interested in the events there occurring.   These were Mary, the mother of Jesus; Salome, mother of James and John and wife of Zebedee; Mary, wife of Alphaeus (or Clopas), and mother of James the Less; and Mary Magdalene.   Three of these women, Mary, mother of Jesus, Salome, and Mary, mother of James the Less, had sons named James.   The author of James was evidently one of these three men.

He was *not* James, son of Zebedee; this disciple and apostle suffered martyrdom at the hand of Herod soon after the church was established, and long before the book of James was written. (Acts 12: 1, 2.)   He was *not* James son of Alphaeus, for that James was an *apostle*.   (Matt. 10: 2-4.)   The brothers of Christ —sons of Mary and Joseph—did not believe in him until *after* his resurrection (John 7: 5); obviously, James, son of Alphaeus, could not have been an apostle and an unbeliever at the same time. Of those mentioned in the New Testament by this name, but one other "James" remains who could have penned the Epistle; James, son of Mary and Joseph, brother in the flesh of our Lord and of "Jude," author of another New Testament book designated *Jude*.

The foregoing view is, on the whole, the most reasonable of the theories advanced regarding the identity of the author of James. We shall, however, set out, for the consideration of the reader, other views which are advocated in order that he may weigh for himself the evidence offered. Actually, the issue turns on the identity of "the brethren" of the Lord (Matt. 13: 55), "the Lord's brother" (Gal. 1: 18, 19). The "James" in the list of those thus designated was evidently the author of the book bearing this name.

What was his relationship to Christ?

One theory alleges that these men—James, Joses, Simon and Judas—were cousins of Jesus, children of a woman named Mary, who was a sister of Mary the mother of Christ! On this assumption, James, "the son of Alphaeus," is to be regarded as the same as James, "the son of Clopas," Alphaeus and Clopas being names derived from the same source, and thus the view is advanced that the James thus mentioned was one of the apostles. In answer to the objection that the brothers of Christ, in the flesh, did not believe on him during his public ministry and were not apostles, it is contended that the word "brethren" by which "James and Joses and Simon and Judas" are identified in Matt. 13: 55, does not necessarily describe the relationship which we ascribe to the term *brothers* today; and, that in reality, they were simply cousins of Jesus—children of a sister of Our Lord's mother, named Mary! This is the Roman Catholic theory (and advocated by many scholars of the Episcopal Church, and the Church of England), and obviously contrived to avoid an insuperable objection to their doctrine of Perpetual Virginity—the theory that Joseph and Mary had no children following the birth of Jesus. The objections which may be levelled at this theory are numerous and weighty indeed. (a) If it is conceded that the names Clopas and Alphaeus derive from the same source, these are distinct appellations and there is no reason to assume that in this, or in any other instance, they refer to the same individual. (b) The theory necessitates the conclusion that in John 19: 25, when it is said that "There stood by the cross of Jesus his mother, and his mother's sister, Mary the wife of Clopas, and Mary Magdalene," there are but three women mentioned, and that "his mother's sister" is identified in this text as Mary "the wife of Clopas." It appears certain that there were four women mentioned in this passage, and arranged in two pairs: (1) the mother of Jesus and his mother's sister; (2) Mary the wife of Clopas, and Mary Magdalene. (c) The theory requires one to believe that *two* sisters were *both* named Mary by the same parents, and were both called *by this name!* Names are assigned for the purpose of distinguishing one individual from another; such a conclusion as the theory necessitates is impossible and absurd. (d) The contention that the word *adelphos* (brother) means cousin is without lexical support, or New Testament example. Moreover, there is a word for cousin (*anepsios*) occurring in the Greek text of Col. 4: 10. (e) In none of the lists of apostles is there any suggestion that two or more of the brothers of the Lord were apostles; indeed, in Acts 1: 13, 14, and 1 Cor. 9: 5, they are expressly differentiated. (f) the most weighty objection to this theory of all, however, is to be seen in the affirmation of John 7: 5: "For neither did his brethren believe on him." It is evident that the fleshly brothers of Jesus did not accept his claim to deity during his public ministry; and that they became his disciples only after his death and resurrection. Yet, if the theory be true, two of his brothers (James and Jude) were among the apostles. We believe that these considerations eliminate the possibility that James, "the brother of the Lord," is the same person as James, the "son of Alphaeus" (or Clopas), one of the apostles.

A second theory, subscribed to by scholars of the Greek Orthodox church, is that "the brethren" of Jesus were sons of Joseph by a former wife. Objections to this view are many. (a) There is not the slightest hint in all of the sacred writings that Joseph had contracted a prior marriage. (b) This theory, as does the foregoing one, requires an arbitrary and unwarranted meaning to be assigned to the "brethren," in the text. (c) On this assumption, these "brethren" were not related to Christ *at all!* Jesus was not related to Joseph by ties of the flesh; *they* (on this hypothesis) would bear no kinship to Mary, mother of Christ; so they would sustain no kinship with him whatsoever. Yet, the text, in simple, direct fashion, describes the members thereof in the same manner a family would be described by us today: "Is not this the carpenter's son? is not his mother called Mary? and his brethren, James, and Joses, and Simon, and Judas? And his sisters, are they not with us?" (Matt. 13: 55, 56.)

A third view, and that advocated herein, is that the "brethren" of Christ mentioned were indeed half-brothers of Jesus, sons of Joseph and Mary, born to them following the birth of Christ, one of whom was James, another Jude, both of whom wrote New Testament Epistles. (a) References to the "brethren" of Jesus are most naturally to be taken in the usual and ordinary import of the term: "After this he went down to Capernaum, he, and his mother, and his brethren, and his disciples; and they continued there not many days." (John 2: 12.) "While he was yet speaking to the multitudes, behold, his mother and his brethren stood without, seeking to speak to him." (Matt. 12: 46.) (b) When Jesus came "into his own country" and taught in the synagogue, he encountered opposition on the part of his country-men; and it was on this occasion that the multitudes identified him as the son of Mary and brother of James, Joses, Simon and Judas (lengthened form of the name Jude). Thereupon Jesus said: "A prophet is not without honor, but in his own country, *and among his own kin*, and in his own house." (Mark 6: 4.) (c) To regard these brethren as sons of Mary and Joseph and hence half-brothers of Jesus is in harmony with the usual significance of the terms used; it is such a view as would ordinarily be accepted by one not possessed of a theory to defend (such as Perpetual Virginity) on reading the passage for the first time. (d) The doctrine of Perpetual Virginity, the chief reason for adopting the views above refuted, was not espoused until centuries after the apostolic age. (e) Ancient writers of near the apostolic age subscribed to the view which we have advanced here. Hegesippus, writing in the last quarter of the second century, in a remarkable statement quoted by Eusebius (Hist. II. 23), identifies James as "the brother of the Lord," and distinguishes him from the apostles.

But, did not Paul say, "Then after three years I went up to Jerusalem to see Peter, and abode with him fifteen days. But other of the apostles saw I none, save James the Lord's brother"? (Gal. 1: 18.) Does this not identify James, "the Lord's brother," *as an apostle?* It should be remembered that, following the early days of Christianity, and long before the end of the apostolic age, the word *apostle* was applied to numerous individuals not of the original twelve, e.g., Barnabas (Acts 14: 14); Andronicus, Junias and others (Rom. 16: 7). (b) The marginal reading of Gal. 1: 19, in the American Standard Version has the phrase, "but only" thus making the passage to mean, "I saw none of the apostles; I saw only James, the Lord's brother."

We may, therefore, properly conclude that (1) there is no reason whatsoever for assuming that James, "the Lord's brother," is to be identified with the son of Alphaeus (or Clopas), or that he was one of the *original* apostles. (2) There is absolutely no basis for the view that "the brethren of the Lord" were *cousins* of Jesus and sons of a sister of Mary, named Mary. (3) James, author of the Epistle which bears his name, was a son of Mary and Joseph, a half-brother of Jesus, and a member of a family that had in it five boys and at least two girls: "Is not this the carpenter's son? is not his mother called Mary? and his brethren, James, and Joseph, and Simon, and Judas? And his *sisters*, are they not all with us?" (Matt. 13: 35.)

The author of James was thus not associated with Christ in his public ministry, nor did he acknowledge the deity of the Lord until after the resurrection. It appears from Acts 1: 13, 14 that it was this event which brought all of the brothers of Jesus, in the flesh, to a recognition of his identity as the Son of God. It is there affirmed that "his brethren" (the sons of Mary and Joseph, Matt. 13: 55, 56) continued with the apostles and others in the "upper room" in the city of Jerusalem. He was privileged to have a vision of the risen Lord (1 Cor. 15: 5, 7), and soon rose to prominence in the early church. If the rendering in the text (in contrast with the margin) of Gal. 1: 18, 19, be correct, he received the title of *apostle* (literally, one sent out), as did other faithful disciples, e.g., Barnabas, Andronicus, Junias, and others. He presided at the council held in Jerusalem and delivered a speech on that occasion (Acts 15: 13) and was a part of the company which received Paul on the return of the apostle from his third missionary journey (Acts 21: 18). Eusebius tells us that he was called "The Just" because of the many virtues which he possessed; and this same historian, "the Father of Church History," preserves a fragment from Hegesippus, a Jewish historian, that James was "wont to go alone into the sanctuary, and used to be found prostrate on his knees, and asking forgiveness for the people, so that his knees grew hard and worn, like a camel's, because he was ever kneeling and worshipping God, and asking forgiveness for the people."

Though a brother of Christ, in the flesh, he chose to identify himself simply as "a servant of God and of the Lord Jesus Christ" (James 1: 1), and to urge acceptance of his message on the grounds of inspiration and truth, rather than only any fleshly relationship to Christ. With Paul he doubtless felt that "we henceforth know no man after the flesh: even though we have known Christ after the flesh, yet now we know him so no more." (2 Cor. 5: 16.)

Traditional reports of his death are conflicting and unreliable, but all bear testimony to a martyr's death for him. He was a great and good man; and the book which bears his name, because of its eminently practical character, continues to be a blessing to mankind.

TO WHOM WRITTEN

The Epistle is addressed to "the twelve tribes which are of the Dispersion." (James 1: 1.) Those thus addressed are not otherwise specifically identified; and there is, therefore, diversity of opinion touching the significance of the phrase, "the Dispersion." The word (*diaspora*) occurs here, in 1 Pet. 1: 1, where it has reference to *spiritual* Israel, the Lord's people, of the areas there designated, and without regard to national or fleshly origins; and in John 7: 35, where it refers to Jews (in the flesh) scattered throughout the Grecian world. The phrases, "the twelve tribes," and "the Dispersion," are, of course, definitely Jewish in background, the details of which are set out in the commentary under James 1: 1. The question turns on whether they are used literally or figuratively here. This matter is discussed in much detail in the comments thereon. On the whole, the most reasonable and satisfactory view of the matter is that the Epistle was addressed to Christians, many of whom were of Jewish descent and perhaps widely scattered.

It is quite certain that it was not addressed to *unbelieving Jews* from repeated statements therein, evidencing the fact that those addressed are Christians (cf. 1: 2, 5, 9, 19; 2: 1, 14; 3: 1; 4: 11; 5: 7, 9, 12, 19), and from the further fact that the writer made no effort to set out the arguments usually made in support of the deity of Christ such as are repeatedly found in the speeches delivered to unbelieving Jews in Acts. The Epistle contains no mention of either the cross of Christ, or his resurrection—unaccountable omissions if the Letter were intended for the edification of Jewish unbelievers. It seems also most unlikely that it was addressed to *unbe-*

lieving Gentiles from the use of the phrases, "the twelve tribes," "the *diaspora*" (1 : 1), "your synagogue" (2 : 2), and other typical Jewish statements; and from the absence of any arguments designed to convince pagans of the One True God, and of His Son, Jesus Christ. In those instances where the writer addresses wicked people, these are directed to apostate members of the church, or are a formal aside (an apostrophe), often characteristic of writers. We thus regard the statement, "the twelve tribes which are of the Dispersion," to be of figurative significance, comparable to Paul's "Israel of God" (Gal. 6: 16), and to embrace Christians, whether of Jewish or Gentile descent.

WHY WRITTEN

Why the Epistle of James was written is closely related to the preceding section, *To Whom Written*, and is to be determined by it. Written, as we believe, and have hereinbefore indicated, to Christians, many of whom—perhaps most of whom—were of Jewish descent as is evidenced by the many references to Israelite worship and history, the purpose of it was evidently intended to instruct them in the Christian faith and to insulate them from all worldly temptation. These to whom James wrote were in frequent contact with rich and arrogant countrymen who continually oppressed and persecuted them, and their trials were thus exceedingly burdensome and painful to bear. It was not always easy to exhibit patience and forbearance in such trying situations and a large measure of Christian endurance and love was necessary in order properly to live the Christian life. Moreover, there were numerous inherent weaknesses and sinful dispositions among them such as censorious judgments, evil speaking, unguarded use of the tongue, a fawning disposition toward the rich and an attitude of contempt toward the poor which needed to be eliminated from their lives before they could reach the plateau of noble, Christ-like conduct. The Epistle of James is not, nor was it intended to be, a formal, theological treatise, but a simple, sober presentation of Christian principles, the design of which was to enable the readers thereof to resist the sins peculiar to the age; to exhort them to live in such fashion as to merit, and to receive the approbation of Christ; and to cope with the difficult social problems then prevailing. The Letter, because of its eminently practical character, has been quite properly styled "the Gospel of Common Sense." It is a wonderful demonstration of the fact that the principles of Christ, properly applied and fully assimilated, will adequately meet the needs of every generation, whatever the period in history may be. This evidences the fact that we of our day do not need a *new* gospel for an alleged modern age; the gospel of Christ, when proclaimed and obeyed in its ancient purity, will satsify every need of every age. It is the only solution of a sick world's problems, the panacea of mankind's diseases, the specific for humanity's ills. It is our solemn and honored obligation to make it available to our age without addition, without subtraction, without modification.

WHEN WRITTEN

It is not possible to fix the *date* of the Epistle of James with any degree of certainty, and any effort to this end is little more than mere surmise. It is usually done by determining the limits in which it could have been written, in the following fashion: James is believed to have been martyred near the middle of the sixth decade of the first century from statements made by Josephus and Hegesippus, which, however are not in agreement, the former placing it about A.D. 62, when he is alleged to have been stoned to death by an edict of Ananus; the latter asserts that it occurred shortly before Jerusalem was beseiged by the Romans, A.D. 65. In either event, it cannot be dated later than A.D. 65. The Letter presupposes that the name Christian had already been given (Acts 11: 26), and was, by the enemies of Christ and Christians, being blasphemed (2: 7). This would eliminate the possibility that it was written before A.D. 40. Moreover, it was after the great wave of persecution which swept over the church under the direction of Saul of Tarsus (Acts 8: 1ff.), because those to whom James wrote were then suffering persecution. In view of the fact that there were fatherless children, needy widows, and poverty-stricken brethren in abundance at the time of writing (James 1: 27; 2: 15-18), and since there was a great dearth in Judaea about A.D. 44, and still another wave of suffering by poor saints in the later years of the fifth decade, the Letter would appear to have been written in one or the other of these periods. Evidently written between A.D. 40 and A.D. 65, and perhaps between A.D. 44 and A.D. 65, any effort to fix a definite date therein is no more than a guess.

Fortunately, the truth of the Epistle and its value to us are not dependent on the date when it was written, and it is therefore not necessary for us to determine it exactly.

WHERE WRITTEN

Though the *place* of composition is not specifically indicated by the author, certain incidental allusions enable us to determine with a fair degree of certainty where the Epistle of James was written. The reference of the writer to the "early and latter rain" (James 5: 7), is a strong intimation that it was written in the land of Palestine. This division of the rainy season was characteristic of the land, and quite familiar to all who lived, or ever had lived, there The "early rain" generally came during the period from October to February, and following the fall sowing of wheat; the "latter rain" came during March and April, and just before the grain ripened for harvest. It was a land which often suffered droughts, with accompanying famines from insufficient rainfall. (5: 7, 8.) There were springs which produced sweet water; others gave forth only salt water (3: 11); and the land produced wine, figs and oil (3: 12). It was a country located near the sea (3: 4; 1: 6); and the dreaded *simoon,* a scorching, blasting east wind from the deserts was well known to author and readers. These considerations point to Palestine as the land in which the author lived; and, inasmuch as James is prominently mentioned in connection with the church in Jerusalem (Acts 15: 13-21), it seems reasonable to suppose that the Epistle was written from Jerusalem in the land of Palestine.

AN ANALYSIS OF THE EPISTLE

The chief aim of the writer was to encourage those to whom he wrote to endure patiently their trials, and to eliminate from their hearts and lives those serious defects which rendered them un-Christian in nature.

Chapter 1. It is the design of trials to make mature Christian character. We may, therefore, rejoice in such. (1: 1-4.) We all need wisdom to recognize this, and God will supply it. (5-7.) Our faith, however, must be stable; and we must not allow outward circumstances to change our status with God. (7-11.) Patient endurance leads to a crown of life. (12.) Evil may not be blamed on God, but results from man's improper desires, and eventually leads to spiritual death. (13-17.) God is the source of all good; and it is through the power of his word that we become spiritual children. (18-21.) But, to be blessed by it, we must both hear and do it; and this includes the practical precepts of Christianity such as providing for the fatherless child and the destitute widow. (22-27.)

Chapter 2. It is sinful to show respect of persons; and to fawn upon the rich and exhibit contempt for the poor is especially reprehensible. (2: 1-4.) There is really more occasion to regard the poor than the rich; the poor are heirs of God's blessings; the rich oppress us and evilly treat us. (5-7) The royal law requires us to treat all alike, and avoid all respect of persons. (8-11.) To obtain mercy, we must be merciful. (12, 13.) Faith, apart from works, is dead; in order to bless us, faith must always be accompanied by obedience to God's commands. (14-26.)

Chapter 3. Teachers have a weighty responsibility. (3: 1.) It is indeed difficult for any of us to control our tongues, and they are possible of great evil. (1-8.) It is absurd to suppose that one is either wise or good who utters curses against others. If what he has is wisdom, it is from below, and not from God. (9-13.) There is a heavenly wisdom and it exhibits itself in kindness toward others and in a life richly filled with good works. (17, 18.)

Chapter 4. Conflicts arise because of improper desire. (4: 1, 2.) Those thus possessed, though ever seeking, are never satisfied; some do not ask God for their needs; others ask, but for the wrong things. (2, 3.) Friendship with the world is enmity with God, and we must ever be on guard lest our lower natures pull us down. (4-6.) The most effective way to do this is to resist the devil and turn to God in humility and contrition. (7-10.) We should avoid all fault-finding and censorious judgments, and not be guilty of attempting to usurp the powers and privileges of God himself. (11, 12.) God must be taken into our plans and purposes, and we should live for today, because we have no assurance that tomorrow will come. (13-17.)

Chapter 5. Let the rich take heed! (5: 1-3.) That which they have obtained by fraud will witness against them in the judgment soon to come upon them. (4-6.) The faithful are to bear

their sufferings patiently, assured that a day of comfort is coming.
(7-11.) They are to avoid unnecessary oaths; they are to find in
prayer and song solace for life's trials and for the expression of its
joys (12-15); the sick are to avail themselves of the miraculous
power of healing then in the hands of the elders of the church (14,
15); all are to confess their faults, and to pray for each other (17,
18); and should a brother fall into sin he is immediately to be assisted in order that his soul may be saved from spiritual and eternal death (19, 20).

A COMMENTARY ON THE
EPISTLE OF JAMES

SECTION 1

THE ADDRESS AND GREETING
1: 1

1 ¹James, a ²servant of God and of the Lord Jesus Christ, to the twelve tribes which are of the Dispersion, ³greeting.

¹Or, *Jacob*
²Gr. *bondservant.*
³Gr. *wisheth joy.*

---

1 **James,**—The author of the book which bears his name was the son of Mary (the mother of our Lord), and Joseph, and thus one of the fleshly brothers of Christ. The grounds on which this conclusion rest are set out in detail in the Introduction to which the reader is referred. It is evident that Mary, the mother of Christ, had at *least* seven children, among whom were five sons and not fewer than two daughters: "Is not this the carpenter's son? is not his mother called Mary? and his brethren, James, and Joseph, and Simon and Judas? And his sisters, are they not all with us?" (Matt. 13: 55.) We thus learn that the brothers of Christ, in the flesh, were James (author of the Epistle of James), Joseph, Simon and Judas, lengthened form of Jude, author of New Testament book bearing that name. Jude, indeed, is identified as the "brother of James." (Jude 1.) Jesus, James, Joseph, Simon and Judas were the five sons; and, inasmuch as *daughters* (plural) are mentioned, there must have been at least two girls in the family thus establishing the fact that there were at least seven children born to Mary. James was, therefore, along with Jude, a half brother of Christ. Reasons for identifying James with the family of Mary and Christ, and his activities in the early church are set out in detail in the Introduction. (Gal. 1: 19.) It is a remarkable fact that our Lord's brothers in the flesh did not acknowledge his deity during his public ministry. (John 7: 5.) It appears that their acceptance of him as the Son of God dates from his resurrection from the dead.

James (Greek *Iakobos,* pronounced ee-ack'-o-bos), is the equivalent of the Old Testament name *Jacob,* and of common usage among the Jewish people. It comes into our language from the Italian *Giacomo.* Other forms in other languages are *Iago* (Spanish), *Hamish* (Scotch), *Jacques* (French), and *Xayme* (Portuguese). The Hebrew form, widely appearing in the Old Testament, is *Yahakov* (pronounced yah-ak-obe') and means *heel-catcher.* In Gen. 25: 26, the definition in the margin reads, "One that takes by the heel or supplants." The name was evidently a favored one among the Jews for many centuries and was borne by at least three prominent characters of the New Testament: James, brother of the Lord (Gal. 1: 19); James, Son of Zebedee and brother of John (Matt. 4: 21; Mark 5: 37); James, the Less, son of Alphaeus (Matt. 10: 3).

Of the last years and death of James, brother of the Lord and author of the New Testament book of James, we have no reliable data. Statements appearing in Josephus, Hegesippus, the Clementine Homilies and other apocryphal sources are open to question regarding the genuineness and authenticity of the passages, the writers too far removed themselves to supply reliable testimony regarding the matters about which they wrote, or obviously distorted and false. Eusebius, not without reason often called "the Father of Church History," informs us that James was designated "The Just" because of his many admirable virtues thus evidencing the fact that he was highly esteemed by his contemporaries.

a servant of God and of the Lord Jesus Christ,—It is especially noteworthy that the author, though a brother of Christ in the flesh, makes no mention of this fact in the Epistle, choosing rather to identify himself simply as a *servant* of God and of Christ. For the probable reasons which prompted this omission, see the Introduction. It is significant that of all the New Testament Epistles, only those which were written by brothers of Christ (James and Jude) have no other identification of the authors save (a) the names; (b) the designation *servant.* Paul occasionally used the term, but associated the word *apostle* with it (Tit. 1: 1; Rom. 1: 1); and Peter described himself as a servant and apostle (2 Pet. 1: 1). The word *servant* is from the Greek *doulos,* a term not easily translated into English, means one "who gives oneself up wholly to another will," serving to the complete disregard of one's own selfish interests.

Our English word *servant* weakens the idea down to one who serves for the wages paid and thus falls far short of the idea of joyous and voluntary submission of one's will to another, inherent in the original word. Our English word *slave* more nearly suggests the idea, *except* for the unwilling and involuntary service indicated in it. If, in contemplating the significance of the term, we can eliminate from the word *slave* the suggestion of unwillingness involved, we have the meaning of the word *doulos* exactly. The American Standard margin approaches it with the word *bondservant*. (Rom. 1:1; James 1:1.)

The faithful *doulos* (servant), far from being a mere hireling, and interested only in the wages to be paid for services rendered, is bound to his master for life in joyous, happy submission in a relationship where his interests and those of his master's are so indissolubly joined that indolence, faithlessness, inattention to duty result in loss not only to the master but to him as well! God's great men, through the ages, have gladly worn this designation of faithful obedience, unquestioned humility, and unswerving loyalty. Among the Old Testament characters who are thus described are Jeremiah (7:25), Amos (3:7), Isaiah (20:3), Abraham, Isaac and Jacob (Deut. 9:7), Joshua and Caleb (Josh. 1:2; Num. 14:24) and Moses (1 Kings 8:53), Paul (Phil. 1:1), Peter (2 Pet. 1:1), and all faithful believers (1 Pet. 2:16), rejoiced to be "bondservants" of God and of Christ in the apostolic age. Inasmuch as Christians are "bought with a price" (the precious blood of our Lord) (1 Cor. 6:20; 7:23; Acts 20:28; 1 Pet. 1:18), it is fitting that the followers of Christ should be thus designated, and should regard all of their personal interests as having been submerged wholly in the interests of Christ.

James declared himself to be a "servant of God and of the Lord Jesus Christ." *God* here refers to the Father, and is to be distinguished from his Son, "the Lord Jesus Christ," thus very clearly indicating the fact that they are *two* persons in refutation of the theory which alleges that they are but one. We serve God only when we serve Christ also, there being no other approach to the Father: "Jesus saith unto him, I am the way, and the truth, and the life: no one cometh unto the Father, but by me." (John 14: 6.) All are servants of God because of creation and providence; but Christians are servants of Christ by virtue of redemption. "And ye are not your own; for ye were bought with a price: glorify God therefore in your body." (1 Cor. 6: 19, 20.) Privileged thus to serve our Creator and His Son we should ever seek to render to him the highest and best service of which we are capable. *Doulos,* translated servant in our text, derives from the verb *deo,* to bind. We are bound in the closest possible relationship with God and Christ; and we should, therefore, be exceedingly careful that we do not profane the Father and His Son through improper conduct. Moroever, there is much significance in the fact that the Spirit chose the word *doulos* (one born a slave), rather than *andrapodon* (one made a slave) to indicate the relation of Christians to Christ and to God. It is a relationship which begins in the new birth and which we are privileged to maintain through life. And, there is great comfort in the realization that a *slave* is free of worries regarding food, shelter and raiment—all of which are provided. Jesus said: "Be not therefore anxious, saying, What shall we eat? or, What shall we drink? or, Wherewithal shall we be clothed? For after all these things do the Gentiles seek; for your heavenly Father knoweth that ye have need of all these things. But seek ye first his kingdom, and his righteousness; *and all these things shall be added unto you.*" (Matt. 6: 31-33.)

to the twelve tribes which are of the Dispersion,—This is the address of the Epistle. Having identified himself, and having indicated his relationship to God and to Christ, the author designates here those to whom he wrote. These were "the twelve tribes" and they are further described as those "which are of the Dispersion." The word "dispersion" from the Greek *diaspora* (pronounced dee-as-por-ah') means *scattered.* The phrase "the twelve tribes" is an exceedingly familiar one to Bible students, and when literally construed has reference to the people of the twelve tribes descended from Jacob (Israel). Here, as indicated in the limiting phrase, are those "which are of the dispersion." Who were they?

The patriarch Abraham, an emigrant from the Ur of the Chaldees, received from God the original promise of a vast posterity and of great blessing (Gen. 17: 1-8) ; and, is therefore, properly regarded as the father of the Chosen People. The promises thus originally made were repeated to Isaac, Abraham's son (Gen. 26: 24), and to Jacob, Isaac's son (Gen. 35: 9-15). At Peniel, where Jacob wrestled with the angel (Gen. 32: 28), his name was changed to Israel (Hebrew yis-raw-ale') a word which means, *power with God*. Jacob (Israel) had twelve sons: "Now the sons of Jacob were twelve: the sons of Leah: Reuben, Jacob's first-born, and Simeon, and Levi, and Judah, and Issachar, and Zebulun; the sons of Rachel: Joseph and Benjamin; and the sons of Bilhah, Rachel's handmaid: Dan and Naphtali; and the sons of Zilpah, Leah's handmaid: Gad and Asher: these are the sons of Jacob, that were born to him in Padan-a-ram." (Gen. 35: 23-26.)

Jacob's descendants formed a vast family variously described as "the house of Israel," "the twelve tribes," or, simply "Israel." The nation was divided genealogically into *tribes,* the tribes into *families*, or clans, and these into *households*. (Josh. 7: 14, 16-18.) The twelve tribes were founded by the twelve sons of Jacob (Israel) who were, in consequence, the tribal heads of their respective groups. There was an exception to this in the case of the sons of Joseph, Ephraim and Manasseh who, having been raised to the position of heads of tribes, were adopted by Jacob as his sons. (Gen. 48: 5.) This arrangement would have made thirteen tribes but only twelve were counted, inasmuch as the tribe of Levi, given the responsibility of conducting the affairs of worship, had no territorial allotment assigned to them, but lived in towns scattered throughout the territory of the other tribes and were supported by tithes from the people of the other tribes. (Ex. 24: 4; Josh. 4: 2; Josh. 13: 14, 33.) In the reckoning of the tribes, Ephraim and Manasseh were included together as the tribe of Joseph. (Josh. 17: 14, 17; Num. 26: 28.) The *twelve tribes* were, therefore, the descendants of Jacob, the people of Israel.

Why are those to whom James addressed his Epistle called "the twelve tribes," instead of the more common designation, "The Jews"? The term *Jew*, properly speaking, may be applied only to the descendants of the tribes of Judah and Benjamin. The more general term for all of Jacob's descendants is *Israel*. The descendants of Abraham are called Hebrews, a term including the Arab

world; the descendants of Jacob are Israelites; the descendants of
the two tribes of the southern kingdom—Judah and Benjamin—
are Jews, from the Hebrew yeh-oo-dee', a Jehudite, that is, a de-
scendant of Judah. Because this tribe constituted by far the greater
portion of the chosen people, following the division of the kingdom
in 975 B.C., the term *Jew* was used to denote all in covenant relationship with God which, of course, included the people of the little
tribe of Benjamin.

Moreover, by no means all of the people of the ten tribes
which, under the leadership of Jeroboam, were induced to follow
him and to adopt a corrupted mode of worship and eventually to
be swallowed up into Assyrian captivity in 721 B.C., thus losing
their tribal identities, abandoned Jehovah; many of these people at-
tached themselves to Judah and continued to worship the God of
their fathers. The Levites, for example, utterly refused to allow
Jeroboam to involve them in the apostate worship he devised; and,
in consequence, they left the cities assigned to them in the territory
of Israel, and thenceforth lived in Judah and Jerusalem. (2
Chron. 11 : 13, 14.) They were indeed, from then on to be most
active in the affairs of the southern kingdom, and were still busily
engaged in performing their duties in connection with the temple
worship at the beginning of the Christian era. (Luke 10: 32.)

The Assyrian captivity was not a single removal accomplished
within a brief period, but consisted of a series of transplantations,
covering a period of 150 years. Tiglath-pileser III, in the reign of
Pekah, king of Israel (about 740 B.C.), carried away the trans-
Jordan tribes (Reuben, Gad, and the half-tribe of Manasseh), and
the people of Galilee. (1 Chron. 5: 26; 2 Kings 15: 29.)
Shalmaneser, king of Assyria, in the reign of Hoshea, king of Israel, on two occasions invaded the realm, laid siege to Samaria,
and carried the people to Assyria. Though the ten tribes ceased to
exist by 721 B.C., as distinct political subdivisions of Israel, not all
of the people suffered their national distinctions to be obliterated.
Some of the people of the ten tribes returned to Judah and com-
mingled with the Jews (Luke 2: 36; Phil. 3: 5); others were permitted to remain in Samaria, where they joined themselves to the
Samaritans and became inveterate enemies of the Jews. Others
were content to live in Assyria, but continued to assert their Isra-

elite characteristics.   (Acts 2: 9; 26: 7.)   These were, of course, exceptions; the majority of the people adopted the idolatrous practices of the peoples among whom they were scattered, intermarried and thus lost their identity.

The Epistle of James is addressed to the twelve tribes "which are of the Dispersion."   Not to all people; not to all the people of the twelve tribes, but only to that portion of the twelve tribes included in the descriptive phrase, "the Dispersion."   We have seen that this word means the *scattered, the dispersed*; and designates the descendants of Jacob who lived *out* of Palestine (then the homeland of the Chosen People).   Then, as now, only a small percentage of the Jews lived in the land of Israel; millions of others were scattered throughout the Gentile world.   Strabo, the Greek geographer, wrote: "It is hard to find a spot in the whole world which is not occupied and dominated by Jews."

These migrations were sometimes voluntary, the restless pioneering spirit of a bold and courageous people urging them forward to new frontiers; but more often than otherwise these transplantations were compulsory.   The history of the Israelite people is replete with instances of great masses of their people being forcibly expelled from the lands in which they formerly dwelt.   Among the most prominent of these was the captivity of the ten tribes by Assyria alluded to above.   (2 Kings 17: 23; 1 Chron. 5: 26.) Another was the Babylonian captivity which involved the Jews of Judah and Benjamin, occurring in 587 B.C., and resulting from the wickedness and rebellion of the people. This captivity involved a period of seventy years, a period prophetically designated by Jeremiah (Jer. 29: 10; 2 Chron. 36: 17-21), but reckoned from the beginning of Babylonian oppression.   A portion of this period was spent under a puppet-ruler in their own land.   Not all of the people were carried away to Babylon; some were left in the land of Palestine, and a governor placed over them by the Babylonians. (2 Kings 25: 22.)   Nor did all of the Jews choose to return to Palestine at the end of their captivity.   We have seen earlier that the people of the Assyrian captivity were absorbed by their captors, thus passing from history as a distinct people.   The Jews in Babylon, however, vigorously resisted all efforts to assimilate them and they maintained their national distinction there where eventually they wielded tremendous power politically, culturally, and socially. It is indeed affirmed by the historians that the Jews in Babylon attained to such eminence and exercised such great powers that at one time Mesopotamia was under Jewish rule. Babylon provided for the Jews the proper cultural atmosphere for learning and letters, and it was there that the monumental Babylonian Talmud, a sixty volume exposition of the laws of the Jews, was produced. While Josephus, the Jewish historian, wrote his *Wars of the Jews*, the first edition was published in Aramaic, rather than in Greek, and was circulated among the educated Jews in Babylon. (It should be observed that reference is to the land of Babylon, not to the great city which bore that name, but which suffered destruction under divine decree. Dan. 5 : 1-30.)

Many Jews moved to the land of Egypt in the days of Nebuchadnezzar. (2 Kings 25 : 26.)

When Jerusalem fell to the Romans in 63 B.C., numbers of Jews were carried as slaves to Rome and, because of their persistence in carrying out their religious ritual, they made poor slaves and were, in consequence, freed. For a time they were segregated in quarters beyond the Tiber river, but they gradually spread over the city and their influence was often felt. For this reason they were often in conflict with their rulers and suffered frequent banishment. But they always returned.

The requirements of business and commerce likewise afforded occasion for wide diffusion of the Jews and wherever business was transacted they were there. On that memorable Pentecost Day of the establishment of the church (Acts 2), Jews were present in Jerusalem for the feast from Parthia, Media, Elam, Mesopotamia, Cappadocia, Pontus, Asia, Phrygia, Pamphylia, Egypt, the part of Libya about Cyrene, Rome, Crete, and Arabia. Stephen's disputants were freedmen of Rome, of Cyrene, Alexandria, Celicia and Asia. (Acts 6 : 9.) Wherever people settled in the centuries immediately preceding the Christian era Jews were there. Ancient writers make mention of them in Egypt, Phoenicia, Syria, Coele-Syria, Europe, Thessaly, Boeotia, Macedonia, Aetolia, Attica, Argos, Corinth, in the lands beyond the Euphrates, indeed, throughout the world. Gentiles not infrequently had themselves circumcised, adopted the Jewish mode of worship and were thenceforth regarded as Jews. Among those present when Peter preached the first gospel sermon in the name of the risen Lord were those of this classification. (Acts 2: 9-11.) Such were regarded as part of the dispersion. This great diffusion of the Jews through the habitable earth was the greatest single factor in the rapid spread of the gospel as it was preached under the Great Commission. (Matt. 28: 18-20; Mark 16: 15, 16.) In every community where Jews resided, though the people about them were pagans, they bore clear and consistent testimony to the doctrine of the One True God; their synagogues afforded a place for preaching for the apostolic preachers (Acts 14: 1), and a congregation of devout worshippers to listen to the presentation of the gospel. To such people and places did the apostles always resort on their missionary tours. (Acts 13: 13-46; 14: 1-17; 17: 1-9.) Only when they were expelled from such quarters did they seek out other places and people. There were, therefore, more Jews scattered throughout the earth than lived in Palestine. James addressed his Epistle to those "which are of the Dispersion." Who were they? There are three possible hypotheses.

(1) We have seen who the "twelve tribes" were, and we have ascertained the significance of the *literal phrase*, "which are of the Dispersion." Shall we thence conclude that the statement, "the twelve tribes which are of the Dispersion," was by the author of James intended to embrace *all* Jews (good and bad, believers and unbelievers) living in lands other than Palestine? We may, without hesitation, reject this hypothesis on the ground that it is shown to be false by the Epistle itself. The document is addressed to those James styles as his "brethren" (1: 2); his readers are privileged to ask of God for wisdom with the assurance it will be bestowed (1: 5); they have regular assemblies for religious activity (2: 1-4); and they are called by the honorable name of Christ which unbelievers blasphemed (2: 7). These considerations appear to eliminate the possibility that the Epistle was addressed to Jews, as such, scattered through the various communities of the world. If to this the objection is raised that the writer did occasionally address himself to those who are rich, who oppress others who, for example, are said to nourish their hearts for "a day of slaughter" (James 5: 5), this "aside," a figure known as apostro-

phe, in which a writer turns away from those directly addressed to another group, is not unusual in the Scriptures. See notes on James 5: 1-5. For an example of apostrophe, see Isa. 14: 12 Moreover, it is not outside the realm of possibility that there were those among the disciples who were rich and who thus lived. We learn from James 1: 10; 4: 3-6, 13-16, that there were rich people among the disciples. We may therefore properly conclude that the letter was chiefly intended for Christians—not unbelievers.

(2) Was the Epistle intended *for all* Christian Jews living away from Jerusalem and the land of Palestine? We have seen that the descendants of Jacob (Israel) were indeed widely scattered throughout the world at that time. If the phrase, "the twelve tribes" is to be construed literally such would be the significance of the statement in view of the fact that it was very evidently intended for Christians, and is addressed to "the twelve tribes which are of the Dispersion."

(3) There is another and more plausible hypothesis. It is to regard the phrase, "the twelve tribes," as figurative, and therefore to embrace the disciples of the Lord of whatever race or nationality. In view of the disposition of the sacred writers to ignore distinctions of the flesh, and to emphasize the fact that there is no respect of persons with God; and that in Christ there is neither Jew nor Greek, bond nor free (Gal. 3: 26-29), such would appear to be the more likely hypothesis.

This conclusion is supported by the following premises: (a) *The true Jew today is the Christian:* "For he is not a Jew who is one outwardly; neither is that circumcision which is outward in the flesh; but he is a Jew who is one inwardly; and circumcision is that of the heart, in the spirit, not in the letter; whose praise is not of men, but of God." (Rom. 2: 28, 29.) (b) *Descent from Abraham, the father of the faithful, is reckoned on the basis of obedience and not genealogy:* "And he received the sign of circumcision, a seal of the righteousness of the faith which he had while he was in uncircumcision; that he might be the father of all them that believe, though they be in uncircumcision, that the righteousness might be reckoned unto them; and the father of circumcision to them who not only are of the circumcision, but who also walk in the steps of that faith of our father Abraham which he had in uncircumcision." (Rom. 4: 11, 12.) "There can be neither Jew nor Greek, there can be neither bond nor free, there can be no male and female: for ye all are one man in Christ Jesus. And if ye are Christ's, then are ye Abraham's seed according to the promise." (Gal. 3: 28, 29.) (c) *The True Israel of God today is the church:* "For they are not all Israel, that are of Israel: neither, because they are Abraham's seed, are they all children. . . ." (Rom. 9: 6.) "Know therefore that they that are of faith, the same are sons of Abraham." (Gal. 3: 7.) "And as many as shall walk by this rule, peace be upon them, and mercy, and upon the Israel of God." (Gal. 6: 16.) In Christ, all rights bestowed because of fleshly distinctions, are eliminated, and all are regarded as equal in privilege before God. "Wherefore we henceforth know no man after the flesh: even though we have known Christ after the flesh, yet now we know him so no more." (2 Cor. 5: 16.) If our Lord is not now regarded thus surely men ought not so to be.

We conclude, therefore, that the book of James was written to Christians scattered throughout the world (whether of Jewish or Gentile origin), among whom were, of course, many descendants of Jacob, and that the phrase the "twelve tribes," because of its obvious significance of totality, is a figurative representation of the true Israel of God. Fleshly Israel was scattered by the various banishments she suffered in her long history; the disciples of the Lord were "scattered abroad" (Acts 8: 4) because of persecution directed largely by Saul of Tarsus (Acts 8: 1-3), and so might also be properly styled "the Dispersion."

greeting.—(*chairein* infinitive of *chairo*, to rejoice.) Though the literal meaning of the word is to rejoice, the infinitive signifies in the compressed form appearing here, *joy to you!* In 2 John 10, the King James' Translation has the rendering, "Godspeed," but the American Standard Translation presents the more literal English equivalent, "greeting." The word is an expressed wish for happiness for those thus greeted, and was common in Greek letters from which numerous instances may be cited in the centuries before Christ. It is remarkable that it occurs in hundreds of payri epistles but in the New Testament only here and in Acts 15: 23, and 23: 26. The former instance is in the Letter from the church in Jerusalem to the brethren in Antioch, Syria, and Cilicia which

may well have been penned by James (with the concurrence of
"the apostles, elders and whole church") who appears to have been
quite prominent in the church in that city at that time. Paul and
Peter, with some variation, use the more familiar greeting, "Grace
to you and peace from God our Father and the Lord Jesus
Christ." (Rom. 1: 7; 1 Cor. 1: 2; 2 Cor. 1: 2; Gal. 1: 3; 1 Pet.
1: 2; 2 Pet. 1: 2.) The fact that this particular form of greeting
is used by *Christian* writers only in Acts 15: 23 (where James is
prominently mentioned), and here (James 1: 1), affords strong
presumptive evidence that the author of the Epistle of James is the
same as the James there mentioned. The Greek word of greeting,
appearing in our text, has been adopted into many tongues, and
has been used by multitudes of people for more than two thousand
years. Our "Cheer up!" derives from the same stem, and reflects
the basic meaning of the word.

SECTION 2
1: 2-18

VALUE OF TRIALS
1: 2-4

2 Count it all joy, my brethren, when ye fall into manifold [1]temptations;

[1]Or, *trials*

---

2 Count it all joy, my brethren, when ye fall into manifold temptations;—Having expressed a wish for joy for his readers, James proceeds to reveal how such may be experienced in a situation which would, by most people, be regarded as the most unlikely one possible to produce such—a state of manifold (many and varied) temptations. If some among his readers were disposed to feel that a *wish* for happiness for people who were then enduring the most severe persecution for their faithfulness and fidelity to Christ was an empty and thoughtless gesture, the writer would have them know that these very trials would provide the occasion for the happiness which he wished for them. "Count" *(hegesasthe,* aorist of *hegeomai)* means to consider, deem, reckon, think, regard; hence, regard it as an occasion for joy when divers temptations come; not merely some joy, but *all* joy! Joy complete, whole, without any admixture of regret or sorrow whatsoever.

Such a disposition was to characterize them when they "fall" into manifold temptations. Fall *(peripipto,* from *peri,* round about, and *pipto,* to fall, "so to fall into; so as to be encompassed about," Thayer), emphasizes (a) the external character of the temptation; (b) the suddenness with which it may entrap; and (c) the inability of one to escape such. These temptations are "manifold," *(poikilois),* hence, of many different kinds. (Matt. 4: 24; 2 Tim. 3: 6; Heb. 2: 4; 1 Pet. 1: 6.) The trials of Christians are of vastly different character and appear in many forms. One must, therefore, maintain a guard against such in every direction.

"Temptations" *(peirasmois)* in both Greek and English can mean (a) inward temptation; (b) outward trial. Here, it is the latter—outward trial—which is meant. While inward temptation is a form of trial, it is apparent from the context that it is a trial in which much suffering is experienced but for which the sufferer

3 knowing that the proving of your faith worketh ⁵patience. 4 And let ⁵patience have *its* perfect work, that ye may be perfect and entire, lacking in nothing.

⁵Or, *stedfastness*

sustains no moral blame that is under contemplation here. James would not bid the brethren rejoice when being subjected to the enticements of sin, Satan and the world. From this, and many other similar statements in the Epistle, it is clear that those to whom the Letter was addressed were experiencing great hardship and severe trial in their efforts to live the Christian life.

Those thus addressed are simply styled "brethren," (*adelphoi*), a word denoting fellow-believers, joined to each other in love, and constituting a single family with God as their Father. It is noteworthy that the inspired writers uniformly avoided the use of terms and designations which would establish class distinctions among the disciples. The terms used, such as disciple, believer, brother, saint, fellow-laborer, beloved brother, etc. denote characteristics, relationships, dispositions, activities, etc.; and all distinctive titles and honorary appellations were eschewed. Here, those to whom James wrote were his "brethren," his "beloved brethren," (1 : 19), and all were regarded as on an equal plane (James 2 : 1, 4, 14; 3 : 1, 10; 4 : 11; 5 : 7, 12, 19). The Hebrew writer referred to "our brother Timothy." (Heb. 13 : 23.) To Paul Tychicus was "the beloved brother and faithful minister and fellow-servant in the Lord" (Col. 4 : 7); Epaphras was "a servant of Christ Jesus" (Col. 4 : 12); and Luke was "the beloved physician" (Col. 4 : 14). Our Lord, on the occasion of the ambitious request of the mother of the sons of Zebedee—that one might sit on the right and the other on the left in his kingdom—renounced all such self-seeking and vain ambition for his followers, and taught them instead that true greatness is along the road to useful service: "Ye know that the rulers of the Gentiles lord it over them, and their great ones exercise authority over them. Not so shall it be among you: but whosoever would become great among you shall be your minister; and whosoever would be first among you shall be your servant: even as the Son of man came not to be ministered unto, but to minister, and to give his life a ransom for many." (Matt. 20 : 20-28.) He thus made it clear that *the way up is first down* and that he who would be truly great must render the greatest possible service to mankind.

3 knowing that the proving of your faith worketh patience.—This is the reason why James' readers were to regard, as an occasion for rejoicing, the varied trials of life. There is, of course, no merit in the mere submission of one's self to difficulties; multitudes of people suffer sorely in life because of their misdeeds, and without profit therefrom. "For let none of you suffer as a murderer, or a thief, or an evil-doer, or as a meddler in other men's matters: but if a man suffer as a Christian, let him not be ashamed; but let him glorify God in this name." (1 Pet. 4: 15, 16.) It is because of the blessing resulting from patient endurance under trial by the faithful Christian that there is occasion for joy in the face of such.

Children of God are *to know* that the proving of their faith produces patience. "Knowing" is from *ginosko,* to learn to know, to understand; knowledge obtained through observation and personal experience. The form of the word which is in our text is the present active participle and which means here, "Ye are continually finding out, and getting to know. . . ." It is therefore progressive knowledge under contemplation here. Christians are to recognize the purpose of trial, and learn a lesson from each conflict they experience. It is indeed this fact that enables one to endure patiently.

"Proving" (*dokimion,* from *dokimos,* the crucible through which ore is made to pass so that the heat thereof separates the genuine ore from the dross, and possibly here the *result* of the smelting), indicates the test to which faith is subjected and out of which it appears fully vindicated. Trials become a furnace through which the Christian passes, and thus demonstrates the genuineness of his faith.

This trial of faith and the assurance of its genuine quality "worketh" patience. "Worketh" is from *katergazetai,* present middle indicative, and means more than merely to work. It signifies to work out (cf. Phil. 2: 12), to accomplish, to bring about, and so assures the success of the proof of faith earlier mentioned. That which is thus successfully brought about is patience.

"Patience" (*hupomone*) resulting from the proof of faith growing out of sore trial is much more than mere submissiveness. The Greek word thus translated has a much more active significance than our English word patience suggests. It means not only the willingness to bear up under the manifold burdens of life, but also indicates the ability to use these burdens as instruments for good and greater glory. This the etymology of the word clearly suggests. It is from the preposition *hupo*, under, and *meno*, to remain, to abide; and thus to stand unwaveringly without yielding to any outside pressure. It denotes the ability to exhibit stedfastness and constancy in the face of the most formidable difficulty. It is this characteristic which, when found in the follower of the Lord, enables him not only to endure the trials of life bravely, but to face up to them and overcome them. It was this which our Lord meant when he said, "In your patience (margin, stedfastness), ye shall win your souls." (Luke 21 : 19.)

It will be observed, from a careful reading of the inspired text, that the test which trials provide is, in this instance, for the *benefit* of *him* whose faith is thus proved, and not as evidence for God. Why does man need to prove (test, establish as genuine) his own faith? Faith is the ground of our hope in God, that upon which our convictions rest. (Heb. 11 : 1.) But for it we would be without assurance, and hence without reason or motive for endurance and patience in the face of trial. Thus, when difficulties assail us, we need first of all to be certain of the genuineness of our faith and to have the assurance that it has laid hold on, and will not relinquish, its aims for the future. Obviously, one who does not believe that it is worthwhile faithfully to endure the afflictions of life incident to Christianity will not fight the good fight of faith. (1 Tim. 6 : 12.) Man must first assure himself of the genuineness and reliability of his own faith if this is the ground on which he is to resist. This may be accomplished only by some such method as is followed when gold ore is made to pass through the fire in order that the genuine metal may be separated from the dross, *and identified* as the pure gold. James thus teaches that life's afflictions become the trials of faith, the fiery furnace through which the individual is made to pass, and in which experience he is enabled to determine whether his faith is sufficiently grounded to guarantee its genuineness and reliability.

The "faith" *(pis' tis)* which trials prove is, in the New Testament, "the conviction or belief respecting man's relationship to God and divine things, generally with the included idea of trust and holy fervor of faith and conjoined with it." (Thayer.) It continues and exhibits the same characteristics of the faith which the alien sinner exercises and which leads him on to salvation, "a conviction full of joyful trust, that Jesus is the Messiah—the divinely appointed author of salvation in the kingdom of God, *conjoined with obedience to Christ."* (Ibid.) Thus faith involves (a) unquestioned acceptance of the truth revealed regarding Christ and God; (b) full and unreserved obedience to their commands; and (c) humble and unreserved reliance on their promises. (Heb. 11: 6; James 2: 20-26.)

Trials prove faith by enabling the believer to determine the extent and degree of willingness to endure and to be obedient to Christ.

4 **And let patience have its perfect work, that ye may be perfect and entire, lacking in nothing.**—We have seen above that the patience of this passage is stedfastness, unwavering constancy in the face of severe and manifold trial. This patience we are to permit to have "its perfect work," *(teleion)*, accomplish its purpose, achieve its end. The word translated "perfect" in this passage does not denote sinlessness, but completeness, wholeness, maturity. It is a term which, in classical Greek, was used of animals which had reached full growth; of scholars past the elementary period of their studies and therefore mature students; of men full-grown. In the New Testament, it is used of those who have attained to spiritual manhood in Christ, to full maturity and understanding in spiritual matters, and are thus no longer babes and immature persons in Christ. It is said of our Lord that he was made "perfect *(teleios)* through sufferings" (Heb. 2: 10), where, of course, it cannot possibly mean that he was made sinless through suffering as if such a state did not obtain before. There, the word has its usual significance of completeness; our Lord accomplished his mission through suffering, and thus perfected (brought to maturity) the plan for which he came into the world. This patience is to be allowed to have its full effect in order that its possessor "may be perfect and entire, lacking in nothing."

In the phrase, "perfect and entire," the Greek is *teleioi kai hokleroi,* signifying that which is complete and without blemish. The words *perfect* and *entire* here are not used synonymously. We have seen that the first as used here denotes maturity, wholeness, completeness. It describes that which has accomplished its purpose, achieved its end; as, for example, a surgeon whose schooling and internship is wholly behind him and he is therefore mature in preparation. The second, *entire* (from the Greek *holokleros),* means that the thing to which it is applied has all that belongs to it, as, for example, a baby, born with all of its parts, and thus in every respect normal. It was used in ancient times of an offering without blemish; of an heir who has received the full portion of his inheritance; of the lame man who had been healed. (Acts 3: 16.) Thus those whose faith is sufficiently strong to enable them to endure trial develop patience which, when allowed to reach maturity, completely equip them, leaving them "lacking in nothing."

These words, "lacking in nothing," (*en medeni leipomenoi,* present passive participle of *leipo,* to leave), mean "not being left behind by another," thus signifying that those who become "perfect and entire" in no sense lag behind, or are inferior to others. Basically, the word is a racing term, and points to the fact that those who develop into mature Christians are not outdistanced by any. This emphasizes the fact that the most advanced children of God may not relax their efforts, but must ever remember that they are engaged in a race which is won only when the entire distance is covered. There is no place in life where one may suspend effort and no longer strive for the victor's laurels. The severe discipline of life does indeed, when properly used, prepare us for continued progress in Christian attainment; and, to terminate the effort before reaching the goal is to lose the crown. "Know ye not that they that run in a race run all, but one receiveth the prize? Even so run that ye may attain." (1 Cor. 9: 24.) "Therefore let us also, seeing we are compassed about with so great a cloud of witnesses, lay aside every weight, and the sin which doth so easily beset us, and let us run with patience the race that is set before us, looking unto Jesus the author and perfecter of our faith, who for the joy that was set before him endured the cross, despising shame, and hath sat down at the right hand of the throne of God." (Heb. 12: 1, 2.)

WISDOM AND FAITH
1: 5-8

5 But if any of you lacketh wisdom, let him ask of God, who giveth to all

---

5 But if any of you lacketh wisdom,—The careful reader will observe that quite often in James the leading word of the clause preceding becomes the chief point with which the verse following begins. This is a figure designated by grammarians as *anadiplosis,* defined by Webster as "Repetition of a word, especially the last word, of one clause, at the beginning of the next." The *greeting* of verse 1 ("joy to you"), is followed by "count it all joy," of verse 2; *temptations* (trials) lead on to "proving" in verse 3; *patience,* in verse 3, to "patience" in verse 4; *lacking in nothing,* in verse 4 to "if any man lack . . ." of verse 5; *if any man lack,* is followed by "let him ask of God who giveth"; *it shall be given him* of verse 5, prompts the statement, *let him ask in faith, nothing doubting* which, in turn, results in "for he that doubteth is like the surge of the sea, driven by the wind and tossed . . ." and so on, frequently in the Epistle.

James had urged his readers to recognize in their varied trials the means by which, through patience, to develop full, spiritual maturity in faith and in life. It would appear that, at this point, he must have anticipated this question: "How is it possible for me to see in my difficulties a blessing? Surely, the ability to do this requires a much greater wisdom than I possess." And, it is as if James answered, "Indeed so! But, do not despair; there is an unfailing and inexhaustible supply available and at hand."

let him ask of God,—The ability to see great blessings in sore trial is not an inherent one, and must, therefore be acquired. It is quite significant that James did not say, "But if any of you lacketh wisdom, *let him study philosophy,* or, *let him meditate,* or, *let him consult the wise."* The wisdom which we need, and must have, to turn our trials into triumphs is available only from God. But, what is this "wisdom" which only God can give? "Wisdom," so Webster says, is the "ability to judge soundly and deal sagaciously with facts, esp. as they relate to life and conduct; discernment and judgment; discretion; sagacity." *Knowledge,* when contemplated apart from *wisdom* is an "acquaintance with fact; hence, scope of information." Knowledge is thus the possession of facts; wisdom the ability of judging soundly and correctly regarding them. Knowledge is obtained only through study, wisdom is a gift of God. One whose desire is to learn mathematical principles would not resort to prayer but to textbooks dealing therewith; one who desires the divine wisdom must get down on his knees. Facts to be stored in the head are obtained only through mental effort; the wisdom which has its home in the depths of the soul only God can bestow. Of the *manner* in which God bestows this wisdom the writer does not deal; it is fact of it which is here affirmed.

who giveth to all liberally and upbraideth not;—If, therefore, we lack wisdom (and all of us do), let us "Ask of God who giveth. . ." The words, "God who giveth" are, in the Greek order, *tou didontos Theou*, literally, THE GIVING GOD! This statement emphasizes the fact that such is characteristic of him; he is revealed to us in the character of a Giver. It is a part of his nature to give. Moreover, he gives to *all*; there are no favored few among the faithful disciples; each is by him regarded with equal favor and his bounties bestowed accordingly. Were we liberal to a fault, our limited means make such widespread bestowal of bounty impossible. But even this does not exhaust the extent of his giving. He gives to all *liberally, haplos,* a word meaning either generously, or without bargaining, either meaning being possible here, and both combining in our word *liberally*, simply, unreservedly, without any material expectation of return. We thus learn that (1) God gives; (2) he gives to all; (3) he gives liberally; and (4) he "upbraideth not" (*me oneidizontos*, present active participle of *oneidizo,* to cast into one's teeth, to reproach) because of our requests. Often, when we give, we do so reluctantly, grudgingly, and with reproaches. Have we known this to happen? It is necessary for us to make a request, and then, later to repeat it, only to be met with this objection: "You were just asking for this yesterday, or last week; you are forever asking for something; are you never satisfied?" God (may his name ever be praised for this fact) never thus upbraids, or casts our requests into our teeth! Nor does he chide us for the misuse of the gracious bounties already received. He does not say when we make request of him,

liberally and upbraideth not; and it shall be given him. 6 But let him ask in faith, nothing doubting: for he that doubteth is like the surge of the sea

"What did you do with the things I have already given you? Make better use of them before you come back asking for more." In truth, *we* should rebuke ourselves for our own misuse of his rich gifts and the poverty which characterizes our efforts in their use.

and it shall be given him.—This reminds us of our Lord's marvelous promise in Matt. 7: 7: "Ask, and it shall be given you." (See, also, Luke 11: 9.) Here is one prayer we may be certain the Father will answer. *And it shall be given him.* The answer to some prayers is conditional. In some instances we are to recognize the contingency of prayer in the petition: "If it please thee, grant our request." For example, it was necessary that our Lord should return to heaven. And, notwithstanding the fact that his disciples earnestly prayed, and fervently hoped that he would remain with them on earth, he departed. It was expedient that he go away. (John 16: 7.) Of course, as is ever the case when a petition of God's faithful children is not granted affirmatively, the sorrowing followers of the Lord ultimately come into possession of a vastly richer blessing than could ever have been theirs had he remained on earth. *There is, indeed, no such thing as an unanswered prayer ever uttered by God's faithful children. He answers every prayer his children pray!* True, he does not always say, "Yes." Often, he says, "No." But the "No" is as much an answer as "Yes" would be, and springs from the same motive. When, for example, a child, because of its immaturity, makes a request of its parents which, for the child's welfare, they must not grant, their refusal to grant the specific request is not a disregard of the petition of the child, *it is an answer to it*, and an answer based upon considerations of the child's welfare. In similar fashion, when we make requests of God which are not for our good; or, because he intends to give us richer blessings later, and he withholds the specific request, this is not a disregard of our prayer, it is an answer to it—an answer grounded in good for us. So it is, and so we should ever regard it, and thus be content with the divine wisdom ever evidenced in such instances.

6 But let him ask in faith, nothing doubting:—Our peti-

driven by the wind and tossed. **7** For let not that man think [6]that he shall

[6]*Or, that a doubleminded man, unstable in all his ways, shall receive anything of the Lord*

tions to the Father must, of course, be made "in faith," inasmuch as "without faith it is impossible to be well-pleasing unto him." (Heb. 11: 6.)   Faith is, as we have seen in our studies of James 1: 3, much more than mere intellectual assent to the truthfulness of a proposition—belief that a statement is true—it is firm reliance upon the Lord, unwavering trust in his word, coupled with the disposition to obey fully his commands. We learn here that, in order to obtain wisdom (a) we must ask; (b) we must ask of God; (c) we must ask of God in faith; and (d) the petition must be made "nothing doubting."   The wisdom which we need to rise to higher plateaus of usefulness, using life's difficulties as steppingstones on which to climb to these higher elevations, must come only from God; he alone can *give* it.   But, we must *receive* it; and to receive it, we must believe in him who alone can bestow it.   Surely it is idle to expect God to give us wisdom if we will not give him trust! "Doubting," (from *diakrinomenos),* the chief idea of which, as used in our text, is inner debate; and it presents the picture of a person torn by conflicting notions, now disposed to feel this way, now that. It is, as Thayer remarks, "to be at variance with one's self," to hesitate, to doubt; and, while it does not denote the utter absence of faith, it describes the disposition of a person who, at one moment, feels God will keep his promise, and, at another moment, that he will not. God's purpose in bestowing wisdom upon his children is to create a better relationship between him and them; and, if his children entertain doubts of the truth and reliability of his promises, the atmosphere is one of suspicion, and not of faith.

for he that doubteth is like the surge of the sea driven by the wind and tossed.—He who doubts is one beset by contradictory notions. The inspired writer compares him to the ceaseless and wild surge of the sea which, at one moment, moves shoreward, and at another moment, in the opposite direction, but always aimlessly and without intelligent direction. One torn by such inner conflict can never lean with confidence on God and on his gracious promises. Utterly wanting, in such a person, is that sense of assurance which would enable such a one to approach God in firm-

receive anything of the Lord; 8 a doubleminded man, unstable in all his ways.

ness of faith and in robustness of hope, confident that he is faithful who promised (1 Cor. 1: 9), and therefore able to keep that which we have committed unto him against that day (2 Tim. 1: 12). We should ever strive to possess that spiritual poise which enables one to weather the winds of trial, temptation and all earthly difficulty and to exhibit that stability of heart and mind which cannot be moved.

7 For let not that man think that he shall receive anything of the Lord;—The second clause of verse 6 describes the restlessness of the man who doubts; the first clause of verse 7 shows that such a one eliminates himself from all special favors from God. A state of mind ranging from hope one moment, to despair through doubt in the next, is not conducive to happiness; and one thus possessed is without claim upon God.(There appears to be some contempt expressed by James in the phrase, *that man*, in this passage. One possessed of such a nature could not possibly be happy in life, and such a one makes no contribution whatsoever of a substantial nature to the times in which he lives. Jacob said of one of his sons, "Unstable as water, thou shalt not excel. . ." (Gen. 49: 4. AV.) Not only is such a man not promised special blessings in wisdom in answer to prayer, he is not to expect them. Let not that man so much as *think* that he shall receive anything of the Lord. "The Lord," as in 4: 15, and 5: 10, 11, is the Father, if James intended any distinction. It is quite likely that he used the term merely to designate deity without designing to distinguish between the members of the godhead.

8 a doubleminded man, unstable in all his ways.—"Doubleminded" in the original text is *dipsuchos,* a man with two minds or souls. The word occurs in no other New Testament book, and in James only here and 4: 8. Inasmuch as there is no clear instance of its use before the Epistle of James was penned this has led to the conclusion that James *coined* it. Following its use in James, it was adopted by numerous later writers, such as Hermas, Clement, Barnabas, etc. A doubter is a doubleminded person and is in the position of attempting to pay homage to two masters. (Matt. 6: 24.) He is, therefore, "unstable," (*akatastatos,* unsteady, wavering, in dispositions and attitude). Such a person is restless, confused in his actions and in all of his ways. A double-minded man is in conflict with himself; this situation makes him *unstable,* a word used to describe a drunk man unable to walk a straight course, swaying now this way, now that, without definite direction in his course, and thus unable to get anywhere. Such a one is unstable "in all his ways," and not merely or solely with reference to petitions for wisdom. A waverer in faith will exhibit instability in every department of religious activity. This, incidentally, is the condition which characterizes a person involved in doubt religiously. While the philosophical world regards such a disposition with favor, James, the inspired writer, held the opposite view. Doubt to him was no evidence of superior learning or unusual intellectual attainment; it was, instead, the mark of mental instability, evidence of confused intellectual processes.

INSTRUCTION TO THE RICH AND POOR
1: 9-11

9 But let the brother of low degree glory in his high estate: 10 and the rich, in that he is made low: because as the flower of the grass he shall pass

---

9 **But let the brother of low degree glory in his high estate:**—From the consideration of trials in general (verses 2-8), the writer, in this section, proceeds to the treatment of those specific problems which result from substantial change in one's economic condition—from poverty to riches and from riches to poverty. So perfectly adapted to *all* of man's needs is Christianity, it enables the faithful child of God immediately to cope with all of life's problems, however varied they may be. The circumstances of life are exceedingly changeful; one may indeed be rich today and poor tomorrow; and the poor may experience similar change in economic station, thus rising to affluence overnight. Such radical alterations in one's mode of living resulting from such changes produce serious problems and often lead to much temptation. The faithful Christian will not allow his relationship to God to be affected by his financial fluctuations but will, in these very changes, find occasion to rejoice.

The one experiencing these changes in his economic situation is a *brother.* Contemplated is "the brother of low degree," and also "the rich" *(brother,* understood). Both are of the great brotherhood of which God is the common Father and Christ the elder brother. All are brothers in Christ. However great is the difference in their financial standing, they meet on a common level in the Lord. *There are no caste systems in Christ.* The disposition to elevate some to positions of eminence in the church and to relegate to the realm of obscurity "the brother of low degree," is wholly opposed to the spirit of Christianity and exceedingly wicked in the eyes of God. (James 2: 1ff.) Some of the most effective work being done for Christ today is by humble, sacrificing servants of the Lord who labor in his cause for sheer love of him, and without desire for public acclaim whatsoever. These, though they may not experience the heady thrill of notoriety characteristic of the more prominent brethren, will nevertheless shine above the brightness of the stars in eternity. (Dan. 12: 3.)

The brother "of low degree" is "to glory in his high estate." The phrase, of low degree," is from *tapeinos,* meaning one of humble position, one who, because of external circumstances, has been brought low. While a brother in such a situation would feel some debasement, the emphasis is not so much on his *inward* attitude, as with reference to his *outward* position. Being poor, he is *low,* in contrast with the rich, who occupy a *high* position in the world. The distinction which the inspired writer at this point emphasizes is in the financial standing obtaining between the rich and the poor.

When the brother of low degree is suddenly thrust into the position of a rich man, he is to "glory in his high estate." Not simply or solely because he is now rich, *not* because he is now freed of the fretting problems which ever plague the poor in life, *not* because his affluence will now enable him to do more in the service of the Savior, *but because he has successfully passed the test of faith which sudden riches afford, and now knows that his faith is genuine.* We must not, in our study of this passage, disregard the force of the context in which these words appear. The general theme is *trials.* (James 1: 2-18.) Trials lead on to patience, and patient endurance supplies the test by which the genuineness of faith is determined. One's faith is never more severely tried than when its possessor suddenly becomes rich and affluent. A brother who has experienced this transition may indeed "glory" *(kauchas-tho,* exult) in his successful change in economic condition inas-

much as his faith is still intact. Many disciples, who suffer great
hardship and want, endure much persecution and remain devoted
to the Lord will, on becoming rich and prosperous, find the temptations resulting from wealth so alluring and seductive that they
surrender to Satan. There are, of course, many proper blessings
resulting from prosperity. Poverty is not an unmixed blessing,
nor are riches an unadulterated evil. There are extremely corrupt
poor men, as there are also wonderfully good rich men. Both poverty and riches involve great temptation; each has its peculiar dangers, but neither necessitates disobedience to God. Perhaps the
safest course, for the Christians, is in moderation. Agur, the son
of Jakeh, "the oracle," made this request of Jehovah before he
died:

> "Two things have I asked of thee;
> Deny me them not before I die:
> Remove far from me falsehood and lies;
> Give me neither poverty nor riches;
> Feed me with the food that is needful for me;
> Lest I be full, and deny thee, and say, Who is Jehovah?
> Or lest I be poor, and steal,
> And use profanely the name of my God."
>
> (Prov. 30: 7-9.)

It is not the amount of money which one has which determines
whether one is rich in the objectionable sense; it is the attitude
which one exhibits thereto. He who "trusts" in his riches is condemned because he expects his riches to accomplish for him only
that which God can do. (Mark 10: 24, see margin.) John, in his
short missive to his friend Gaius, informs us how safely rich one
may be: "Beloved, I pray that in all things thou mayest prosper
and be in health, even as thy soul prospereth." (3 John 2.) The
brother of low degree may indeed rejoice because his faith has endured the test of both poverty and riches! Now possessed of a
sizable store of this world's goods, his horizons have been lifted,
his potential for good enhanced and his responsibility increased.
While he may not be able actually to do more *good* for the Saviour
in his affluence, he is equipped to labor in fields formerly closed to
him. He may, therefore, properly "glory" (exult) in his "high estate."

10 **and the rich, in that he is made low:**—The "rich" (brother) is likewise to "glory" (rejoice, be glad) that he is made low. That the rich man contemplated in the passage *is a brother* seems not open to serious question. Obviously, the inspired writer would not direct such an edict to the worldly rich, nor could he reasonably expect those of that class either to heed his admonition or to regard the loss of riches as an occasion for rejoicing. Men of the world regard the loss of riches as a major catastrophe. When the stock market broke in the ill-fated financial crash of 1929, numbers of men, their entire fortunes wiped out in an hour, lost their reason and leaped from tall buildings in New York City to their deaths. Life to them without their former affluence was no longer desirable. Only a brother (a child of God) can see in financial disaster a blessing. Brought low by his losses, he is nevertheless in position—as a faithful disciple of Christ—to see the deceitfulness of riches (Matt. 13: 22), to know their evanescent nature, and to recognize their powerlessness to bring happiness to the human heart. The *trial* of the brother brought low is doubtless harder to bear than is that characteristic of the brother of low degree who has been raised to financial prosperity. The latter may indeed find, in his improved circumstances, occasion to rejoice; but it is most difficult for one who has seen his riches take wings to feel that in their departure he has experienced a great blessing! But, inasmuch as all things work together for good to those who love the Lord and who are called according to his purpose (Rom. 8: 28), in the wisdom which God will give him (verse 5), he will be able to see that since such has happened it must be for his good, and he can therein rejoice.

Such a one may thenceforth reason that (1) the loss of riches is, in his case, providential and therefore for his good; (2) his association with the world and with worldly men must thenceforth be less intimate; (3) the burdens borne by men in the business world —which often operate to shorten life—have been listed and he may expect to live longer; and (4) he is in position henceforth to fix his attention more thoroughly on the things which endure. In so doing, he is now able to appreciate more fully Paul's affirmation that true values are not those which are tangible and may be seen: "While we look not at the things which are seen, but at the things which are not seen: for the things which are seen are temporal;

but the things which are not seen are eternal." (2 Cor. 4: 18.) One of the most vital lessons in life to learn is that "a man's life consisteth not in the abundance of things which he possesseth." (Luke 12: 15.)

because as the flower of the grass he shall pass away.—Not only are riches disposed to vanish, he who possesses them is not more enduring; as the tender, fragile flower of the grass appears only to be crushed or to wither so also does the rich man "pass away." This verb, *pareleusetai*, in the future tense, compounded from *para*, by, besides, and *erchomai*, to come or to go, denotes, in impressive fashion, the frailty of human nature, and rapidity with which men, however rich they may be, are made to pass from life. As a slender and delicate blade of grass withers and is gone, so the rich man passes by and is no more. Such a one is not to feel that the loss of riches is fatal; he, too, cannot long remain on the earth and would not therefore reasonably expect to retain his riches and to enjoy them forever. Inasmuch as his life here is "but for a moment," let him recognize that, whatever his earthly circumstances, his riches are not essential to his happiness or well being here, nor can their loss in any fashion defeat him in his efforts to gain heaven and eternal life. The things of this life are so transient in nature that it is of little consequence whether we have abundance or are in want, provided we "put first things first," and enthrone the Lord Jesus Christ in our hearts and lives.

(Note: Other interpretations proposed for this passage are, (1) the brother of "low degree" is, because he is a brother, to glory in his high estate; i.e., because he is a Christian, he is to find in this fact occasion for joy whatever his outward circumstances may be. The rich brother is similarly to glory (exult) because, as a Christian he has accepted a state of humiliation which will operate ultimately for his good enabling him to be saved despite his riches. *Objection:* all brothers in Christ are on the same level; there is no respect of persons with God. (Gal. 3: 28, 29; Rom. 2: 11.) Throughout the Epistle James deplores the disposition to create distinctions between brethren. (2) The rich man is not a brother at all but one who, because he is rich, rejoices in the abandonment of life (through yielding to the allurements of the world) which his riches makes possible. *Objection:* Both classes are addressed

away. 11 For the sun ariseth with the scorching wind, and withereth the grass; and the flower thereof falleth, and the grace of the fashion of it perisheth: so also shall the rich man fade away in his goings.

---

in the same fashion as if they were equally related to the writer. The rich would see no occasion for rejoicing in the loss of possessions, nor would such be disposed to heed the injunctions issued. The context is against both of these interpretations. The objection, that elsewhere in the Epistle the writer condemns the rich, is to beg the question. That wicked rich men are elsewhere condemned does not necessarily require that the conclusion be drawn that James does so here, unless, of course, one subscribes to the view that the mere fact that one is rich means that one is wicked, an absurd conclusion, truly!

We conclude, therefore, that both the poor and the rich, under contemplation in our text, are children of God; and, that it was James' design to show that however changing and changeable the outward circumstances of life may be, those who are faithful to the Lord may find occasion to rejoice and be happy. We thus learn that the rich and the poor both have their trials; and, while they are not the same trials, the road to heaven is not smooth for either. Each may, however, in spite of his peculiar temptations, find satisfaction in service to his Saviour, and ultimately receive eternal bliss.

11 **For the sun ariseth with the scorching wind, and withereth the grass; and the flower thereof falleth, and the grace of the fashion of it perisheth: so also shall the rich man fade away in his goings.**—Eastern peoples would be especially familiar with this illustration taken from nature. A scorching wind, called the *simoom,* frequently begins with the coming up of the sun; and the heat which it brings is often so intense that the green vegetation withers and eventually dies. The "grass" of the passage *(choroton)* is from a comprehensive term for vegetation; and, "the flower of the grass" *(anthos)* does not refer to the bloom but to wild flowers which often grow up in the midst of the grass in Palestine. Lilies were by our Lord called "the grass of the field" in his Sermon on the Mount. (Matt. 6: 28, 30.)

This blast of hot air, called "the scorching wind" in the text, comes in from the deserts east of the Jordan valley, and up from the burning sands of Egypt. The destructive character of "the east wind" is often mentioned in the Scriptures. "Yea, behold, being planted, shall it prosper? shall it not utterly wither, when the *east wind* toucheth it? it shall wither in the beds where it grew." (Ezek. 17: 10.) "And it came to pass, when the sun arose, that God prepared a sultry *east wind*; and the sun beat upon the head of Jonah, that he fainted, and requested that he might die, and said, It is better for me to die than to live." (Jonah 4: 8.) This entire section in James appears to be based upon a quite similar affirmation from the prophet Isaiah: "The voice of one saying, Cry. And one said, What shall I cry? All flesh is grass, and all the goodliness thereof is as the flower of the field. The grass withereth, the flower fadeth, because the breath of Jehovah bloweth upon it; surely the people is as grass. The grass withereth, the flower fadeth; but the word of our God shall stand forever." (Isa. 40: 6-8.)

Because of the extremely barren nature of much of the soil in Palestine, the scarcity of water and the scorching, burning winds, grass in that country remains green but a short time. Its fragile character and its short life afford an excellent illustration of the brevity of man's existence on earth, and the rapidity with which men are cut down and are no more. As the tender grass withers and perishes in the burning blasts of the east wind, "so also shall the rich man fade away in his goings." The figure is a familiar one: "Man, that is born of a woman, is of few days, and full of trouble. He cometh forth like a flower, and is cut down. . ." (Job 14: 1, 2.) "As for man, his days are as grass; as a flower of the field, so he flourisheth. For the wind passeth over it, and it is gone; and the place thereof shall know it no more." (Psalm 103: 15, 16.)

James has earlier shown (verses 2-4), that the loss of riches is not to be regarded as a catastrophe; on the contrary, one experiencing this is to rejoice in it, provided that his faith is sufficiently strong to enable him to endure the trial such an experience brings. Here, he emphasizes the fact that the rich will die as do other men as surely as the grass of the field withers and dies. He, too, will "fade away" (*maranthesetai*, future passive indicative of *maraino*, to extinguish a light, to put out a flame), like a light which flickers and goes out, a vivid figure of speech for the suddenness with which life can vanish. Man is thus like a candle which, for the moment, is seen, and then is snuffed out and is no more. Such a one will fade away "in his goings," as he goes about his tasks, as the poorest do, he shall die, there is no difference between the rich and the poor in this respect. Like the flower of the field, today alive and beautiful, but tomorrow withered and sere, like a light which flames forth in brilliance one moment, and is out the next, so the rich man dies "in the midst of his goings," and is seen no more.

THE CROWN OF LIFE
1: 12

12 Blessed is the man that endureth temptation; for when he hath been approved, he shall receive the crown of life, which *the Lord* promised to

12 **Blessed is the man that endureth temptation;**—Verse 12 reverts to the theme of *temptation* first introduced in verse 2, where it is affirmed that temptation supplies an occasion for joy inasmuch as it proves our faith and leads on to patience and thus to spiritual maturity. It will be recalled, from the comments there, that the temptation contemplated is not a solicitation to do evil, but *outward trial,* a fact evident from the context. The temptation under consideration enables one to be "approved" *(tried,* King James' Version), when the one subjected thereto endures it properly; and it produces for such a one a crown of life. It is for this reason that one called upon to endure temptation (trial, hardship, difficulty) is regarded as "blessed."

"Blessed" *(makarios)* is the word with which the "beatitudes" begin. (Matt. 5: 2-11.) There are indeed many points of resemblance between the Epistle of James and the Sermon on the Mount and to these attention will be hereafter directed. The word *makairios,* translated "blessed" in the text, describes one who is in a state of blessing, sometimes declared to be a *happy* one. However, our English word "happy" is an inadequate term to denote the state of blessedness which the original word describes. Blessedness is a condition resulting from a state of inner peace; whereas, happiness (derived from *hap,* chance) is dependent on external circumstances. The former is in the heart and not subject to interference from, or the whims of, others; the latter involves matters over which one cannot always maintain control. Happiness is more often produced by material affairs; blessedness is much more spiritual, and therefore of a far more enduring quality. Happiness, closely related to the world, cannot always be enjoyed; blessedness, not dependent on material matters, may ever be the cherished possession of the faithful, however poor they may be in this world's goods. Blessedness is a characteristic of God himself. (1 Tim. 1: 11.) Thus, the more we become like God, the more blessed we are. (Matt. 5: 8.)

We have seen that (a) the difficulties of life are the means which prove faith; (b) produce maturity in the Christian character; and (c) enable one to possess an abiding inner peace described as *blessed*. However, the mere fact that one is subjected to trial does not mean that this state of blessedness always results. Only those who *endure* trial are declared to inherit the blessing. "Endureth," *(hupomenei,* present active indicative of *hupomeno,* patience), is derived from the same source as the word translated "patience" in verse 3. Thus the one who endures is the one who patiently submits to the trials of life, knowing that they are the furnace of fire which tests (proves) faith and strengthens character. Etymologically, the word *hupomeno* (patience) signifies *to remain under,* and thus denotes the determination of its possessor to bear up under any and all of life's difficulties which he may be called upon to bear. It vividly describes that quality of endurance which distinguishes the faithful disciple from the superficial one. (Luke 8: 13.)

The word translated "endureth" *(hypomenei)* does not contain a compulsive concept; it is rather a type of stedfastness sustained by one who regards the trials of life as necessary to patience and to maturity of character and therefore readily accepted as a means to future blessing. It must, of course, be kept continually in mind that the inspired writer does not, in this verse, deal with inner solicitations to evil, but to outward trials which, because we are human beings, are an inevitable portion of our heritage. The former must ever be stoutly repelled, not merely suffered. Affirmed here is the fact that trials are (a) common to us all; (b) they must be endured; (c) when successfully borne they produce in one a state of blessedness.

for when he hath been approved, he shall receive the crown of life,—"Hath been approved," is, literally, "having become approved," *(dokimos genomenos);* a fact accomplished by having successfully passed the test of faithfulness and fidelity to God which outward trial affords. Under the figure of the crucible (a furnace of fire) in which ore is melted and the dross eliminated, the faithful disciple is, by his trials, enabled to have eliminated from his character the dross of life, and thus privileged to appear approved before God. Evidence of having been able successfully to pass the test is to be seen in the fact that he has, by his patience in affliction, endured. Like metal which has passed through the fiery furnace, and has been cleansed of all impurity, he now possesses a character wholly unalloyed, and therefore pure. Some suffer and do not endure and thus fail the test. (1 Pet. 4: 15.) Only those who are faithful in the face of trial evidence their sonship: "My son, regard not lightly the chastening of the Lord, nor faint when thou art reproved of him; for whom the Lord loveth he chasteneth, and scourgeth every son whom he receiveth. It is for chastening that ye endure; God dealeth with you as sons; for what son is there whom his father chasteneth not? But if ye are without chastening, whereof all have been made partakers, then are ye bastards, and not sons." (Heb. 12: 5-8.)

In truth, only those who faithfully endure are promised salvation (1 Cor. 11: 19), a salvation tendered only on evidence of unwavering stedfastness: "Beloved, think it not strange concerning *the fiery trial* among you, which cometh upon you to prove you, as though a strange thing happened unto you: but insomuch as ye are partakers of Christ's sufferings, rejoice: that at the revelation of his glory also ye may rejoice with exceeding joy." (1 Pet. 4: 12, 13.) For these alone is the symbol of success in patient endurance reserved.

which the Lord promised to them that love him.—He who shall receive "the crown of life" is the one successfully passing the test inherent in trial. He *shall* receive (future tense) it, at the end of the examination, and not at its beginning, as is by some affirmed. Jesus said, "Verily I say unto you, There is no man that hath left house, or brethren, or sisters, or mother, or father, or children, or lands, for my sake, and for the gospel's sake, but he shall receive a hundredfold now in this time, houses, and brethren, and sisters, and mothers, and children, and lands, with persecutions; and in the world to come eternal life." (Mark 10: 30.) The "crown of life," *ton stephanon tes zoes,* genitive of apposition, literally, the life crown, thus life itself, is the crown promised. "And this is the promise which he promised us, even the life eternal." (1 John : 25.) "In hope of eternal life, which God, who cannot lie, promised before times eternal. . . ." (Tit. 1: 2.) See Rev. 2: 10, the only other instance where the phrase occurs. Compare, however, Paul's reference to the "crown of righteousness" (2 Tim. 4: 8), and Peter's allusion to "the crown of glory" (1 Pet. 5: 4). In all these instances, it is clear that the reception of the *crown* is conditioned on faithfulness and patient endurance. Literally, the crown *(stephanos)* signified the wreath of victory to the winner in the ancient games (1 Cor. 9: 25); it also was an ornament to evidence the bestowal of honor (Prov. 1: 9), and a sign of dignity (2 Sam. 12: 30). As those in the ancient games were qualified to receive the crown only when they had complied with the rules thereof, so now only those who conform to the conditions which the Lord himself formulated are privileged to receive the crown of life at the last day. (1 Tim. 2: 5.) "Faithful is the saying, For if we died with him, we shall also live with him: if we endure, we shall also reign with him. . ." (1 Tim. 2: 11.)

The Lord has promised this crown of life to "them that love him," *(tois agaposin auton),* literally, to those loving him—not those who once loved him, but to those who *now* love him. It was promised either in (a) some extra-biblical statement, not preserved for us, but known to those of the apostolic age (cf. Acts 20: 35), or, what is more likely, (b) embraced, in principle, again and again in his teaching. (Matt. 19: 28.) It will be observed that, in addition to the condition of patient endurance set out at length by James in verses preceding this, he adds here *love for Christ* as a condition precedent to the crown of life. Actually, the two are closely related and cannot be separated. "For this is the love 'of God, that we keep his commandments: and his commandments are not grievous." (1 John 5: 3.) The Bible abounds with promises to those who love God, because those who truly love him, obey him and endure faithfully to the end—the conditions essential to receiving the crown. (See, also, Ex. 20: 6; Deut. 7: 7-11; 1 Cor. 2: 9.)

Those who affect to know him, but refuse to obey him, are by John said to be liars. (1 John 2: 4.)

We may, therefore, rejoice that (a) if we endure, we are by him regarded as faithful; (b) if faithful, we are assured of the life crown at the end of life's journey; (c) in view of this we may rejoice even in the midst of grievous trial. "Wherein ye greatly rejoice, though now for a little while, if need be, ye have been put to grief in manifold trials, that the proof of your faith, being more precious than gold that perisheth though it be proved by fire, may be found unto praise and glory and honor at the revelation of Jesus Christ: whom not having seen ye love; and whom, though now ye see him not, yet believing, ye rejoice greatly with joy unspeakable and full of glory: receiving the end of your faith, even the salvation of your souls." (1 Pet. 1: 6-9.) The love *under* consideration here is not a vague sentiment or a passing emotion; it is a robust affection which prompts the possessor to be obedient to all of the Lord's commands. It is idle for one to profess devotion for Christ while refusing to do his will. Faithful obedience is the *test* of love. "Ye are my friends, if ye do the things which I command you." (John 15: 14.)

TEMPTATION AND SIN
1: 13-15

them that love them. 13 Let no man say when he is tempted, I am tempted [7]of God; for God [8]cannot be tempted with [9]evil, and he himself tempteth no

---

[7]Gr. *from.*
[8]Or, *is untried in evil*
[9]Gr. *evil things.*

---

13 **Let no man say when he is tempted, I am tempted of God;**—Thus far in his treatment of *temptation,* James has dealt with it from the viewpoint of outward trial. (James 1: 2-12.) *Here, a significant change occurs.* No longer does he use the noun form for temptation; thenceforth, a verbal form is used *(Peirazomenos,* present passive participle of *peirazo,* to solicit to do evil), an example of which may be seen in Satan's solicitation to evil on the occasion of our Lord's temptation in the mount. (Matt. 4: 1ff.) The shift is a natural one, and to be expected. From the contemplation of those outward trials which inevitably beset men in life, it is an easy transition to the inner conflicts which are no less serious obstacles to faithfulness and piety on the part of the

disciples of the Lord. There is, indeed, the disposition on the part
of some to hold God responsible for the adversities which assail us,
and to accuse him of producing the circumstances which result in
hardship and trial. Adam did it in Eden when he sought to shift
the blame to God for his evil action by saying, "The woman whom
thou gavest to be with me, she gave me of the tree and I did eat"
(Gen. 3: 12), and his posterity has followed this pattern ever
since.

Every evil act is by some justified on the ground that God
created our bodies and placed in them desires which he should not
have done if he is to regard their gratification as sinful! Such reasoning is, of course, done by those who conveniently forget there is
a fundamental difference between the proper *use* and *abuse* of privilege; and is grossly fallacious. Opium, for example, medicinally
used, is a blessing to humanity; improperly taken into one's body
it becomes a destructive and deadly poison. The effort to pass on
to God responsibility for humanity's difficulties is a comfortable
and common one; it is a convenient method by which man absolves
himself of all moral responsibility for his actions. It is not surprising that the theory has a theological application and that there
are those who advocate the view that God is the author of every
act of man and that all such was predestined from eternity. The
doctrine of predestination and reprobation, set out in some of the
older creeds, is an example of this view. A more modern version
of the doctrine, stripped of theological implication, and of a philosophical flavor, affirms that man is a creature of his origin and sur-
roundings (heredity and environment), neither of which he was
privileged to choose, and that any evil which may reside in him is
the product of forces over which he has no control, and for which
he should not be held responsible. This evasion of personal responsibility is a persistent one, and finds expression not only in
Theology and Philosophy but also in Literature, Drama and Poetry.
For example, Robert Burns, the plowman poet of Scotland, wrote:

> "Thou knowest thou hast formed me
> With passions wild and strong;
> And listening to their witching voice
> Has often led me wrong."

This dangerous and deadly view James strikes down in a single affirmation in this section. (Verses 13-15.)

No one may properly say, "I am tempted of God" *(apo tou Theou peirazomai); i.e.,* from God I am tempted. It is interesting and highly significant that the phrase, *from God,* is, in the Greek Testament, *apo theou,* rather than *hupo theou.* The use of *apo* (ablative) indicates origin, not agency; were the phrase to read, *hupo tou Theou peirazomai,* the meaning would be that God is directly the cause of temptation; as it is, it insinuates that (though he did not directly order our temptation) he is responsible for it in some remote sense. We must, of course, remember that James is affirming *neither;* instead, he is denying the charge which some made in that day (and continue to make in this) that God is at least remotely responsible for our sins. The meaning is, *Let no man say that God tempts us to do evil in any sense, remote or otherwise.* Temptation (solicitations to evil) is neither from *(apo),* nor by *(hupo)* the Father.

for God cannot be tempted with evil,—God is beyond the area of temptation, being untemptable. The word thus translated occurs nowhere else in the Scriptures, but a similar one *(apeiratos),* is common in ancient Greek writings. A compound term, it is made up of *"a"* (not) and *peirao,* one of the meanings of which is "to be familiar with"; "to have experience in." It would therefore appear that, when it is affirmed that God is untemptable, it is meant that having no experience in any evil thing, there can be in him no desire for evil, and thus no ground for temptation. One who is himself wholly removed from evil could never desire to see it, or to cause it to appear in others. God neither tempts, nor is tempted.

and he himself tempteth no man:—Not only is God himself not susceptible of evil through temptation, he tempts no one. Untemptable himself, because of his inherent goodness and eternal abstinence from every evil thing, he does not thrust into the lives of others that which is wholly foreign to his own. It would be wholly inconsistent with his character, his goodness and his love for man whom he desires to imitate himself to be responsible for creating a condition in his creatures which would alienate them from him. If to this the objection is raised that in the King James Translation of Gen. 22: 1, it is said that "God tempted Abraham," it should be recalled that the word *tempt* means (a) trials; (b)

man : 14 but each man is [10]tempted, when he is drawn away by his own lust,

[10]Or, *tempted by his own lust, being drawn away* by it, *and enticed.*

evil suggestions; (c) solicitations to evil. Verses 2-12, of James 1, involves the first of these meanings; verses 13-15, the second and third. James affirms that God tries men for the purpose of determining the genuineness of their faith, but he denies that he does so for the purpose of seducing them to sin. God tested, tried, proved Abraham; the American Standard Version renders Gen. 22 : 1, "God did prove Abraham. . . ." God proves us, i.e., he tests our faith; and this is for our good; but he never leads us to sin. The author of all good cannot be the source of sin in us.

14 but each man is tempted, when he is drawn away by his own lust, and enticed.—Here, the writer states the real source of temptation. One is tempted when (a) he is drawn away (b) by his own lust and (c) enticed. One is "drawn away" *(exelkomenos,* from *ek,* out of, and *helkomai,* to draw), "by" *(hupo,* the agent involved) "his own lust" *(epithumia,* desire), "and enticed," *(deleazomenos,* present passive participle of *deleazo,* literally, to bait, figuratively, as used here, to trap by enticing delights). Desire, seeking satisfaction, prompts to sin; and the individual is caught, trapped, ensnared, or, as we sometimes say, *hooked!* Forbidden pleasure, however great the desire for it may be, should be rigidly excluded from our lives, lest we be caught in Satan's snare. The illustration which James uses of enticement is that of the blandishments of a harlot; and the means used, those common to fishermen and hunters. As a fisherman uses the most attractive sort of bait, or the most alluring fly to induce the fish to strike, so Satan tempts us by means of those things which are to us most desirable.

It is good for us, in this connection, to note that desire must first be drawn away, before there is enticement. It is the function of a fisherman's fly to induce the fish to forsake the safety of the rock or the weeds, and to come within reach of the hidden hook in the enticing lure. We must stay away from those places where we may be easily hooked. Christians should never go to any place where there is the possibility they may be tempted to do wrong. They should abstain from all association with those who are disposed to exercise the wrong influence over them. We should not

and enticed. 15 Then the lust, when it hath conceived, beareth sin: and the

only avoid those places and practices which we *know* to be wrong; we should shun all of *those which we do not know* to be right!

The influence of Satan is universal. No one capable of sinning is removed from the area of his wooing. "Every man," *(hekastos,* each one) is, tempted; tempted by being drawn away by evil desire induced by the desirable bait which the devil dangles before the unwary. It is vitally important to observe that the first step to sin consists in being *drawn away,* drawn away from our place of safety. The other steps could not follow but for this. Here, indeed, is the threshold Satan must first invade. He must call us forth from our shelter of safety before he can seduce us to sin. The corruptor of morals does not attempt to accomplish his designs *in church,* in the company of the good, or where the pure of heart gather. His first aim is to draw us away from our spiritual defenses, induce us to go where we ought not, and where we are helpless to resist his advances.

How sad indeed it is to be *drawn away* from God, drawn away from all that is good, drawn away from the church, drawn away from the Bible, drawn away from the road to heaven. Bad as it is to be drawn away from that which is good, this is but the first step in Satan's sinful designs, the prelude to even more serious action. Not content with merely drawing us away from that which is good, he then launches us on a course of positive evil. Few drawn away from that which is good stop there; soon they advance to active evil. This, the writer next affirms.

15 **Then the lust, when it hath conceived, beareth sin:—** "Lust" is evil desire *(epithumia).* This desire conceives. The figure is a familiar one. The hapless individual, his defenses abandoned by being drawn away from them, and hooked by his evil desires, discovers that from the union of improper desire and his yielding will, a conception has occurred. The will yields to lust and when "it hath conceived," *(sullabousa,* second aorist active participle of *sullambano,* to conceive), the monstrous offspring is born. The lust (evil desire) thus becomes the mother of sin because the will surrendered to the desire, and suffered seduction. It should be observed that James does not affirm that sin sprang into life at the moment desire was experienced. It is, alas, impossible

for us to purge our minds of fleeting desires, improper thoughts, and questionable ideas. These appear unwanted, and without prior notice. We must, when such occur, rigidly exclude them, and never harbor and entertain them. It is good to know that their appearance does not of itself constitute sin. The appearance of sin is described by the inspired writer under the figure of a conception and birth. And, as two people are required before a normal conception and birth can take place, so there must be the action and concurrence of two parties operating in the individual before the conception and birth of sin can follow. Desire is one, the influence of Satan over the will is the other. When the will surrenders, through the prompting of evil desire, and Satan moves into the heart, conception takes place. The natural and inevitable fruit thereof is sin.

So long as we are in the flesh it is impossible to avoid *all* sin. John said, "If we say that we have no sin, we deceive ourselves, and the truth is not in us. . . . If we say that we have not sinned, we make him a liar, and his word is not in us." (1 John 1: 8, 10.) One simply adds sin to sin in denying sin; *it is a sin to say that one does not sin!* There is (may God be praised for it) a remedy provided: "If we confess our sins, he is faithful and righteous to forgive us our sins, and to cleanse us from all unrighteousness." (1 John 1: 9.) These words are, of course, applicable *only* to those who have obeyed the gospel, and have fallen into sin after having become Christians. Sinners, who have never been children of God, must, in order to be saved from their past, or alien, sins, *believe the gospel* (Mark 16: 15, 16); *repent of their sins* (Luke 13: 3; Acts 2: 38); *confess their faith in the Lord* (Rom. 10: 19), *and be buried with him in baptism into the body of Christ* (Rom. 6: 3, 4). Then, the remedy set out in 1 John 1: 7 becomes to them available.

Children of God should ever remember that the devil, "as a roaring lion," goes about seeking whom he may devour, and thus be ever on guard against his evil devices. (1 Pet. 4: 8; 2 Cor. 2: 11.) It should grieve the hearts of Christians when they sin, and should prompt them to strenuous efforts in the future to avoid similar lapses. It has been truly said that, "He who falls into sin is a man, he who grieves at sin is a saint, but he who boasts of sin is a demon."

We have seen that the offspring of evil desire and the will yielded to Satan is sin. James tells us that lust when it conceives "beareth sin." Such is its evil progeny. "Beareth is from *tiktei*, present active indicative of *tikto,* the ordinary word for bringing one into the world in childbirth. Such a birth is the natural result of the conception earlier occurring. And, just as that which is conceived *must* eventually be born, so it is not possible to hide evil desire long in the heart, it must ultimately spring forth into life, fullborn.

and the sin, when it is fullgrown, bringeth forth death.— Sin, when thus born, proceeds to maturity, becoming "fullgrown." Far from remaining in a rudimentary state, it goes on to full development. Here, too, James continues the figure of birth to illustrate the *beginning, progress,* and *full maturity* of sin. The word translated "fullgrown," is *apotelestheisa,* first aorist passive participle of *apoteleo,* that which is complete, fully developed. There is yet another act in this drama of the conception, birth and growth of sin. When fullgrown, it brings forth death. "Bringeth forth," in the text, is from *apokuei,* from *apo,* from, and *kueo,* to be pregnant. This is a medical term often used in Greek literature of unusual or monstrous births. Here, at the consummation of birth, the child is dead. The birth necessarily results in death. The "death" here *(thanatos)* is separation from God and all that is good. The basic meaning of death is *separation.* Physical death results from the separation of body and spirit (James 2: 26); a death *in* sin is separation from that which is good (1 Tim. 5: 6); and a death *to* sin is separation from the practice of sin (Rom. 6: 1-4). Sin, when it becomes fully developed produces death in the individual who harbors it.

We have, in this section, one of the most remarkable pictures of sin in the *Scriptures.* Improper desire has seduced the will and tempted it to submit to impure contact. From this wicked union sin is conceived, and ultimately born. From babyhood it develops into vigorous manhood and slays eternally him who harbored it. This amazing genealogy each one should contemplate before launching out into a life of sin. Far from blaming God with the result of sin, he who sins should recognize the fact that he is the begettor of his own sin, and the ancestor of his own demise!

The steps of sin are as follows: (1) temptation begins when one is drawn away from the course of right and rectitude; (2) that which prompts one to move away from the position of safety and into an area where danger exists is the enticement (bait) which Satan dangles; (3) the lust which influences one conceives in the union between the evil desire and the submission of the will to Satan; (4) sin is born; (5) this sin grows to full stature; (6) its consummation is spiritual death. Thus, evil desire leads to the birth of sin; and sin, in turn, gives birth to death. Such is the remarkable description of sin so impressively outlined by James in this section. Death, as the natural consequence of sin, is often dwelt upon by the sacred writers. "For when ye were servants of sin, ye were freed in regard of righteousness. What fruit then had ye at that time in the things whereof ye are now ashamed? for the end of these things is death." (Rom. 6: 20, 21.) See, also, Rom. 6: 22, 23; 8: 6; Eph. 2: 1ff.; Rom. 5: 12.

From these affirmations of James we learn that we must never dally with temptation nor entertain improper desire. He who dwells upon evil, nourishes it in his heart and suffers it to settle down in permanent abode, will eventually yield to his desires and translate them into action. Sin does not begin with normal desire. It is when this desire gets out of bounds, clamors for satisfaction, and leads its possessor into a course of action the design of which is to secure such satisfaction that the evil progeny of sin is spawned. Eve is an excellent illustration of the truth taught by James. She looked longingly upon the fruit of the tree of death; but, so long as she looked, and did not eat, sin remained in the shadows. Unable to resist the lure which Satan dangled before her eyes, she ate, Adam was induced to do likewise and the race was plunged into unspeakable misery. Achan, in spite of the specific injunction touching the spoils of Jericho, could not resist the desire for the goodly Babylonish mantle, and the wedge of gold. Said he, "When I *saw* among the spoil a goodly Babylonish mantle, and two hundred shekels of silver, and a wedge of gold of fifty shekels weight, then I *coveted* them, and *took* them. . ." (Josh. 7: 21.) See Josh. 6: 15-21; Gen. 3: 1-8.

GOD THE SOURCE OF ALL GOOD
1: 16, 17

sin, when it is full grown, bringeth forth death. 16 Be not deceived, my

---

16 **Be not deceived, my beloved brethren.**—The words of this verse are closely related in thought, and should be considered with the section immediately preceding. Those to whom James wrote, identified here as his "beloved brethren," are not to allow themselves to be deceived into thinking that God originates temptation and sin in them and thus separation from him. To subscribe to such a view is to be deceived *(planasthe,* literally, to wander about, to stray from the right course). Figuratively used in this instance, it is an injunction designed to keep the brethren from allowing their minds to be led away from the truth and into a sphere of thinking which would blame God for their conduct! The words, "be not deceived," are of frequent occurrence in the New Testament. (1 Cor. 6: 9; 15: 33; Gal. 6: 7.) Satan labors diligently to deceive the saints about sin, and he seeks to accomplish his purpose by inducing them to abandon the stable principles of the Word of Truth anchored in their minds, and to wander away from them. (2 Cor. 4: 4; Rom. 1: 27; Eph. 4: 4; Col. 3: 5.) Satan successfully seduces people when he prompts them to abandon the principles of Christianity for the philosophies of men; and many an unwary soul has been lost to the cause of Christ under the pretext of a search for truth. We should, of course, be ever ready to accept *truth* wherever found; but we should never forget that any philosophy which is opposed to the teaching of the Scriptures is vicious and false and will, if accepted, plunge its dupes into destruction and perdition. Paul declared that all of "the treasures of wisdom and knowledge" are hidden in Christ, and he warns us not to be deluded with "persuasiveness of speech" originating in the wisdom, philosophy and tradition of men. (Col. 2: 1-9.)

The warning issued by James is to his "beloved brethren." The mere fact that one is in Christ does not create immunity to deception and delusion. Were Satan able to convince the saints that God is the author of sin in them, his work would thenceforth be easy and multitudes would slide unsuspectingly into his snare. *There are more than twenty-five hundred warnings* to the saints of

beloved brethren. 17 Every good ¹¹gift and every perfect gift is from above, coming down from the Father of lights, with whom can be no variation, nei-

¹¹Or, *giving*

the possibility of apostasy in the Scriptures. One can scarcely open the pages of the Bible without having the eyes fall upon some such injunction as the following: "Take heed, brethren, lest haply there shall be in any one of you an evil heart of unbelief in falling away from the living God: but exhort one another day by day, so long as it is called Today; lest any one of you be hardened by the deceitfulness of sin." (Heb. 3: 12, 13.) Satan deceived and deluded Eve through his subtlety, and thus thrust the human family into speakable misery (2 Cor. 11: 2); and he has, through the ages, continued this device to entrap the saints (2 Cor. 2: 11).

James regarded those to whom he wrote as "beloved *brethren,*" *(adelphoi,* from "a" copulative, and *"delphos,"* from the same womb). Here, the term denotes fellow-believers united to others by a bond of affection, of Christians constituting a single family. (Thayer.) From its literal significance of male members of the same family and with a common parentage, it has come to mean, metaphorically, those with the same ancestry spiritually, and is thus descriptive of all those who are with us in Christ, whatever their national and racial origins. It is a term of affection, denoting that close relationship which obtains between those of the same family. With God as our Father, and Christ as our elder brother, all who have obeyed the gospel sustain this relationship. Being brothers, we should conduct ourselves accordingly, bearing one another's burdens and so fulfilling the law of Christ. (Gal. 6: 2.) Wholly foreign to this relationship is that disposition of mind and heart which prompts brethren to bite and devour one another. (Gal. 5: 13-15.) "If we live by the Spirit, by the Spirit let us also walk. Let us not become vainglorious, provoking one another, envying one another." (Gal. 5: 25, 26.) "We know that we have passed out of death into life, because we love the brethren. He that loveth not abideth in death. Whosoever hateth his brother is a murderer; and ye know that no murderer hath eternal life abiding in him." (1 John 3: 14, 15.)

17 Every good gift and every perfect gift is from above,—It will be observed that the noun *gift* occurs twice in this clause; and though both of the Greek words thus translated derive from the same original verb *(didomi,* to give), they differ in form, in spelling, and in meaning. In the phrase, "every good gift," the word is *dosis,* signifying the *act* of giving; in the phrase, "every perfect gift," the word is *dorema,* indicating the *result* of the act of giving, that is, *the gift* itself. The word "good," modifying gift, in the first part of the clause, is predicative in nature, and points to the fact that all giving is good; and the adjective "perfect" modifying gift in the second instance, (every perfect gift), emphasizes the fullness, the completeness of that which is given. Of course, the two ideas are closely related. The gift is complete because of the goodness of the giver. The motive which prompts liberality, on the part of men, may be good, but there must be lacking, in the nature of the case, the wholeness, the completeness and the thoroughness of the gift which God bestows.

Such giving and gifts, as are those described above, come "from above," that is, from heaven. (James 3: 15; John 3: 31; 19: 11.) What is meant is that the motive which prompts such giving, as well as the gifts themselves, originates, not with men who can never approach such high ideals in giving, but with God who is in heaven. The Greek word translated "from above," in our text, is the same as that occurring in John 3: 3, where Jesus told Nicodemus that he must be born "anew," *(another,* margin, "from above"). All that is good ultimately derives from God, the inexhaustible source of all blessing. For this fact we should ever be grateful; and we should express and exhibit our gratitude in word and in deed daily. Many people never pause to express thanks for the bounties which they regularly receive from God's hand. Like pigs, they eat their food, never lifting their eyes to the tree from which the acorns fall! A father, in the presence of his family, boasted that he offered thanks for their food every Christmas day. It is for them quite fortunate that God does not forget to feed them *except* on "Christmas day!"

The words, "every good gift and every perfect gift," of our text, translate a phrase which, in Greek, forms a hexameter line with a short syllable lengthened, and this has led to the supposition that this is a brief quotation from some ancient poem or early song. Brief quotations from such sources are not unknown in the New

Testament.   (Tit. 1: 2; 1 Cor. 15: 33; Acts 17: 28.)   No original source can be cited for the line which appears here, and it may simply be accidental that this particular cadence occurs. Whether it is a quotation from some ancient source not now known to us, or is an accidental metrical line is not important. In either instance, the Holy Spirit selected the *words* (1 Cor. 2: 13), when penned by James, and they thus became a part of the inspired deposit of truth, whatever their former usage.

coming down from the Father of lights,—This statement is to be construed with the word *another* (from above), which it explains and expands. Good giving and good gifts that are complete and perfect are from above; they come *down* to us from their divine source. Again, emphasis is given to the fact that the truly valuable things available to men are not of the earth; they do not find their origin on earth, but descend *(katabaino)* from him who is in heaven. Inasmuch as all good things from him *come down,* surely simple gratitude suggests that we *send up* our thanks!

Him from whom they issue is described as "the Father of lights." "Lights," in the text, refers to the heavenly bodies—the sun, the moon and the stars—which provide light for us. God is styled the Father of these heavenly bodies because he is the ultimate source of them. The word "father," in the sense of *creator,* is by no means unknown in the sacred writings. (Job 38: 24; 2 Cor. 1: 3; Eph. 1: 17.) While it appears that the best exegesis regards this statement (the Father of lights) as literal, the lesson intended goes beyond the reference to literal lights in the skies and embraces all light, light both literal and figurative. God is, of course, the originator of lights and light. As he produced the heavenly bodies by waves of his omnipotent hand, so he also originates and freely bestows upon his children every perfect gift. From whatever source blessing may appear, it must ultimately be traced to him.

> "Back of the loaf is the snowy flour
>   And back of the flour is the mill;
> And back of the mill is the wheat and the shower,
>   And the sun and the Father's will."

God is light and in him "there is no darkness at all." (1 John 1: 5.) Because God, whom man cannot see, made *the lights* and men can see them, some yield to the temptation to forget God and reverence the creation instead of the Creator. Through the centuries men have often paid homage to the handiwork of God in the heavens rather than to him. They have worshipped nature rather than the Creator of nature. This is sinful in the highest degree. "While we look not at the things which are seen, but at the things which are not seen: for the things which are seen are temporal; but the things which are not seen are eternal." (2 Cor. 4: 18.) The things which abide are not those material matters of the earth which may be seen with the natural eye; such matters perish with the using, and must eventually suffer the dissolution which awaits all worldly things. Our interests should be centered in the things which cannot be shaken and which will remain intact amid the crash of dissolving worlds at the last day.

with whom can be no variation, neither shadow that is cast by turning.—Continuing his illustration of the "lights" of which God is Father (creator), James asserts that (1) there is no variation nor (2) shadow cast by turning with God, as appears to be characteristic of these "lights" (heavenly bodies). In this respect, God differs greatly from them. With him, there is no "variation" *(parallage,* a word signifying the change, in position, from hour to hour, through which the sun *appears* to pass in its relationship to the earth). God does not reflect such variations in his dealing with us. Though the celestial bodies alter their relation to the earth, and the changes appear from day to day and from season to season, no such variation in God is noted; he is ever constant and unvarying in his attitude toward us, and in his bestowal of good gifts upon us. "For I, Jehovah, change not. . . ." (Mal. 3: 6.)

Nor is there "shadow that is cast by turning" with him. The word translated "turning" here is used in the Greek Old Testament (Septuagint Version), in Job 38: 33 and Deut. 33: 14, for the changes which appear in the relative positions of the heavenly bodies. It is as if James were saying: *The phenomena of nature are, of necessity, changeable; the phenomena of God are unchangeable. All material things are mutable; God is immutable. Though the lights of the heavens change with the hours and the seasons, he who created them changes not. It must therefore follow that only that which is good can originate with him, and he can never be the*

occasion of placing temptation and sin in the path of his creatures.
(Verses 13-15.)

Two wonderful truths are thus affirmed of God in this section:
(1) There is no admixture of evil in the goodness which he bestows; (2) no obscuring shadow ever falls over him, hiding his
goodness. He is ever at the zenith; he occupies the position of the
sun at high noon in the steadying and unvarying light with which
he shines so benignly upon the race. It is therefore beyond belief
that such a one as thus described could ever lead those who are in
his image astray.

BROUGHT FORTH BY THE WORD
1: 18

ther shadow that is cast by turning. 18 Of his own will he brought us forth
by the word of truth, that we should be a kind of firstfruits of his creatures.

**18 Of his own will he brought us forth by the word of
truth,**—The phrase, "of his own will," is participial, and means:
"willing, he brought us forth, . . ." and is to be closely construed
with the verses preceding. The thought runs thus: instead of regarding God as the source of temptation (and consequent sin), he
it is who willed to give us life by means of the truth. The evil
offspring of sin is death. God, under the same figure (conception
and birth) is a parent, too. But, how vastly different the progeny!
That which is born of him possesses life. This evidences the fact
that the process of conversion is not accidental or of chance; it involves the exercise of the divine will, and according to a plan previously adopted. "He came unto his own, and they that were his
own received him not. But as many as received him, to them gave
he the right to become children of God, even to them that believe
on his name: who were born, not of blood, nor of the will of man,
but of God." (John 1: 11-13.)

This does not mean that the selection is arbitrary or that God
wills to save only a predetermined number; on the contrary, it is
his desire that all should be saved, and come to the *full* knowledge
of the truth. (1 Tim. 2: 4.) Provision has been made for all
(John 3: 16); the invitation has been extended to all (Matt. 11:
28; Rev. 22: 17); and, the gospel is applicable to all (Matt. 28:
18-20; Mark 16: 15, 16). That there are those not saved is not a

matter involving the opposition of God's will to them, but of the opposition of their own wills to God: "And ye *will not* come unto me that ye may have life." (John 5: 40.) The reason some do not come to the Lord, even though the gospel is preached to them, and the Lord's gracious invitation is extended to them is by him thus explained: "For this people's heart is waxed gross, and their ears are dull of hearing. And their eyes they have closed; lest haply they should perceive with their eyes, and hear with their ears, and understand with their heart, and should turn again, and I should heal them." (Matt. 13: 15.)

That our salvation results from the free determination of the will of God does not necessitate the conclusion that his will is arbitrarily exercised, or that the choice is made independently of human agency and responsibility. The Lord calls; but he calls by the gospel (2 Thess. 2: 14); and the gospel is to be preached to all, and may be obeyed by all (Mark 16: 15, 16). The saved have been chosen; but the choice was not capricious or arbitrary; it requires belief of the truth: "But we are bound to give thanks to God always for you, brethren beloved of the Lord, for that God chose you from the beginning unto salvation in sanctification of the Spirit and belief of the truth: whereunto he called you through our gospel, to the obtaining of the glory of our Lord Jesus Christ." (2 Thess. 2: 13, 14.) God *wills* the salvation of *all* who believe his word and obey his will. (Heb. 5: 8, 9.)

"He brought us forth," is "begat he us," in the King James' Version, and, in the Greek text, *apekuesen*, first aorist active indicative of *apokueo*, the word occurring in James 1: 15, and though not indicating any abnormality here, as there, it does suggest the idea that the action of birth was not the usual, natural one (of a mother), it being, in this instance, affirmed of God (a masculine personality). That the verb is *aorist* points to a specific act in the past which is a reference to the time when they were born again, saved. The "us" of the passage includes all the Christians to whom James wrote.

The instrument by which God effects the "new birth" is declared to be "the word of truth" *(logoi aletheias,* genitive), a word originating in truth. This is, of course, the gospel: "Seeing ye have purified your souls in your obedience to the truth unto unfeigned

love of the brethren, love one another from the heart fervently:
having been begotten again, not of corruptible seed, but of incorruptible, through the word of God which liveth and abideth. . .
And this is the word of good tidings which was preached unto
you." (1 Pet. 1 : 22, 23, 25.) It follows, therefore, that the words,
"He brought us forth by the word of truth," describe that part of
the conversion process in which the word of truth (the gospel) is
involved. Under the figure of birth, we are begotten and born,
and so become children of God. We are begotten when we believe; and the birth process is completed when we have been baptized in water. "Whosoever believeth that Jesus is the Christ is
begotten of God." (1 John 5 : 1.) "In Christ Jesus I begat you
through the gospel." (1 Cor. 4 : 16.) "Except one be born of
water and the Spirit he cannot enter into the kingdom of God."
(John 3 : 5.)

that we should be a kind of firstfruits of his creatures.—The
words, "that we should be," *(eis to einai,* purpose clause with the
verb) indicate the aim of God's will exercised as described in the
preceding portion of the verse. The figure is that of the sheaf of
firstfruits of the harvest which were offered in the passover cele-
bration. (Lev. 23 : 10; Deut. 26 : 2.) The "firstfruits" were a
token and pledge of the fuller harvest to follow; and, as the sheaf
of the wave offering presented to the Lord foreshadowed the bountiful harvest to follow, so the early disciples to whom James wrote
were among the first of a vaster company which would follow
them. Further, the offering was not only an earnest (part pay-
ment) of that which was to follow, it was the consecration of the
entire harvest. The figure is not an unusual one in the New Testament. Paul declared that the house of Stephanas were "the firstfruits of Achaia" (1 Cor. 16 : 15); and John, in The Revelation,
makes mention of those who "are firstfruits unto God and unto
the Lamb" (Rev. 14 : 4). Our Lord, in triumphing over the grave
and Hades, is by Paul affirmed to be "the firstfruits of them that
are asleep." (1 Cor. 15 : 20.)

It is not improbable that James had particularly in mind the
Jewish Christians, in this verse, who were first in Christ Jesus our
Lord. To the Jews were committed the oracles of God (Rom. 3 :
1), and it was long ago ordained that out of Judah the lawgiver

should come (Gen. 49: 10). When God's plan was fully mature, and the Savior came into the world, it was fitting that those who had borne the banner of Jehovah through the centuries in the midst of a pagan world should enjoy the distinction of having the gospel first preached to them, of becoming the first Christians, and thus to be a "a kind of firstfruits" of the Lord's people. To the Jews in Antioch in Pisidia, Paul and Barnabas said, "It was necessary that the word of God should first be spoken to you. . . ." (Acts 13: 46.) This allusion to the "firstfruits" would be very meaningful to the Jews, not only from their familiarity with the Hebrew ritual regularly engaged in at the passover feast, but from the further fact that Israel herself had by her ancient prophets been referred to as "the firstfruits of his increase." (Jer. 2: 3.)

The word "creatures," from *ktismaton,* the most comprehensive term possible, is used to indicate the relationship of these early Christians to all other things. As such, their position was unique among all the rest of creation, including not only men, but all created beings. The whole of God's creation partakes in the blessings of redemption, and patiently waits for the consummation thereof. (Rom. 8: 19-22.)

We learn, (1) it was God's will that those to whom James wrote should become his children; (2) these became his children by being born by the word of truth—the gospel; (3) those who thus did became the "firstfruits" in pledge of a greater harvest.

Inasmuch as it is by the word *of truth* we are brought forth into spiritual life, it is vitally important that the truth be preached, believed, and obeyed. Jesus said, "And ye shall know the truth and the truth shall make you free." (John 8: 32.) The truth is the means to spiritual freedom; and it ought, therefore, to be preached and taught in its primitive purity without admixture of human opinion or the doctrines and commandments of men. The gospel is the hope of the world; it is the panacea of humanity's diseases, the specific for mankind's ills. It is a sad commentary on human nature that many people today prefer to listen to pleasing falsehoods rather than what to them is unpleasant truth. And, as there are always those who desire error rather than truth, so those can be found, who for a price, will supply the preaching desired. Paul admonished Timothy to preach the word, because the time would come when men would not "endure the sound doctrine, but having itching ears, will heap to themselves teachers after their own lusts; and will turn away their ears from the truth, and turn aside unto fables." (2 Tim. 4: 1-4.)

What a glorious parentage is ours through being privileged to be "brought forth" (born of God). Inasmuch as God is our Father, we partake of his nature, the divine nature; and we are, in consequence, expected to conduct ourselves in keeping with our heritage. "And if ye call on him as Father, who without respect of persons judgeth according to each man's work, pass the time of your sojourning in fear: knowing that ye were redeemed, not with corruptible things, with silver or gold, from your vain manner of life handed down from your fathers; but with precious blood, as of a lamb without blemish and without spot, even the blood of Christ. . ." (1 Pet. 1: 17-19.)

SECTION 3
1: 19-27

MAN'S WRATH, GOD'S RIGHTEOUSNESS
1: 19, 20

19 [12]Ye know *this*, my beloved brethren. But let every man be swift to

[12]Or, *Know ye*

---

19 **Ye know this, my beloved brethren.**—Whether this is an injunction, signifying, "know this," (imperative), or "ye know this," (indicative), cannot be definitely determined, inasmuch as the form for both constructions is the same, in this instance. It is likely that the Greek *iste* is to be construed as indicative; and, that it was James' design to point out that his readers were familiar with the fact to which he referred in the verses preceding, and he enjoins them to act accordingly. On this hypothesis, the meaning is: *You are well aware of the fact that we were brought forth into spiritual life by the word of truth; therefore, let your life, in word and in deed, reflect the knowledge you have gained therefrom.* From a general statement of their knowledge of the noble ideals which should characterize them in their acknowledged familiarity with the word of truth, the writer proceeds to detail what such involves. Here, again, those addressed are the writer's "beloved brethren," a phrase repeatedly occurring in the Epistles. It indicates, (a) the same parentage; (b) the closest kinship; (c) deep and abiding affection.

But let every man be swift to hear, slow to speak, slow to wrath:—Here, the verb "let . . . be" *(esto)* is imperative. James thus *commands* each of those to whom he wrote to be (a) swift to hear, (b) slow to speak; (c) slow to wrath. The word "swift" is from the Greek *tachus*, occurring only here in the New Testament, and signifying that which is fleet of foot, quick, speedy; and it introduces a remarkable phrase urging a fast and attentive mind, *tachus eis to akousai*, a ready disposition to listen. The second phrase, "slow to speak," is of similar construction, the meaning of which is, *slow to begin speaking*, not of course, slow while speaking! "To speak," is *lalesai*, ingressive aorist active infinitive. "Slow to wrath" follows the injunctions to be swift to hear and slow to speak. "Wrath" *(orgen)* is violent emotion resulting in uncontrolled anger and improper indignation, and renders one thus possessed wholly incapable of receiving the word of truth without which one cannot be saved. Men will not, and cannot, properly listen to God when they entertain bitterness, malice, and hatred in their hearts toward their fellows. While it is likely that these words of James primarily refer to hearing the word of God, in a secondary sense they are applicable also to that which we hear from others.

The disposition to speak rashly and thoughtlessly and not always to weigh one's words is a besetting sin of many races and was especially characteristic of the Jewish people of the period in which James wrote. There is, therefore, much teaching in the Scriptures regarding the proper use of the tongue. (Prov. 13: 3; 14: 29; 17: 27; Eccles. 5: 2); and to this subject James himself devoted considerable space (1: 26; 3: 1-18; 4: 11, 12; 5: 9). It has often been observed that the writer, in this passage, gives us his version of the maxim, "Speech is silver; silence is golden." Ancient writers, both sacred and profane, have often dwelt upon the importance of constant vigilance in speech, and many interesting and pithy sayings have come down to us expressing sentiments similar to that of James: "Men have two ears, and but one tongue, that they should hear more than they speak." "The ears are always open, ever ready to receive instruction; but the tongue is surrounded with a double row of teeth, to hedge it in and to keep it within proper bounds." "How noble was the response of Xenocrates! When he met the reproaches of others with a profound silence, some one asked him why he alone was silent. 'Because,' says he, 'I have sometimes had occasion to regret that I have spoken, never that I was silent. . .'" "Talk little, and work much."

Socrates, the great Greek philosopher and educator, was once approached by a young fellow who asked the ancient sage to teach him oratory. The young man rattled away at great length; and when, at last, the philosopher was able to speak, he informed the voluble fellow that he would be required to charge him a double fee. "Why a double fee?" he asked. "Because," the famous teacher replied, "I shall have to teach you two sciences; first, how to hold your tongue, and second, how to use it."

Solomon said, "In the multitude of words there wanteth not

hear, slow to speak, slow to wrath: 20 for the wrath of man worketh not the

transgression; but he that refraineth his lips doeth wisely."
(Prov. 10: 19.)   "He that guardeth his mouth keepeth his life;
but he that openeth wide his lips shall have destruction."   (Prov.
13: 3.)   "See thou a man that is hasty in his words?   There is
more hope of a fool than of him."   (Prov. 29: 20.)

The degree to which one adheres to the precept, "Swift to hear,
slow to speak, slow to wrath," will, in large measure, reveal how
stable one's character is. The respect people are disposed to give to
our opinions will depend largely on the amount of thought we give
to the utterance of these opinions—and not the rapidity with which
we express them!   And, those who are impatient of the views of
others, and who can scarcely refrain from the expression of their
own, will quickly be regarded as uncharitable and unthoughtful of
others, and possessed of much conceit and immodesty themselves.

**20 for the wrath of man worketh not the righteousness of
God.**—This is the reason the Holy Spirit assigns why we are to be
"swift to hear, slow to speak, slow to wrath."   Those who are full
of wrath (violent, mental agitation, resulting in uncontrolled
anger), are wholly unequipped to listen to the presentation of the
truth; or, for that matter, to do anything that is right.   One of the
most famous of the Old Testament's maxims of conduct is expressed by Micah as follows: "He hath showed thee, O man, what
is good; and what doth Jehovah require of thee, but to do justly,
and to love kindness, and to walk humbly with thy God?" (Mic.
6: 8.)   One who is a battleground of violent passion finds it impossible to conform to this standard of right; and the conflict
which rages in such a person makes it far more difficult for those
about him to serve God acceptably.   A "man's wrath," (so the
Greek phrase runs), is put in contrast with "the righteousness of
God."   The *wrath* described here differs from "righteous indignation," which is, on some occasions, proper; condemned here is personal anger which, when it boils up and over, makes it impossible
for those thus possessed to "work the righteousness of God," that
is, the righteousness which God requires.

What is "the righteousness of God" *(dikaiosunen Theou)?*
Thayer, in an unusually fine statement, says that *righteousness,*

"denotes the state acceptable to God which becomes a sinner's possession through that faith by which he embraces the grace of God offered him in the expiatory death of Jesus Christ." By *faith*, this lexicographer means "a conviction, full of joyful trust, that Jesus is the Messiah—the divinely appointed author of eternal salvation in the kingdom of God, *conjoined with obedience to Christ.*" The same authority says that righteousness *(dikaiosune)* in "the broad sense" is the state of one "who is such as he ought to be, . . . the condition acceptable to God." It is, then, simply and solely a state of justification established on the basis of the sacrifice of Christ and man's acceptance thereof through the conditions required.

This lexical definition is completely and fully confirmed by affirmations of inspired writers. "Then Peter opened his mouth, and said, Of a truth I perceive that God is no respecter of persons: but in every nation he that feareth him, *and worketh righteousness,* is accepted with him." (Acts 10: 34, 35.) Righteousness is thus that state or condition wherein one is in a *right* relationship with God. Our English word "righteousness" derives from the word "right," which, in turn, literally suggests that which is straight (as, for example, a straight line), and so designates a relationship with God which he approves. A "righteous man" is, therefore, one who is *straight,* lined up properly with God! (Psalm 119: 172; 1 John 2: 29.)

A simple and brief definition of righteousness is, therefore, *right-doing*; to be righteous one must do right. "He that doeth righteousness is righteous, even as he is righteous." (1 John 3: 7.) Of a certain type of character it is affirmed that he is righteous. Who is he? He that *doeth* righteousness. No other is. He who does righteousness is righteous; but he who is righteous is one who does right; therefore, he who does right possesses righteousness. Conversely, an unrighteous person is a perverse one; a perverse one is an individual in a twisted (as opposed to a straight) relationship with God. It is hence clear that righteousness is that state or condition wherein one is approved of God; but God approves of those only who do right (keep his commandments); therefore, to possess the approval of God and the righteousness which he requires one must do right, by keeping his commandments.

Here is unmistakable evidence of the falsity of the denominational doctrine of *transferred* righteousness. It is by some alleged
that in the process of conversion Christ transfers to the sinner the
righteousness which he possesses, and thenceforth the sinner is
clothed in the righteousness which Christ himself exhibits! One
can only sadly wonder what the future holds for us as more and
more writers among us, following the lead of denominational theologians, adopt the view of an imputation of righteousness on this
basis, an idea repugnant to both reason and Scripture. It is absurd to assume that one person is good *because* another is. True,
through the merits of Christ's blood shed in our behalf, our guilt is
cancelled and through obedience to his will we are privileged to go
free; but this is far from declaring that we thereupon become positively good in the absence of good works. There is a vast difference between (a) *not* imputing guilt (this, the Lord does for us)
and (b) in conferring merit (this, the Lord does *not*) in the process of salvation. The primary import of the word translated righteousness indicates a change in position and in relationship to God,
and not, *on that basis alone,* a life of personal purity. A pardoned
criminal is no longer regarded as guilty of the crimes which led to
his arrest and conviction, but he is thence by no means a valuable
citizen with a long record of civic goodness back of him simply because he has been pardoned. Righteousness is right-doing. *To be
righteous, one must do right.*

But, was not Abraham's faith reckoned (imputed, counted) to
him for righteousness? Yes. In the absence of further duties at
the moment God accepted Abraham's faith as an *act* of righteousness itself. Thus faith itself became *the act of obedience,* on
the basis of which God accepted Abraham as in a right relationship
with him. (James 2: 20-22.) Did not David speak of "'the
blessedness of the man, unto whom God imputeth righteousness
without works?" (Rom. 4: 6.) The works contemplated here
(as the context clearly shows) were the works of the law. The
man to whom the Lord imputes righteousness is the one whose "iniquities are forgiven, and whose sins are covered." (Psalm 32: 1,
2; Rom. 4: 8.) Such a one actively complies with God's plan for
his forgiveness, and is thus declared righteous (justified). *We
must distinguish between a righteousness imputed to (credited to)*

*man because he has a right relationship with God through obedi-
ence to his will, and a righteousness which Christ (through his
own submission to the will of the Father), is alleged to transfer to
the sinner. The former the New Testament teaches; the latter is
Calvinism.*

But was not Christ made "righteousness" for us? (1 Cor. 1:
30.) The Lord became *the means* of righteousness for us; i.e., it is
through him that we are privileged to receive "the gift of righteousness" (Rom. 5: 17); but this is accomplished through compliance with his will, and in obedience to his commandments, and
not through some mysterious bestowal of merit. We should ever
remember that justification does not eliminate the fact of sin; it
simply releases the sinner from the guilt thereof. The history of the
act must forevermore remain. Paul, though mindful of the great
grace which he had experienced, was never without the consciousness of the fact that he had persecuted the church of God and
wasted it. Pardoned, saved, justified, acquitted, no longer under
guilt, it now remained for him, through faithful adherence to the
Lord's will to exhibit personal righteousness, "right standing" with
God. And so with us all. The marvelous blessing of salvation is
available through Christ. He is the means of righteousness,
through him we receive the gift of righteousness, and in him we
partake of God's righteousness; i.e., the righteousness which God
makes available to us, through unswerving allegiance to his will.
The law of Moses was powerless to provide justification. It provided a perfect standard to which man, in sin, could never measure. A measuring cup will indicate the amount of the substance
it contains, but it will not increase it; a tapeline will reveal the
length of a string, but it cannot make it longer. It was, therefore,
necessary that justification "apart from the law" be provided for
man. This, we rejoice to say, was accomplished in Christ.

DOERS OF THE WORD
1: 21-25

righteousness of God. 21 Wherefore putting away all filthiness and overflowing of [13]wickedness, receive with meekness the [14]implanted word, which

[13]Or, *malice*
[14]Or, *inborn*

Wherefore—That is, for the reasons just assigned. That our hearts may be properly prepared for the word which alone can supply us with the knowledge of salvation, let us eliminate everything which would hinder or defeat its operation. A stubborn disposition is wholly foreign to that spirit of docility which must ever characterize us if we are to profit by the word in our hearts, and he who would be blessed of God must exhibit that spirit which ever says, "Speak, Lord, thy servant heareth; command, and I will obey." Only those who thus do qualify as the friends of Christ (John 15: 4); and those who affect to know him while refusing to obey his commandments are, in the words of John, "liars" (1 John 2: 4). Jesus reserved one of his severest rebukes for those who give lip service to him, but refuse to do what he says: "And why call ye me, Lord, Lord, and do not the things which I say?" (Luke 6: 46.)

putting away all filthiness and overflowing of wickedness, —"Filthiness" (*ruparian,* that which is dirty) occurs only here in the New Testament, but a form of the word appears in the Septuagint Translation of the Old Testament in Zech. 3: 3, 4, where the reference is to filthy garments. There is, in the word, a suggestion of *loathesomeness,* and it seems likely that in his use of this term it was the writer's design to create in his readers a deep sense of abhorrence of sin, all sin, any sin. Such is God's attitude toward such, and such should also be our attitude toward it. God regards all sin as a filthy rag, disgusting and sickening, and so should we. Here is indisputable evidence of the fact (often taught in the Scriptures), that sin pollutes the soul, renders it unclean, and creates a condition in a person wholly unlike him whom we affect to serve: "Thou that art of purer eyes than to behold evil, and that canst not look on perverseness." (Hab. 1: 13.)

We should be impressed with the fact that James did not seek to soften the character of sin or to obscure God's unwavering opposition to it. There is the disposition today to dally with sin, to excuse it, to resort to euphemisms in referring to it, to speak of "inhibitions," psychological weaknesses, reversions, environmental influences, hereditary factors, etc., the design of which is to render it less objectionable in the individual, and so to make sin appear to be less sinful! The New Testament writers never attempted to present the matter other than it is—filthiness and overflowing of wickedness.

"Overflowing of wickedness," *(perisseian kakias,* superabundance of evil), denotes that state in which the heart is filled with evil, and which exhibits itself in ungodliness of life. The picture is of such an abundance of evil in the heart that it bubbles up and overflows in its wicked manifestations. It is by some believed, and with reason, that the first of these statements, "filthiness," describes sins of the flesh; and the second, "overflowing of wickedness," sins of the heart. Obviously, while harboring malice in the heart, or allowing sin to control our members, we are wholly unfitted to receive the word of truth into our hearts and lives. We must, therefore, put all such away.

"Putting away," *(apothemenoi,* aorist middle participle of *apotithemi,* to put off, as one removes clothing), indicates (a) in the significance of the word the act of stripping oneself completely of every evil thought and act; (b) the tense (aorist), points to a once-for-all-act to be performed before the word can accomplish its full work in the heart; and (c) the middle voice emphasizes that the *putting away* is something we must do for ourselves, since God *will* not, and others *cannot,* do it for us.

receive with meekness the implanted word,—Thus, the word (a) must be *received*; (b) the word must be received *with meekness.* The word, in the Scriptures, is often compared to seed (Luke 8: 11); and seed, in order to germinate, must enter the soil. The seed-bed for the word of truth is the human heart; and into the heart the seed must fall; it is powerless to spring up into life otherwise. Those with hearts comparable to the wayside soil do not receive it; or if they receive it, in the rocky, barren ground into which it falls, it soon withers and dies; or, if it is received and springs up, the thorns (cares of this world, the deceitfulness of riches and the pleasures of this life), eventually choke it out. (Matt. 13: 1-9, 16-23.) Only those who receive the word "into an honest and good heart" bring forth fruit. (Luke 8: 15.) It would be well for each reader of these notes to ask himself or herself the question: "Do I profit by the word sown in my heart, or have I allowed my soul to become a roadway for the world until the seed (which is the word of God) cannot enter; or, if it enters is the ground so barren that it soon withers and fades; or, if it enters and grows, is it in danger of being crowded out by worldly affairs?"

The order of the words, in the Greek text, suggests a more emphatic statement than our translation, "In meekness receive ye . . ." *(en prauteti,* in a docile manner, in contrast with the *wrath* earlier alluded to, often characteristic of men). One must be meek as well as pure in order for the word to have its full effect in the heart. Those who approach the study of the Scriptures with arrogance may discover the proof texts they seek (as a lawyer seeks precedents to sustain his case from previous court decisions), but such can never imbibe the spirit which pervades the holy pages thereof. One who studies the Bible ought to do so for the purpose of discovering God's will, in order that one may first practice it in one's own life, and *then* teach it to others. Our approach to it should be with the disposition of docility characteristic of little children. This, indeed, is precisely what our Lord taught: "Verily I say unto you, Except ye turn, and become as little children, ye shall in no wise enter into the kingdom of heaven. Whosoever therefore shall humble himself as this little child, the same is the greatest in the kingdom of heaven. And whoso shall receive one such little child in my name receiveth me." (Matt. 18 : 3-5.)

No partial, superficial reception of the word will suffice. "Receive" is from *dexasthe,* aorist imperative, a positive, once for all action. Moreover, it is the *word* which is to be received. James would have no sympathy whatsoever with those who would minimize the importance of the *written word,* and who seek to assign to it a place of relative unimportance. The "word" is the body of truth contained in the Scriptures—the word which constitutes the Scriptures—and is that by which we are saved (James 1 : 21) ; born again (1 Pet. 1 : 22-25 ; 1 Cor. 4 : 15) ; directed through life (Psalm 119 : 105) ; and strengthened (1 Pet. 2 : 1 ; Heb. 5 : 2-14) ; the gospel, revealed to us in his word, is God's power to save (Rom. 1 : 16), and it *pleases* God to accomplish salvation in this way (1 Cor. 1 : 21).

Further, it is the "implanted word" *(ton emphuton logon);* i.e., rooted, fixed, grown strong, thus emphasizing the necessity of a thorough reception of the word in the heart before it can accomplish its purpose. Other definitions of the word translated "implanted" are inborn, innate, ingrafted. The word, deposited superficially in the heart, can never properly seed and grow into a strong, healthy plant. Here again is positive proof of the absolute necessity of preaching and teaching the truth fully, firmly, and plainly, in order that it may be understood, received without reservation, and thus permitted to have its full influence in the heart. When the soil (which is the heart) is properly prepared, the seed (which is the word of God) will readily spring into spiritual life, and yield its rich fruitage in Christian activity. It is not without much significance that Paul refers to the activities of the Christian life as *fruit*, the happy result of seedtime, and harvest. (Gal. 5: 22.)

which is able to save your souls.—The word of God is *able*, powerful, dynamic in its operation, from *dunamenon*, from *dunamis*, whence our words dynamic, dynamo, dynamite derive. There is power, limitless, inexhaustible power, in the word; and this power is released when received into an honest and good heart. This is in irreconcilable conflict with the view that the word of God is a dead letter, and without inherent power. It operated effectively, when used by our Lord, to still the tempestuous seas, to feed the famishing multitudes, to restore and heal broken bodies, and to raise the dead. It is, therefore, able to *save* the soul.

"Save," from *sosai*, aorist active infinitive, means much more than (though it of course also includes) the forgiveness of past, or alien, sins. James was addressing people already forgiven of their alien sins; hence, the salvation here primarily refers to a deliverance following pardon. The Greek verb means *to keep safe, preserve;* and this is precisely what the implanted word does for us, —it preserves us from a life of habitual sin, and it keeps us pure and holy. David said, "Thy word have I laid up in my heart, that I might not sin against thee." (Psalm 119: 11.) We are privileged to see, in this section, a principle repeatedly taught in the sacred writings: *the necessity of the concurrence of both the divine and the human wills in order to man's salvation.* The word is *able* to save; but, it saves only those who *receive* it. God wills the salvation of all men; but men must will to be saved themselves in order for the word to work effectively in their hearts. (1 Tim. 2: 4; John 5: 40.)

That which the implanted word saves is the *soul.* The word "soul" is from the Greek *psuche,* a generic term, the meaning of

is able to save your souls. 22 But be ye doers of the word, and not hearers

---

which must be ascertained from the text in which it appears. It is variously used in the Scriptures to denote the whole person (Acts 2: 41), the life which ends at death (Psalm 78: 50), and the spirit —the immortal nature—of man (Acts 2: 27). Here, the most simple explanation appears to be that James refers to the immortal nature—the spirit of man—which is saved from eternal separation from God by the word received into the heart, and translated into faithful obedience to his will, in the life.

We are, therefore, to rid ourselves of all sinful defilment and with great gentleness take once for all the seeded word which is fully able to accomplish the salvation of the soul. We have seen that James sets out, as a condition precedent to the reception of the word, the removal of "all filthiness." The word "filthiness is *ruparian*, from *rupos*, that which is soiled, dirty, filthy. Another instance of the wondrous wisdom of the Scriptures, and the penetrating analyses always characteristic of the Holy Spirit in the words which he selected to convey the message of the Bible (1 Cor. 2: 13), is to be seen here in the fact that in classical Greek the word *rupos*, when used in the field of medicine, has reference to *wax in the ear!* It is not without design that the Spirit chose this particular word, out of many which might have been selected to convey the idea of filth or dirt, to indicate to us that sin in the soul is comparable to wax in the ear—it renders impossible the reception of the word into the heart. As wax in the ear prevents sound impulses from entering the brain, so sin in the life effectively blocks the hearing of the word and its reception into the heart. Jesus said of some in this condition: "For this people's heart is waxed gross, *and their ears are dull of hearing,* and their eyes have they closed; lest haply they should perceive with their eyes, and hear with their ears, and understand with their heart, and should turn again, and I should heal them." (Matt. 13: 15.)

22 But be ye doers of the word,—"Be ye," *(ginesthe,* present middle imperative), means much more than simply *be,* it means "to exhibit yourselves as doers of the word." Moreover, the tense of the verb, denoting continuous action, means, *"keep on demonstrating* yourselves as doers of the word." Earlier in the chapter,

James had emphasized that the word must be received into the heart (implanted there) in order to spring forth into spiritual life; here, he directs attention to the fact that it is not sufficient merely to hear and to receive it, one must also be obedient to it. It is significant that God has never blessed anybody in any age or dispensation because of his faith until such time as his faith exhibited itself in obedience to his will. One is not simply or solely to keep on hearing the word, or even to keep on receiving it; it must express itself in action in the life in order to bless and to save. Further, the verb is middle, emphasizing the fact that the action required is that which one must do for one's self. Others can teach us; but we must, each one for himself, see to it that the word taught issues in life.

The word "doer," *(poietai)*, derives from *poieo,* a term denoting creative action. Had James intended merely to indicate that we are to be active, the word *prasso,* to do, to act, would have sufficed. There must, however, be more than mere mechanical action to discharge the obligations inherent in the word; it denotes a type of action wherein the heart is exercised and where motivation results from such participation. It is noteworthy that from the word translated *doer (poietai)* comes our word *poet.* Poetry is regarded as one of the most creative fields in all literature. A faithful Christian *poetizes;* his life is a perpetual poem, exhibiting therein the beauty and symmetry of a harmonious life, and demonstrating always and everywhere the creative action of a productive life.

and not hearers only,—The word rendered "hearers" *(akroatai)* was used in the early centuries to designate those attending lectures who heard, but never became genuine disciples. There are those, in every congregation, who attend services regularly, and who sit passively where the truth is preached, but who never profit by the word preached, nor translate into life the things heard. Many regard hearing the word as sufficient within itself, and feel no sense of obligation further. Our Lord often refuted this assumption. "Not every one that saith unto me, Lord, Lord, shall enter into the kingdom of heaven; but he that doeth the will of my Father who is in heaven. . . . Every one therefore that heareth these words of mine, and doeth them, shall be likened unto a wise man, who built his house upon the rock: and the rain descended, and the floods came, and the winds blew, and beat upon that house; and it fell not: for it was founded upon the rock. And every one that heareth these words of mine, and doeth them not, shall be likened unto a foolish man, who built his house upon the sand: and the rain descended, and the floods came, and the winds blew, and smote upon that house: and it fell; and great was the fall thereof." (Matt. 7: 21-27.) Paul said, "For not the hearers *(akroatai)* of the law are just before God but the doers of the law shall be justified." (Rom. 2:13.) Our Lord pronounced a blessing upon those who "hear the word of God, and keep it." (Luke 11: 28.)

It would be well for us to take notice of the fact that the *hearer only* of which James speaks is not a person who listens with little or no interest; on the contrary, the word *(akroatai)* denotes those who listen avidly and feel great interest in the things being presented, but who think that the blessing therein derives from the listening and who make no effort to express in life the things heard. One who audits a course in college may derive momentary benefit from the things heard, but he will not be on the stage when the diplomas are handed out! In like fashion, it is impossible for one to acquire considerable knowledge of the Scriptures by attentively listening to their presentation; but, those who make no effort to inculcate into life the principles learned will be missing when the Diplomas are handed out on the Great Examination Day.

deluding your own selves.—Those who hear, but do not, are not only without promise for the future, they are under a delusion. The word "deluding" is from *paralogizomenoi,* present middle participle of *paralogizomai,* from *para,* "beside," and *logizomai,* to "reckon," literally, to reckon sideways, and then to cheat, to deceive. Thus, a person who assumes that he can derive sufficient benefit from the word by merely listening to it simply cheats and deludes himself. The word occurs only here and in Col. 2: 4, where the meaning appears to be: "Led astray by unsound argument." He who thinks that it is enough merely to hear the word from week to week is resorting to fallacious reasoning; he is using arguments that are illogical; and, in so doing, is deceiving and deluding himself. This is not to minimize the importance of learning the truth. This, indeed, is the first step to faithful service.

only, deluding your own selves. 23 For if any one is a hearer of the word
and not a doer, he is like unto a man beholding [15]his natural face in a mir-

[15]Gr. *the face of his birth.*

But, of what avail is it, though one can quote every verse in the
New Testament, if one practices none of them? Of what value is it
to be able to silence every opponent with a thus saith the Lord, if
the one so doing refuses to heed the admonitions oneself? He who
thus does increases his own guilt: "for it were better for them not
to have known the way of righteousness, than, after knowing it, to
turn back from the holy commandment delivered unto them." (2
Pet. 2: 21.) The mere fact that one can quote the Great Commission does not assure salvation; it must be believed and obeyed to
produce spiritual life. John said, "He that saith, I know him, and
keepeth not his commandments, is a liar, and the truth is not in
him." (1 John 2: 4.)

It should be observed that this verse under consideration bids us
not only to *do, but to be doers.* The substantive is stronger than
the verb; there is in the construction the suggestion of persistence
and continuation. "Let this be your constant pursuit," is the
meaning thereof. Such is to be continued in as if it were one's
main purpose in life, as indeed it should be. Those who hear, but
do not do, delude themselves, by assuming that they shall receive
the blessing from the mere fact of hearing, when in reality, the
blessing is promised only to those who obey. (1 Pet. 4: 7; 2
Thess. 1: 7-9.) *Let it be remembered that James is not addressing the alien sinner primarily here. These words are addressed to
Christians!* One who merely listens to a doctor, but never takes his
course of treatment, need not hope to profit thereby; and a disciple
of our Lord is by him regarded as a genuine one only if he abides
in his word; i.e., conforms completely to it. (John 8: 31, 32.)

23 **For if any one is a hearer of the word and not a doer,—**
The first clause is, literally, "if any one is a hearer of the word,
and a *not-doer,*" thus contrasting those who hear and do with
those who hear and do not. The construction is an interesting one
—a condition of the first class with the statement assumed as true,
and thus with the conclusion following. He who hears and does
not is like the man whom James describes later in the verse.
Because that which we hear, but do not allow to take root in our

ror : 24 for he beholdeth himself, and goeth away, and straightway forgetteth

hearts, is soon forgotten and can never be a blessing, it is vitally important for every disciple to take special pains to see to it that the truth heard is also heeded. Otherwise, he is merely a hearer and a not-doer.

he is like unto a man beholding his natural face in a mirror : —"His natural face," is, literally, the face of his birth *(prosopon tes geneseos autou)*. The "mirror," to which the writer alludes, was not made of glass, but of some sort of polished metal, usually copper or tin, and sometimes silver, and highly burnished to reflect. One who hears and does not is like *a man* (not a woman, strangely enough!) who sees the reflection of his face in the mirror. One would suppose, from the nature of the illustration, that James intended to indicate that the man idly and carelessly *glanced* at his face in the mirror and that the effort was so momentary and brief that there was not sufficient time for an impression to be made. On the contrary, the word "beholding" is from *katanoeo*, to fix the mind definitely on, to regard attentively, to take careful note of. We shall see that it was not a defective look which led to forgetfulness, but the fact that he turned from the mirror to other things!

24 for he beholdeth himself, and goeth away, and straightway forgetteth what manner of man he was.—The tense of the verbs in this graphic illustration are highly significant. He looked (aorist) at himself, and has gone away (perfect active), and immediately forgot (aorist middle indicative) what kind of man he was. Thus, even the verbs of the passage provide a lifelike representation of the man who hears but does not. The man looked but did not linger ; he went away, and the state of abandonment continues to be present ; and he therefore forgot the impression received when he looked. Lessons merely listened to, and not allowed to sink deeply into the heart, are quickly forgotten and they influence the life no more than a glance into a mirror. The parallels are important and should not be lost upon us. The glance into the glass represents the listener who hears the word ; the going away is the wandering of the mind from that which is heard ; and, the result, in each instance, is forgetfulness. The effort of some to see in this illustration the effect of sin in the life, such as the marks of dissipa-

what manner of man he was. 25 But he that looketh into the perfect law, the *law* of liberty, and *so* continueth, being not a hearer that forgetteth but a doer that worketh, this man shall be blessed in his doing. 26 If any man

---

tion in the countenance, is fanciful; it was simply James' purpose to compare the quick glance and the equally speedy removal of the impression thus received with the loss sustained by the superficial hearers who listen to the word but soon forget it.

We are taught in the word to take heed *how* we hear as well as to be careful *what* we hear. This lesson our Lord taught in the parable of the sower, one of the most striking and impressive parables of the New Testament. (Matt. 13: 1-9, 19-23; Luke 8: 4-15.) The hearer sustains a tremendous responsibility to translate into life the lessons which he learns; and he must answer in judgment for his increased opportunities. (Matt. 11: 21-24; 2 Pet. 2: 20-22.) Nor, are those who teach and preach the word without great responsibility. (James 3: 1.) It is the obligation of all of those who thus do to present the truth in interesting and simple fashion so that those who hear may readily grasp it. Slovenliness, whether in the pulpit or in the pew, is inexcusable, highly objectionable to God, and a serious barrier to the spread of the gospel.

25 But he that looketh into the perfect law,—Here begins the application of the illustration of the man who looks but forgets his reflection in the mirror, set out in verses 23, 24. It is presented as a contrast, as evidenced by the word "but" with which the verse begins. Actually, the illustration of the mirror is mingled with the lesson and the figure is dropped. A man looks into his mirror and for a moment sees his reflection, but passes on, forgetting what he saw. Such is characteristic of one who hears the word of truth, but soon forgets it, and is thus wholly uninfluenced by it. The genuine listener is far more interested. The verb "looketh" clearly indicates this. It is from *parakupas,* aorist active participle, from *parakupto,* to stoop and look, to gaze intently. It is the term used to describe the actions of Peter and Mary as they peered into the empty tomb of Christ on the morning of his resurrection. (John 20: 5, 11.) It describes, in vivid detail, one who stoops down, as it were, in order to get the closest possible look; and, as used in our text, denotes one who is highly interested in the word of truth. It is a stronger term, and indicates a much more minute look, than that suggested by "beholding" in verse 24. It reveals (a) an abiding interest on the part of the viewer; (b) a recognition that there is something vitally important to see. It is this disposition which characterizes the interested listener.

That into which such a one intently looks is "the perfect law." It is well to observe first that it is *law* into which one is to look. James would be utterly without sympathy with that school of thought which alleges that the Old Testament consisted wholly of law, but no grace; the New Testament wholly of grace, but no law! *Law* is "a rule of action"; to insist that there is no law in the new covenant is to urge that there is no rule by which we are to walk today. In complete contrast with such a view, there is a "law of Christ" (Gal. 6: 2; 1 Cor. 9: 21); a "law of the Spirit of life" (Rom. 8: 2); a "law of liberty" (James 1: 25; 2: 12); the "law of love" (Rom. 13: 10); and, to insist that there is *no law* in the New Testament is (a) in conflict with these plain affirmations of inspiration; (b) implies that we are without an enforceable standard of conduct; and (c) disregards the significance of the word *law*.

But did not Paul declare that children of God are not under law, but under grace? (Rom. 6: 14.) The statement, "Ye are not under law, but under grace," is either (a) limited by the context; or (b) it is not. If *it is not*, Christians are a lawless people. Those who are under no law are lawless. It is absurd to affirm, in one breath, that children of God are not under law, any law, law of any kind, and then to concede that they are under restraint. Law is restraint. Those who are restrained are under law. Where there is no law there is no restraint. Moreover, those who are without law are without sin. Sin is the transgression of the law. "Where there is no law, neither is there transgression." (Rom. 4: 15.) Where there is no law, there is nothing to transgress; where there is nothing to transgress, there is no sin. Hence, where there is no law, there is no sin. This conclusion is irresistible. What is sin? It is lawlessness. (1 John 3: 4.) What is lawlessness? Lawlessness is an offense against law. But, where there is no law, there can be no offense against it. Those incapable of offending are either (a) perfect, thus *above* law; or (b) they are wholly *without* law. How can one transgress that which does

not exist? We are under some law; or, we are not. If we are
not, then it is impossible for us to sin; if we are under some sort of
law, then those who affirm otherwise are in grave error.

That Paul, in the passage alluded to, (Rom. 6: 14), did not intend to affirm that children of God are wholly without law *of any
kind* is evident from (a) the fact that he himself said that we are
under law to Christ and to God (1 Cor. 9: 21); and (b) from the
context in which the statement appears. The *thesis* of Romans is
that justification is through the system of faith which originated
with Christ, and not by means of the law of *Moses*. (Rom. 1: 16,
17.) In much detail, and with many contrasts, does he pursue this
argument from Rom. 1: 13 through 8: 25. The law which the
Gentiles did not have (2: 12-16) was the law of Moses. That
upon which the Jew rested, in which he found instruction, gloried
in, and often transgressed (2: 17-24), was the law of Moses. The
ordinances of the law (2: 25-28) were of the law of Moses. The
works of the law (3: 19, 20), which could not justify, were the
works of the law of Moses. The righteousness, in Christ, apart
from the law (2: 21-26), is that which is apart from the law of
Moses. The law of works, contrasted with the law of faith (Rom.
3: 27, 28), was the law of Moses. The law which issued in, and
was established by faith (4: 31), was the law of Moses. The
blessing pronounced upon Abraham, because of his faith (cited by
the apostle to sustain the view that justification was not by the law
of Moses), which was exercised anterior to the giving of the law
(4: 9-14), was declared to be apart from, and before the law of
Moses. The law to which the Jews were made dead, in order that
they might properly be joined to Christ (Rom. 7: 1-6), was the
law of Moses. The law which said, "Thou shalt not covet" (Rom.
7: 7), was the law of Moses. The commandment, which Paul
found to be death to him (Rom. 7: 7-25), was the law of Moses.
The law which was weak, through the flesh (Rom. 8: 2), was the
law of Moses. It is, therefore, an exceedingly careless and confused exegesis which would take from such a context a statement
which says, "For ye are not under law, but under grace," and deny
that the law referred to is *the law of Moses!* Here, the contrast
intended is exactly the same as that of John 1: 17: "For the law
was given through Moses; grace and truth came through Jesus

Christ." The conclusion is irresistible that the statement (Rom. 6: 14: "For ye are not under law, but under grace,") is limited to the contextual significance of the term; and, that Paul, continuing his thesis that Christians are not under the law of Moses, but are, in this dispensation, wholly answerable to Christ, meant by the statement, *You are not under the law of Moses; you are amenable to Christ through the system of grace originating with him.* This is, however, far from affirming that, in consequence, Christians are not under *any* law today. (Gal. 6: 2; James 2: 12; 1 Cor. 9: 21.)

Children of God have been, by the precious blood of Christ, redeemed from the *curse* of the law (of Moses), and are privileged, in Christ, to share in the blessings of salvation available through conformity to "the *law* of the Spirit of life." (Rom. 8: 2.) Through the freedom from the law of Moses children of God today enjoy, they may pursue their obligations under the law of love, realizing that the law by which they shall be judged (James 2: 12) is not one of slavery, but one of freedom. By this rule (of law) let us ever walk. (Gal. 6: 16.)

The *law,* into which Christians are to look intently, is a *perfect* one. "Perfect," in this passage, is from *teleion,* from *telos,* end, thus indicating, completeness, fullness, wholeness. The law of Christ is full, complete, embodying all that is necessary to accomplish its purpose.

the law of liberty,—This statement is further explanatory of why the law is designated as perfect, in the statement preceding. It is *law,* it is a *perfect* law, it is a perfect law *of liberty.* It is law, because it is "a rule of action" the design of which is to govern our lives; it is a perfect law, because it is (a) without defect; (b) it is all-sufficient to accomplish the purpose for which it was designed. It is a law of liberty, because obedience thereto sets one free from the bondage of sin and Satan, and spiritual death.

The view obtains with some that *law* and *liberty* are contradictory terms. The Holy Spirit, through James, envisioned no such difficulty. With him it is perfectly consistent to speak of law and liberty in the same breath, and to join them in the same phrase. Indeed, there can be true liberty only where there is law; law is restraint; where there is no restraint there is the most hopeless and abject slavery. A dope addict, for example, defies law, and thus operates without restraint, and thereby suffers the most rigorous bondage. Denominational theologians, laboring under the prepossessions of their creeds, seek to eliminate all law from God's plan today, and in this fashion attempt to avoid the essentiality of baptism, and other acts of obedience, as conditions precedent to the forgiveness of sins.

It is by such contended that law excludes grace; and that to insist on adherence to law, as a condition of salvation, makes the redemptive plan a system of works instead of faith. It is strange that those who thus reason (and who place such great confidence in the efficacy of faith, apart from all work) fail to observe that on this hypothesis, faith itself is excluded! "They said therefore unto him, What must we do, that we may work the works of God? Jesus answered and said unto them, This is the work of God, that ye believe on him whom he hath sent. " (John 6: 28, 29.) Belief itself is thus declared to be a work of God. It is, therefore, highhanded presumption on the one hand, and a denial of the plain affirmations of Scripture, on the other, to insist that there is efficacy in one work of God (faith), but not in another (baptism) in order to salvation. The truth is, neither is efficacious in *obtaining* salvation for us; we are saved on the merits of Christ's blood shed in our behalf, but appropriated on compliance with the conditions which the Lord himself gave. These are belief in his deity (Mark 16: 15, 16), repentance from every sin (Luke 13: 3), confession of him before men (Rom. 10: 9, 10), and baptism in water (Acts 2: 38). The Lord saves us; but he saves us only when we believe, repent, confess and are baptized in water for the remission of sins! To allege that such is legalism is to level the charge against the Lord himself who is the author of the plan of salvation applicable to us today.

To object to this on the ground that it involves a *plan* is absurd; a "plan" is "a proposed method of action or procedure" (Webster); the Lord requires of us the foregoing "method of action, or procedure" in order to our salvation. To charge that emphasis on the *Plan* is to minimize the *Man* is opposed to common sense; we magnify the Man in exact ratio to the respect we exhibit for his Plan. The confidence we have in our physician is indicated by the degree of faithfulness which characterizes our adherence to his instructions. We evidence our respect for Christ in the care we exercise in doing what he said. *We honor the Man in respecting and obeying the Plan!* The effort to draw away attention from the plan on the allegation that such should be focused on the Man usually has as its aim deemphasis of the commands of Christ, particularly baptism. We implore our readers to avoid and repudiate this hurtful and dangerous heresy. If it is legalism to insist that every command of Christ should be equally respected and faithfully obeyed, then let us all be legalists! Far better this than to deny the plain affirmations of his word and thus, in effect, to become infidels!

and so continueth,—It is not enough merely to look, or to look intently into the "perfect law of liberty"; one must continue therein. "Continueth" is from *parameinas,* an aorist active participle, meaning to "stay close." It is to be closely construed with *parakupsas,* "to look into," in the preceding clause of the verse. The "law of liberty" is set out in the New Testament; and, one who has the proper attitude toward it will stay close to it; i.e., he is never far from contemplation thereon, and he returns again and again to that in which he finds chief delight. In harmony with the Psalmist's observation, such a one's delight "is in the law of Jehovah, and on his law doth he meditate day and night." It is psychologically true that we forget more in the *first eight hours* after the study of a lesson, than we do in the *three weeks* following; and it is, therefore, of prime importance that we study regularly and review frequently the matters studied. It is interesting to note the relation which obtains between the approach which James mentions and the resulting action: The good hearer (1) looks deeply and with much thought into the Scriptures; (2) he remains with them, not allowing matters of the world to distract him from his study, nor to take from him that which he has learned.

being not a hearer that forgetteth but a doer that worketh, —"A hearer that forgetteth" is one whose disposition is to hear and to forget; such is characteristic of him; and such he always does. *He is simply a forgetful hearer.* Many are in this class today. They sit quietly and politely under the sound of gospel preaching, but their thoughts are far away and on material matters, and the word of truth finds no room to settle down and stay in hearts already filled with worldly affairs. The "doer that worketh," *(alla poietes ergon,* genitive of description), is literally a "doer of work," one whose characteristic is to work. Thus, people with totally opposite dispositions are here contrasted: (a) the hearer who forgets; (b) the hearer who puts into practice the things heard. Only the latter is promised blessing.

this man shall be blessed in his doing.—Blessedness belongs only to those who are obedient to the Lord's will. Jesus said, "If ye know these things, blessed are ye if ye do them." (John 13: 17.) There is no promise in the word of truth to indolent and indifferent individuals. Both by precept and by example our Lord emphasized the essentiality of faithful obedience to his will as a prerequisite to blessing.

Let us then be impressed with two things in this section of James: (1) There is a law *of liberty* to which all are today answerable; (2) this law of liberty is *perfect.* It is a law of liberty because it enables the ones obedient thereto to enjoy true freedom. Far from enslaving men, the law of God liberates them, enabling them to be truly free. The ancient Greeks were agreed on this premise and often expressed themselves to this end. "To obey God is liberty," said the scholarly Seneca. The Stoics declared that "The wise man alone is free, and every foolish man is a slave." He who is dominated by his desires is a slave to them; he who has surrendered his life to Christ, *has been set free,* through conformity to the Lord's law, from them! Moreover, the law of liberty is a *perfect* law, because it issues from a perfect source; it can never be amended, improved or transcended; it is fully able to accomplish all that it was designed to do, and is thus entirely adequate for every need of man.

PURE RELIGION
1: 26, 27

[16]thinketh himself to be religious, while he bridleth not his tongue but deceiv-

---

[16]Or, *seemeth to be*

---

26 If any man thinketh himself to be religious,—Verses 20-25 are an inspired commentary on James 1: 19. These verses deal particularly with being "swift to hear," mentioned there. Verse 26 begins with the consideration of another portion of verse 19, "slow to speak." "If any man thinketh" is a condition of the first class. "Thinketh," from *dokei,* has the marginal reading, "or seemeth to be," and, "thinketh," in the text, or *seemeth* (a less likely rendering) equally make good sense. The latter would refer to the impression such a one would make upon others; the former, the impression entertained by oneself, the more likely meaning here. The context suggests that the reference is to the man's attitude toward himself, rather than as he may appear to others. It is quite possible for one to deem himself religious when he is far from such. We shall see later in more detail that the reason for this deception is that such a one fails to exercise the control over his speech which he should, thus nullifying his claim to effective religion.

"Religious," from *threskos,* derived from *threskeia,* designates piety as it manifests itself outwardly—external devotion. It includes such activities as public prayer, observance of the Lord's supper, church attendance, and the like. There is in the word some suggestion of scrupulosity, the disposition to be particularly concerned with the most minute details; and it is very possible for one to be extremely careful in such activities and at other times to indulge in unbridled speech highly displeasing to God. In these one may engage quite freely, yet unacceptably, and under a delusion regarding one's true condition. One may think himself to be wholly pleasing to God, in these respects, yet fail in others, and so be out of harmony with the Creator. We thus learn that however scrupulous one may be in the observance of the outward forms of religious activity, if one does not control the tongue one is self deceived and displeasing to God. It is the design of Christianity to bring our whole being into harmony with Jehovah; and, if the tongue is unrestrained, this is sufficient evidence that in such a person the influence which Christianity normally exercises is wanting, and the man's religion is vain.

while he bridleth not his tongue but deceiveth his heart, this man's religion is vain.—"Bridleth" *(chalinagogeo,* from *chalinos,* a bridle, and *ago,* to lead) graphically portrays a man putting a bridle in his own mouth, and not in another. He who does not bridle (exercise complete control of) his tongue is, in consequence, deceived, and has a religion that is vain. "Deceived" here is from *apaton,* present active participle of *apatao,* to deceive, trick. Such a one is not only deceived; he keeps on tricking himself under the delusion that he is an acceptable religious character. "Religion," from *threskeia,* is devotion in outward manifestation; and is translated "worshipping" in Col. 2: 18. The word "worshipping" in this instance has, in the American Standard Version, a footnote which says, "The Greek word denotes an act of reverence, whether paid to a creature, or to the Creator." This emphasizes that the word means outward devotion, external religious actions.

Such religion is "vain," *mataios,* empty, valueless, without benefit to man, and unacceptable to God. The word thus translated indicates that which fails to produce the desired result and is thus fruitless. It follows, therefore, that however punctual in the performance of the external duties of Christianity one may be, if the tongue is not rigidly controlled, such a one's religion is profitless and vain. This is a lesson sorely needed. There is the disposition to feel that it is enough if one conforms to the rituals and ceremonials of Christianity; and but little importance, in the minds of many, attaches to the condition of heart characteristic of those participating. Some religions, indeed, are founded on the premise that a mere profession is sufficient, and that the blessing of God falls upon those who engage in a prescribed number of devotions without regard to the condition of heart of those thus engaging. This persistent view Jesus repeatedly refuted. Among the final warnings issued in the Sermon on the Mount, he said, "Not every one that saith unto me, Lord, Lord, shall enter into the kingdom of heaven, but he that doeth the will of my Father in heaven. Many will say to me in that day, Lord, Lord, did we not prophesy by thy name, and by thy name cast out demons, and by thy name do many mighty works? And then will I profess unto them, I never knew you: depart from me, ye that work iniquity." (Matt. 7: 21, 22.) Of others similarly influenced, it was said, "This people draweth nigh unto me with their mouth, and honoreth me with their lips; but their heart is far from me. But in vain do they worship me, teaching as their doctrines the precepts of men." (Matt. 15: 8, 9.)

eth his heart, this man's religion is vain. **27** Pure religion and undefiled before our God and Father is this, to visit the fatherless and widows in their affliction, *and* to keep oneself unspotted from the world.

It will be seen that the reason such religion is *vain* is that it does not *please* God. Though it highly pleases the worshipper, unless God is pleased, no blessing derives therefrom. It is the end and aim of religion to satisfy the requirements of Jehovah; and when men follow a course the design of which is to *please* them, on the assumption that such is sufficient to please God, they are under a delusion. We are assured of pleasing God only when we do exactly what he said in his word and that without addition, without subtraction, without modification.

27 Pure religion and undefiled before our God and Father is this,—The adjectives "pure," and "undefiled," describe an approved kind of religion, now to be contrasted, by James, with the "vain" religion characteristic of a person with an unbridled tongue and a deceived heart. "Pure," from *kathara*, denotes that which is clean; "undefiled," from *amiantos*, that which is without contamination. The two words often appear together; and they evidence the fact that the religion which pleases God is in sharp contrast with the devotions which rely, for their efficacy, on ritual and ceremonial, and are without regard for the purity of heart and the sincerity of soul which the New Testament throughout enjoins. It is idle for one to expect God to be pleased with outward acts of religion when the heart is not pure. (Matt. 5: 8.) The disposition to feel that mere mechanical performance suffices is a persistent and stubborn one, and is often inveighed against by writers in both of the Testaments. Against this unwarranted assumption Micah thundered in one of the most impressive passages in the Old Testament: "Wherewith shall I come before Jehovah, and bow myself before the high God? shall I come before him with burnt-offerings, with calves a year old? will Jehovah be pleased with thousands of rams, or with ten thousands of rivers of oil? shall I give my firstborn for my transgression, the fruit of my body for the sin of my soul? He hath showed thee, O man, what is good; and what doth Jehovah require of thee, but to do justly, and to love kindness, and to walk humbly with thy God?" (Mic. 6: 7, 8.) Our Lord's most severe denunciations were reserved for religious men who made long prayers, but who devoured widows' houses! (Matt. 23 : 25, 26.)

The religion contemplated here is "before our God and Father." "Before" is from *para*, by the side of, i.e., the rule of measurement which God keeps, as it were, by *his* side, to determine such. Whatever men may affirm regarding the attributes and characteristics of religion, this passage is God's standard; and, of course, the only right one. He is "our" God and is further identified, in the passage, as "Father," quite significantly in view of the injunction regarding fatherless ones and widows in need: "His name is Jehovah; and exult ye before him. A father of the fatherless, and a judge of widows, is God in his holy habitation. God setteth the solitary in families. . . ." (margin, *maketh the solitary to dwell in a house*). (Psalm 68: 4, 5.) "Jehovah preserveth the sojourners: he upholdeth the fatherless and widow, but the way of the wicked he turneth upside down." (Psalm 146: 9.)

We have earlier observed that the word translated religion *(threskia)* denotes external actions, outward devotions. This, then emphasizes the fact that benevolence is by our Lord regarded as *worship*, and that those who neglect to provide for the fatherless and widow, however punctilious they may be in the observance of the visible forms of worship, such as prayer, singing, the Lord's supper, and the like, are without the approval of God. What is "pure and undefiled religion before our God and Father"? It is "this," *haute*, a demonstrative pronoun, in agreement with "religion" *(threskeia)*:

to visit the fatherless and widows in their affliction,—"To visit," is from *episkeptesthai,* present middle infinitive of *episkeptomai*, to see, to inspect, with a view of assisting. It is used figuratively here to designate the assistance which pure and undefiled religion requires of the Lord's people regarding "the fatherless and widows." It is quite obviously not limited to a social call; an orphaned or abandoned child would find little solace in such! God "visited" his people by sending his Son into the world to bless and to save them (Luke 1: 68); the "fatherless and widow" are "visited" when we do what we can to comfort and sustain them. The infinitive, "to visit," is in the present tense, thus indicating a continuous and habitual action, *"Keep on* visiting the fatherless and widow. . ." Jesus said, "For ye have the poor always with you, and whensoever ye will ye can do them good. . ." (Mark 14: 7.) The obligation remains so long as the need continues; and, since the need always exists, the obligation continues.

The "fatherless" *(orphanos)* are those "bereft of parents," whether because of death, disease, divorce, desertion or delinquency; children without parents, children whose parents either cannot, or will not, provide for them fall within the purview of this word. The "widows" *(cheras)* are women who have lost their husbands (either by death or desertion), and are without the means of support. It is interesting to observe that the word has a metaphorical significance of abandonment; i.e., of one forsaken. (Cf. Rev. 18: 7.) The phrase, "in their affliction," describes the status of both fatherless and widows, and that which necessitates the "visiting." James does not, of course, imply here that orphaned children with a trust fund set up for their support or rich widows are to be provided for financially. Those to be "visited" (sustained and supported) are children without parents to provide (for any of the reasons above designated), and widows in destitution.

There are those who have objected to the orphan homes among us on the ground that there are children in them with one or more parents living; and, that such children are not orphans. This objection is wholly without merit in that (a) it disregards the meaning of the word *orphanos,* translated fatherless (see above); (b) such children are often the most destitute and needy of any. Every one recognizes the needs of a child which suffers the loss of both parents in death, and loving arms are quickly outstretched to receive it, but the truly destitute child is the one whose parents either will not, or cannot, provide but because they live others cannot take the children into their own homes and support them. Here, especially, the *legal* homes (homes such as the Tennessee Orphan Home, set up in harmony with state law, and operated accordingly), fulfill a need which *private* homes simply cannot meet. A child with worthless parents, on becoming a ward of the state, can seldom be placed in a private home; the children our "orphan" homes receive in this category would, did we not have such homes, go into Catholic or denominational institutions.

It is alleged that this passage is exclusively individual; i.e., the duties here enjoined are obligatory upon individuals *only*, and that the church cannot scripturally participate in such. The objection is invalid because (a) there is nothing in the passage or its context which justifies such a conclusion; if it be urged that James has in mind only the individual from his use of the word "oneself," in the final clause of the verse, it should be noted that the context deals with the "church assembly" (James 2 : 1ff.), in the verses following which, as James penned the statement, was without chapter and verse division; (b) such a conclusion would mean that the church is forbidden to practice pure and undefiled religion; (c) such would require that each individual member of the church must, if able, take at least *two* orphans and at least *two* widows (the words are plural), into his own home and support them, in order to engage in pure and undefiled religion; (d) If it is alleged that James designates by the word "oneself" in the last clause of the verse a duty which only an individual may perform, and which bears no relationship to *church* duties, would not Paul's statement, "But let a man prove *himself*, and so let *him* eat of the bread and drink of the cup. For *he* that eateth and drinketh, eateth and drinketh judgment unto *himself*, if he discern not the body" exclude the church? (1 Cor. 11 : 28, 29.) If "oneself" in James 1 : 27 excludes the church from all participation in the matters mentioned, why would not "himself," from the same mode of reasoning, eliminate the Lord's supper from *church* action? Is the Lord's supper exclusively individual action, and from which the church must abstain? If not, why does "oneself" eliminate it, but "himself" include it? The effort to exclude the church from such participation, on the basis of this argument, is obviously a failure!

The truth is, it was not James' design to indicate the *who* in the passage under study, but the *what*. It was doubtless assumed by him that those to whom he wrote would understand that these injunctions were obligatory upon them whether collectively or individually. However poor one may be, one who belongs to a congregation which supports the fatherless and widow participates therein, inasmuch as we are all members of the same body. (1 Cor. 12 : 1ff.) Paul designates the *who* in 1 Tim. 5 : 16, when he charged the *church* with the responsibility of providing for the widow "indeed." Since widows and orphans are to be provided for some way, and inasmuch as Paul designates that such is the responsibility of the church, the church may properly provide funds to support the destitute. So Paul taught in Gal. 6: 10: "So then, as we have opportunity, let us work that which is good toward all men, *especially* toward them that are of the household of the faith." The effort to make this passage exclusively individual is absurd; it requires the conclusion that Paul, in a letter specifically addressed to "the churches of Galatia" (Gal. 1: 2), gave them instruction therein *which it would be sinful for these churches to follow!* It is clearly the responsibility of the church to provide for the needy. (James 1: 27; Gal. 6: 10; 1 Tim. 5: 16.)

Whether the church supports the needy in a *legal* home (one licensed by the state for the purpose of providing for the destitute), operating in harmony with state law, as in the case of the homes for the fatherless and the aged being operated by faithful Christian men and women and supported by the churches of Christ, or in a *natural* home (their own, or some others), the principle is precisely the same. A great (though temporary) need arose in the Jerusalem church, shortly after the day of Pentecost, which the disciples of that congregation sacrificially met by selling their possessions and placing the proceeds thereof into the hands of the apostles to be disbursed for the poor among them as the need arose. (Acts 6: 1-6.) The needy thus provided for continued to exercise the autonomy of their families; the mere fact that they were being thus supported does not mean that the church took these homes into the congregations where the elders exercised oversight of the family structure in the same manner as they oversaw the operation of the Bible school. The *church* and the *home* are separate institutions; each has its distinctive and peculiar duties; and, in this area the church cannot properly usurp the functions of the home. To the *home* God assigned the duties and responsibilities of child care; the church was not organized to engage in such. *The home cannot scripturally operate as a church; neither can the church operate as a home.* When the home falls into the need, it is the duty of the church to come to its aid; but, in so doing, it does not dissolve the home, and assume its functions. The church has no more right to attempt to operate as a *home* than it does as a *state!* The doctrine of the union of church and state is Catholicism; the theory that the church can take over the home and operate it *as a part of the church* is hobbyism.

The "orphan homes" (the term is a misnomer, the children received into them are no longer orphans; i.e., bereft of parental care, but are being lovingly cared for by tender, Christian hands, and supported by the churches of Christ), are not in conflict with the church, because these institutions are not doing the work of *the church,* they are performing the functions of *the home;* they are not in conflict with the *home*, because the home, which they replace for the child, is gone. What is an "orphan" home? It is the home which the child had, but lost, and which has been restored. It is God's will that "the solitary" should be placed "in families" (Psalm 68: 6), and this is precisely what is done for them when they are placed in these homes and are provided for there. It follows, therefore, that these homes, every one of them today being supported by the churches of Christ, are scriptural ones, and deserving of our liberal financial support, our prayers and our encouragement. May the "God of the fatherless and the judge of widows" bless every one of them

and to keep oneself unspotted from the world.—This is the second aspect of the religion (outward devotion) which is pure and undefiled. "To keep," *(terein,* present active infinitive), means *to keep on* keeping oneself unspotted from the world! Children of God are members of the church *(ecclesia,* from *ek*, out of, and *kaleo,* to call); and have been called out from the world; they are, therefore not to love it (1 John 2: 15), to have friendship with it (James 4: 4), but to separate themselves from it. The "world" *(kosmos)* denotes that which is peculiar to this existence, in contrast with the realm of the spirit; the domain of Satan, that over which he rules, and in which his spirit is the dominating factor. It is the world of the unbelieving, the corrupt of heart and life; and Christians are to have no concourse with those who are of it, lest they suffer contamination. One keeps "unspotted" from the world by not allowing the spots of the world to be transferred to him. One cannot come into contact with dirt, without becoming dirty; in like fashion, it is impossible to participate in the things of the world, without being worldly. Paul solemnly admonished:

"Have no fellowship (partnership, joint participation) with the unfruitful works of darkness, but rather even reprove (expose, bring to light) them." (Eph. 5: 11.) Paul's admonition to Timothy, "Keep thyself pure" (1 Tim. 5: 22), is as applicable to all of us today, as to him to whom it was originally penned. Only those who thus do shall see God. (Matt. 5: 8.) "Having therefore these promises, beloved, let us cleanse ourselves from all defilement of flesh and spirit, perfecting holiness in the fear of God." (2 Cor. 7: 1.) "But like as he who called you is holy, be ye yourselves also holy in all manner of living; because it is written, Ye shall be holy; for I am holy." (1 Pet. 1: 15, 16.)

SECTION 4
2: 1-13

RESPECT OF PERSONS
2: 1-4

1 My brethren, [1]hold not the faith of our Lord Jesus Christ, *the Lord* of

[1]Or, *do ye, in accepting persons, hold the faith . . . glory?*

1 **My brethren,**—With this warm and friendly phrase, characteristic of James, a new theme begins. This brotherly address was the manner in which the writer often began a fresh topic. (James 1: 19; 2: 5, 14; 3: 1; 5: 7.) Inasmuch as it was his intention to rebuke the brethren to whom he wrote for serious and repeated infractions of the law of love, it was fitting that this subdivision should thus begin. For the significance of the word "brethren," the implications involved in its use, and the lessons applicable to us to-day therein, see the comments on James 1: 2.

hold not the faith of our Lord Jesus Christ, the Lord of glory, with respect of persons.—"The faith of our Lord Jesus Christ" *(ten pistin tou kuriou hemon Iesou Christou)* is not, of course, the faith which Christ exercises; it is the whole of the Christian religion, represented under the phrase, "the faith," where a vital part thereof is made to stand for, and represent, the whole of it. James is saying here, "My brethren, do not hold to Christianity and at the same time show partiality and special concern for those who are rich or highly favored of the world." It is, in effect, to say: *Don't try to be a Christian and a hypocrite at the same time!* The disposition which prompts one disciple of the Lord to entertain and exhibit favoritism for another, on external grounds, and because of worldly considerations, is wholly foreign to the spirit of Christianity, and a violent perversion of genuine religion. Christ is identified in the passage as "the Lord of glory," not without much significance in the connection in which it appears. Its meaning is much the same as "the glorious Lord," and was doubtless introduced to show that in spite of, and despite the poverty and extreme humiliation to which he was subjected while on earth, his is now a position of great glory, a glory which he offers to his *humble* disciples, and grounded in Christian character, not on fame or worldly possessions.

This "faith" Christians are not to *hold* "with respect of persons." "Hold not" is *me echete,* present active imperative of *echo,* with the negative; i.e., *quit having the habit* of holding the faith in such fashion. It will be observed that here, and often elsewhere in the Epistle, the writer repeatedly returns to his theme that it is impossible for one properly to approach God in worship if the heart is not right, or if the conduct is corrupt. Though James is filled with injunctions the design of which was to impress his readers with the necessity of *practical* religion, ever emphasized is the fact that such will result in a blessing only when purity of heart and life characterize the worshipper.

"With respect of persons" is from *en prosopolepsiais,* compounded from the nouns *prosopon* (which means face, countenance), and *lempsia,* derived from *lambano,* to receive, thus, literally, to receive face! As used here, it signifies to show regard for the external circumstances of another, and to exhibit favoritism on the ground of rank, wealth, social position, worldly attainment and fame. It is this disposition which James condemns, and which our Lord so sharply rebuked while on earth. (Luke 20: 21.) Partiality, based on wordly or material considerations, is so far removed from the true spirit of Christ, that for any of the disciples to exhibit such is a violent perversion of the Christian religion. For other instances of the word, see Rom. 2: 11; Eph. 6: 9; Col. 3: 25. God does not show respect of persons, and neither may we. It was this which impressed Peter in the incident of the great sheet: "Of a truth I perceive that God is no respecter of persons: but in every nation he that feareth him, and worketh righteousness, is acceptable to him." (Acts 10: 34.)

Having seen that all are *equal* before God, and that it is sinful to show respect of persons from wordly considerations, inasmuch as every disciple is entitled to the same privileges in Christ (Gal. 3: 26-29), it is an extension of this beyond proper bounds to imply that there are no differences obtaining between men. We are taught, in the New Testament to "honor the king" (1 Pet. 2: 13), and to pray for those in high places (1 Tim. 2: 2).

Elders, deacons, aged men and women, dignitaries, men of great

glory, with respect of persons. 2 For if there come into your ⁂synagogue a
man with a gold ring, in fine clothing, and there come in also a poor man in

⁂Or, *assembly* Comp. Heb. 10. 25 (Gr.).

faith and courage, are often singled out, in the Scriptures, and declared to be worthy of special regard for their works of faith, their
labors of love, and patience in hope they exhibit. (1 Tim. 5: 17;
3: 13; 1 Tim. 5: 1-3; Heb. 11: 1ff.; 2 Pet. 2: 10, 11.) What is
taught is that there is no place for worldly acclaim in Christianity,
and that all such reverence in public worship is unseemly and sinful. Inasmuch as God is no respecter of persons, neither should
we be.

2 For if there come into your synagogue—"Synagogue,"
(sunagogen), from *sun*, with, and *ago*, to gather, thus, literally, to
assemble with, meant, in the apostolic age, (a) a congregation assembled; (b) the place where the assembly took place. It seems
quite obvious, from the context, that it is the first of these meetings—a congregation assembled—which is intended here. If to us
today it appears strange that a Christian writer, addressing Christians regarding conduct in a Christian assembly should, nevertheless, refer to the event under a Jewish appellation, let it be remembered that the religious background of the writer and the people to
whom he wrote was wholly Jewish; that these impressions lingered
for a long time; that the Jewish influence was strongly felt and exhibited throughout the apostolic age; and that terms were of necessity used which would convey as fully as possible to Jewish people
the mind and message of the Spirit through James.

a man with a gold ring, in fine clothing,—Occasionally a man
of means would visit the assemblies of the saints and, as has ever
been characteristic of many people, the disposition to fawn upon
such, and to show them special honors, was a temptation to which
men in every age have been subjected, and to which they sometimes yielded. The phrase, "a man with a gold ring," is, in the
Greek Testament, *aner chrusodaktulios*, literally, *a gold ringed
man!* This indicates that such a one would be possessed of many
rings, and would wear them in ostentatious fashion. An ancient
writer mentions one man who wore six rings on each finger, day
and night, and did not remove them when he bathed. The histori-

vile clothing; 3 and ye have regard to him that weareth the fine clothing, and say, Sit thou here in a good place; and ye say to the poor man, Stand

---

ans record that Hannibal, after a great battle in which his forces were successful, sent three bushels of gold rings from the fingers of Roman knights killed in the conflict as a trophy to Carthage. Moreover, the man in the mind of the writer, in addition to the grand display of rings which he wore, was arrayed "in fine clothing," *(en estheti lampria,* brilliant, gaily colored garments), which attracted much attention from those less endowed.

and there come in also a poor man in vile clothing;—This poor man, in the illustration, was much worse off than we ordinarily mean by the adjective *poor* today. The word is *ptochos,* a beggar (Matt. 19: 21), one dependent on the charity of others for his very livelihood, not simply one with but little of this world's goods, yet with a sufficiency for living. His apparel, in sharp contrast with that of the richly bedecked man described above, is described as "vile clothing," *(en ruparai estheta,* squalid, cheap, perhaps dirty). Though their economic status is as different as day and night, and though, in social rank, they are as far apart as the poles, they are both in church, and there stand equal before God who respects not the persons of men.

3 and ye have regard to him that weareth the fine clothing, —How characteristic of men so to do, and what common human weakness is here evidenced! "Ye have regard for," is *epiblepsete de epi,* aorist active subjunctive of *epibelpo,* to gaze with favor upon, and thus to be impressed, as in this instance, with the dazzling gold ornaments, and the brilliant display of clothing worn by the affluent man.

and say, Sit thou here in a good place;—*(Su kathou hode kalos),* "*You* (emphatic) sit here in a good place"; i.e., a place of honor and prestige. The most coveted place in a synagogue, to a Jew, was near the end of the building, facing Jerusalem, and where the ark in which the sacred roll of the law was kept. In the illustration which James uses, of course based upon actual observance, the visitor is escorted to the most favored place in the building and with great deference there seated.

and ye say to the poor man, stand thou there, or sit under

thou there, or sit under my footstool; 4 [3]do ye not make distinctions [4]among
yourselves, and become judges with evil thoughts? 5 Hearken, my beloved

[3]Or, *are ye not divided*
[4]Or, *in your own mind*

my footstool;—There is thinly veiled contempt in the words of
the usher to the poor man, and no regard whatsoever shown for
his comfort. He is not invited to sit in the usual places at all; he
is rudely told to stand; he is not escorted to any place; but coldly
instructed to find his own; with a contemptuous wave of the hand,
the usher says, in effect, "Stand there, or sit, if you must, under
my footstool, the place where I rest my feet." For a visitor to be
required to stand, while the regular attendants sat was extreme
discourtesy; and it was little better to be permitted, grudgingly, to
sit under the stall where the people usually placed their feet. It
was James' intention to show, in this striking contrast, the difference people are disposed to make between the rich and the poor,
and to condemn such. In view of this, what must our Lord think
of that attitude of mind and heart which often prompts people,
themselves alleged suppliants before the throne of grace and in
need of much mercy, to array themselves in the most ostentatious
garments possible, and to parade down the aisles of New Testament church buildings preening like peacocks to the admiration of
some and the envy of others?

4 do ye not make distinctions among yourselves,—The
phrases "do ye not make distinctions," and "among yourselves,"
both have marginal readings, in the American Standard Version of
the Scriptures, thus indicating a difference in view among the
translators as to the preferred rendering. For, "do you not make
distinctions," there is the footnote, "are ye not divided," and for
"among yourselves," the footnote reads, "in your own mind."
Were the footnotes placed in the text, the passage would read,
"Are ye not divided in your own mind. . ." The verb, "make distinctions," is, in the Greek text, *diekrithete*, first aorist passive indicative of *diakrino*, to separate; and, the construction of the sentence is such that an affirmative answer was expected from the
question raised. The verb is translated "doubteth," in James 1 : 6,
and in similar fashion in Acts 10 : 20, and Rom. 14 : 23.

There is, therefore, two possible interpretations, depending on whether the translation in the text, or in the footnotes, is followed. If the first, the meaning is, "Do you not recognize differences among you based upon material considerations? Is it not true that you fawn upon the rich, when they enter your assemblies, and do you not treat with contempt the poor?" If the second, the meaning is, "When you show partiality, on the basis of economic standing or other material and worldly considerations, are you not exhibiting doubt (disbelief) in the teaching of our Lord who straitly forbade all such in his teaching?" In view of the fact that the word translated "distinctions" is used uniformly to express doubt, in the New Testament, it would appear that the second of these interpretations is the more probable one. The phrase which follows, "and become judges of evil thoughts," supports this view. The conduct of those to whom James wrote (the verb indicates that they were practicing the things which he condemned here) was such that they were wavering between what the Lord taught regarding fame, riches, social standing, and the like, and the temptation to show special favors to those well circumstanced. To use one of James' phrases, they were men of *two minds;* i.e., "double-minded." (James 1 : 8.)

and become judges with evil thoughts?—These people had, by their exhibition of favoritism toward the rich, resulting from the wavering of their faith, become "judges with evil thoughts." The word "judges" is from *dialogismon,* from *dialogismos,* reasoning. The word is a legal term; and, as here used, describes the litigation which resulted from the conflicting views which they felt, producing the doubt earlier mentioned. The conflict which existed in their minds, between what they knew the Lord taught regarding the rich and riches, and their desire to show preferential regard for such made them a court of conflict! These conflicts were as pronounced as would be the opposing views of lawyers arguing a case in court.

From this section we learn that it was evidently quite unusual for a rich man to visit an assembly of the saints. The appearance of such a man was so exceptional that when it occurred considerable excitement prevailed, prompting the brethren to exercise themselves unduly in assigning to him the most honorable seat possible. Such a disposition was highly displeasing to God with whom there

is no respect of persons. In his sight, all men are equal in privilege and promise; and with him, one soul is as precious as another.
It is evil to show honor to any man simply because he wears better
clothing, lives in a more pretentious house, or has a bigger bank
account. What prompts people to show special regard for the
rich? Usually the motive is a selfish one. There is lurking in the
back of the mind the idea that some day it may be necessary to ask
favors of the rich, and it is therefore expedient to flatter them.
Why bother with the poor? They can never do anything for us,
anyway. Ah, how many sins stem from simple selfishness!

GOD'S REGARD FOR THE POOR
2: 5

brethren; did not God choose them that are poor as to the world *to be* rich
in faith, and heirs of the kingdom which he promised to them that love him?

---

5 **Hearken, my beloved brethren;**—Compare statements beginning, in similar fashion, at James 1: 2, 19; 2: 1, 14; 3: 1, 10;
4: 11; 5: 7, 12, 19. To "hearken" is to hear with attention.
James would have his readers to give special attention to what he
was about to write, in view of the practices which he was rebuking.
Immediately preceding this is a sharp reprimand; it is followed by
this brotherly and tender address, breathing the very spirit of love,
interest and concern for those to whom he wrote. These contrasts
appear regularly in the Epistle. All of us should give careful attention to these matters. They are as important and pertinent to
us today as for those originally addressed. The sins which the sacred writer condemns are no less common now.

**did not God choose them that are poor as to the world to be
rich in faith,**—This question is cast in a form requiring an affirmative answer. That God has indeed chosen the "poor as to the
world," is evident from the fact that far more poor people serve
him than do the rich. The Lord has ordained that the poor shall
be possessors of the blessings of his kingdom; and, of this fact he
frequently made mention. (Luke 6: 20; cf. 1 Cor. 1: 26-30.)
This, of course, does not mean that the choice was arbitrary and
without regard for the character of those chosen; indeed, the passage declares that those thus chosen are "rich in faith," a phrase
which contrasts their spiritual endowments with the preceding one,

"poor as to the world." The manner in which God *chooses* people is clearly indicated in 2 Thess. 2: 13, 14, where it is affirmed that the divine call is through the gospel (which is to all men, Mark 16: 15, 16), and that belief of the truth (an act of men) is essential thereto. The poor outnumber the rich among those God has thus chosen simply *because the poor are much more likely to obey God than the rich are.* This passage does not assert that the Lord chooses people *because* they are poor; poverty, of itself, is not a blessing; nor, is the mere possession of wealth a sin. There is exceedingly good rich men, and extremely bad poor men. The meaning is that the poor are much more likely to be "rich in faith," than the rich are (who have far greater temptation), and inasmuch as God favors the poor for this reason, we ought not to reverse his order and favor the rich over the poor. The choice should always be made on the ground of richness of faith rather than on the basis of worldly and material possessions. Far better it is to be "poor as to the world," and "rich in faith," with the blessings which attend such, than to be possessed of all the gold of Ophir and the cattle on a thousand hills and to be impoverished in faith.

and heirs of the kingdom which he promised to them that love him?—A second characteristic of those who are "poor as to the world," but "rich in faith," is that they are "heirs of the kingdom," *(kleronomous tes basileias,* inheritors of the kingdom, those who shall some day receive the blessings thereof by right of descent). To be an *heir,* in New Testament usage, is to be related to God in such fashion as properly to receive that which descends from a father-son relationship. (1 Pet. 3: 9.) This relationship begins with the new birth (John 3: 3-5; cf. Col. 3: 24; Eph. 1: 18; Matt. 5: 5), and such expressions as "eternal life," (Matt. 19: 29), "an inheritance incorruptible," (1 Pet. 1: 4), and the "eternal inheritance," (Heb. 9: 15), are based on this relationship, and they continue and extend the figure thus used. To be an heir of the kingdom is, therefore, to be in that line of descent from God so as to be properly entitled to inherit that which belongs to him, and which he holds for his children.

It is important to take note of the fact that the kingdom contemplated here *is not* the kingdom set up on the first Pentecost following our Lord's resurrection, but the eternal kingdom which will result from the abdication of Christ at the end of this, the Christian age. (1 Cor. 15: 20-28.) That the kingdom referred to here is the heavenly aspect of Christ's kingdom is evident from the fact that those who love him, who are rich in faith, and have been chosen, are already in the kingdom which had its beginning on the eventful Pentecost day. (Acts 2: 1-47.) See Matt. 16: 18-20; Mark 9: 1; Col. 1: 13, 14; Heb. 12: 28; Rev. 1: 9. The kingdom, now in existence, is entered when one becomes a subject of Christ; the aspect of the kingdom mentioned in our text is that which Christians shall be privileged to enter at the last day, provided they have added to their faith the graces which adorn the Christian character. (2 Pet. 1: 5-11.)

It is this kingdom which God has *promised* to the poor who are rich in faith, though poor as to the world. It is to such that the kingdom of heaven belongs, a fact often asserted and emphasized in the Scriptures. (Matt. 5: 3; Luke 6: 20; 12: 32.) However, the future aspect of the kingdom, and the blessings associated therewith, exist only in promise, and it is a perversion of the Scriptures to insist that that which is only in promise is, at the same time, enjoyed in realization. The eternal *life* which begins with the realization of the promise will be enjoyed only on entrance into the future kingdom. (Mark 10: 30; Tit. 1: 2; 1 John 2: 25.) Those passages which assert that children of God are in possession of eternal life now (John 3: 16) must, in harmony with the foregoing considerations, be regarded as teaching that such life is enjoyed *in prospect*—not in actuality. Life that is eternal never ends. If Christians possess such today, it is impossible for them to lose it, and thus fall from grace. It is absurd for one to affirm today that one is in actual and literal possession of eternal life, yet concede the possibility of apostasy. *How can that which is eternal end?* There are more than twenty-five hundred warnings to the saints in the Scriptures touching the possibility of apostasy. One meets such on every page; it is not possible to open the Scriptures without seeing either directly or indirectly this fact taught. For example, "Ye are severed from Christ, ye who would be justified by the law; ye are fallen away from grace." (Gal. 5: 4.) "And thou Solomon, my son know thou the God of thy father, and serve him with a perfect heart and with a willing mind; for Jehovah searcheth all hearts and understandeth all the imaginations of the thoughts. If thou seek him he will be found of thee; but if thou forsake him, he will cast thee off for ever." (1 Chron. 28:9.)

We may, therefore, from the foregoing premises conclude that (a) the father-son relationship begins with the new birth; (b) those born again enter the kingdom of Christ on earth over which our Lord reigns today, and in which the Spirit dwells; (c) those thus positioned are *heirs* and, consequently, inheritors of the blessings of the future kingdom; (d) for them that divine inheritance awaits; (e) while on earth and before the consummation of all matters to occur when the Lord returns they are in possession of the promise of these future blessings which, in summary, consist of eternal life; (f) actual realization will be when they are granted the abundant entrance into "the everlasting kingdom of our Lord and Saviour Jesus Christ." (2 Pet. 1:5-11.)

Though these blessings are *in promise* today, of the ultimate fulfillment thereof, we may entertain no doubt whatsoever, *provided* we are faithful and persevere to the end. (Rev. 2:10.) The promise of God is sure, and on it we may safely rely. (2 Pet. 3:9.) God is faithful who promised; and, he will not fail us, if we do not fail him! "Behold then the goodness and severity of God: toward them that fell, severity; but toward thee, God's goodness, if thou continue in his goodness: otherwise thou also shalt be cut off." (Rom. 11:22.)

The promise is to those who *love* him. Here, indeed is the acid test; for it is love *for* him which prompts to faithful obedience *to* him: "He that saith, I know him, and keepeth not his commandments, is a liar, and the truth is not in him; but whoso keepeth his word, in him verily hath the love of God been perfected." (1 John 2:4, 5.) The phrase, "to them that love him," is, literally, *to those loving him, (tois agaposin auton)*; i.e., to those who continue to love him, and who evidence this love by faithful obedience to his will.

OPPRESSION BY THE RICH
2: 6, 7

6 But ye have dishonored the poor man. Do not the rich oppress you, and themselves drag you before the judgment-seats? 7 Do not they blaspheme

6 **But ye have dishonored the poor man.**—These to whom

James wrote had done this by giving preferential consideration to the rich, and by treating the poor with contempt. Notwithstanding the fact that the poor were far more likely to obey the Lord than the rich, there were those among James' readers who exhibited favoritism for the rich *because they were rich*, and showed disdain for the poor *because* they were poor. In so doing, they "dishonored" the poor man. The word translated "dishonored," *(etimasate,* aorist active indicative of *atimazo,* to degrade), means much more than merely to ignore, disregard; as here used, it signifies to put the poor in a state of degradation and to withhold from them the respect which they deserved. The attitude was more than a passive one; these thus rebuked *showed* contempt for the poor, and this involved active disrespect. This was to reverse God's attitude in such matters. "Thou, O God, did prepare of thy goodness for the poor." (Psalm 68: 10.) "For Jehovah heareth the needy." (69: 33.) "I know that Jehovah will maintain the cause of the afflicted, and justice for the needy." (140: 12.) See, also, Job 5: 15, 16; 36: 15; Psalm 9: 18; 72: 12, 13; 109: 31; Jer. 10: 13.

The statement, "But ye have dishonored the poor man," is an exceedingly vivid and impressive one in the original text. "But," (in contrast with the way God feels about such matters), "You," (emphatic), "on your part, far from exhibiting the same high regard for the poor that God does, have treated him with the grossest disrespect and contempt." Their actions, in the matter, were wicked, because they were at variance with God's will and way; and, as the next verse indicates, were lacking in good judgment. To dishonor the poor is a grievous sin, because it is an officious intermeddling with the plan of God. If God assigns to the poor a position of honor, how dare mere man to disregard it, and to set up a standard of his own? Solomon said, "He that despiseth his neighbor sinneth; but he that hath pity on the poor, happy is he." (Prov. 14: 21.) Distinctions among men, of whatever nature other than on Christian character, were especially obnoxious to James, and by him frequently condemned in the Epistle.

Do not the rich oppress you,—In addition to the lack of Christian charity evidenced in the fawning favoritism some were manifesting toward the rich, the attitude was one of absurdity, and wanting in good sense! The rich, whom they were favoring over the poor, were the very ones who had added to their misery through much persecution and oppression. The word for "oppress" in the text is a significant one, being *katadunasteuousin,* compounded from *kata,* down; and *dunastes,* ruler, potentate; and reveals that already the early Christians were suffering tyranny from the hands of rich Jews in positions of authority and influence. The Greek, freely rendered, is, "Do not the rich lord it over you?" Among the Sadducees of that period were many powerful Jews who were privileged by the Roman government to exercise considerable authority in the local courts of the Jews. There are numerous instances of such persecution from this source in Luke's inspired history of the early church. (Acts 4: 1-3; 13: 50; 19: 19.)

and themselves drag you before the judgment-seats?—Not only did these wealthy Jews oppress (bear down hard upon) the poor of the period, they frequently "dragged" (a vivid expression which continues in use to this day of individuals brought into court against their wills), where, under the pretense of legality, there was exacted from them what little they possessed. The "judgment seats," before which they were "dragged," were probably synagogue courts. Though the Jewish people were under the subjection of the Roman government (which maintained an army of occupation in Palestine at the time), they were permitted the privilege of conducting both civil and religious courts in which were heard matters of litigation involving the religion and business affairs of the Jewish people. Into these courts rich Jews often had the poor brought and by their power and influence had actions decided in their favor and against the poor, however just the cause of the latter might be. It should be noted that these were not Christian rich men, but unbelieving Jews who oppressed and evilly treated the Christian Jews among the early disciples. This situation is cited by James to show the absurdity of the practice which prevailed among some Christians of the time to show undue regard for the rich because they were rich, and to despise the poor because they were poor.

It is worthy of note that the only other instance in which the word translated "oppress" in the text occurs, is in Acts 10: 38,

the honorable name [5]by which ye are called?   8 Howbeit if ye fulfil the royal

[5]Gr. *which was called upon you?* See Acts 15. 17.

where it is said that Christ healed all that "were oppressed" of the devil. The actions of the heartless rich people of the period were comparable to that of the devil himself. How lacking in good sense it was to show servility to such characters solely on the ground that they were rich.

7 Do not they blaspheme the honorable name by which ye are called?—The antecedent of "they" is the rich. (Verse 5.) In addition to the oppression and exactions characteristic of those people they blasphemed the good name by which the early disciples were called. "Blaspheme" is from *blasphemousin,* present active indicative of *blasphemeo,* derived from *blasphemos,* evil speaking. They slandered the name which the disciples wore; and this evil speaking was not momentary or occasional, they did it over and over so the tense of the verb indicates. They habitually blasphemed the name. This name is described as *"honorable,"* from *kalos,* good, noble, excellent. The phrase, "by which ye are called," is, *to epiklethen eph' humas,* literally, *which is called upon you,* and such is the marginal rendering in the American Standard Version. The verb *called* is from *epikaleo,* aorist passive participle, and signifies to assign a name to, to place a name upon. This name was most surely that of *Christ,* pronounced upon us in baptism (Matt. 28: 19, 20; Acts 2: 38), and which Christians gladly wear because given by divine authority (Acts 11: 26; 26: 28; 1 Pet. 4: 14, 16). It is a further indication of the fact that James, who was prominent in the Jerusalem church, is the author of the book which bears his name, that an expression similar to the words *to epiklethen eph' humas,* "which is called upon you," occurs from his mouth in Acts 15: 17, it being a quotation from The Septuagint (the translation of the Old Testament from Hebrew into Greek) in Amos 9: 12.

THE ROYAL LAW
2: 8-13

law, according to the scripture, [6]Thou shalt love thy neighbor as thyself, ye

[6]Lev. xix. 18.

8 Howbeit.—This word, (not translated in the King James' Version), from the Greek *mentoi,* indicates the connection between that which follows, and that which precedes it, in the text. It appears to be used adversatively, and to imply that James' readers were attempting to justify their conduct toward the rich on the ground that they were simply obeying the royal law of love which requires one to love one's neighbor as one's self. In this event, the statement is to be understood in the light of the following facts: The writer had condemned all undue regard for men simply because they are rich. The disciples might say, in reply: "Our regard for them is no more than we are expected to exhibit, in view of the fact that the law requires us to love our neighbor as our selves." The apostle answers: "It is good if you keep the law; however, since your neighbors include those both rich and poor, why have you honored those who are rich, and have despised the poor? It is all very well to plead the law in justification of your acts, but 'If ye have respect of persons, ye commit sin, being convicted by the law as transgressors.' Thus, the very law which you offer as justification of your act condemns you because it forbids respect of persons, and so convicts you of being transgressors of the law."

Less likely is the view that the statement is designed merely to confirm what had earlier been penned. Favoritism and partiality toward the rich, and a corresponding disregard for the poor, by Christians, is a violent perversion of the law of love, and is thus sinful. In this event, the meaning would be: "If you really fulfill the royal law, which requires you to love your neighbor as yourself, it is good; but, if you continue to show respect of persons, as you have been doing by favoring the rich and dishonoring the poor, you commit sin, and transgress the law of God yourselves." The law, which they affected to observe, positively forbade all such distinctions: "Thou shalt not wrest justice: *thou shalt not respect persons;* neither shalt thou take a bribe; for a bribe doth blind the eyes of the wise, and pervert the words of the righteous." (Deut. 16: 19, 20.) It is highly inconsistent to cite the law in justification of one's actions in one matter, and disregard and violate the law in another matter.

if ye fulfil the royal law, according to the scripture,—"Fulfil," *(teleite,* present active indicative of *teleo,* to bring to completion, perfect, *fill full),* designates the obligation all sustain to the law. It is our responsibility to permit it to accomplish in us its full purpose, and to see to it that its requirements are met as fully as it is possible for us so to do. "If ye fulfil" is a condition of the first class, and thus the conclusion which follows is assumed to be true; i.e., if the law is fulfilled, "ye do well." It is always well to do right. One who fulfills the law does right. James' readers might properly feel secure in any course which involved fulfilling the law. In showing respect of persons, however, they were not fulfilling the law; they were, instead, disobeying it which forbade all such distinctions.

That which Christians are to fulfill is the "royal law," *(nomon basilikon),* a kingly law. Why is it thus designated? There are numerous reasons why it may be so described. (1) It is the law of the kingdom of Christ; and, in summary, involves man's entire duty to those about him; (2) it is a law which originates with the King of the universe; (3) it stands at the head of all other laws respecting man's obligation to his fellows; (4) it surpasses in nobility, all other obligations, and leads to the fulfillment of all others. (Gal. 6: 2.) Thus, whether James meant that it is a law such as is proper even for kings to follow; or, that it is the king of all other laws, his purpose is quite obvious, the design being to indicate the supreme position which this law should have in the hearts and lives of us all. Notwithstanding its greatness, it must be obeyed; and, any action which violates its spirit, such as favoritism for the rich, because they are rich, is a violation of it.

Thou shalt love thy neighbor as thyself,—This is a portion (by no means all) of the "royal law," and that portion especially involved in the matter under discussion—respect of persons. This law is timeless in nature, it being incorporated in the law of Moses (Lev. 19: 18), and confirmed, sanctioned and made a part of the New Covenant by our Lord. (Luke 10: 28.) Jesus, indeed, taught that love is at the base of every duty, whether to God or man. In response to the lawyer's query, "Teacher, which is the great commandment of the law?" Jesus answered, "Thou shalt love the Lord thy God with all thy heart, and with all thy soul, and with all thy mind. This is the great and first commandment. And a second like unto it is this, Thou shalt love thy neighbor as thyself. On these two commandments the whole law hangeth, and the prophets." (Matt. 22: 35-40.) Let us imagine a nail driven into the wall, and a string draped over it, the two ends hanging downward. Let one of these strings represent the command to love God supremely; the other, our neighbor as ourselves. Jesus tells us that these two commandments hold up all that is in the law and the prophets. The law, comprising the five books of Moses, constitutes a vast segment of the Old Testament; and, when to this is added the prophets, major and minor, the mass is greatly enlarged; yet, the Lord declares that these two embrace the whole of the law and the prophets. The meaning is that these two duties are so comprehensive they sum up, and include, all else. He who loves God supremely will discharge fully his duty to God; he who loves his neighbor as himself will, in similar fashion, perform every obligation owed to his neighbor. A Gentile, desiring to make fun of the tremendous mass of material assembled by the Jews in their traditions, once said to a rabbi, "Rabbi, teach me the law, provided you can do so while standing on one foot!" (The Gentile felt that the eminent scholar could not long speak in this position!) The rabbi answered, "Love God with all your heart, mind, strength and soul; and your neighbor as yourself; that is all of the law; the rest is mere commentary."

The first appearance of the statement, "Thou shalt love thy neighbor as thy self," is in the Old Testament (Lev. 19: 18), but Jesus quoted, confirmed and ratified it, and made it a part of the "law of liberty" applicable to us today. (Matt. 18: 19; 22: 34-40; Luke 10: 26-28; Mark 12: 28-34.) It is significant that Jesus designated, as the foundation of all true religion, these basic principles involving love for God and man which, when properly observed, lead to the performance of every duty in both spheres, and neither of which was a part of the decalogue (the ten commandments). It is noteworthy that Jesus said, "Thou shalt love thy neighbor *as* thy self,"—not *instead* of thyself! It is not wrong for one to entertain proper regard for one's self; indeed, this becomes the standard by which we are to gauge our actions toward others. It is the application of the Golden Rule to life; which, when faithfully followed, will prompt to the performance of every duty owed. "And as ye would that men should do to you, do ye also to them likewise." (Luke 6: 31.)

do well: 9 but if ye have respect of persons, ye commit sin, being convicted
by the law as transgressors. 10 For whosoever shall keep the whole law,

---

ye do well:—Your actions are approved and are above reproach. Far from being subjects of rebuke, as in the case involving an unseemly attitude toward the rich, if you obey the royal law
which bids you to love your neighbor as yourselves, you shall
enjoy the approbation of both God and men. To love others less
than we love ourselves is to fail to measure to the standard offered; and, he who fails so to do, is in disobedience to him who
erected the standard; i.e., to God himself. Hence, to fall short of
this requirement is to be deficient in the performance of duty to
God and man. On the other hand, he who properly fulfills his obligation in this area, will be blessed in the fact that in doing his
duty to his neighbor he is also obeying God. (1 Pet. 2: 20.)
Compare, also, Phil. 4: 14; 1 Cor. 7: 37; and Acts 10: 33. Any
action, which has, as its design, the fulfillment of the law of God, is
excellent; James had no word of condemnation for any who thus
did; it was the violation of the law of love (as evidenced in favoritism for the rich and contempt for the poor) being practiced by
those to whom he wrote which occasioned his treatment of the
matter. One does not obey one portion of the law of God by disobeying another; and, it is highly inconsistent to quote one law in
an effort to justify the violation of another law. Balaam, who
wanted to see what the Lord had more to say, has had imitators in
every age and dispensation. (Num. 22: 1-41.)

9 **but if ye have respect of persons,**—*(ei de prosopolepteite,*
condition of the first class, and thus assumed as true that they were
doing this), the verb of which is from the same root as the noun in
James 2: 1. It means to judge people on the basis of outward
appearance, rather than on the condition of the heart. The Greek
verb is a compound term, occurring nowhere else in the New Testament, and signifying, literally, *face-accepting.* This, those to
whom James wrote, were doing, in the contrasting attitudes they
were exhibiting toward the rich and the poor. This is not an unusual attitude on the part of people of the world. Many are much
more interested in what people appear to be, than in what they
really are. The accidental circumstances of life, including wealth,
fame, social position, and the like, are to many people of greater

and yet stumble in one *point*, he is become guilty of all. 11 For he that said,

---

value than the enduring qualities of the soul and of the heart. To honor one person more than another simply because one has material means, and the other does not, is to be "face-accepting," and is sinful.

ye commit sin,—*(hamartian ergazesthe)*, literally, "Ye work sin," you participate habitually in it. It was not an occasional lapse into the very human weaknesses, of which James deals; it was a deliberate and calculated course of action which these disciples followed in fawning upon the rich and in showing contempt and disregard for the poor. Moreover, it was not simply or merely a "fault," in which they were engaging; it is by James designated as *sin*. The word "sin," being without the article in the Greek text, signifies it in the abstract; they were not only committing *acts* of sin (earlier described), they were *in sin,* in the practice which the writer so severely condemns.

being convicted by the law as transgressors.—The law which bade them to love their neighbor as themselves convicted them in their practice, inasmuch as it forbade all respect of persons. (Lev. 19: 15.) It was therefore, not possible for them properly to appeal to the law in support of their conduct, since the law to which they would thus appeal, condemned them. *To transgress* is to cross over; i.e., to violate; sin is the transgression of the law. (1 John 3: 4.) Thus, when these to whom James wrote violated such laws as that set out in Lev. 19: 15 (forbidding respect of persons), they demonstrated themselves to be sinners. However much they may have adhered to the law *in other matters,* in this respect they stood condemned by it. The condition of one who thus does is clearly indicated in the verse following.

 10 **For whosoever shall keep the whole law,**—"For," *(gar),* introduces the reason for the conclusion drawn in the verse preceding. "Whosoever shall keep . . ." is an indefinite relative clause, the verb of which ("shall keep," aorist active subjunctive of *tereo,* to guard), means to observe carefully with the view of adhering tenaciously to that which is kept; "the law," is the royal law earlier mentioned, and summed up, as it relates to duties by men to men, in the edict, "Thou shalt love thy neighbor as thyself." The argu-

ment of James here appears to be this: "You appeal, for support for your practice (in showing special regard for rich people), to the law which you claim to be observing. But, if you are to justify your action by the law, you must keep the law perfectly. It is most inconsistent for you to claim justification for your acts by quoting the law, when your actions are flagrant violations of this same law which you affect to follow, with reference to showing respect of persons." (Lev. 19: 18.)

and yet stumble in one point,—"Stumble," *(ptaisei,* first aorist active subjunctive of *ptaio,* to trip), denotes a lapse from that which is right. (James 3: 2; Rom. 11: 11.) It will be observed that the word "point," in our English text, is in italics, thus indicating that there is no corresponding word for it in the Greek text. "Trip, moreover, in one," is the literal rendering of the phrase; however, the context clearly shows that some such word is needed to complete the sense. One might properly translate, "Stumble in one precept."

he is become guilty of all.—"He"; i.e., the one who claims to be keeping all of the law, and yet is violating one of its precepts. Such a one has become guilty *(gegonen,* second perfect indicative of *ginomai,* stands guilty) of all. That is, the position which he occupies is that of one who is guilty of all. All of what? Certainly not guilty of having *transgressed* every specific commandment of the law. Obviously, one who steals does not, by such an act, become a murderer; one who lies does not, in so doing, become a drunkard. How then does one become guilty of "all," by violating one precept of the law? The meaning is, he stands condemned by all of the law when he violates any portion of it. This principle is universally recognized. Some members of our society are styled criminals. These are those who violate the law of the land. What makes them criminals? Their infractions of the law. How much of the law? *Any portion thereof.* A murderer is no less a criminal because his only crime is murder. He need not to this add other violations of the law in order to acquire this classification. A lawbreaker is one who breaks the law. There may be, and doubtless often is, but one law involved; nonetheless, such a person is properly regarded as a lawbreaker. What is the relationship of such a person to the law? He is a law violator. While

⁷Do not commit adultery, said also, Do not kill. Now if thou dost not commit adultery, but killest, thou art become a transgressor of the law. 12 So

⁷Ex. xx. 13 f. Dt. v. 17 f.

one must keep all of the law to be lawful; one need break only one precept of it to be a law violator. Thus, one may keep much of the law with great consistency, yet violate one portion of it, and stand condemned by the law as a breaker of it. To illustrate: A flock of sheep in a pasture surrounded by a paneled fence are *in* the pasture. If they leap over one of the panels, they are *out* of the pasture. It is, of course, not necessary for them to leap over every section of the fence around the pasture to be outside. One leap puts them out. Similarly, one violation of God's law, unforgiven, puts one in the position of being condemned by it as a violator of it; disobedience to one precept puts the person who thus does in an area outside that which is characteristic of those who keep it.

The vital lesson taught here is that *all* of the law of God is pertinent to us, and that we must not feel at liberty to tamper with any portion thereof. He who seeks to pass judgment on the validity of God's laws, and to regard some as essential and others as unnecessary, is most presumptuous, and has officiously invaded the realm of God. One does not justify the violation of one law, by citing another observed. It is not a valid defense against the charge of theft that one did not get drunk, slander another, or commit murder. Obedience to God's law involves submission of the will. Those who keep only such laws as those which they approve, or in which they find satisfaction, have repudiated the will of God, and substituted their own. Such a disposition is presumption of the most objectionable type. It is not our prerogative and privilege to pass judgment on the propriety of any law of God. The fact that they are his is sufficient reason for unquestioned obedience thereto. God's will must be obeyed, not because it commends itself to our sense of what is right and proper, *but because it is God's will!* No other reason need be assigned. Here, indeed, is the acid test of faith. Here, too, many stumble and fall, because such walk by sight and not by faith. Only those who can truly say, "Speak, Lord; thy servant heareth; command, and he will obey," can ever get to heaven.

11 **For he that said, Do not commit adultery, said also, Do**

not kill.—These two commandments, from the second table of the law (man's duty to man), are cited to show that the law is *one,* because it originated from *one* source. Inasmuch as the whole of it came from the same God, whatever portion one violates is transgression of the will of the *one* God. It is, therefore, absurd to assume that one portion of the law, issuing from such a lawgiver, is valid and vital, whereas, another from the same divine source may be disregarded with impunity. The law of Jehovah is one; it is the single expression of the divine will. It must be regarded as a unit, and respected on this basis.

The order in which these commandments appear is not significant; here the seventh comes before the sixth (the arrangement in which they originally appear in the decalogue), but the order followed here is that of the Greek Version of the Old Testament. Jesus cited them in this order in Luke 18 : 20, as did Paul in Rom. 13 : 9.

now if thou dost not commit adultery, but killest, thou art become a transgressor of the law.—The meaning is, Though you meticulously observe the first of these commandments, but disregard and disobey the second, you are a transgressor of the law, because the law which forbids adultery *also forbids* the unlawful taking of human life. It is all the same law; and, it originated with the same lawgiver. It is no defense against the charge of drunkenness, that one is not a thief, not a murderer, not an embezzler, etc.; the law which forbids *these* forbade *that* also. In the final analysis, law exists as a disciplinary measure for the good of man. In an important sense, all commandments are, in principle, included in each one, inasmuch as each is an expression of the authority of the lawgiver; and, to violate one puts the violator in conflict with the will of him who originated all of them.

It would be an extension of the principle here taught beyond that intended and beyond that which is right to assume from this that one is *as guilty* who violates but one precept of Jehovah as one who has violated a thousand such precepts; or, that there is but one plateau of depravity, and that one reaches it on the occasion of the first sin. Such is not taught, in any sense, here. What is taught is that any sin, however insignificant it may appear to the sinner, or to those about him, is as much a violation of God's will,

speak ye, and so do, as men that are to be judged by a law of liberty.   13

(which is an expression of his authority and sovereignty), as any other would be. It is obvious that James has under consideration here presumptuous actions engaged in by individuals who have passed judgment on God's laws, and who have decided *some* of them are important, and others not. These considerations could not apply to good people who are sincerely desirous of doing all of the will of God, and who seek daily to do exactly this, but who through weakness, inadvertence, and ignorance unwittingly transgress his will. For these, a provision has been made through the continuous cleansing of the blood of Christ to those who *keep on walking* in the light. (1 John 1: 7-9; 2: 1-4.) The writer has under contemplation here those who keep the law in those instances in which *they approve* of what God has said, and who hesitate not to violate it in those instances in which *they disapprove,* or which they regard as of little consequence. David said, "Blessed is the man that feareth Jehovah, that delighteth greatly in his commandments." (Psalm 112: 1.) "I have rejoiced in the way of thy testimonies, as much as in all riches. I will meditate on thy precepts, and have respect unto thy ways. I will delight myself in thy statutes: I will not forget thy word." (Psalm 119: 14-16.) May we ever seek to imitate the Psalmist in this respect.

12 So speak ye and so do, as men that are to be judged by a law of liberty.—The verbs "speak," and "do," are present active imperatives, and thus designate habitual activity. "Ever speak and ever do as men that are to be judged. . ." There *is* a day of judgment coming. (Dan. 12: 2; Rom. 14: 12; 2 Cor. 5: 10.) It is, therefore, vitally important that we should keep on speaking and keep on doing in a fashion dictated by the realization that one day we must give an account for our speaking and our doing before the Judge of all the earth. To *speak* and to do sums up all that we do and all that we say. Here, as often elsewhere in the Epistle, the writer emphasizes the importance of proper speaking and doing; and, thus repeats the principles which the Lord himself taught: "And I say unto you, that every idle word that men shall speak, they shall give account thereof in the day of judgment. For by thy words thou shalt be justified, and by thy words thou shalt be condemned." (Matt. 12: 36, 37.)

For judgment *is* without mercy to him that hath showed no mercy: mercy glorieth against judgment.

That by which all men are to be judged is "a law of liberty." It is, therefore (a) law (a rule of action); (b) a law of liberty, in that it leads to liberty for those formerly enslaved by sin. For the significance of the word *law*, see comments on James 1: 25. The "law of liberty" is the same as the gospel, "the implanted word" (James 1: 21), and the "word of good tidings" (1 Pet. 1: 25). Those who humbly submit their wills to Christ, and who become obedient to the principles contained in the law of God, do not enslave themselves; on the contrary, they come into possession of true liberty, obtainable in no other way. This liberty is not license; the ideas are mutually exclusive; the liberty thus enjoyed necessitates restraints without which man could not survive in a state of society, nor be happy. "For ye, brethren, were called for freedom; only use not your freedom for an occasion to the flesh, but through love, be servants one to another. For the whole law is fulfilled in one word, even in this: Thou shalt love thy neighbor as thyself. But if ye bite and devour one another, take heed that ye be not consumed one of another." (Gal. 5: 13, 14.) By the law of liberty we are to live, and by it we are to be judged. Fortunate indeed are we that it is not the law of Moses, since none can keep it perfectly today (Acts 15: 10); and, since any violation thereof puts us under the condemnation of the whole. We may indeed rejoice that in Christ we have been delivered from the law of Moses and are privileged to approach God through the great sacrifice which he made in our behalf. "There is therefore now no condemnation to them that are in Christ Jesus. For the law of the Spirit of life in Christ Jesus made me free from the law of sin and death. . . ." (Rom. 8: 1, 2.)

13 For judgment is without mercy to him that hath showed no mercy:—There will be mercy shown in judgment for those who have faithfully served the Lord, and whose lapses were unintentional and absolved in the blood of Christ; but, those who have shown others no mercy need not expect mercy themselves when before the judgment seat of Christ they come to stand. (Acts 17: 30; 1 Cor. 5: 10.) The word translated "mercy," *eleos,* means pity for those in distress. The close connection between this statement and that appearing in James 2: 2 should be observed. Instead of showing compassion on the poor, as they ought to have done, James' readers had treated them with contempt, and had turned their attention to the rich simply because they were rich. They had shown no pity for the poor; if they persisted in this course, no pity would be shown for them in the judgment! It is remarkable that our Lord, in his description of the Judgment, affirmed precisely this same principle: "Then shall he say also unto them on the left hand, Depart from me, ye cursed, into the eternal fire which is prepared for the devil and his angels; for I was hungry, and ye did not give me to eat; I was thirsty, and ye gave me no drink; I was a stranger, and ye took me not in; naked, and ye clothed me not; sick, and in prison, and ye visited me not. Then shall they also answer, saying, Lord, when saw we thee hungry, or athirst, or a stranger, or naked, or sick, or in prison, and did not minister unto thee? Then shall he answer them, saying, Verily I say unto you, Inasmuch as ye did it not unto one of these least, ye did it not unto me." (Matt. 25: 41-45.) It is the *merciful* who shall obtain *mercy* (Matt. 5: 7), those who have been merciless need not expect it when they need it most. To be forgiven, we must forgive others; to avoid condemnation, we must not exercise adverse judgment toward others. (Matt. 6: 15; 7: 1.) The debtor, forgiven of his great and hopeless debt, need not expect God, at the last day, to lift his own tremendous obligation, if he will not mark off an insignificant debt (of sin) owed him by one of his brothers. (Matt. 18: 23-25.) This principle the text teaches with great clarity. Indeed, the Greek is even more emphatic than the English translation, signifying, "For the judgment shall be merciless to him that worketh no mercy." Here, again, there is obvious reference to our Lord's teaching in the mountain instruction (Matt. 5, 6, 7), to which James so often reverts.

mercy glorieth against judgment.—For "glorieth," some translations have "rejoiceth," "triumphs," "exults over," and the like, all of which point to the fact that where mercy can express itself, it always transcends judgment. Mercy cancels out judgment (condemnation); those who have been merciful may properly exult in the mercy which they shall receive at the judgment. None of us can hope to stand before God on our own merit; we all are in need of the divine mercy. But, to enjoy it ourselves, we must show it to others.   Mercilessness in us toward others, whether rich or poor, will effectively close the door of mercy to us when we need it most.   Let us, at this moment, memorize the following words, and make them a part of our daily devotions: "Blessed are the merciful: for they shall obtain mercy."   (Matt. 5: 7.)

SECTION 5
2: 14-26

FAITH, WITHOUT WORKS, IS DEAD
2: 14-17

14 What doth it profit, my brethren, if a man say he hath faith, but have

---

14 **What doth it profit, my brethren,**—We have had occasion to observe quite often in these notes that it was James' design to emphasize the practical aspects of Christianity in his Epistle, and to teach his readers that it is the *doer* and not the *hearer alone* who enjoys the approbation of God. It is from the eminently practical character of the Epistle that it has been styled "The Gospel of Common Sense." In the verses immediately preceding it was shown that one who loves his neighbor as himself will show mercy to his neighbor though the neighbor be poor and not rich; and, here it is demonstrated that where one is indifferent to the needs of those about him such is clear proof of the want of true faith on the part of the one exhibiting such indifference.

For centuries James 2: 14-26, has been the occasion of much controversy; and, it was this passage which prompted Martin Luther to regard the Epistle of James with considerable contempt, and to describe it as "a right strawy one." Others, who entertain no doubts regarding the inspiration of the book and passage, have nevertheless engaged in much useless and vain speculation thereon in an effort to *harmonize an alleged conflict of teaching between James and Paul!* There are those who believe that Paul, in Rom. 4: 1-6, teaches that justification is by faith *without* works of any kind; and, inasmuch as James, in this passage (2: 14-26), quite obviously affirms that there is no justification *apart* from works, it poses quite a problem for the advocates of the doctrine of salvation by faith only. Moreover, Paul, in Eph. 2: 8, 9, wrote: "For by grace have ye been saved through faith; and that not of yourselves, it is the gift of God; not of works that no man should glory." Yet, James asserted: "Was not Abraham our father justified by works, in that he offered up Isaac his son upon the altar? Thou seest that faith wrought with his works, and by works was faith made perfect." (James 2: 21, 22.)

It should be apparent to the most casual reader that Paul and James are discussing *two different kinds of works in these passages*. Paul refers to works which are *excluded* from God's plan to save; James discusses works which are *included* in it. Each writer gives the characteristics of the works under consideration. Those *excluded*, discussed by Paul, are works in which one might *glory* (exult in, boast of); the works *included* (mentioned by James) are those which *perfect* faith. Of the first category, works of which a man might boast and in which he might glory, are human, meritorious works, works of human achievement, works the design of which is to earn salvation. Were it possible for man to devise a plan by which he could save himself, he could dispense with grace, accomplish his own deliverance from sin, and glory in God's presence. Such of course, is utterly impossible. All such works are *excluded*. The works included, and discussed by James, are the *commandments* of the Lord, obedience to which is absolutely essential to salvation. (1 John 2: 4; 2 Thess. 1: 7-9.) Humble submission to the will of God as expressed in his commandments, far from involving works of the type *excluded*, demonstrate complete reliance upon God, and not upon one's self. Only those who seek to exclude all work, even the commandments of the Lord, such as baptism in water for the remission of sins (Mark 16: 15, 16; Acts 2: 38), have any difficulty in harmonizing Paul and James! Paul taught the necessity of obedience to the commands of Christ as plainly, positively and emphatically as did James. (Rom. 6: 3, 4.)

The alleged difficulties in this section are not of the inspired writer's making, but stem from the erroneous view that salvation is by faith *alone*, before and without other acts of obedience. Because James teaches that faith, apart from works, is dead, the passage does indeed pose a serious problem for those who teach that "the doctrine of faith, and faith only, is a most wholesome doctrine, and very full of comfort." (Methodist, Discipline, Art. 9.) We shall have occasion, in these notes, to observe some of the efforts put forth by denominational theologians to avoid the obvious difficulty which they face here.

if a man say he hath faith, but have not works? can that faith save him?—Two questions are raised: (1) Of what profit is there to a man who says he has faith, but does not have works? (2) Can that faith save him? "Profit," is from *ophelos,* increase; and, as here used, denotes advantage, blessing, good, etc. What good is to be derived by the man who has faith but not works? Can *that* faith save him? It should be carefully noted that James does not minimize the importance of faith. The doctrine of salvation by faith is clearly and repeatedly taught in the New Testament. (Rom. 5: 1; 1 John 5: 1; John 3: 16; 3: 36.) In none of these passages, nor elsewhere in the Testament, is the doctrine of salvation by faith *only* taught. Inasmuch as faith is the great principle of salvation on the basis of which its possessor is led to do the will of God, it is often made to stand for all of the conditions of salvation,—indeed for the entire Christian system. (Gal. 3: 23-29.) The faith that saves is of the type which expresses itself in obedience to the commandments of the Lord; and it produces a blessing only when it so does,—a proposition which James proceeds to prove.

A man says, "I have faith, but not works." James asks, "Can *that* faith save him?" The statement is rhetorical; it is put in question form for emphasis. The Greek sentence is *me dunatai he pistis sosai auton,* and is so constructed (with *me*) that a negative answer is expected. The meaning is, *That* faith cannot save him! Note that James does not deny the efficacy of faith. Under consideration is a special kind of faith. What kind is it? That which is *without* works. James picks out this particular kind of faith and says that it cannot save. Note the use of the demonstrative *that.* *That* what? *That* faith! What kind of faith is *that?* The kind of faith that is without works. What is affirmed of it? It cannot save. What cannot save? Faith without works. What works? The commandments of the Lord! This is decisive of the matter in issue. It makes clear the fact that faith, apart from, and without works, is profitless, barren, vain and dead, all of which James later affirms. (Verses 17, 20, 26.)

It is noteworthy that the verbs in the statement, "If a man say he hath faith and have not works," are present active subjunctives, thus, "If one keeps on saying he has faith, but keeps on not having works. . ." Mere profession, without obedience to God's commands, is worthless. Chapter eleven, of Hebrews, is Inspiration's

not works? can that faith save him? 15 If a brother or sister be naked and

Hall of Fame. There the wonderful worthies of the illustrious past are made to appear in demonstration of the tremendous faith and humble obedience which ever characterized them as they sought to discharge the will of God in their day. It will be observed that the mention of their faith is followed by *a verb of action,* thus evidencing the fact that faith blesses only when it leads its possessor to obedience. God has never blessed anybody, in any age or dispensation, *because of faith,* until the faith exhibited itself in action. Faith saves; but only when it prompts to faithful and unquestioning obedience to the will of God. Proof of this James demonstrates in the verses following.

15 If a brother or sister be naked and in lack of daily food, —In view of the fact that those to whom James wrote were disposed to treat with contempt the poor among them, and to show servile favoritism for the rich, it may well be that the writer, in this instance, brings forth an actual incident. It is, in any event, a practical demonstration of the principle that he is impressing in these verses; viz., that faith, apart from works (of obedience), is profitless, barren, vain, and dead. James, to illustrate his principle that faith, apart from work, cannot bless, introduces an instance of the most inexcusable kind. A "brother," or "sister," is (a) "naked," and (b) "in lack of daily food." "Naked" here does not mean utterly without clothing, but nearly so; i.e., without sufficient clothing. (Matt. 25 : 36; John 21 : 7; Acts 19 : 16.) "In lack of daily food" indicates that the person under consideration is in the greatest possible destitution, in a condition of want that would touch the hearts of all but the hardest. Under contemplation is "a brother," or "a sister." While these words do not *require* the conclusion that they were members of the body of Christ (see Acts 9 : 17, where Ananias addressed Saul of Tarsus, before he obeyed the gospel, as "Brother Saul. . ." because he was a brother Israelite, and compare Matt. 5 : 23, Acts 2 : 29; 3 : 17), it is likely that they were Christians, although our obligation to assist the needy and destitute is not limited to those who are members of the church. Paul wrote to the *churches* of Galatia, and instructed them "to work that which is good toward all men, and especially toward them that are of the household of faith" (Gal. 1 : 1ff.; 6 :

in lack of daily food, 16 and one of you say unto them, Go in peace, be ye warmed and filled; and yet ye give them not the things needful to the body;

10), in which instance it is absurd to assume that it is wrong for churches of Christ to do what Paul *commanded* the churches in Galatia to do.

16 and one of you say unto them, Go in peace, be ye warmed and filled;—The verbs of the first two clauses are quite significant, and make more vivid the lesson intended. In the first, *(eipei de tis autois ex humon),* the verb is an aorist active subjunctive, in effect, "Let us be done with this matter *at once;* in the second, *(hupagete en eirenei),* it is a present active imperative *"keep on going* in peace!" This phrase translated, "Go in peace," was the usual Jewish expression of farewell. (Luke 7: 50; 8: 48; Acts 16: 36; 1 Sam. 1: 17; 20: 42.) In the third clause, "be ye warmed and filled," *(thermainesthe kai chortazesthe),* the verbs may be either middle or passive; if middle, the meaning is "Get yourselves warmed and filled"; if passive, "Be warmed and filled yourselves." The middle voice is the more probable in view of the context. It was James' design to show the heartlessness of the disposition which bids a sister or brother to go his way, and to shift for himself; and the middle more nearly conforms to this design. Far from assisting the destitute in their distress, empty words were substituted for good deeds. Those with insufficient clothing are bidden to "Warm yourselves!" Those in need of food to "Fill yourselves!" And, with a wave of the hand and a dismissal of all responsibility, the poor are told "Farewell! Be off. Best wishes. Feed and fill your own selves."

and yet ye give them not the things needful to the body; —The "things needful to the body" include the food and clothing implied in the preceding statement. The "things" mentioned would not be limited to this, but would include whatever is essential to meet the needs of the persons under contemplation, such as medicine, professional attention, nursing care, and the like. The words, "Go in peace, be ye warmed and filled," are empty, meaningless gestures; warm words, resulting in icy rejection of duty and responsibility.

what doth it profit?—Put in question form for emphasis, the meaning is, There is *no* profit in such. One is not warmed by good

what doth it profit?   17 Even so faith, if it have not works, is dead in itself.

wishes; one cannot fill an empty stomach with greetings. The application follows in the next verse.

17 Even so faith, if it have not works, is dead in itself.— Here the writer returns to the theme of verse 14 ("What doth it profit, my brethren, if a man say he hath faith, but have not works? Can that faith save him?"). The verses which intervene are designed to illustrate the fact that there is no profit in faith without works. "Even so" means *in like manner;* that is, as there is no benefit whatsoever in good works, when not attended by deeds, neither is there any profit in faith, if it "have not works. . ." The phrase, "have not works," *(ean me erga echei),* is a condition of the third class, the verb being a present active subjunctive; i.e., "if it keep on not having works. . ." There is no profit in faith which is without works.

It is evident that the "works" of which James writes are the commandments of the Lord. (James 2: 20-22.) It is indeed such "works" which demonstrate faith. Our confidence (faith) in our physician is evidenced by our willingness to *do* what he *says.* In like manner, he who affects to believe in the Lord, yet refuses to do what the Lord commands, or doing it, does so on other grounds, demonstrates that his faith is vain, fruitless, dead. James affirms that "faith, if it have not works, is dead in itself." "In itself," is *kath' heauten,* of itself, according to itself, by the utter absence of "works." Because it is lacking in that which evidences life in faith (works), it is dead, being incomplete, partial, fragmentary; no more alive than a body from which the spirit has flown. As a dead body is lacking in that which gives it life (the spirit), so faith, without works, is dead, being deficient in that which gives life to faith. It is dead, not only with reference to outward signs of life, it is dead *in itself.* A rose bush, in the cold, dark days of winter exhibits no signs of life, but it is not dead in itself; when the warmth of lovely spring days falls upon it, it buds and blooms and flowers forth into life and beauty. Faith, *without works,* has no winter, and consequently, no flowering spring.

The lesson is obvious. As one who is in need and hungry cannot profit from kind words and fair speeches, neither is there any blessing in faith which does not prompt to faithful obedience to the Lord's commandments. We prove that our good wishes for others are genuine when we translate them into golden deeds of mercy and good will; and we prove our faith when we are obedient to the will of him whose word prompts to faith. We should be deeply impressed with the lesson which James teaches here that faith, unattended by unquestioning obedience to the Lord's will, is as worthless and vain as the expression of empty wishes for the needy with no effort expended to relieve their distressed condition. There is no help for a sick, hungry family in pious platitudes, unaccompanied by assistance; and there is no blessing promised or salvation available to people on the basis of faith without works. We have earlier observed that the works under consideration are not the works of the law of Moses, or of human merit; but, the commandments of the Lord. Peter said, "Of a truth I perceive that God is no respecter of persons: but in every nation he that feareth him, *and worketh righteousness,* is acceptable to him." (Acts 10: 34, 35.) Righteousness is the keeping of God's commandments. (Psalm 119: 172.)

WORKS PROVE FAITH
2: 18-20

18 [8]Yea, a man will say, Thou hast faith, and I have works: show me thy faith apart from *thy* works, and I by my works will show thee *my* faith. 19

[8]Or, *But some one will say*

---

18 **Yea, a man will say,**—James, in order further to emphasize his thesis that faith, apart from works, is dead, and to prove that works demonstrate faith, imagines an objector to appear with an argument the design of which is to try to prove the inspired writer's reasoning wrong. James is quite willing to listen to the objection because his position is secure. It will indeed enable him more fully to establish his contention that there is no value whatsoever in faith which does not demonstrate itself in works. What does the objector have to say?

Thou hast faith, and I have works:—Were the New Testament to follow modern methods of punctuation, these words would be in quotation marks, thus indicating that they are the words of the objector to James' position. It is idle to speculate whether

"Thou" means James specifically; and "I" the objector; more likely the meaning is, "One person has faith, and another works; one emphasizes the faith which he has; the other, the works which he possesses; each is good and effective; and neither should be minimized," the objector argues. It is as if James should say, "Suppose some one comes forth with the objection that one's piety and devotion to God are not always exhibited in the same fashion; one may show his loyalty to God by faith, another by works; yet, both be equally pious and devout in God's sight." Inasmuch as this challenge of the objector to James' reasoning is on the ground that faith can exist apart from works, the inspired writer answers with a challenge of his own!

show me thy faith apart from thy works, and I by my works will show thee my faith.—Faith, actually and literally, cannot be seen; its existence is evidenced only through the works which it produces. Hence, James demands of his objector that he *show* his faith (if he thinks it can exist in this fashion) apart from works. This, of course, was impossible; and thus constituted additional evidence of the truth of the thesis, that faith, without works, is dead. Faith and works, in the religious realm, are so related, that one cannot long exist without the other. One springs from the other, and each depends, for its effectiveness, on the other. Faith, without works, is dead; works, without faith, cannot bless, either. So the objection is invalid, in that it is based on the erroneous assumption that faith can exist apart from works,—an untrue premise. Works may be seen; these may be offered in evidence of faith which cannot be seen. Faith, however, cannot be seen; one without works cannot offer proof of the faith which he alleges to have. It follows, therefore, that one who disparages works *must resort to them to prove that he has any faith at all!*

It seems not possible to overemphasize these matters in our day. We should learn them well for our own good; and, that we may be able also to teach them effectively to others. In view of the fact that the denominational system alleges that salvation is by faith without works and to it multitudes about us subscribe, it is important that every member of the body of Christ should be able to explain clearly the kind of works *included* in the plan of salvation (the commandments of the Lord), and the kind of works

Thou believest that ⁰God is one; thou doest well: the demons also believe,

⁰Some ancient authorities read *there is one God.*

excluded (those involving merit, the law of Moses, and the like). It is idle for one to expect salvation short of complete submission to God's will. (Matt. 7: 21; 1 John 2: 4; Heb. 5: 9.) It is also vitally important to remember that these words are not limited to the alien sinner; faith, apart from works, whether possessed by an alien or a member of the church is powerless to bless. As Christians, we are to "work out" our own salvation with fear and trembling (Phil. 2: 12), and those ultimately to be privileged to enjoy the bliss of the eternal city are those who have kept his commandments (Rev. 22: 13, 14).

19 **Thou believest that God is one;**—The address here is to the objector to whom James, in verse 18, said: "Thou hast faith, and I have works: show me thy faith apart from thy works, and I by my works will show thee my faith." This is to say, in effect, "You contend that faith, apart from works—the mere intellectual assent of the mind—is sufficient to save. Let us test your thesis. Basic among the things one must believe to be saved is that 'God is one. . .' This, you believe. It is good that you so do. But, is this enough? Remember that the demons believe and shudder. You do not argue that demons are saved. It follows, therefore, that one may believe, and yet not be saved. Belief, unattended by good works, is no more effectual in saving the sinner (or the Christian) than the demons who exercise it."

It is clear that the verb "believest" here signifies no more than intellectual assent to the truthfulness of a proposition—in this case, that *God is one.* It is, in this instance, contemplated apart from love, obedience, trust, and submission—being an action of the mind alone. And, while the acceptance of the doctrine of the One True God is the fundamental premise of all genuine religion, mere lip service thereto will not suffice. James selects this as an illustration of what mere belief—if it could of itself produce a blessing—might do, in saving the soul. If the simple exercise of belief is sufficient, surely those who subscribe to the basic premise of all religion worthy of the name should be saved by it. "No," the writer hastens to add; "It is not enough; even the demons believe, and shudder at the destiny which awaits them."

That "God is one" is taught repeatedly in the Scriptures, Old and New. The *Shema* of Israel (Deut. 6: 4), uttered morning and evening by every devout Jew, and endlessly recited in the synagogues, kept this fundamental fact of all true religion constantly in the minds of the worshippers. So important was it regarded in the religion of Israel that the rabbis taught that those who prolonged the word "one" in the recitation thereof would have their days and years prolonged upon the earth!

"God," (Greek *theos*), denotes deity. (Thayer). It is the Greek name of the divine nature. There is but one divine nature. Hence, there is but one God. There are, however, three Persons who possess this divine nature—the Father, the Son and the Holy Spirit—the Godhead. Hence all are God. Since there is but one divine nature, and this nature is named God, there is but one God. Thus, the three Persons of the Godhead constitute the One God. This is demonstrated (a) in the plural pronouns used to designate the activity of God: "And *God* said, Let *us* make man in *our* own image, after *our* likeness. . . ." (Gen. 1: 26.) (b) In the designation of Christ as God: ("In the beginning was the Word and the Word was with God, and the Word was God. . . . And the Word became flesh and dwelt among us (and we behold his glory, glory as of the only begotten from the Father), full of grace and truth." (John 1: 1, 14.) (c) In the plural form of the Hebrew word *Eloheem* (God) appearing in Gen. 1: 1: "In the beginning God *(Eloheem,* plural form of *El,* God), created the heavens and the earth." (d) In the reference to the Father as God: "Blessed be the God and Father of our Lord Jesus Christ. . ." (1 Pet. 1: 3.) (e) In the reference to the Holy Spirit as God: "But Peter said, Ananias, why hath Satan filled thy heart to lie to the Holy Spirit . . . thou hast not lied unto men, but unto God." (Acts 5: 3, 4.) To believe that *God is one* is a basic doctrine of the Bible. (Ex. 34: 14; Psalm 90: 1; Jer. 43: 3, 10-13; John 4: 24; 1 John 4: 6.)

thou doest well:—The writer is careful to make it clear that the acceptance of the premise that God is one is not under criticism. It is absolutely necessary for one to believe that God is one in order to be saved. James does not minimize the importance of the doctrine of the One True God. He is simply showing that such is not sufficient in order to salvation. "Thou doest well" is, in the Greek, *kalos poieis.* It is beautifully good for you to do this. The word for "good," *(kalos),* signifies a type or kind of goodness which allures, attracts, and woos; one who believes in the One God is to be commended for this if one does not rest there; it is good to do this and it is fine so far as it goes. But, it does not go far enough.

the demons also believe, and shudder.—To believe that God is one is simply not enough because the demons of the unseen realm—the imps of Satan—do as much; they believe so strongly in God that they tremble with fear in their contemplation of the terrible destiny which awaits them. The word "shudder," *(phrissousin,* present active indicative of *phrisso,* to bristle up,) indicates the kind of terror which makes one's hair to stand on end (Job 4: 14, 15), thus emphasizing how strongly the demons subscribed to the doctrine of One God. It should be observed that the kind of faith which the demons have is exactly that which James declares to be profitless—faith which does not express itself in humble obedience to the commands of the Lord. Demons believe, but will not obey; those exercising faith, without works, thus exhibit the same kind of profitless faith which the demons have. *They* know that they are lost; and they tremble at their inevitable destruction. There is no more hope for those who depend upon faith only as the basis of salvation than there is for the salvation of the demons.

Who were the demons of whom James writes? The question is not an easy one to answer; and the subject of demonology is fraught with many difficulties. The word *demon,* from the Greek *daimon,* and its derivative *daimonion,* is used in a variety of senses in the New Testament: (a) of idols (Acts 17: 18); (b) angels which kept not their first estate (Matt. 25: 41; Rev. 12: 7, 8); (c) ministers of Satan (Luke 4: 35; John 10: 21); (d) Satan, the prince of demons (Matt. 9: 34; Mark 3: 22; Luke 11: 15).

Demons, in the first century, were able to enter individuals and vex them (Luke 8: 30, 32); interfere with their thinking and reasoning (Luke 7: 33; John 7: 20), and cause men to do and to think evil (Matt. 8: 31; Mark 3: 11).

Numerous efforts have been made to explain their existence

such as (1) the allegation that demon possession was a popular superstition without any basis of fact but at which Jesus winked, knowing better himself, thus apparently accepting a common error which, in reality, he did not believe. (a) Such a theory seriously reflects on the integrity of Christ and imputes to him deceit, hypocrisy and falsehood. (b) Moreover, it is in conflict with established facts. Jesus charged, rebuked, commanded, and cast out demons; they recognized his deity and obeyed his commands. (Mark 5: 9-12; Matt. 8: 29-32; Mark 1: 25; Luke 4: 34; Matt. 12: 23-37; Luke 11: 17-23.) (c) The apostles were given power to cast out demons. (Mark 3: 14, 15.) Thus, Jesus recognized the reality of demoniac possession and it cannot be questioned without reflection on his credibility. (2) Others have attempted to explain this strange matter as mental sickness resulting from diseased minds and bodies. This is shown to be false in the fact that people were said to be sick *and demon possessed*. (Matt. 8: 16; Mark 1: 32, esp. verse 34.) (3) Jesus based an argument on the fact of demoniac possession in his contentions with the Jews, declaring that casting them out by the Spirit of God proved his deity. (Matt. 12: 23-27; Mark 9: 29.) We may be certain that our Lord would not have rested the case of his deity on a popular superstition!

We may, therefore, conclude that (a) the demons of the apostolic age were real and not fanciful; (b) they were wicked spirits (Acts 19: 13-17); (c) judgment upon them was impending; they recognized the justice of such, but insisted that the time was not yet (Matt. 8: 29); (d) they were possessed of consciousness and intelligence (Luke 4: 41); (e) they acknowledged the deity of Christ; (f) they deliberately taught false doctrines, and circulated them among the early disciples (perhaps by influencing men whom they possessed, 1 Tim. 4: 1; 1 John 4: 1).

Who were they? Where did they come from? Where did they go? are questions which cannot be fully answered today. It is quite obvious, from the New Testament description of them and of their activities, that they are not *equally* active in the world today. Efforts to explain their existence have been many, none of which settles the question satisfactorily. Among the views advanced thereon are, (1) the demons were wicked angels which

and shudder. 20 But wilt thou know, O vain man, that faith apart from

kept not their first estate and in some manner not known to us were suffered to come out of the place where they were restrained and to vex human beings. (Jude 6; 2 Pet. 2: 4.) (2) The demons were disembodied spirits of evil men which, after death and their descent into Hades, escaped the Hadean realm, returned to earth, and seized the minds and bodies of live people. Josephus, the Jewish historian, advanced this view. Compare, also, Thayer, under *daimonion.* If either view is correct, the second would appear the more probable.

As interesting as these questions are, and however much we might desire to have correct answers thereto, they are not pertinent to our study of the text of James. The meaning of the sacred writer is clear: *Demons believe in the doctrine of the One True God, and tremble at the thought of their impending destruction. Their faith does not express itself in obedience; and is, hence, dead. But this is precisely the kind of faith that the objector* (who subscribes to the doctrine of faith only) *alleges to be sufficient!* (Verse 18.) Therefore, the conclusion of verse 20 is obvious.

20 But wilt thou know, O vain man, that faith apart from works is barren?—"But wilt thou know . . ." is *theleis de gnonai,* ingressive active aorist infinitive of *ginosko,* to come to know, and here in the sense of to realize, to recognize the truth of that affirmed. The conclusion which the writer is about to draw is so obvious that he calls upon the objector to acknowledge the truth of his proposition which, thus far, he has not; and is consequently, "a vain man," (literally, an empty-headed fellow) who has not properly considered the matter under consideration. He who would attempt to reason that faith, apart from works, is efficacious, is empty-headed, devoid of those qualities which are essential to proper reasoning. Faith, apart from works, *is faith only.* Such a faith is "barren," *(argen,* unproductive), because it is dead. That which is dead is incapable of producing; and is thus barren. Earlier, and in much detail, James shows that faith, without works, is dead; here, he indicates that it is without the *outward* evidence of life (productivity) which demonstrates that life exists. (James 2: 17, 20.) The kind of faith described here—faith apart from

works is barren?   21 Was not Abraham our father justified by works, in

works,—is the kind which the denominational world urges is that which saves. The Scriptures, on the contrary, establish the fact that in the hands of a person exercising such faith there are no sheaves whatsoever!

TRUE FAITH ILLUSTRATED
2 : 21-26

(a) In The Case of Abraham

21 Was not Abraham our father justified by works,—To establish his thesis that faith, apart from works, is useless and vain, James turns to the father of the Hebrew race (Abraham), and offers him as an example of the fact that works are vital in God's plan.   These to whom James wrote included many Jewish people; and those who were not would, as Christians, be interested in, and would soon acquire a knowledge of, one who occupied such a prominent place in the history of the Lord's people in earlier dispensations; and his example would, therefore, be most impressive. Further Abraham is the spiritual ancestor of all "who walk in the steps of" his faith today (Rom. 4: 1-25); and all who are Christ's, are "Abraham's seed, and heirs according to the promise" (Gal. 3: 29).   The principle involved in Abraham's justification is, therefore, illustrative of the manner in which all men are justified today.   The case of the illustrious father of the Jewish people is frequently cited, for this purpose, in the Scriptures both Old and New. (Gen. 12: 1-3; 15: 1-20; 17: 1-8; Heb. 11: 8-18; Gal. 3: 15-29); and James' reference thereto was neither novel nor unusual.   It was just the instance which would be the most impressive to the people to whom he wrote.

(1) Abraham was "justified," *(edikaiothe,* first aorist passive indicative of *dikaio,* to pronounce or declare one to be just); i.e., he was counted, reckoned, pronounced, declared to be *in a right relationship with God.*   The basic significance of the word translated "justified" is that of acquittal; one justified is not regarded as an enemy of God; thenceforth no state of alienation between such a man and God exists.   Thus, to be justified is to be acquitted —thereafter to be in a relationship with God which he approves. "For by thy words thou shalt be *justified,* and by thy words thou

that he offered up Isaac his son upon the altar? 22 [10]Thou seest that faith
wrought with his works, and by works was faith made perfect; 23 and the

[10]Or, *Seest thou . . . perfect?*

shalt be condemned." (Matt. 12: 37.) "And by him every one
that believeth is justified from all things, from which ye could not
be *justified* by the law of Moses." (Acts 13: 39.) It follows,
therefore, that one who is justified is by the Lord regarded
(counted, reckoned, declared to be) innocent of any charges formerly made. The *verdict* has been rendered; one justified is *declared* not guilty.

(2) Abraham was justified "by works." The words, "Was not
Abraham our father justified by works," translate the Greek
phrase, *Abraam ho pater hemon ouk ex ergon edikaiothe*, the negative *ouk* indicating that an affirmative answer is expected. Thus,
even the objector—who alleges that faith, without works, produces
a blessing,—must concede that, in Abraham's case, justification
was by works. The preposition "by" (Greek, *ex*, out of), points to
the source of Abraham's justification; it was *out* of *works* that he
was justified, not *by means* of works. Works, as such, are not efficacious; God, it is, who declares one just; but God does it *out of*
works—that is, he issues the verdict when the works appear.
Only God can justify; but God justifies *only* when the works,
which he prescribes, appear. The verdict of justification results
from the works. Hence, no works, no justification! There was a
definite time and place when Abraham was justified. When was
it?

in that he offered up Isaac his son upon the altar?—It will
be noted that the phrase "in that," with which this portion of the
verse begins, is, in the King James Translation, "When. . . ."
The meaning is the same. Inasmuch as the verb is *aorist* (which
indicates an action contemporary with, or prior to the action of the
main verb), the meaning here is that the declaration of Abraham's
justification and his offering of Isaac were simultaneous; i.e., out
of *(ek)* the one—the offering—the other—justification—occurred.
For the story of Abraham and his offering of his son Isaac, see
Gen. 22: 19, and compare Heb. 11: 17-19.

22 Thou seest that faith wrought with his works,—James
points his objector to the obvious truth of that he had just penned.

scripture was fulfilled which saith, [11]And Abraham believed God, and it was reckoned unto him for righteousness; and he was called the friend

[11]Gen. xv. 6.
[12]Is. xli. 8; 2 Chr. xx. 7.

It was easy to see, in this historic incident, that Abraham's faith wrought (exercised itself) with his works in offering up his son Isaac. "Wrought with" is from *sunergei,* imperfect active of *sunergeo,* to cooperate with; hence, faith and works *kept on cooperating with each other* to produce the result—Abraham's justification.

and by works was faith made perfect;—It was "by" (Greek, *ek,* out of) works that faith, in Abraham's case, was "made perfect." The phrase, "made perfect," is from *eteleiothe,* aorist passive indicative of *telfio,* to consummate, to complete, to finish. The tenses in this verse are highly significant. Faith was continually exercising itself (imperfect tense) with works (the command to offer up Isaac on the altar), and out of these works faith was perfected *at once* (aorist tense). Neither works nor faith operating alone can justify; each in cooperation with the other produces that status wherein God justifies.

23 and the scripture was fulfilled which saith, And Abraham believed God, and it was reckoned unto him for righteousness;—The Scripture alluded to here is that found in Gen. 15: 6: "And he believed in Jehovah; and he reckoned it to him for righteousness." This was affirmed of Abraham after the illustrious patriarch had accepted, without question, and despite his childlessness, and the advanced ages of himself and his wife Sarah, God's promise of vast posterity. Not knowing at the time how such could be, he nevertheless *believed* that it would be and stumbled not at the promise of God in unbelief. This scripture (Gen. 15: 6) is declared to have been fulfilled when Abraham's faith was made perfect. It is vitally important to observe *when* the scripture referred to was fulfilled. Though Abraham was *earlier* (Gen. 15: 6) acknowledged as a believer, and his faith "reckoned" for righteousness, it was not until *later* (Gen. 22: 1-19) that his faith was consummated (made perfect) in the act of obedience involving Isaac. Abraham believed God, prior to this act of obedience; i.e., he fully accepted God's word, and relied implicitly on the promises which it contained; and, as a result, his faith "was reckoned unto

of God. 24 Ye see that by works a man is justified, and not only by faith.

---

him for righteousness. . . ." "To reckon" *(elogisthe)* is to regard, deem, consider, account; hence, God deemed, considered, regarded Abraham's faith as righteousness (right-doing). *Faith itself thus became an act of obedience which, in its exercise, and when, at the moment, there were no additional duties devolving upon Abraham, God accepted as proof of Abraham's devotion.* One must not from this assume that the exercise of belief bestowed upon Abraham blessings apart from and independent of any obedience; though this conclusion is often drawn, it is an erroneous and hurtful one. In the nature of the case, the promise of great posterity involved matters which would require considerable time for their development; hence, there was nothing more, at the moment, for Abraham to do but to accept, without hesitation, the assurances of such from God. This, he did; and his acceptance thereof became *an act of righteousness* which God, in his turn, accepted, and put to Abraham's account for righteousness (right-doing). It is a violent perversion of this passage and historic incident from it to assume that because Abraham's faith was accepted as an act of righteousness when there was *nothing else required* of him *at the time* that in our case faith will suffice *without* the performance of those conditions which *are required of us now.* Even in Abraham's case, as James so clearly shows, the patriarch's faith did not reach its consummation, its fulfillment, until it had translated itself into action in the offering of Isaac.

and he was called the friend of God.—That is, Abraham was, and *was called* "the friend of God"; i.e., God's friend. The phrase, "of God," is not an objective genitive, "friend of God," meaning that Abraham regarded God as *his* friend (though doubtless he did), but a subjective genitive, he was one whom God considered as his friend! "Didst not thou, O our God, drive out the inhabitants of this land before thy people Israel, and give it to the seed of Abraham, thy friend for ever?" (2 Chron. 20: 7.) God regarded Abraham as his friend because he was ever faithful to God, and always submitted his will to God's. Jesus said, "Ye are my friends if ye do the things which I command you." (John 15: 14.)

24 Ye see that by works a man is justified, and not only by faith.—This is the irresistible conclusion to be drawn from the preceding premises. Any reasonable person must, on careful and prayerful consideration of the foregoing affirmations of the sacred writer, readily see that faith blesses only when it leads the one exercising it to faithful compliance with the commands of God. James' conclusion is established (1) by analogy (verses 14, 15); (2) by demonstration (verses 17, 18); (3) by example (a) in the case of the demons (verse 19); (b) in the case of Abraham (verses 21-23); (4) by inspired affirmation (verses 14-26); (5) by an appeal to common sense (verse 24). "Ye see" (from the array of evidence presented) that it is "by works," (obedience to the commandments of the Lord, Acts 10: 34, 35), that "a man is justified" (declared to be innocent), "and not only by faith," (not by faith only). The inference is obvious. There is no more important matter taught in the New Testament.

Justification *is not by faith only!* "It is by works a man is justified, and not only by faith." The allegation that Paul taught justification by faith only and is in conflict with James is utterly false; there is a vast difference between the doctrine of justification by faith (which Paul and James both taught, Rom. 5: 1; James 2: 20-22) and the doctrine of justification by faith only, which neither of them taught. We have seen earlier that the faith that saves is one that expresses itself in obedience to the commands of God. Faith, apart from works, is dead, barren, vain. (James 2: 17, 20, 26.) Justification is by faith. (Rom. 3: 28; 5: 1.) This faith which justifies is either *with*, or *without*, works. If it is *with* works, it is not by faith only; and it blesses only when accompanied by the works which perfect it. If it is *without* works, salvation results from a faith that is dead. But, a faith that is dead is barren (unproductive of life whatsoever). There is no salvation on the basis of a dead faith. A faith that can save is neither barren nor dead. But, faith, without works, is both barren and dead. It follows, therefore, that salvation is not by faith only.

Those whose doctrine it is that salvation is at the point and moment of faith, and without any additional acts of obedience, have found this passage to be exceedingly difficult to reconcile *with their view* that Paul taught justification by faith only. The methods have been many and the efforts to this end varied and novel.

(1) Luther, the leading light of the Reformation movement,

made short work of the effort by denying, for a time at least, that the Epistle of James is worthy of a place in the sacred canon of *Scripture*, on the allegation that in the section which we have been considering, (James 2: 14-26), its teaching conflicts with Paul, whose words in Rom. 3: 28 read: "We reckon therefore that a man is justified by faith apart from the works of the law," but which the fiery Reformer changed to read, ". . . a man is justified by faith *alone*, . . ." an unwarranted and unjustified rendering without lexical support. He referred to James as a "right strawy epistle," said it had "no gospel character in it," and added, "I will not have it in my Bible in the number of the proper chief books." He admitted that "there is many a good saying in it," but he was unable to harmonize his doctrine of justification by faith only with it. The views are indeed irreconcilable; and, the stout-hearted Luther was honest enough not to attempt such. More recent theologians, while holding to the same view of justification as Luther, have attempted to reconcile the difference in the following ways:

(2) "Paul refers to the justification of a sinner; where, James regards the matter from the viewpoint of the justification of a Christian." This answer is both fanciful and false; there is no such distinction between the two New Testament writers as is here affirmed; both refer to the *same* passage of Scripture to establish Abraham's justification. Paul, in Rom. 4: 1-5, refers to Gen. 15: 6, *to prove that Abraham was not justified by works.* James, (2: 20-22), refers to Gen. 15: 6, *to prove that Abraham was justified by works!* Abraham *was* justified by works, affirmed James. Abraham *was not* justified by works, declared Paul. By what scripture do they prove their contentions? The *same* scripture, Gen. 15: 6. It should be quite obvious that Paul and James have under consideration *two different kinds* of works. Paul, in Rom. 3: 28, tells us that "a man" is justified "apart from the works of the law." What law? The law of Moses, of course. James informs us that Abraham was justified by works which perfected his faith. What particular work was alluded to? The offering of Isaac. But, this was a commandment of God. It follows, therefore, that the works which are *excluded* (by Paul) from the plan of salvation are works such as the law of Moses, and the works which are *included* (by James) are the commandments of Christ and of God.

(3) "The justification of which James writes is before men ('Ye see . . .' verse 24), and not before God. Abraham's act justified him in the eyes of men, not God." This effort is both completely absurd and obviously false. Who, among men, *saw* the offering of Isaac? Not the young men who accompanied Abraham and Isaac to the place of offering; they were sent away. (Gen 22: 3, 5.) They were not present to *see* Abraham's justification in the act. No others were present save the patriarch and his son. If it is alleged that the justification came *after* the event, then it was neither at the point of faith *or* works!

(4) "Paul writes of true, justifying faith; whereas, James deals with a faith that is false and feigned." If so, Abraham was justified by a spurious and counterfeit faith! Desperate indeed must one be to entertain for a moment such a view. The faith of which James writes is invalid only when it is separated from works. Paul penned nothing in conflict with this view; on the contrary, he made obedience to the commands of God essential to salvation. (Rom. 6: 1-7; Gal. 3: 26, 27; 2 Thess. 1: 7-9.) Inasmuch as both James and Paul were inspired writers, neither wrote a line in conflict with the other. All truth harmonizes. Paul, in Rom. 3, 4, demonstrates that salvation is through Christ by faith and apart from the works of the law of Moses; James shows that salvation is by a faith which expresses itself in humble and unquestioning obedience to the will of the Lord. (James 2: 14-26.)

Strange indeed that men would insist, in the light of this section of Scripture, that salvation is by faith only; but so all denominational bodies do which deny the essentiality of water baptism. Stranger still that men who are members of the body of Christ and who accept the view that baptism sustains some relation to the plan of salvation would assert that there is *some sense* in which salvation is by faith only! Salvation is not by faith alone; salvation is not by works alone; the former view is that of the major Protestant denominations; the latter view is that of the Roman Catholic Church! The truth is, as illustrated in the case of Abraham (James 2: 20-22), faith exercises itself with works, and in works it is perfected: "Thou seest that faith wrought with his works, and by works was faith made perfect." Legalism, does some one shout? Then let the charge be levelled at James, who *penned*

25 And in like manner was not also Rahab the harlot justified by works, in that she received the messengers, and sent them out another way? 26 For as

these words, and not at those of us who *believe* them! Highly suspicious is any effort, however much piety its advocates may affect, which has, as its design, the aim to minimize *any* of the commandments of Christ. The same Lord which commanded faith requires baptism in water (Matt. 28: 18-20) ; it is an officious intermeddling with the will of God to magnify one and minimize the other. Those who thus do are spiritual ancestors of the Pharisees who had developed the practice into a profession! (Matt. 23: 1ff.)

(b) In The Case of Rahab

25 **And in like manner was not also Rahab the harlot justified by works,**—"In like manner," means, in this instance, *in the same way.* Rahab affords another example of that which James, in this section of his Epistle, affirms—that justification is not by faith only, but is also dependent on acts of obedience to God's will. It is not improbable that James deliberately selected two instances from Old Testament history—Abraham and Rahab—the former from the highest ranks of the most illustrious, the second from one who had been on the lowest rung of the social ladder, to show that in neither instance was salvation by faith only, and that each perfected the faith exercised in works. Rahab was an inhabitant of Jericho, a heathen before her contact with the messengers, and it is possible that her case was cited, in addition to that of Abraham, for the further design of showing that the principle of justification is the same whether applied to those in the family especially favored of God or those out of it. We are not, of course, to assume that Rahab was a harlot *at the time* she was justified by works; formerly a pagan, she had lived as many pagans did, a life of loose, dissolute activity ; and though she had ceased that manner of living, the identifying phrase by which she had been known, clung to her. For the details of her life, see Josh. 2: 1-24.

in that she received the messengers, and sent them out another way?—This woman of the ancient past, a harlot (a prostitute, a woman who sold her body for immoral purposes), was living in Jericho, in the Jordan valley, during the conquest of Canaan

the body apart from the spirit is dead, even so faith apart from works is dead.

by the Israelites. When Joshua sent spies into the city to obtain information on the basis of which the city was later to be besieged and taken, she received them into her house, welcomed them, hid them, protected them, and then enabled them to escape safely, having elicited from them a promise of deliverance for her loved ones, when the Israelites had taken the city. (Josh. 2: 1-14.) In these actions she evidenced her faith, a faith which expressed itself in the actions above outlined. Hers was not a vain and empty faith; it busied itself in performing those actions which validated it. Hundreds of years later, the Hebrew writer, in detailing the heroic acts of faith in Israel's history, did not overlook this impressive incident, but cited it as an example of genuine faith and great courage: "By faith Rahab the harlot perished not with them that were disobedient, having received the spies in peace." (Heb. 11: 31.)

The verbs of action, in verse 25 are significant. Rahab "received" *(hupodexamene,* aorist middle participle, to welcome) the messengers and "sent them out" *(exbalousa,* aorist active participle to hurry away) another way. Her's was an invaluable service which she performed gladly and effectively. Thus, she, like Abraham, afforded James with another excellent example of true, justifying faith (faith expressing itself in works). Rahab is listed in the genealogy of our Lord, having married Salmon. (Matt. 1: 5.)

26 **For as the body apart from the spirit is dead,**—The body *(soma)* is the animal frame of man which houses the spirit—the immortal nature—and which is temporal, frail, subject to deterioration and decay. In death it is dissolved (2 Cor. 5: 1); it is a "tabernacle" which must be put off (2 Pet. 1: 13, 14); it is made from the dust of the ground (Gen. 2: 7), to which is returns at death (Eccles. 12: 7). The word *soma,* translated "body" in our text, does not denote the *material* substance (this is the *sarx,* flesh, and its related substances), as much as it indicates the composition of the flesh into an organism which, when united with the spirit, constitutes *life.* The "spirit" *(pneuma)* is the "vital principle by which the body is animated" (Thayer); and, in this instance, refers to the immortal nature of man. The *soul,* not mentioned here,

but often elsewhere in the sacred writings; is a *generic* term, the context determining its significance, in any given instance. It is used (a) to designate the whole person (Acts 2: 41; 1 Pet. 3: 20); (b) the animal life which man possesses, and which ends in death (Psalm 78: 50); (c) in contradistinction to the spirit, the intellectual nature (1 Cor. 2: 14, Greek; Heb. 4: 12; 1 Thess. 5: 21); and (d) the *spirit,* the immortal nature (Acts 2: 31).

The body is temporal and frail and eventually falls into the grave; the spirit (and *soul,* when used as a synonym of the spirit), is eternal and therefore not subject to dissolution or decay. Our bodies we receive from our earthly parents; our spirits are infused into us, and fathered for us, by God himself. (Heb. 12: 9.) Were it possible, in view of this fact, (which *it is not),* to prove that there is some moral taint hereditarily transmitted from parent to child (which theologians style Original Sin, the Adamic Nature, etc.,) the doctrine of Total Depravity would still not be established, because our spirits come to us directly from God, and not from our parents. Inasmuch as "like begets like" (Gen. 1: 9-25, everything brings forth after its own kind), and since God begets our spirits, they are, at birth, as pure as the source from which they spring, and become sinful only through personal transgression.

The body, "apart from the spirit," is dead. "Dead" *(nekron)* signifies one whose life is extinct, "one that has breathed his last, lifeless." (Thayer.) One who is dead is, therefore, destitute of life. Here, incidentally, is the best brief, practical definition of death (and, by implication, *life*) which can be formulated. *What is life?* It is that state or condition which obtains while the body and spirit are united. *What is death?* It is the resulting condition when the spirit is no longer in the body. Death is then, simply the separation of body and spirit. The body, the outward frame of man, without the spirit which animates it, is dead, lifeless, henceforth inactive.

even so faith apart from works is dead.—This is the conclusion, which inspiration draws from the foregoing premises. Faith, without works, is as lifeless as the body without the spirit. Compared here are two things, *both* dead. One is spiritually dead, the other is physically dead. Faith, without works, is as destitute of life as is a fleshly body with the spirit. Separate faith and works, and the faith remaining is as lifeless as a body from which the spirit has departed. What are the works which must be joined to faith to make it alive? The commandments of the Lord. (Acts 10: 34, 35.) These commandments are righteousness. (Psalm 119: 172.) Only those who work righteousness are acceptable to him. "Whosoever doeth not righteousness is not of God. . ." (1 John 3: 10.)

While the principles herein taught by James are of course applicable to alien sinners—those who have never obeyed the gospel— we must not assume that they are limited to such. As a matter of fact, these words were penned especially to Christians; and are designed to impress believers with the fact that their faith must evidence itself in action to be a blessing to them. Members of the church whose faith does not prompt them to faithfulness in the Lord's work, and to regular Christian activity such as consistent church attendance, liberality in giving, and personal work, are spiritual corpses, possessed of a faith which is destitute of all life.

SECTION 6
3: 1-12

RESPONSIBILITY OF TEACHERS
3: 1

1 Be not many *of you* teachers, my brethren, knowing that we shall re-

1 **Be not many of you teachers,**—The verb "be not," *(me
. . . ginesthe),* a present middle imperative, with the negative,
signifies "stop becoming many teachers. . . ." This prohibition is
to be closely construed with the theme which characterizes the
Epistle through most of chapters 2 and 3. Words are worthless
without acts; faith apart from works is dead; blessings are to be
bestowed upon those who hear and do, and not upon those who
hear and do not. Even those whose *work* it is to use *words* are
ever to remember that a weighty responsibility attaches thereto,
and they are not to rush into the teaching office without proper
preparation and a due regard for the importance of the work in
which they are to engage.

It would appear that there was a disposition on the part of many
of the early converts to the word to desire the attention and influence which attended its teaching; and these, without sufficient
preparation, were disposed to attempt that which they were not
qualified to do. The influence which teachers exercise upon their
pupils is often immeasurable; and, the impressions which they
make on the impressionable minds of their students, either for
good or ill, are far-reaching in nature. It is, therefore, vitally important for those who thus do to be duly conscious of the importance of the work to which they aspire, and to make the requisite
preparation thereto. Inasmuch as all faithful disciples of the Lord
are, as far as they are able, to teach his word whenever and wherever opportunity offers, it was not James' design to discourage any
one who has the capacity to teach, then or now; it is the obligation
of us all to utilize our talents in this, and in all other areas, of the
work of the church, to the extent of our ability; but, we must take
that we are *able* properly to instruct and edify. In the days of
spiritual gifts, some were disposed to rise in the assembly and to
attempt to speak, whether they were qualified or not (1 Cor. 14:

1-33), and this created confusion and discord. If we keep in mind that James does not condemn teachers *who are able* to teach, and is warning those whose sole motive is the desire for notoriety, we have his meaning exactly. This disposition to desire the place of a teacher, and the acclaim which attended such, seems to have been exceedingly widespread in the early church. Paul, in his Epistle to Timothy, wrote: "But the end of the charge is love out of a pure heart and a good conscience and faith unfeigned: from which things some having swerved have turned aside unto vain talking; desiring to be teachers of the law, though they understand neither what they say, nor whereof they confidently affirm." The ambition to teach is a worthy one, and should be encouraged, provided the person so aspiring is willing to make the necessary preparation to accomplish the desired end. A failure so to do subjects one to the displeasure of the Lord. The Hebrew writer had especially severe words of censure for those who neglected such preparation: "For when by reason of the time ye ought to be teachers, ye have need again that some one teach you the rudiments of the first principle of the oracles of God; and are become such as have need of milk, and not of solid food. For everyone that partaketh of milk is without experience of the word of righteousness; for he is a babe. But solid food is for fullgrown men, even those who by reason of use have their senses exercised to discern good and evil." (Heb. 5: 12-14.)

Not all disciples can be public teachers of the word (1 Cor. 12: 28ff.; 14: 26), and not all should aspire to be. "If the whole body were an eye, where were the hearing?" (1 Cor. 12: 17.) There are other duties and activities in the church which are equally vital; and, those without special ability in one field may possess unusual talents in some other. What is condemned here is self-appointed teachers motivated by desires not worthy of those who teach and preach the word of God. Jesus positively forbade any unseemly seeking for prominence in teaching (Matt. 23: 8-10); and some wise man in Israel penned the maxim: "Love the work but strive not after the honor of a teacher." A "teacher," *(didaskalos),* is an instructor in righteousness, and his work is vital to New Testament Christianity. Teaching is, indeed, basic to its existence; and, it flourishes only where it is assiduously taught. The early church depended on its teachers for edification, and these men are prominently mentioned through the sacred writings. (Acts 13: 1; 1 Cor. 12: 28.) The faithful teachers of the apostolic age were highly regarded and specially honored for their works' sake; and, James (by the use of the plural pronoun "we,") in the clause following, included himself in the number. It is the work of teachers to *edify*. (1 Cor. 14: 26.) It follows, therefore, that unless those who affect to teach are able to edify (instruct, build up, strengthen), their effort is unsuccessful. There are special qualifications which ought to characterize all members of the body of Christ, and which *must* be possessed by all who would teach effectively. Paul wrote Timothy, "Till I come, give heed to reading, to exhortation, to teaching. . . . Be diligent in these things; give thyself wholly to them; that thy progress may be manifest unto all. Take heed to thyself, and to thy teaching. Continue in these things; for in doing this thou shalt save both thyself and them that hear thee. And the things which thou hast heard from me among many witnesses, the same commit thou to faithful men who shall be able to teach others also." (1 Tim. 4: 13-16; 2 Tim. 2: 2.) The minimum qualifications, as indicated here, are, (1) *faithfulness;* (2) ability to teach others. Where either is lacking the results will be far short of what is desirable. However, faithful one may be, without the ability to instruct, it is impossible to edify; and though great ability to teach is possessed, unfaithfulness on the part of the teacher nullifies much of the good which otherwise may be done. Our Lord was preeminently a *teacher* (Master, in the Authorized Version), and the verb "teach" is used in connection with his work many times. As a matter of fact, Jesus is never called a "preacher" in the books of the gospel (Matthew, Mark, Luke and John), and only eleven times is it said that he "preached" *(kerusso)* his message. Only five times, and these in Luke, is he said to have "evangelized" *(euangelizomai)* or announced good tidings. It is thus apparent that neither Jesus, nor the above mentioned writers, regarded his work as chiefly preaching, but rather as teaching men. Forty-five times in the books of the gospel he is called a teacher; six times he refers to himself in this fashion; twenty-three times his disciples, and those friendly to his cause to style him, and twelve times his enemies, the Pharisees, Sadducees, Herodians, and others, call him a teacher.

my brethren,—This phrase recurs with great regularity in the Epistle of James. (1: 2, 19, 21; 2: 1, 14; 3: 1, 10; 5: 7, 12, 19.) It denotes (a) the close relationship of fraternalism which obtains between the disciples; (b) the brotherly love which should ever characterize them; and (c) the common level all enjoy in Christ. It was James' purpose throughout the Epistle to condemn the disposition which some among his readers regularly exhibited of assigning to some people places of preference, and to treat others (because they were lacking in the worldly attainments possessed by those honored) with contempt. *There is no caste system in Christ.* Inasmuch as we are all brethren, it behooves us to conduct ourselves as brethren should, and to eschew all bitterness and envy, and "to love one another from the heart fervently." (1 Pet. 1: 22.) Accidental accomplishments, such as wealth, social position, and fame, count for nothing in Christ. "While we look not at the things which are seen, but at the things which are not seen: for the things which are seen are temporal; but the things which are not seen are eternal." (2 Cor. 4: 18.)

knowing that we shall receive heavier judgment.—This is the reason why one should not rashly assume the work of a teacher. He is to know that his judgment will be heavier if he fails in the proper discharge thereof. "Heavier judgment" *(meizon krima)* is, literally, greater judgment (condemnation). The word translated judgment here almost always means condemnation. The word thus translated *(krima)* is from *krino*, to separate, distinguish. Thus, at the great judgment day, the Lord *will separate* those who have been teachers of his word from those who have not, and will then pass on them by far stricter standards than those applicable to non-teachers. The consequences involved in teaching that which is false are fatal; and those who have not properly prepared themselves for such work, and who thus mislead those whom they affect to teach, must answer under "a heavier judgment," than those not thus engaged. "But whoso shall cause one of these little ones that believe on me to stumble, it is profitable for him that a great millstone should be hanged about his neck, and that he should be sunk in the depth of the sea. Woe unto the world because of occasions of stumbling! for it must needs be that the occasions come; but woe to that man through whom the occasion com-

ceive [13]heavier judgment. 2 For in many things we all stumble. If any stumbleth not in word, the same is a perfect man, able to bridle the whole

---

[13]Gr. *greater.*

---

eth!" (Matt. 18: 6, 7.) The lesson for us is that leadership involves responsibility; and the greater the area of leadership the greater the responsibility. Teachers must, therefore, answer for a great deal more than those engaged in other Christian work. But, if the responsibility is greater, and the judgment heavier for those who misuse or do not properly use the occasion, the reward is greater for those who do properly teach and edify others. Paul described the Philippians as his "brethren beloved and longed for," his "joy and crown." (Phil. 4: 1.) And John said, "Greater joy have I not than this, to hear of my children walking in the truth." (3 John 4.) Daniel said that they "that are wise shall shine as the brightness of the firmament; and they that turn many to righteousness as the stars for ever and ever." (Dan. 12: 3.)

Teachers, preachers, elders, all who have the obligation to instruct others, should take these matters carefully to heart, and to be mindful always of the weighty responsibility which is theirs in this respect. All of us, whatever our lot in life, should be desirous of becoming more proficient in the word of truth, and we should labor diligently to this end. A well-stocked library of good religious books and periodicals, regular periods of study, and love for truth are prime requisites to this end. We must answer, in the judgment, not only for what we know, but for what we could have found out by reasonable effort; and it will not suffice for us, of this day, to plead ignorance of God's will and way, when the means by which we may become efficient teachers are readily at hand.

CONTROL OF THE TONGUE
3: 28

2 For in many things we all stumble.—"In many things," (from *polla,* an adverbial accusative), means "with reference to many things." For the significance of the word "stumble," see James 2: 10, and comments thereon. It will be observed that the writer affirms *two* things here, and includes himself among those who thus stumble: (1) "We all stumble"; (2) "We all stumble in many things." "To stumble" is to trip, to fall; and here refers to the mistakes all of us make, particularly where the use of the tongue is involved. The fact that James includes himself among those who trip in this manner is no reflection on the inspiration which guarded his writings from all error. We must ever remember to distinguish between what the inspired penmen *wrote* under the direction of the Holy Spirit and their own personal and individual activity as Christians. They had no more protection against the possibility of sinning—as Christians—than do we; otherwise, in their case at least, the doctrine of the impossibility of apostasy would be true. The people of Israel "angered" Moses at "the waters of Meribah," and "it went ill with Moses for their sakes; because they were rebellious against his spirit, and he spake unadvisedly with his lips." (Psalm 106: 32, 33.) Paul resisted Peter "to the face" in Antioch, when he and Barnabas "walked not uprightly according to the truth of the gospel." (Gal. 2: 11-21.)

Because all stumble in this respect, all need provision for their sins; and this the Lord has marvelously provided. "If we walk in the light, as he is in the light, we have fellowship one with another, and the blood of Jesus his Son cleanseth (literally, keeps on cleansing) us from all sin. . . . If we say that we have no sin, we deceive ourselves, and the truth is not in us. If we confess our sins, he is faithful and righteous to forgive us our sins, and to cleanse us from all unrighteousness." (1 John 1: 7-9.) The tense of the verb *ptaiomen* (stumble) denotes continuous action, but (thank God!) the tense of the verb *cleanseth* signifies the same; and when, in our weakness, we *keep on* stumbling, the blood of Jesus *keeps on* cleansing! We must not, of course, suppose that the stumbling here is deliberate; no such provision exists for those who set out on a calculated course of sin. Represented is a difficult road beset by many dangers and containing many pitfalls. The faithful disciple, forced to follow it through life, often trips over unseen obstacles therein, and stumps his toe on the stones of sin which are frequently in his path. He is headed for heaven however; and, obviously, does not deliberately trip and fall in the way. His is not a voluntary stumbling, but that which is occasioned by the difficulties of the path he follows, and the disposition of the devil to place in his way as many obstacles as possible.

If any stumbleth not in word,—Here James returns to his special theme—the proper use of the tongue—which is to be particularly dealt with in this chapter, and teaches us that it is possible to "trip" with the tongue in word, as well as in life and in action. "In word" means in what we *say*. The word "stumbleth" signifies the same as it does in the first clause of the verse, and in James 2: 10. "Any" here means any *person*—old, young, rich, poor, wise, unwise, all—thus evidencing the fact that here is a matter to which every disciple must give constant attention. Though verse 1 is devoted exclusively to "teachers," the writer broadens the application, and admonishes all in the church to be wary of temptations involving the tongue. Teachers especially need the instruction given, inasmuch as speaking is an indispensable and major part of their activity; but the lesson is not limited to them, and the application is thus expanded to embrace all.

the same is a perfect man,—That is, the one who stumbles not in word "is a perfect man," *(teleios aner),* one who has reached full maturity in spiritual growth. This term does not denote sinlessness, so much as full development, mature growth. The meaning is, "If any man does not keep on stumbling in word, he has reached that status in life where he is fully mature." The word translated "perfect" might properly be rendered *goal.* One who has attained to such complete mastery over his tongue has truly reached the goal in spiritual achievement. This does not mean that he is above the possibility of sinning; it means that he has acquired such mastery over his tongue that he is able to control it. He is like David in "Fulfilling all of God's will and having respect for his commandment" (Psalm 119: 6), and like Zacharias and Elizabeth in walking "in all the commandments and ordinances of the Lord blameless" (Luke 1: 6). Such also is affirmed of Noah, Abraham and Job. (Gen. 6: 9; Job 1: 1). See, also, Phil. 3: 12, 13.

able to bridle the whole body also.—So disposed is man to use his tongue improperly, and to say things which he ought not, that he who is able to restrain himself in *word* would evidence such remarkable self-control that it might properly be assumed that he is able "to bridle" (keep under rein) his entire body. To exercise restraint over it is to demonstrate the ability to keep under

body also. 3 Now if we put the horses' bridles into their mouths that they may obey us, we turn about their whole body also. 4 Behold, the ships also, though they are so great and are driven by rough winds, are yet turned about by a very small rudder, whither the impulse of the steersman willeth.

---

control all the other members of the body, inasmuch as it requires greater effort to keep the tongue under control than any other member of the body. We must not from this assume that it is more important to do this than to exercise restraint in any other area; or, that in this field alone mastery means perfection, but that it is a test which determines whether control over the body is being exercised. The phrase, "the whole body," is used here to designate the sum of all the sins of which man is capable; that is, if one can control his tongue, he will have attained to such mastery over himself that other temptations will be easily repelled. The figure of the "bridle" is an impressive one, and suggestive of the same meaning as in James 1: 26. Inasmuch as one who has control of the bridle controls the horse, so one who controls his tongue may be expected to keep in check the rest of the body.

3 **Now if we put the horses' bridles into their mouths that they may obey us, we turn about their whole body also.**—This illustrates that which James has just affirmed: to control the tongue is, in effect, to exercise restraint over the whole body. A horse, though large, is controlled by a comparatively tiny bridle; this, indeed, is the reason why the bridle is used—in order that the entire body may be easily turned and controlled.

4 **Behold, the ships also, though they are so great and are driven by rough winds, are yet turned about by a very small rudder, whither the impulse of the steersman willeth.**—In James' first exemplification, the illustration of bridled horses is used; here, the figure is that of great ships which are steered by a small rudder, in harmony with the will of "the steersman." With both of these figures the writer's readers would be perfectly familiar, and would readily grasp the lesson intended. In the first, a spirited animal is used; in the second, an inanimate object, but one nevertheless subject to the influences of the winds and the seas. Notwithstanding the will of the first, the horse, and the brute forces—the winds and the seas—operating upon the second, both are easily controlled, and that by a small object; in the first in-

5 So the tongue also is a little member, and boasteth great things.   Behold

---

stance, a bridle; in the second, a rudder; according to the will of man in both. The meaning of both illustrations is: We are able to control large animals and huge ships with very small objects; how much more ought we to be able to govern ourselves! For, if we are able to exercise similar rule over our tongues, we govern our whole being.

5 **So the tongue also is a little member,**—This is the application of the illustrations of the bridle and the rudder. Though small, each is exceedingly effective, thus demonstrating the fact that a thing may be little yet powerful and influential. The tongue is a small object compared to the whole body, just as a bridle is small in comparison to the horse and the rudder to the ship; but, as the bridle and the rudder are capable of exercising great influence upon that which they influence, so the tongue, notwithstanding its insignificance in size, possesses great potential. The contrast drawn here is between the tiny character of the tongue and the hugeness of the body and the effect which the tongue exercises, despite this great disparity in size.

and boasteth great things—(*megalaauchei,* present active indicative), it continually boasts; i.e., it is a characteristic of this *little* member of the body to *talk big,* to be arrogant and boastful in its action. While there is a very proper sense in which the highest possible honor is due the tongue—because of the ennobling sentiments it is capable of expressing—it is most likely that here it was the design of the writer to carry through the point which the illustrations emphasize: the disparity in the size of the tongue and the possibilities of which it is capable. Its power and influence are exceedingly great. It is capable of the greatest good, and of the most far-reaching harm. The extent of its influence is indicated in the statement following.

Behold, how much wood is kindled by how small a fire!—Here is a *third* illustration used by James to denote the potency and power of the tongue. The construction of this sentence is unusual and informative. The same relative form occurs for the two indirect questions: "What sized fire kindles what sized wood." The writer's chief point continues to be impressed: The vast difference in size between the cause and the effect; but, there is an additional characteristic injected here. In the illustration of the horse and bridle, and the ship and rudder, there is *controlled* effect; here, the effect of the little fire and the resulting tremendous destruction are *uncontrolled*.

A huge factory, a mighty forest, a whole city may go up in flames from the effects of one tiny match. There is a legend that the great Chicago fire started when a cow, being milked, kicked over a lantern, and when the flames had wrought their great and terrible destruction, and had finally burned out, hundreds of blocks of homes and vast areas of the city were no more. "How much wood is kindled by how small a fire!" In similar fashion, one improper statement by the tongue, small though that member of the body is, may start a furious flame that will consume and destroy individuals, families, and whole congregations. A deceitful tongue is often condemned in Scripture: "Deliver my soul, O Jehovah, from lying lips, and from a deceitful tongue." (Psalm 120: 2.) "As a madman who casteth firebrands, arrows, and death, so is the man that deceiveth his neighbor, and saith, Am I not in sport? For lack of wood the fire goeth out; and where there is no whisperer, contention ceaseth. As coals are to hot embers, and wood to fire, so is a contentious man to inflame strife. The words of a whisperer are as dainty morsels, and they go down into the innermost parts. Fervent lips and a wicked heart are like an earthen vessel overlaid with silver dross. He that hateth dissembleth with his lips; but he layeth up deceit within him: when he speaketh fair believe him not; for there are seven abominations in his heart." (Prov. 26: 18-25.)

Backbiting with the tongue is one of the most common of sins. (Psalm 15: 4.) The word "backbite" is an Anglo-Saxon term, with three inherent ideas: (1) Knavery, (2) cowardice, (3) brutality. (1) A backbiter is a knave, a low-born person. People of good breeding do not find pleasure in, and therefore, do not indulge the temptation to engage in malicious gossip. (2) A backbiter is a coward, always saying that behind one's back, and in one's absence, what would never be said to one's face. (3) A backbiter is a brutish person, being wholly insensible of the feelings of others. "He that backbiteth not with his tongue," is, in the Hebrew

[14]how much wood is kindled by how small a fire! 6 And the tongue is [15]a fire: [16]the world of iniquity among our members is the tongue, which defileth the whole body, and setteth on fire the wheel of [1]nature, and is set on

[14]Or, *how great a forest*
[15]Or, *a fire, that world of iniquity: the tongue is among our members that which &c.*
[16]Or, *that world of iniquity, the tongue, is among our members that which &c.*
[1]Or, *birth*

text, "He foots not upon his tongue"; i.e., he does not *kick about*, as a football, the character of an absent person. It is virtually impossible to counteract the effects of slander and malicious gossip; and those guilty inflict injury the effects of which extend through time into eternity. And, if people are to be judged on the basis of *the effects* of their activities this undoubtedly will be one of the most grievous sins for which to answer at the judgment.

6 **And the tongue is a fire:**—Having shown the devastating effects of fire, when raging out of control, James tells us that this is what the tongue is, in the improper consequences of its use. The figure is not an unusual one in the Scriptures. "A worthless man deviseth mischief; and in his lips there is a scorching fire." (Prov. 16: 27.) See, also Prov. 26: 18-22. This statement, "and the tongue is a fire," identifies the tongue, in its effects, with the fire which begins as a tiny flame, but immediately becomes a great conflagration, as indicated in the verse preceding. The tongue is like a fire in this respect. It is a "fire," (a) in the pain it inflicts; (b) in the destruction which attends it; (c) in the effects which follow it.

the world of iniquity among our members is the tongue,—
We must, of course, remember that it is the *improper* use of the tongue which is contemplated here. Among all the members of the body the tongue is, when improperly exercised, the most wicked of all. The phrase, "world of iniquity," is an expression, the design of which is to indicate the *sum* of evil; and the tongue, because of its great powers, becomes such in its evil activity. It is "a world of iniquity" among the members of the body, because of the incalculable harm which it produces; it is utterly impossible to measure, in this life, the harm which grows out of the slander, the profanity, the falsehood, the blasphemy and the scandal of which it is capable. History is replete with instances of wars, strifes, alienations resulting from its evil work. *Were all men suddenly to lose the faculty*

*of speech, the number of sins of which men are continually guilty
would be sharply reduced!* In view of this fact, how important it
is that we speak only what we ought to, and that what we say be
soberly considered.

which defileth the whole body,—"Defileth" is from *spilo,* to
spot, to stain. The meaning is that the improper use of the tongue
besmirches, stains, renders defiled, the entire body. A slanderer
eventually exhibits the effects of his sin in his own personality.
His outlook on life becomes polluted, his confidence in his fellows
vanishes, and his spiritual life dwarfs and dies. A mechanic may be
capable of doing excellent work; but, if we catch him lying to us,
we immediately regard his work as untrustworthy. It is an ancient and true adage that one is no better than his word.

and setteth on fire the wheel of nature,—This clause is not
easy of interpretation because of the obscurity of the phrase, "the
wheel of nature," *(ton trochon geneseos,* the wheel of birth). The
marginal reading is "birth." Birth is that which ushers us into
life; and, "the wheel of birth" may well signify our entire existence, beginning with birth and ending with death. A "wheel" is
that which is round, hence, "the round of existence," that is, the
whole period of our lives. All of it is set on fire by the improper
use of the tongue, "Setteth on fire" is from *phlogizousa,* present
active participle of *phlogizo,* to ignite, from *phlox,* a flame. We
shall have no difficulty in understanding the passage if we keep in
mind that it was the design of James to show the far-reaching effects of the abuse of the tongue, and thus the need of constant restraint thereof. So potent is it in its effects that it can, and often
does, influence man's entire round (period) of existence. An in-
flamed speech, intolerant words, a false rumor may set on fire an
individual, a city and even a nation. We recall only too well the
rabble-rousing speeches of Hitler, and the overwhelming wave of
the war spirit which swept over the German nation as a result.
Banks have been broken, financial institutions driven to bankruptcy
by thoughtless words spoken over a back fence.

and is set on fire by hell.—*(Kai phlogizomene hupo tes ge-
hennes,* present passive participle of *phlogizo,* is continually set on
fire by hell.) The fire which results from the tongue is comparable only to that which arises in hell (Greek, *Gehenna).* This term

fire by ²hell. 7 For every ³kind of beasts and birds, of creeping things and things in the sea, is tamed, and hath been tamed ⁴by ⁵mankind: 8 but the

²Gr. *Gehenna.*
³Gr. *nature.*
⁴Or, *unto*
⁵Gr. *the human nature.*

—Gehenna—originally was the name of the valley just outside, and to the southeast of the city of Jerusalem, where the children of Israel practiced the idolatrous rites of Moloch, which they borrowed from their heathen neighbors. There, the children of Israel sacrificed their own offspring to the fire god Moloch. When Josiah instituted reforms, he destroyed the altars, broke down the high places, and that the valley might be wholly unsuited for such practices, caused it to be turned into the garbage dump of Jerusalem. The garbage of the city was carted out there and in sufficient quantity that it had to be burned, and thus fires were continually burning. Occasionally bodies were thrown there and burned. Thus, the place served as a fitting symbol of the place of future punishment, and the Lord so applied it hundreds of years later when he came to the earth. (1 Kings 11: 7; 2 Kings 23: 13, 14; Matt. 5: 22, 29, 30; 10: 28; 18: 9; 23: 15, 33; Mark 9: 43, 45, 47; Luke 12: 5.) It is important to distinguish between *Hades,* the realm of departed spirits between death and the resurrection, and *Gehenna,* the eternal abode of the finally disobedient. *Sheol,* occurring often in the Old Testament, is the equivalent of Hades in the New Testament. Hades is the intermediate state of the dead, between death and the resurrection, and contains the good and the bad who are, nevertheless, separated there, the good in a place of blessing, the wicked in torment. (Luke 16: 23.)

It is of interest to observe the care which James used in presenting these symbols. An evil tongue defiles the entire body. A defiled body is fit only to be thrown on the refuse dump (as was often done in early centuries), and there burned. It is truly a sobering thought that the fire which (figuratively) issues from our tongues when improperly used originates in hell, and will lead us there if we do not learn to extinguish it. Hell is truly the garbage dump of the world and such is the destiny of all who die in disobedience. It has been truly said that one should never throw mud because one may miss the mark thrown at, but will always wind up with dirty hands!

7 **For every kind of beasts and birds, of creeping things and things in the sea, is tamed,**—"Kind" is from phusis, literally nature. All of brute nature has been brought under the dominion of man: "And God created man in his own image, in the image of God created he him; male and female created he them. And God blessed them: and God said unto them, Be fruitful, and multiply, and replenish the earth, and subdue it; and have dominion over the fish of the sea, and over the birds of the heavens, and over every living thing that moveth upon the earth." (Gen. 1: 27, 28.) God said to Noah, "Be fruitful, and multiply, and replenish the earth. And the fear of you and the dread of you shall be upon every beast of the earth, and upon every bird of the heavens; with all wherewith the ground teemeth, and all the fishes of the sea, into your hand are they delivered." (Gen. 9: 1, 2.) This dominion thus granted to man had to be exercised and retained. James does not say that every wild thing has been tamed; affirmed is the fact that every *kind* of creature has been brought under subjection to man. The most ferocious of beasts, the fishes of the deep, blue sea, the birds which soar high in the skies, and even the slimy serpents, have yielded to the superiority of man, and have been made subordinate to him.

The "beasts" designated here are quadrupeds, four legged animals *(therion)*. "Birds" *(petomai,* to fly) designates creatures which are able to fly; "creeping things," *(herpeton,* to crawl), serpents which slither along the ground, and "things of the sea," of course, the fishes. It will be seen that the four classes of created things are much the same as those designated in Gen. 9: 2. There are two pairs of four groups: (1) beasts and birds; (2) creeping things and things in the sea.

"Is tamed" *(damazetai,* present passive indicative) is, literally, "is continually being tamed." The dominion which Adam was to exercise over all the animals was not to be limited to him, or to his day; it was to be exercised by mankind through all succeeding ages.

and hath been tamed by mankind:—*(Dedamastai,* perfect passive indicative, of the verb translated "tamed" in the clause preceding, thus indicating a past fact general in character.) "By mankind" is *tei phusei tei anthropinei,* instrumental case, "by the

tongue can no man tame; *it is* a restless evil, *it is* full of deadly poison.　9

nature of the human." That is, every kind of brute nature has been subjected to, and subdued by the human nature. It was James' design to emphasize the fact that the taming process has been exercised in this fashion from the beginning of creation. *Though able to subdue the brute creation, man does not always control himself!* Because of the fall, and the consequent moral weakness thus experienced, he has ceased to be in control of his own members, and particularly, his tongue. It is a sad commentary on man, and an embarrassing exhibition of his moral and spiritual degradation that though able to tame the wildest animals, he cannot tame his own tongue!

8 **but the tongue can no man tame;**—Here, the tense of the verb is momentary, and not continuous action. It is impossible for *man* to accomplish the taming of his own tongue. Though exceedingly powerful in his exercise of dominion over the brute creation, he is helpless when it comes to his own *little* tongue. Why cannot he accomplish this? The answer is that it is a *human* tongue, and not merely or solely an animal's tongue. Human nature can easily subdue the animal nature, but it is powerless of itself to subdue the Satanic nature which has moved in because of a life of sin. When James said, "The tongue can no man tame," he did not mean (a) that man, being unable to control his tongue, is therefore excused for any abuses which may result from its improper use; nor (b) that God assigns an impossible task, yet demands that it be done. The meaning is that birds and beasts, however wild and fierce they may be in their native habitat, *when tamed,* are no longer dangerous. One does not keep a tamed beast chained! The tongue, however, can never be tamed. It may be successfully restrained for forty years, but in an unguarded moment leap out a dangerous and hurtful thing. This statement of James was intended to teach us that we must ever exercise ceaseless vigilance in all matters pertaining to the tongue. How conscious all of us ought always to be of this painful fact. How often do we thoughtlessly give utterance to sentiments the moment said we would give the world to recall. It is impossible to bring back the spoken word.

> The Moving Finger writes; and, having writ
> Moves on: nor all your Piety nor Wit
> Shall lure it back to cancel half a Line,
> Nor all your Tears wash out a Word of it.

It is a revealing and profitable exercise in Bible study, to gather up, by means of a concordance, or similar word book, all of the passages of the Bible dealing with the abuses of the tongue, and the evils which may result therefrom. The terms used to describe these sins make a lengthy and exceedingly ugly catalog. The word, "devil," is translated from the Greek *diabolos,* means a calumniator, slanderer, accuser, false witness. He is also called a liar, and "the father of lies." Among the sins possible to be committed with the tongue are blasphemy (to speak evil of God and of sacred matters), sacrilege (an offense against God), perjury (false witness in the limited, legal sense), slander, flattery, backbiting, whispering, false suggestions and, of course, many others.

There are those whose chief joy in life is the accumulation of malicious matter against every person of their acquaintance, and who relish the recitation thereof on every possible occasion. Such are ever with us; and we must be careful that we do not become their instruments in passing on their slanderous tidbits. Two questions we should raise on hearing something of an injurious character regarding others: (1) *Is it true?* There is a rather common type of small-souled individual who seems to think that he lifts himself from the anonymity he deserves by attacking others, and who appears to feel that besmirching and discrediting others brings credit to himself. We should, therefore, raise the question, *Do I know that this thing is so?* Unless I have sufficient evidence of the correctness of the report, I should throw the mantle of forgetfulness about it, and relegate it to the realm of forgotten things. But, granting that it is true, I should ask this additional question, (2) *Will it do any good to tell it?* Will it aid the church, the community, the nation? If not, let it be forgotten forever!

it is a restless evil,—*(Akatascheton kakon,* an evil ever turbulent, agitated, unstable, like a wild beast continually moving up and down in his cage, resisting, as far as possible, all restraint.) With what vividness does James describe the tumultuous tongue! It is

(a) an evil thing when uncontrolled, capable of the greatest possible injury. Those who would shrink in horror from the thought of plunging a sword into the heart of another will, nevertheless, indulge in malicious gossip that drives a sword through the heart in a manner far more painful than any possible physical injury. In Cymbeline, Act III, Scene IV, Shakespeare tells of a husband who, believing his wife to be disloyal, writes to his servant accusing her of infidelity, and commands him to kill her. The servant shows the letter to the accused woman whom he believes to be innocent. Watching the effect of the letter upon her as she reads, the servant says,

> "What, shall I draw my sword? The paper
> Hath cut her throat already. No 'tis slander
> Whose edge is sharper than the sword; whose tongue
> Outvenoms all the worms of the Nile; whose breath
> Rides on the posting winds, and doth belie
> All corners of the world; kings, queens and states,
> Maids, matrons, nay the secrets of the grave
> This viperous slander enters."

It is said that the great theologian Augustine had enscribed over his dining room table the following couplet, in Latin, reading:

> "He that is wont to slander absent men
> May never at this table sit again!"

Were this rule to be invariably followed today, many would never dine at the same place twice.

(b) The tongue is a restless evil, continually chafing against any restraint which may be exercised upon it. It fights against any effort to corner it and is thus an untamed thing. It is impossible to restrain a calumnious tongue as it is impossible to overtake and restrain the calumny itself. It is of course possible to refute the slanderer and to prove his calumny false, but the originator will simply move into new areas and resume his favorite avocation. Moreover, the consequences of such are far-reaching and impossible to eliminate; those who heard the calumny but not the refutation will be disposed to associate the name and the calumny, when either is heard, and so the evil work of the slanderer continues.

it is full of deadly poison.—*(Meste iou thanatephorou,* full of death-bringing poison.)   The effects of its improper use are deadly and the reason is that it is filled with a poison that is death-dealing in nature.   We are to understand, of course, that James is discussing the improper use of the tongue here; and, is by these figures of speech indicating the far-reaching effects of such use.   There is here a possible reference to Psalm 140: 3: "They have sharpened their tongue like a serpent; adders' poison is under their lips." The phrase, "full of," indicates that such is the character of the tongue under consideration.   This form of expression is not uncommon in the sacred writings.   Peter writes of those who are "full of adultery" (2 Pet. 2: 14), and Paul of some who were "full of envy" (Rom. 1: 29).   It was not James' design, in this instance, to describe the effects of the tongue on the individual guilty of its abuses, but upon those who are victims of it.   Those possessed of such tongues are like slithering snakes carrying a sac of virulent poison which they are ready to inject at the first opportunity.   There is no more contemptible character, and it is not to be wondered at that the Scriptures represent such as snakes.

If those whose delight it is to engage in slander are thus described, what of the individual who listens to, and thus encourages, the slanderer in his evil work?   Were there no listeners there would be no slanderers!   He who encourages another in his calumny is about as guilty as he who commits it.   The receiver of stolen goods is, under the law, as much of a criminal as the thief himself; why not then, the receiver of false and malicious gossip. Were all such intercourse eliminated, the world would improve one hundred per cent over night. And many, whose chief interest consists in dwelling on the weaknesses and foibles of others, would find themselves barren of useful ideas, and without an avocation in life. Those who have hitherto allowed their minds to become garbage cans for the collection of every foul and filthy thing would suddenly discover themselves to be in the position of the man out of whom seven demons were cast—swept and garnished.

Therewith bless we the Lord and Father; and therewith curse we men, who

CONTRADICTIONS OF THE TONGUE
3: 9-12

9 Therewith bless we the Lord and Father;—The verb "bless" is from *eulogoumen,* present active indicative of *eulogeo,* to speak well of. This is, of course, the noblest and highest use of the tongue. It is, however, not surprising that the tongue is thus used with reference to God. Believers, at least, would be expected to speak well of God if they speak of him at all. This common use of the tongue by those who believe does not justify its improper use with reference to men, and emphasizes the glaring inconsistency often characteristic of men to which this verse alludes. It cannot possibly be pleasing to the Father to be addressed in words of praise by a tongue which, preceding and following the ascription of praise, is used to pronounce curses and maledictions upon men. It is a strange form of logic which prompts a man to believe that God is pleased with praises addressed to him by a tongue which regularly slanders others. Man is made in God's image; and, he who despises man, the handiwork of God, despises God himself. John said, "If a man say, I love God, and hateth his brother, he is a liar: for he that loveth not his brother whom he hath seen, cannot love God whom he hath not seen. And this commandment have we from him, that he who loveth God love his brother also." (1 John 4: 20, 21; Matt. 25: 45.) It is idle for one to expect to be pleasing to God, though disposed to express words of devotion, when the same tongue is used to curse others, to slander their names, and to destroy their reputations. The word "bless," the general meaning of which is to speak well of, is used more specifically elsewhere in the New Testament for the giving of thanks. (Matt. 26: 26; 1 Cor. 14: 16.)

The phrase, "The Lord and Father," *(ton kurion kai patara),* means "the Lord who is our Father," both terms referring to the same person. It will be observed that in the Greek phrase the article appears before the word Lord only, and thus the reference is to God. God is styled Father here to emphasize the fact that man is in his image, a fact indicated also in the last clause of the verse.

and therewith curse we men,—("And therewith," *kai en aute.)* The two statements—this and that occurring in the preceding portion of the verse—are joined by the copulative *kai,* and are thus paralleled. The tongue is used to say good things of God, and it is the same tongue which is used to curse men. "Curse," *(katarometha,* present middle indicative of *kataraomai),* indicates not an occasional lapse into this vice, but an habitual practice. The tenses in the statements thus placed side by side are the same. It is, so James affirms, a characteristic of some men habitually to praise God with a tongue which is also used *regularly* to pronounce curses upon other men. Such contradictions are common to men who are possessed of evil hearts, and a constant temptation to all, whether good or bad. The Psalmist wrote of some who "delight in lies," who "bless with their mouth, but they curse inwardly." (Psalm 62: 4.)   And, Paul admonished the Romans, "Bless them that persecute you; bless, and curse not." (Rom. 12: 14.)

The etymology of the word translated "curse" is interesting and significant. It is compounded from *kata,* down, and *araomai,* to curse. One who feels disposed so to do regards himself as occupying a higher position than other men, and privileged to deal thus with his fellows. He considers himself as able to look *up* to God, and bless him; and *down* to men and curse them. It is a presumptuous and high-handed disposition wholly displeasing to God. James' word, *katarometha,* from *kataraomai,* is derived from *katara,* a curse. This word, *etymologically,* is made up of the preposition *kata,* down, and *ara,* a prayer. It is therefore, an address to God in the form of a prayer that he will bring evil upon men. The noun *ara* was originally used by the Greeks to designate the goddess of destruction. A curse is, therefore, a petition to God to destroy men made in his own image. Such is sinful and wrong. We must distinguish between such maledictions uttered by men against other men and the legitimate curses often mentioned in Scripture. God cursed the serpent which tempted Eve and which became the instrument of sin and death in the human family. (Gen. 3: 14.)   He also pronounced a curse upon Cain, who slew his brother Abel. (Gen. 4: 11.)   God promised Abraham that he would curse those who cursed him. (Gen. 15: 1-6.)   These divine curses were not simply and solely imprecations, nor the utterance of evil desires, they carried their effects with them, and were accompanied by the sufferings which they foretold. There are also numerous instances of curses delivered against individuals and nations by the servants of God. (Gen. 9: 25; 49: 7; Deut. 27: 15; Josh. 6: 26.) These curses did not develop from feelings of passion, revenge, and malice; they were prophecies of impending doom upon people who were highly disobedient to God. The law of Moses positively forbade all unjustified cursing; and one who cursed his father or mother committed a capital crime. (Ex. 21: 17.)

who are made after the likeness of God:—The antecedent of "who" is the word *men,* whom some were disposed to curse with a tongue at other times used to bless God. These men thus cursed are made after God's likeness, a fact which points up the grave crime of speaking against them. The phrase is the translation of *tous kath' homoiosin Theou gegonotas,* the perfect tense—*gegonotas,* from *ginomai*—denoting that man *was* made in, and *continues to be* in the likeness of God. This image is not physical but moral and spiritual; and, though marred greatly in the fall, is still apparent in man, and is that which elevates him above the animal creation. (2 Cor. 3: 18.) There is in men, even the worst of them, traces of their divine origin, and this fact must ever be kept in mind in our dealings one with another. Inasmuch as man is in the likeness of God (Gen. 1: 27), and since God desires the salvation of all men (1 Tim. 2: 4), it is the responsibility of every child of God to establish and maintain a relationship toward others that will enable him to influence them for good.

The image of God in man has long been a fruitful field of controversy, and study, and many questions remain unanswered, due to the fact that the Scriptures have little to say thereon. It is idle to speculate as to the *manner, extent* and *present character* of it. Man is said to have been made in the image of, and after the likeness of, God (Gen. 1: 26; 5: 1), and it has been a favorite exercise of theologians to search out what they regard as distinctions between these two terms. It is by no means certain that there is any essential difference between *likeness* and *image* in the passage cited above; and it may well be that the twofold expression is used merely to give emphasis to the idea of *godlikeness* set forth in

are made after the likeness of God: 10 out of the same mouth cometh forth
blessing and cursing.   My brethren, these things ought not so to be.   11

these passages.   Those who wish to pursue the matter to the extent possible from the sparcity of scripture thereon will consider
Gen. 9: 6; Psalm 8; James 3: 9; Eph. 4: 24; Col. 3: 10; 1 Pet. 1:
15, 16; 2 Pet. 1: 4.   The *fact* of such likeness is clearly taught,
and many considerations are based upon it. The sacredness of
human life issues from this fact (Gen. 9: 6), and as the avenging
hand is not to be raised against our fellow human beings for this
reason, so the slanderous tongue is also to be restrained from in-
flicting injury.   Paul informs us that "all have sinned and fall
short of the glory of God" (Rom. 3: 23), a passage which appears
to suggest that the image of man, though yet discernible, is not as
glorious as it was before the fall.   References to the "new man"
(Eph. 4: 24; Col. 3: 10); "partakers of the divine nature," (2
Pet. 1: 4), and similar affirmations, definitely indicate that man
has lost much of what he once had in this respect, but which may
be regained in Christ.

10 **out of the same mouth cometh forth blessing and cursing.**—The absurdity of such a situation is glaring, and is alluded to
by statement and by illustration again and again in this section.   It
is sinful for many reasons: (1) The mouth was created for holy
purposes and not for base and sinful ones; (2) it is highly inconsistent for the mouth to utter praise to God, and then to curse men
made in God's likeness; (3) it is contrary to nature (emphasized
in verse 11), for the mouth to give utterance to sentiments so contradictory.   Though the sinfulness of such a practice is apparent to
every thoughtful person, the evil alluded to is well nigh universal
and the warnings of the sacred writer are by no means superfluous.
If those most prominent among the early disciples often erred in
this respect, and were rebuked for such, we would do well to give
the most serious attention to these matters that we may avoid them
in our own lives.   Peter, for example, assured the Lord that "If all
men shall be offended (margin, *caused to stumble*), in thee, I will
never be offended" (*caused to stumble*).   (Matt. 26: 33.)   Yet,
just a few short hours later, this same apostle "denied with an
oath" that he was acquainted with Jesus, and re-enforced his de-

Doth the fountain send forth from the same opening sweet *water* and bitter?

---

nials with curses. (Matt. 26: 69-75.) John, often called the "apostle of love," was so incensed on one occasion he asked the Lord to call down fire out of heaven upon a Samaritan village which he fancied had shown disrespect to them, yet could later write, "He that loveth not, knoweth not God, for God is love." (1 John 4: 8.) If the best of men were guilty of occasional lapses in this respect, we must ever be on our guard that we do not sin even more grievously.

My brethren, these things ought not so to be—A conclusion drawn from the preceding premises. The verb indicates the coming into a situation, rather than the situation itself, thus signifying, "These things ought not to begin to be." The word rendered "ought" means that aside from the consideration of *right* and *wrong* (with which the writer had already fully dealt), it is contrary to the fitness of things for us to bless God and to curse men from the same mouth. It is not even in harmony with good sense! The word translated "ought" is from a root from which another Greek word, *chresis*, meaning *use*, comes. Thus implied is the uselessness of such actions, aside from their sinfulness. Why pronounce evil maledictions upon another? They do not harm him; God is not influenced against another thereby; and, it is idle to engage in that which is both senseless and without profit. When, to this is added the fact that the action reverts upon the head of the one doing the cursing, and places him under the condemnation of God, it is seen to be both senseless and sinful.

11 **Doth the fountain send forth from the same opening sweet water and bitter?**—The illustration of the fountain to which James alludes here would be especially familiar and impressive to his readers. In a land where rainfall is sparse, where wells are few and costly, and where the people are poor, multitudes of them depended on springs flowing out of the earth for their water supply. Access to an abundant supply of *good* water was one of the greatest blessings to people thus situated. "The fountain" *(he pege)* is, literally, the spring, a source of water springing forth from the ground. The verb *(bruei)* is a present active indicative, meaning to bubble up and to gush forth. "The same opening,"

12 can a fig tree, my brethren, yield olives, or a vine figs?   neither *can* salt water yield sweet.

(opes) a word indicating a break or fissure in the earth, is translated *cave* in Heb. 11: 38. "Sweet," *(glukus),* is from the same root as our word *glucose,* and "bitter" is from *pikron,* the root of which means to cut or prick, indicating the effect of the thing so designated on the tongue and tastebuds. The question is rhetorical, and in a construction where a negative answer is expected. "No; a fountain does not send forth from the same opening water that is both sweet and bitter!"

Many springs in Palestine are brackish and bitter; and often water there and elsewhere over the earth is of such character that it is not fit for human consumption. The Israelites were not unacquainted with the bitter waters of Marah (Ex. 15: 23); travelers in the Holy Land have discovered that most of the springs on the eastern side of Judah and Benjamin are hardly fit for use; and water tasting of sulphur or salt is commonly found there. Some springs are good; others, bad; but it is not characteristic of the same spring to supply both good water *and* bad.

A spring known to supply good water may be depended on to continue to do so. One would be most surprised after drinking deeply of the waters of a cold, refreshing mountain spring, to discover that, on a second imbibing, they had turned brackish and bitter. Nature is consistent in its bestowal of blessings. God does not mock us by making good water turn into bad, while we drink.

12 can a fig tree, my brethren, yield olives, or a vine figs?— This, too, is in a construction where a negative answer is expected. "A fig tree cannot yield olives, nor a vine figs, my brethren, can it?" It is quite likely that James, if he looked out of his window when he penned these words, could see fig trees, olive trees and vines from where he sat, since all of these are most common in Palestine. The yard of practically every house in Palestine had a vine and fig tree, and vines of various kinds grew on the hills round about. (2 Kings 18: 31.) There is an unchanging law of nature that like produces like; and to this law the sacred writers often alluded. Jesus taught this same lesson, in principle, when he said, "Either make the tree good, and its fruit good; or make the tree corrupt and its fruit corrupt; for the tree is known by its fruit. Ye offspring of vipers, how can ye, being evil, speak good things? for out of the abundance of the heart the mouth speaketh. The good man out of his good treasure bringeth forth good things; and the evil man out of his evil treasure bringeth forth evil things." (Matt. 12: 33-35.) In the Sermon on the Mount he said, "By their fruits ye shall know them. Do men gather grapes of thorns, or figs of thistles? Even so every good tree bringeth forth good fruit; but the corrupt tree bringeth forth evil fruit. A good tree cannot bring forth evil fruit, neither can a corrupt tree bring forth good fruit." (Matt. 7: 16-18.)

It is contrary to nature for a fig tree to produce olives or a vine figs. If to this the objection is raised that by grafting a tree may be made to produce a variety of fruit different from the parent root, it should be noted that James' illustration deals with the *nature* of things. A tree which, when planted, is a fig, will not later produce olives, nor will a vine yield figs. Figs *and* olives are desirable, but each must be produced from its own kind. There is a fixed and invariable law of nature in this respect, but for which one could never sow with any certainty that the kind of harvest desired would be produced. Therefore, the practice of the tongue in giving utterance to sentiments wholly opposite, as blessing and cursing, is contrary to all nature, a violation of the will of him who created it and when allowed to operate unrestrained, will eventually result in the destruction of him who is thus guilty. Such a person demonstrates that he is out of harmony with the law of God in nature and revelation.

neither can salt water yield sweet.—A spring, whose water is salty, does not yield sweet water, good for human consumption. If this statement appears to be in conflict with earlier affirmations of James that "blessing" and "cursing" proceed from the same mouth, it is important to note that the "blessing" which issues from such a source is itself corrupted by the cursing which also issues, and thus loses its character of true blessing. The lesson is that a thing must produce according to its own nature; and, if blessings and curses appear to come from the same mouth, there is something seriously wrong. Either the blessing *or* the cursing must be defective; it cannot, in the nature of the case, be the cursing; therefore, it is the blessing. Prayer and praise, from the same heart, indicate that the one thus engaging is hypocritical; blessing and cursing from the same mouth reveal that the blessing is corrupted. As a fountain which yields salt water does not give forth fresh water, so a mouth which curses cannot properly bless. Though both may be attempted, it is the cursing which reveals the true character of the heart.

It is, therefore, vitally important that the tongue be restrained, and this lesson James repeatedly teaches in his Epistle. Reasons assigned are, (1) the tongue is a little member, though capable of exercising the most far-reaching effects; (2) it is the most difficult member of the body to restrain and control; (3) it is impossible to tame it so that it may be left unguarded; (4) it is "a world of iniquity," because of its potentiality for evil; (5) unrestrained, it will defile the whole body, "set on fire the wheel of nature," and itself be "set on fire by hell." Jesus said, "And I say unto you, that every idle word that men shall speak, they shall give account thereof in the day of judgment. For by thy words thou shalt be justified, and by thy words thou shalt be condemned." (Matt. 12: 36, 37.) "A soft answer turneth away wrath; but a grievous word stirreth up anger. The tongue of the wise uttereth knowledge aright: but the mouth of fools poureth out folly." (Prov. 15: 1, 2.)

SECTION 7
3: 13-18

THE WISE AND THE UNDERSTANDING
3: 13, 14

13 Who is wise and understanding among you?   let him show by his

---

13 **Who is wise and understanding among you?**—We have seen, in the comments thereon, that James 3: 1 was addressed primarily to *teachers*, and was designed to emphasize the great responsibility which is theirs in influencing others in this manner. From the discussion of the teacher's responsibility and work, involving the use of the tongue, the sacred writer extended his treatment to include all disciples; and James 3: 2-12 deals directly with the abuses of the tongue and the evil effects which follow. It is indeed remarkable how much of the Epistle is devoted to *words* and *works*. Shown clearly is the worthlessness of being a hearer of words, and not a doer of works (1: 19-27); next is revealed the glaring inconsistency of loving one's neighbor as one's self *if* the neighbor happens to be a rich man, and neglecting another neighbor who happens to be poor (2: 1-13); then discussed is the emptiness and barrenness of faith apart from works (2: 14-26); and in 3: 2-12, the abuses of the tongue are particularly dealt with. In all of the Epistle, the writer makes clear that the disposition to avoid the practical duties of the Christian life, on the allegation of one's religion or faith, is a token of wickedness and sin, and not a manifestation of Christian character. Without such practical devotion, evidenced in deeds, such profession is worthless and vain. "And why call ye me, Lord, Lord, and do not the things which I say?" (Luke 6: 46.)

Here, then, is a reversion to verse 1, "Be not many of you teachers, my brethren, knowing that we shall receive heavier judgment." For the reason which prompted James to pen these words see the notes there. But, suppose some teacher says, "Such advise is good for those not qualified to teach; but, I do not need it, inasmuch as I am a wise and understanding man." James raises the question, "Who is wise and understanding among you?" The word "wise" is from *sophos,* a teacher; and "understanding" is from *epistemon*, one skilled. Thus, the question raised is, *Who is really a skilled teacher?*

We should not overlook the additional important consideration that James, by implication, designates here the essential qualifications of *all* teachers, including those of our day. They are to be (a) *wise;* (b) *understanding.* (See Deut. 1: 13; 4: 6.) It is to be observed that there is a great deal of difference between *wisdom* and *knowledge.* One may, indeed, be exceedingly wise, yet unlearned; on the other hand, it is possible to be highly learned, yet exceedingly unwise. One becomes learned through diligent study; wisdom is acquired only from God. (James 1: 5.) Knowledge is the possession of facts; wisdom their proper application. Essential to the erection of a building is (a) a contractor; (b) building materials. Neither is of value to the purpose at hand without the other; yet, the contractor (source of the wisdom) is vastly superior to the material which makes up the building. In like manner, the wise need learning to enable them properly to use the wisdom which God bestows.

let him show by his good life his works in meekness of wisdom.—Here is the way in which the possession of wisdom and understanding may be demonstrated. If the teacher claims to be possessed of a superior knowledge by which he believes himself to be capable of instructing others, let him prove it by a godly life, richly filled with good works! It is to be seen that James thus gives two tokens which evidence wisdom and understanding: (1) "good deeds"; (2) "meekness of wisdom." This, incidentally, is a test which may be applied under all circumstances, at all times, and to all people, including ourselves! One's wisdom is evidenced, not by argument or assertion, but by a godly life garnished with good deeds. It is interesting to note that here, as often elsewhere in the New Testament, (Matt. 20: 20-28), the world's standard and rule of measurement differs greatly from that of inspiration. We are disposed to regard men as wise as they are able to impress us with their learned oratory, or wit; James makes it clear that it is not by *words,* but by *works* that true nobility of character is exhibited. We thus have a rule by which to determine whether we are wise and understanding. Do we seek constantly to practice the practi-

good life his works in meekness of wisdom. 14 But if ye have bitter jeal-

---

cal precepts of Christianity in ministering to those about us? Do we show meekness in our dealings one with another; and, do we avoid an arrogant, proud and unrestrained spirit? If not, then we are not possessed of the wisdom which is from above. While these considerations apply primarily to public teachers of the word, they are applicable, in principle, to all, and should be so regarded.

We learn, (1) wisdom may be *shown* (exhibited, revealed, manifested) in life; (2) it is shown by *a good life (kales anastrophes,* a walk attractive in nature); (3) it is to be done in *meekness of wisdom* (wisdom stripped of all arrogance, pride and desire for worldly acclaim). Here, again, as he has so often done before, the writer rebukes, by implication, the disposition of any disciple to parade his accomplishments, whether they be mental, physical or material. One may indeed be meek and not wise; but, one who is truly wise will be meek; and, where meekness is wanting there is evidence of the lack of wisdom also. We must avoid the conclusion that James is teaching that if one is wise, he *ought* to demonstrate it by good works, as if it were possible to be wise, yet fruitless in life; what he is teaching is that where there is wisdom there *will be* good works, inasmuch as the latter is the inevitable fruit of the former. Where there are no works, there is no wisdom. Is one wise? He will exhibit it by the works which follow. Are there no works to follow? Then there is no wisdom.

The "meekness of wisdom" which the truly wise will exhibit is a reflection of the wisdom which characterized our Lord, who is "meek and lowly in heart" (Matt. 11 : 29); and which he desires to see demonstrated in the lives of all of his followers. An arrogant and proud spirit is, indeed, farther removed, in spirit, from our Lord, than any other disposition. In this, as in all similar matters, Christ is our example and pattern (1 Pet. 2 : 21); and, insofar as it is humanly possible, we should imitate the meekness he ever exhibited in his relationships with his Father and with men.

14 But if ye have bitter jealously and faction in your heart, —This is, grammatically, a condition of the first class, and therefore assumed as true. Such was indeed characteristic of some of

James' readers, as it is, alas, occasionally true of some of the Lord's followers today. "Bitter jealously" *(zelon pikron)* is translated from two words of significance. Jealousy is from *zelos* a word used in the New Testament in both good and bad sense. (John 2: 17; Acts 5: 17.) It denotes, when good, the desire one feels to emulate another whose attainments are of noble order; and, when bad, the envy and jealousy one experiences in the contemplation of another's possessions, or accomplishments. The two ideas are closely related; and often there is only a little difference between a legitimate ambition to be like another, and envy over the attainments of another which one is without but greatly desires. This disposition is described as "bitter" *(pikron)*, in that it leaves the heart with an unpleasant sensation, as our tastebuds react to a bitter substance in the mouth. The Hebrew writer warns against allowing "any root of bitterness" to arise (Heb. 12: 15); and Paul instructed the Ephesians to "let all bitterness, and wrath, and anger and clamor, and railing, be put away from you. . . ." (Eph. 4: 31.)

"Faction" *(eritheian)* is from the Greek word *erithos,* a hireling, which, in turn, is derived from the word *eritheuo,* to spin wool. This word affords an excellent and interesting illustration of the manner in which usage causes a term to bear a variety of related meanings through the years. It has meant (1) a spinner of wool; (2) one hired to spin wool; (3) a hireling; (4) a selfish person interested only in wages; (5) a partisan concerned with one's own affairs; (6) one who resorts to evil measures to accomplish one's desires. The word in the text *(eritheian)* denotes the state or condition in the heart where such a disposition exists. It describes the spirit of partisanship, or selfishness which exists in the heart where such desires motivate the possessor. It is a condition produced by improper zeal which has as its aim the acquisition of that possessed by others. Jealousy and envy lead to faction. Not one of us is wholly removed from the dangers of which James writes, and all should be exceedingly careful to keep the heart free of such unseemly dispositions. This condition characterized some of those to whom James addressed his Epistle. That which he condemns was not an outward form of jealousy, but one lodged in the heart *(en tei kardiai humon),* the basic character of which is *selfishness.* All factions, all party-spirit, and all envying issue from selfishness, a desire to put one's self forward, and to go ahead of others. We are not to overlook the fact that these words were penned primarily with teachers in view, whose activities afford frequent occasion for the temptations against which he warns. Teachers, preachers, writers, editors are all in a position where humility is often difficult and where selfish ambition is a constant temptation. There is a conceit of knowledge which is as real and wrong as the pride of worldly possession; and both dispositions must be rigidly expelled and avoided by all who would be pleasing to the Lord. But, whether teachers or not, we must all be careful lest an unseemly zeal, which has as its aim selfish ambition, prompts us to entertain a feeling toward others in, or out of the church, which is selfish and sinful. There is no place in the body of Christ for those motivated by the desire to be leaders of a party, or to secure for themselves, and for selfish reasons, a place of prominence in the church of our Lord. Paul, in 1 Cor. 1: 12, 13, demonstrates the fact that the party-spirit is an exhibition of *carnality;* and it thus falls into the class of such sins as fornication, adultery, drunkenness, and the like. It is difficult to conceive of a more grievous sin than that which results from the deliberate efforts of a man or group of men who, for the sake of selfish ambition and personal gains, will cause division among the people of God. Far better to be the Roman soldier who thrust a spear into the side of the fleshly body of Christ on the cross, than to be one who drives a sword of division into his spiritual body—the church. (Eph. 1: 19-23.) Jealousy and faction are works of the flesh (Gal. 5: 20); and those who engage in such "cannot inherit the kingdom of God." Those who, despite the warnings of Holy Writ, persist in such a course are as sure for hell as if they were already there.

glory not and lie not against the truth.—"Glory not," *me katakauchasthe,* present middle imperative of *katakauchaomai,* means to exult over. Additional evidence of the incisiveness of the words which the Holy Spirit selects is to be seen in the fact that the phrase, "glory not," indicates not so much the mere fact of glorying, but the exulting over somebody else, because of the possession of real or fancied advantages. The teacher, preacher, elder, dea-

ousy and faction in your heart, glory not and lie not against the truth.   15
This wisdom is not a *wisdom* that cometh down from above, but is earthly,

---

con, Bible school instructor, editor, writer, or whoever he may be who exults (glories) in the thought that he is superior to some other because of his attainments in this, or some other field, falls under the ban of this passage. The present middle imperative means, "Stop glorying and lying against the truth. . . ," thus evidencing the fact that some among his readers were guilty of pride and selfish ambition resulting from their achievements. The etymology of the word translated "glory" in our text is interesting and quite significant. It is compounded of *kata,* against, and, *kauchaomai,* to boast. It thus really means to boast of one's affairs to the hurt of another. It should be considered here in the light of the use of the word "faction" in preceding clauses. One possessed of the spirit of faction entertains the desire to obtain a goal without regard for, and often in violation of, all honorable ethics. It is, alas, all too often true that one person pushes himself *upward* by propelling another in the opposite direction—*downward;* and it is this disposition which James so straitly condemns here and throughout the Epistle.

Those who entertain bitterness and the party-spirit in their hearts, and who glory over others, are also disposed to "lie against the truth." The phrase, "lie against the truth," *(pseudesthe kata tes aletheias),* means to be false to the truth. Obviously, he who violates the truth, as to envy, jealousy, and faction, is not true to it, though he may affect to be greatly devoted to it in other areas. One who claims to teach the truth must certainly practice it, else his efforts are as a sounding brass and a tinkling cymbal. For one to glory with the tongue because of the possession of an alleged or genuine superior knowledge, while entertaining jealousy and envy in the heart, is to be guilty of falsehood and manifestly opposed to the truth which such affect to believe. Such thus become unfaithful to the very cause which they profess to serve. Advocacy of a party-spirit in the church is never right; and where such a condition exists, those responsible are actually acting out a lie, inasmuch as they oppose the truth which they pretend to believe and to defend.

THE WISDOM FROM BELOW
3: 15, 16

15 **This wisdom is not a wisdom that cometh down from above**—"This wisdom," *(haute he sophia),* is the wisdom possessed by those who have in their hearts bitterness, jealousy, envy and the party-spirit, who glory over others, and who lie against the truth which they pretend to preach and teach. "This" wisdom does not come down from above *(katerchomene anothen),* as does that which is promised in James 1: 5, 17, where the word is the same. This wisdom, in contrast with the true wisdom promised in these passages, *does not keep on coming down,* thus implying that the genuine wisdom, which is from God, does. Inasmuch as it does not derive from God, it is, as the remainder of the verse declares, of an origin below heaven and thus sinful in nature. In view of the fact that it exhibits an evil disposition of men, it ultimately derives from the devil. Since the "teachers" (3: 1), whom James so severely rebukes in this section, exhibited the "wisdom" which involved bitterness, envy, and the like, their wisdom was not that from above, thus not from God, and hence from men, ultimately from Satan. It was, in reality, a spurious wisdom, which prompted its possessors to entertain feelings, and to be influenced by motives, wholly foreign to the "wisdom which is from above." A wisdom which creates factions and parties in the church cannot come from God who is "not a God of confusion, but of peace." (1 Cor. 14: 33.) To claim to be in possession of a superior wisdom, the fruits of which are alienation, division, and disruption of the body of Christ, is to demonstrate that the alleged wisdom possessed is not the heavenly wisdom, is not from above, thus not from God.

but is earthly, sensual, devilish.—This is the true character of such a wisdom. It is "earthly," *(epigeios,* of the earth), because it has its origin here, and not in heaven; it is "sensual," *(psuchike,* belonging to the sensuous or animal life), because it embodies motives of a base origin; and it is "devilish," *(daimoniodes,* demon-like), because it partakes of the nature and character of demons, and not of God.

The word "earthly," when put in contrast with that which is "heavenly," as here, designates that which is worldly (Phil. 3:

19), and which is, therefore, to be avoided. (Cf. Col. 3: 1, 2.)
Neither it, nor the things characteristic of it, are to be loved (1
John 2: 15), and with it we are not to be friendly (James 4: 4).
From all such things Christians are to separate themselves (2 Cor.
6: 16, 17), and to cleanse themselves from the defilement which
results from contact with such (2 Cor. 7: 1). The "wisdom"
which James condemns is of the earth, because it sets its affection
on things of the earth and in only such finds satisfaction. The motives which prompt it to action are from below, and it hesitates
not to use the basest of reasons even in matters of a spiritual nature. It is for this reason that it does not shrink from effecting the
greatest harm in the body of Christ, often under the pretense of
great loyalty thereto.

The "wisdom" which James condemns is also "sensual" *(psuchike,* from *psuche,* the soul). The margin of the ASV has, "Or,
natural. Or, animal." Man is a *triune* being. He is possessed of
(1) a body; (2) a soul; (3) a spirit. Often, the word *soul* is
used to designate the *spirit;* but, when one is distinguished from
the other, the spirit *(pneuma)* is the immortal nature, (that which
is infused in us directly from God the Father); and, the soul
(psuche) is the animal life. (Psalm 78: 50.) Inasmuch as the word
soul is thus used, the adjective *psuchike* is literally, *soulish, natural,* or *animal.* Thus, the word (as an adjective) describes the
condition of man when he is governed by the lower impulses of his
nature, and not by his spirit, his higher being. Paul uses the same
term to designate "the natural man," (the man dominated by the
soulish disposition), in contrast with the "spiritual man," (the
man influenced by his better or higher nature), in 1 Cor. 2: 14,
and to indicate the difference between natural and spiritual bodies
in 1 Cor. 15: 44, 46. In a remarkable passage, (Jude 19), the
fleshly brother of our Lord writes of those "who make separations,
sensual, *(soulish),* having not the spirit." It was James' design
here to show us that the wisdom which is not from above and is,
consequently, from below influences the lower and baser nature of
man, and hence does not originate with God.

This "wisdom" is also "devilish," *(daimoniodes,* demon-like), in
character. For a discussion of the subject of *demons,* see comments on James 2: 19. It is devilish because it prompts those pos-

⁶sensual, ⁷devilish. 16 For where jealousy and faction are, there is confu-

⁶Or, *natural* Or, *animal*
⁷Gr. *demoniacal.*

---

sessed of it to act like demons, being full of malice, ambition, egotism, malignity and pride. There is a doctrine of demons (1 Tim. 4: 1ff.), and those who follow their pattern are demon-like (devilish). There is but one devil; there are many demons. The King James Translation does not make this distinction, sometimes rendering the word *daimonion* by the word "devil." The Greek word for "devil" is *diabolos* (a slanderer); and, when it is used to refer to Satan it is always singular; whereas, the word for demons is, in the Greek, usually plural. The "wisdom" which James condemns is from *below*, and not from *above;* and is worldly, sensual and demoniacal. Its sphere of activity is in the animal nature, and its motives are of the basest type. It seeks for the gratification of the flesh, and its chief characteristic is pride. It will resort to anything to accomplish its desired ends, even to effecting division among the Lord's people. It may enable a man to be shrewd, cunning, adroit, and to attract the attention of other worldly-wise people, but it is wholly foreign to that spirit which motivated the lowly Nazarene, and which he desires to see in his followers today. It can lead one *down* only to the source from which it comes, and never *up* to God.

The order of the words, "earthly, sensual, devilish," is significan. In each there is a progressiveness of sin, an advance to deeper guilt and thus to greater condemnation. (1) Those who are earthly are of the earth; (2) those who are sensual are influenced by the baser desires of the flesh; (3) those who are devilish are of the nature of demons. This order designates the course of every individual who follows the lead of, and ultimately surrenders to, Satan. First worldly in disposition, he then easily yields to the desires of his lower nature, and finally partakes of the character of the evil in which he finds his greatest pleasure.

16 **For where jealousy and faction are, there is confusion and every vile deed.**—"For," *(gar,* to introduce the reason), indicates why the "wisdom" which is not from above is earthly, sensual and devilish. Its existence is ever marked by "jealousy," and "faction"; these are its invariable associates. For the meaning of these

words, see comments on verse 14, above. Where jealousy and faction dominate, "there is confusion and every vile deed." Such is the bitter fruit of jealousy and faction. "Confusion," *(akatastasia)* is translated from the noun form of a word which occurs, as an adjective, in James 1: 8, and 3: 8. It designates a state of disorder and disturbance and mental conflict which leads to confusion and tumult in the church. It is clear that such a situation does not develop from the exercise of true wisdom, but results from a "wisdom" which is "earthly, sensual and devilish." Because God is "not a God of confusion, but of peace" (1 Cor. 14: 33), a "wisdom" which produces such a state cannot be from him. Moreover, from such a situation "every vile deed" proceeds. The word for "vile" *(phaulon)* denotes that which is tawdry, cheap, originally that which is of no value. It came eventually to mean something cheap in a bad sense; and thus, anything bad; and "deed" is from *pragma,* something done or accomplished (cf. Thayer), hence, a thing, a matter, an affair. Where jealousy, envy and the spirit of rivalry exist, there is disorder, division and disruption of all that is good and right. Under such circumstances, those thus possessed lose all sense of proper values, and resort to whatever is necessary in order to achieve their factious designs. The scene of our Lord's body, divided and bleeding from the wounds of its "friends" before a scoffing world, moves them not; they must have their way whatever the price involved. It is no wonder that James says that where "jealousy and faction are, there is confusion and every vile deed."

A tree may be known by its fruit. That which results in division and disorder cannot originate with him who desires his people to be one, and who labored and prayed to that end. (John 17: 1ff.) The "wisdom" which James condemns, far from fostering peace, unity and fellowship, foments warfare, division and alienation. One may be possessed of a sharp tongue, a shrewd mind, and a ready wit; his accomplishments and talents may secure for him much worldly acclaim; but, if his efforts cause trouble among brethren, drive them apart, and make them enemies, his "wisdom" is not from above, but is "earthly, sensual, devilish." Such a one serves not God, but Satan, and is an enemy to the cause of truth. The sooner such a one is recognized, marked as such, and avoided

sion and every vile deed. 17 But the wisdom that is from above is first pure,
then peaceable, gentle, easy to be entreated, full of mercy and good fruits,

---

(Rom. 16: 17, 18), the better it is for the cause of Christ. Those
thus motivated "serve not our Lord Christ, but their own belly;
and by their smooth and fair speech they beguile the hearts of the
innocent." (Rom. 16: 18.) "A factious man after a first and second admonition refuse; knowing that such a one is perverted, and
sinneth, being self-condemned." (Tit. 3: 10, 11.)

THE WISDOM FROM ABOVE
3: 17, 18

17 But the wisdom that is from above is first pure,—The
wisdom that is from above is, by James, put in contrast with that
"wisdom" described by him earlier as "earthly, sensual, devilish"
(verse 15), which produces jealousy and faction and results in
confusion and every vile deed (verse 16). This wisdom to which
James is now to give special attention is "from above," because it
originates with God and not with men; and, being from above is
heavenly in character and not earthly. Because it comes from
above, it is God's gift (cf. "the giving God," Greek of James 1: 5),
and must be sought from him. It comes down from him "with
whom can be no variation, neither shadow that is cast by turning."
(1: 17.) Solomon said, "My son, if thou wilt receive my word,
and lay up my commandments with thee; so as to incline thine ear
unto wisdom, and apply thy heart to understanding; yea, if thou
cry after discernment, and lift up thy voice for understanding; if
thou seek her as silver, and search for her as hid treasure, then
shalt thou understand the fear of Jehovah, and find the knowledge
of God. *For Jehovah giveth wisdom; and out of his mouth cometh knowledge and understanding.*" (Prov. 2: 1-6.)

This wisdom is "first pure, *then* peaceable. . ." This is sometimes explained to mean that no peace can exist until purity has
been obtained; and as applied to the church, it is our obligation
first to attain to purity in doctrine and teaching, in the absence of
which there can be no peace between brethren. On this ground,
disturbances in the church, on the pretense of attaining to purity in
doctrine, are justified. There are two basic errors involved in such
reasoning: (1) James' teaching here applies to peace *in the heart*

of the individual, and was designed to emphasize the fact that peace cannot there reign until purity controls the heart; it is, therefore, an incorrect exegesis which would apply it to the church; (2) purity is first for logical rather than chronological reasons; for if we were the only persons on earth, and there was no one else to be gentle to, no one coming to us to be entreated, no one needing mercy, the wisdom from above *would still be pure!* The word "pure" *(hagnos,* from *hagios)* denotes that which is uncontaminated, without fault, wholly good. It is a kind of good-ness which shrinks from any pollution whatsoever. It is such a state of mind and of heart without which one cannot see God. (Matt. 5: 8.)

Purity of doctrine and practice on the part of the church is, of course, absolutely essential and must be sought after by all who love the Lord. We must ever contend earnestly for the faith once delivered to the saints. (Jude 3.) A pure faith and a faultless practice may be enjoyed only by constant vigilance against every suggestion and semblance of error. We must not, however, fall into the error of assuming that because others hold to error, we cannot enjoy peace in Christ. An alleged defense of the truth, at the expense of a sincere heart and a peaceful disposition, is illogical and irrational. It is absurd to attempt to do right by doing wrong! Men have made murderers of themselves on the pretense of doing God's will. (Matt. 10: 17, 21; 24: 9, 10.) The wisdom that is from above is pure, free from all defilement.

then peaceable,—*(epeita eirenike).* The wisdom that is from above is first pure, "then peaceable," peace-loving, exhibiting that disposition in the individual which produces and maintains peace. (Heb. 12: 11.) It is peaceable because its basic characteristic is purity. It is impossible for a factious spirit and a fractious disposition to issue from a pure heart. It is significant that James, who so often reflects, in his writings, the teaching of our Lord in the Sermon on the Mount, follows the same order as designated there in the Beatitudes. Here, as there, purity precedes peace: (1) "Blessed are the pure in heart: for they shall see God." (Matt. 5: 8.) (2) "Blessed are the peacemakers: for they shall be called sons of God." (Matt. 5: 9.) Because the wisdom which is from above is "peaceable," it not only instills peace in the hearts of its possessors, it also exhibits itself in peaceful pursuits in life. There is no blessing pronounced upon those who cause dissension, and whose activities produce strife; God, who is "the Lord of Peace" (2 Thess. 3: 16), gives peace only to the peaceable. Men yearn for peace; peace in the heart, peace in the life, peace "in our time." The ancient benediction was a pronouncement of peace: "Jehovah bless thee, and keep thee: Jehovah make his face to shine upon thee, and be gracious unto thee: Jehovah lift up his countenance upon thee, and give thee peace." (Num. 6: 24-26.) The Hebrew word of greeting is, to this day, *Shalom!* which means *peace*. When the writer of these notes was in Israel some months ago, he heard this salutation repeatedly expressed. When people meet you there, they say, *Shalom!* When they bid you goodby they repeat the salutation. It is an expression of a wish for peace for friends. Jesus promised his disciples peace: "Peace I leave with you; my peace I give unto you; not as the world giveth, give I unto you." (John 14: 27.) Paul wrote, "And let the peace of Christ rule in your hearts, to the which also ye were called in one body; and be ye thankful." (Col. 3: 15.) The Greek for the word "rule" in this passage means to "arbitrate," (the margin), *to umpire* (so Williams translates). Where peace is the arbitrator, serenity of life prevails and contentment reigns. This is the kind of peace which the "wisdom" that is "from above" produces in the heart.

gentle, easy to be entreated,—These are the third and fourth characteristics of the "wisdom which is from above." "Gentle," *(epieikes,* from *eikos,* that which is reasonable, fair in dealing,) designates an attitude of forbearance, the exhibition of a disposition which does not *demand* its rights, but is willing, if necessary, to suffer wrong in the cause of right. The word appears in Phil. 4: 5 and 1 Tim. 3: 3. We ought always to be fair and reasonable in our dealings one with another. It is highly absurd for one who fancies that truth is all on his side to be unwilling to consider the views of those who oppose him. One may entertain pity for an opponent for holding inconsistent and contradictory opinions, but should not despise him for it. We feel the most sincere concern for a friend afflicted with a serious malady, and we should be equally exercised regarding one whose mental and spiritual health is impaired. Some shrink from gentleness on the ground that it

is weakness under another name; but, the truth is, a gentle disposition results from strength, and is maintained thereby. One sure
of his position does not feel the necessity of defending it with passion; he maintains it from premises wrought out by reason from
revelation and arrived at calmly and soberly. Some assume they
are *strong* in argument only if they are violent in argument.
Some seek to make up in thunder what they lack in lightning; but,
it should be remembered that it is the lightning that kills! He
who has established a sincere conviction of the truth in his heart,
and possesses a genuine faith in the ultimate triumph of right, will
disdain such efforts, and be content to speak the truth in love.
Gentleness is not a natural characteristic; men are not born gentle.
It results from wisdom; wisdom is a gift from God (James 1: 5);
therefore gentleness is a gift from God.

This wisdom is also "easy to be entreated," *(eupeithes,* from *eu,*
easy, and *peithomai,* to persuade, hence, persuadable, willing to
consider). This is a word occurring nowhere else in Scripture. One
easy to be entreated is open to reason, ever ready to hear what
others have to say, and willing to yield to what is right. It is
not to be interpreted as meaning that one is susceptible to every
vagrant impulse, or carried about by every wind of doctrine (Eph.
4: 14); there is no weakness or deficiency of courage inherent in
the word. He who is thus influenced will listen carefully to what
others have to say and, if it appears that the course he has adopted
is an erroneous one, he will not hesitate to abandon it, and to accept
that which is right. Such a one will not persist in a course that is
wrong, simply because it is that originally launched; he will readily
yield to convincing argument and sound logic. This disposition
will exhibit itself both inwardly and outwardly. One who is "easy
to be entreated" will utilize the same gentle forbearance and persuasiveness toward others.

full of mercy and good fruits,—The foregoing characteristics
of "the wisdom which is from above" are attitudes and dispositions of the heart; here, the writer moves to an area of *conduct* on
the part of the Christian, and designates the practical, outward,
visible aspects of this wisdom. The gentle, pure, persuasive soul is
also "full of mercy," and "good fruits,"—is active in the performance of those deeds earlier described as "pure religion and unde-

filed before God and the Father." (James 1: 27.) "Mercy" here *(eleous)* is compassion, the disposition to desire to help those in distress; and, the "good fruits" *(karpon agathon)* result from such an attitude of heart. A man possessed of such a disposition is like a tree ever in bloom, and ever bestowing its blessed fruits upon those about it. This, indeed, is the test of the heart's status; one cannot always know the condition of the tree, but one can easily determine the character of the tree by the nature of the fruit. As James 1: 27 affords an example of the manner in which this mercy exhibits itself, so James 2: 15 indicates the situation where such is wanting. It should be remembered that this entire section of the Epistle is by James addressed primarily to *teachers* who are expected to exhibit in their lives the principles herein outlined. If such is to be characteristic of those who teach and preach his word, with what great severity must the Lord regard those who not only do not do such themselves, but who seek to discourage others in the performance thereof!

without variance,—"Variance, *(adiakriots,* from *a,* not, and *diakrino,* to distinguish), means to hesitate, to doubt; and has the marginal reading, "doubtfulness or partiality." Thus, one without variance does not doubt, is not drawn by divided opinions, and is stable in his views regarding religion. His attitude is exactly opposite to that of the "double-minded man" mentioned in James 1: 8. Compare, also, James 1: 6, and 2: 4, where the verb form of the same word appears.

The wisdom which is from above enables one to be firm in his views, and to entertain complete confidence in God and in his word. It is good for us to keep an open mind regarding all matters which we have not thoroughly explored, and to be willing to bring our views into harmony with any new truth we may acquire; but, we must recognize the fact that the fundamentals of the faith, which are neither obscure nor difficult, are easily grasped, and from these we should never move away, nor suffer them to be taken from us. The faithful disciple of the Lord has confirmed convictions; these convictions are grounded in a robust faith in God's word; and to question them is to question the word, and ultimately, the Lord himself. A vacillating, changeable disposition is neither conducive to Christian growth, nor to useful service in the

without [8]variance, without hypocrisy. 18 And the fruit of righteousness is sown in peace [9]for them that make peace.

[8]Or, *doubtfulness* Or, *partiality*
[9]Or, *by*

vineyard of the Lord; and does not originate in the heavenly wisdom. We should all acquire and maintain principles by which to guide our lives and these may be properly obtained only from God. Those thus directed follow a compass which is not deflected by worldly acclaim or selfish interests, nor by current views announced by favorite preachers. They recognize that truth is unchangeable, and that the New Testament reads exactly the same as it did a quarter of a century ago. They are consistent in attitude toward the principles of true religion because they obtained them at the source.

without hypocrisy.—(*Anupokritos,* from *a,* not; and *hupokrino,* hypocrisy.) The word *hypokrites* (a hypocrite) meant originally a play-actor, i.e., one who plays a part, and thus does not reflect his true situation. A hypocrite is, therefore, one who practices deception, one who appears to be other than what he really is. The wisdom which is from above does not prompt one *to wear a mask,* but to appear in one's own true character—a character based upon the principles of true Christianity. Hypocrisy was exceedingly common among the Jews; and our Lord's most severe denunciations were leveled against them because of this sin. (Matt. 23: 1ff.) Those who are without hypocrisy are sincere, open in their dealings, and without pretense. Hypocrisy is dishonesty; it deceives and misleads others for selfish ends, and must, therefore, be strictly avoided by all who would please the Lord. It is possible to be hypocritical not only in action but also in attitude. Feigned piety and an affected holiness are as contemptible in God's sight as deceptive actions. Neither has any place in the lives of Christians.

18 **And the fruit of righteousness is sown in peace**—"And" *(de,* moreover), indicates something to be considered besides the products of the "wisdom which is from above." It is a reference to the "good fruits," which do result from such wisdom, and here summed up in "the fruit of righteousness," *(karpos . . . dikaiosunes,* fruit growing out of righteousness). "Righteousness" is right-doing, (Psalm 119: 172; Acts 10: 34, 35; see, also the com-

ments on James 1: 20). Thus, the "fruit of righteousness" is the good which righteousness prompts its possessor to do. It is not correct to say that "the fruit of righteousness" is righteousness itself. "Of righteousness" is genitive of origin, that which issues from righteousness, in this case, fruit produced by righteousness. All the good we do issues from righteousness, which in turn flows out of the wisdom which is from above. All that is bad issues from that "wisdom" which is from below, and which is earthly, sensual, devilish. Isaiah said, "And the work of righteousness *shall be peace;* and the effect of righteousness, quietness and confidence for ever." (Isa. 32: 17.) Thus, the fruit is that which comes from the tree—righteousness. For comparable expressions, see "fruits worthy of repentance" (Luke 3: 8), and "the fruit of light" (Eph. 5: 9), where, in the former instance the fruit is to be distinguished from the repentance, and in the latter from the light. The meaning is that the blessed results of righteousness can never prosper except in an atmosphere of peace.

The "fruit of righteousness" is "sown in peace," *(en eirenei speiretai,* sown in the sphere of peace). Peace is its rightful and proper habitat; it is the realm where righteousness grows and flourishes, and where its fruit—good deeds—abound. Righteousness is the seed from which good deeds grow, and the good deeds then become seeds from which further fruit springs. It is the responsibility of all—particularly teachers and preachers—to cultivate peace by sowing good deeds which are expressions of righteousness. The fruit of righteousness is a holy life. This is sown in peace, not in strife, conflict, and war. Peace is conducive to the spread of the truth, and contributes to it; whereas, strife, division, faction and partyism hinder and restrain it. Here, again, we observe the close connection between the Epistle of James and the Sermon on the Mount:

"Blessed are the peacemakers:
   For they shall be called
     sons of God."
(Matt. 5: 9.)
	"The fruit of righteousness
	    is sown in peace
	    For them that make peace."
	(James 3: 18.)

Peacemakers are intimately related to God; being acknowledged by him as "sons"; and the harvest of that which is sown in peace is the "fruit of righteousness." David said, "Light is sown for the righteous, and gladness for the upright in heart." (Psalm 97 : 11.)

for them that make peace.—*(Tois poiousin eirenen,* by the ones making peace.)   See Eph. 2 : 15, where a similar phrase occurs.   Peace was, by the ancient Hebrew writers, regarded as one of the most desirable forms of blessedness; and, those possessed of this grace would be those who sowed the seed of, and later harvested, "the fruit of righteousness."   Peace is, indeed, a fruit of righteousness; and it, in turn, becomes the sphere in which righteousness and all which issues from it grows and flourishes.   To this the true wisdom leads, and in it finds its noblest accomplishments.   Christ is our peace (Eph. 2 : 14), and through him we are reconciled to God.   The peace which he gives is available through righteousness—the keeping of his commandments.   In him we have peace, peace with ourselves, peace with one another, peace with God.   "Mercy and truth are met together; righteousness and peace have kissed each other."   Whether the phrase should be rendered, *"for* them that make peace," or *"by* them that make peace," (the question cannot be definitely decided), it is clear that what is taught here is that peacemakers are the ones who sow the seed the fruit of which is righteousness.   It is an action which finds its origin in, develops by, and ends in a state of peace.

SECTION 8
4: 1-10

CAUSE OF CONFLICTS
4: 1

1 Whence *come* wars and whence *come* fightings among you? *come they*

---

1 **Whence come wars**—Following his discussion of *peace* in the final verses of the third chapter, the writer passes, by an easy transition, to that of *war* and *conflict* in this portion of the Epistle. In the preceding section there is a sharply drawn contrast between two kinds of wisdom, each of which is traced to its source, and its characteristics designated. Here, he points his readers to the disastrous consequences involved in following the dictates of that "wisdom" which is not from above, but which is earthly, sensual and devilish. It appears quite certain that the sacred writer has under consideration here strife, dissension, and warfare in the church, and *in* and *between* individuals, and that the words, "wars," and "fightings," are to be construed figuratively, although his analysis of the real causes of war is applicable to any kind of warfare, whether figurative or literal, and whether in the individual himself, between individuals, or between nations. His words were especially applicable to the situation which widely prevailed in the day when he lived. There were many bitter contentions in the world in the first century; and, the Jews, particularly, were divided into numerous warring camps, such as Pharisees, Sadducees, Herodians, Essenes, Zealots, and the like, each of which fought all the rest with great industry and effort. And, there is ample evidence in the New Testament that converts to Christianity from Judaism often brought with them their contentious spirit and urged their views upon their brethren to the point of division. (Cf. Col. 2: 20-22.) James provides clear evidence here, and often elsewhere in his Epistle, that such difficulties were not confined to those congregations composed of people lately out of heathenism, such as the Corinthians, Galatians, etc., but that among the Christians of the "circumcision," there were dissensions, divisions, and factious groups. The early church was thus by no means free of difficulty; and, while we may properly deplore trou-

ble in the church at any time or place, we may at least conclude that such is not peculiar to our day, and that the congregations of the apostolic age wrestled with this vexing problem. Here, James traces to their source these difficulties, and designates the real reason for them.

"Whence," *(pothen)*, is an interrogative adverb, signifying, "from what source." Thus is raised the question, "what is the *source*, the origin of, war? The word "war," from *polemos* here, means a quarrel, a wrangle, and denotes a prevailing state of strife as distinguished from specific conflicts designated in the second phrase of the sentence.

and whence come fightings among you?—"Fightings," from *mache*, denotes separate conflicts, all of which are summed up in the word "war" of the preceding phrase. War is that state or condition resulting from a series of clashes; "fightings," that which produces this state. The horror of war has long been painfully felt, and multitudes wearily and often hopelessly seek for the solution. How may war be forever eliminated is a question on the lips of millions throughout the world today. Peace is life's greatest temporal blessing; peace with oneself, peace among men, peace in the world. It rarely exists on any of these levels. It is a tragic commentary on man's inability to live at peace with his fellows that there has been open, armed conflict between men and nations in every generation since our Lord was here upon the earth. However, in the efforts put forth to eliminate it, men seldom seek out the real reasons therefor. This, James proceeds to do in the statement which follows.

come they not hence, even of your pleasures that war in your members?—Thus, the writer answers, with this rhetorical question, the queries raised in the first part of the passage. Wars and fightings do originate in the "pleasures" which cause conflicts among our "members." The word "pleasures," from *hedonon*, a word designating desire and lust (the effects put for the cause), denotes the *source* of conflict; and "in your members," the *place* or *sphere* of it. Pleasures, as used here, mean the satisfaction men seek from the senses and oftentimes the impelling desire for the gratification thereof. In this impressive passage, the writer represents pleasures as soldiers spread out among the members of the

not hence, *even* of your pleasures that war in your members? 2 Ye lust, and
have not: ye kill, and [10]covet, and cannot obtain: ye fight and war; ye have

[10]Gr. *are jealous.*

body, and using them as instruments to accomplish their ends.
Often the individual is the seat of such conflict, and finds himself a
battleground of conflict. Peter wrote, "Beloved, I beseech you as
sojourners and pilgrims, to abstain from fleshly lust, which *war*
against the soul. . ." (1 Pet. 2: 11.) And, in the church such
often occurs. The lust for power, the desire for acclaim, and the
overpowering pride of opinion have propelled men into the most
vicious and hurtful state of war, thus disgracing the cause of
Christ, discouraging the good, and providing infidelity with one of
its most effective arguments.

The desire to get, at all odds, what one does not have, but
greatly desires, is at the root of most difficulties between nations
and men. The acid test of life's motives is thus provided. Is our
chief concern pleasure? If yes, then in order to secure and maintain it, clashes and conflicts must inevitably arise, and nothing will
be permitted to interfere with the effort. Some, indeed, become
slaves to lust and pleasure, and the battleground of conflict all of
their lives. Paul, in describing the status of one without the gospel, and the assurance it provides, wrote: "But I see a different
law in my members, warring against the law of my mind, and
bringing me into captivity under the law of sin which is in my
members." (Rom. 7: 23.) Desire of the wrong kind will inevitably lead to conflict. Money, prestige, the desire for a place of
prominence and influence are all sources of conflict; and men frequently seek to climb up in the world on the bodies of those they
have pulled down! Desire of the type condemned by James is responsible for the gravest of crimes, and men have not hesitated to
commit murder to secure their coveted ends. Where then is
strife? It is in the individual. Why is it there? Because of
man's desire to gratify his senses. What prompts to such desire?
The pleasures derived from such gratification. What is the result
of such? The writer answers in the verse which follows.

UNASKED AND UNANSWERED PRAYER
4: 2, 3

2 **Ye lust, and have not:**—The word "lust," *(epithumeite,* pres-

ent active indicative of *epithumeo,* from *epi* and *thumos,* to have a strong passion for), denotes the intensity of feeling characteristic of those to whom James wrote, and explains why "wars" and "fightings" alluded to in verse 1 often arose among them. Coveting what another has, whether on an individual, national or international level, is the basic cause of war, whether such warfare be literal or figurative; and James thus traces to its source the evil which results from such unlawful desire. This lust for what one does not have has led to the gravest of crimes, examples of which may be seen in David, in the matter of Bathsheba (2 Sam. 11: 1), and Ahab, in the matter of Naboth's vineyard (1 Kings 21: 2-4). When desire of this character is entertained and encouraged, it becomes overpowering and the dominant feature in one's life. In such a case, desire is the master of the soul; and the individual thus possessed is enslaved and helplessly propelled to the very vortex of sin. Here, indeed, is the test by which all of us may easily and accurately determine the principle by which our lives are governed. May we truly say, *"Thy* will be done"; or, *"My* desires be satisfied"? It should be remembered that the rich man of Luke 16 was not charged with serious crimes against man or God; it is not affirmed of him that he engaged in *bad* things; he is said to have had his *good* things here; yet, he was rejected because fleshly gratification and the love of things material were the dominant factors of his life. *He who would gain heaven must sacrifice the things of the world.* We must choose whether to have our good things here, *or* hereafter; we cannot have them *both* here and hereafter!

Those particularly in the mind of James when he wrote, despite their burning desire, did not obtain the things which they coveted. And why did they not? The answer is that they did not seek for the things for which they might properly ask God. Here, we meet with another vital test in the realm of religion. When faced with the necessity of deciding whether any given act is open to participation for the faithful Christian, one need only ask. Will God approve? Seldom is it difficult to find the answer to this question. And, where any doubt whatever exists, it is the part of prudence to refrain. The devoted disciple will not attempt to force the Scripture into support of his position; he will seek only to be sure that his position is on the side of Scripture! These of whom James wrote, notwithstanding their intense desires, and the efforts expended to realize them, were without that upon which they had set their hearts.

ye kill, and covet, and cannot obtain:—This statement, insofar as it refers to *murder,* would best be construed as figurative; it is most unlikely that James intended to charge wholesale murder upon the people to whom he wrote. If the word "kill" is to be interpreted literally, then the writer was describing the situation which normally follows when men are influenced by evil desire. What James appears to mean here is that the motive which urged them on was murderous in its nature, and the disposition which leads men to murder. A further difficulty arises in the order of words here which, on the surface, would appear to be transposed, inasmuch as killing is regarded as a more serious crime than coveting. Why "kill and covet," rather than "Covet and kill"? A simple solution is to be found in the rearrangement of the punctuation of the passage, thus making it to read,

> "Ye lust, and have not!
> Ye kill;
> Ye covet and cannot obtain. . ."

In which case, killing, whether literal or figurative, is thus shown to be the result of improper desire and the failure to obtain that thus coveted; and avoided is the inversion which the punctuation of the ASV (uninspired, of course), creates.

"Ye kill," *(phoneuete,* present active indicative of *phoneuo,* to murder), is literally, "You engage continuously in killing," and thus indicates that such was the constant practice of this people. But, even this did not secure for them that which they so passionately wanted. "Ye kill, and covet, and cannot obtain."

ye fight and war;—A constant state of conflict prevailed from their efforts to satisfy desire, yet this failed to accomplish their aims. James thus vividly and impressively describes the vicious circles into which these people were caught. They passionately desire things they ought not; to satisfy the desire, they maintain a constant state of strife and warfare; but, this does not obtain for them their wants. Verse 2 is thus in close connection with verse 1, and denotes the relationship obtaining between *desire* and *conflict.* The latter is the result of the former, and its inevitable fruit.

Where improper desire obtains, there will be strife. Thus shown is the certain consequence of choosing pleasure to the neglect of God. The Bible abounds with illustrations indicating the fatal consequence of such a choice. Among them are Cain, Balaam, and the Israelites in the wilderness.

ye have not, because ye ask not.—From this section we learn that there are not only *unanswered* prayers, there are also *unasked* prayers! It is evident that proper desire may be experienced and satisfied by praying to God who alone can supply the soul's innermost need. There are some things it is entirely proper for us to have; God wants us to have them; and he freely bestows them upon those who ask. Some seek to secure to themselves the things they want and perhaps need by methods which avoid God; and thus often fail to have such—not because they are forbidden to them, but because they simply do not go to the right source for them. We must, of course, (a) desire the *right* things; (b) we must ask God for the things which he graciously has for us (James 1: 5); (c) and we must have confidence that he will hear and answer our petitions (1 John 4: 14, 15). God will answer the prayer of the penitent (Luke 18: 14), the cry of the righteous (Psalm 34: 15), and those who *keep on asking* for their needs (Matt. 7: 7). Here, indeed, is indisputable evidence of the efficacy of prayer. In its effectiveness James believed implicitly, and was, by the Holy Spirit, led to pen one of the strongest statements in Scripture regarding it: "The supplication of a righteous man availeth much in its working." (James 5: 16.) "Ye ask not," in our text, is in a construction where the action is performed in behalf of one's own self; and thus indicates a disregard for that which would be for their good were they to follow the Lord's way. They *would* not pray for legitimate needs; therefore, God *would* not give them such; and they *could* not obtain them in other ways. Men who disregard God and seek by short-cuts, as did Esau, to obtain that which God will, under proper circumstances, bestow, must always find the satisfaction for which the heart sighs just beyond reach. Thus, the right way to obtain anything we need is to ask God for it; and, when we have so done, and the petition is not granted, we should conclude that God does not regard the object as necessary for our need; or, that he intends to give us something far better later.

not, because ye ask not. 3 Ye ask, and receive not, because ye ask amiss,

We learn here, (1) those of whom James wrote were guilty of lust, murder, covetousness, fighting and strife. Though continuously torn by overwhelming desires, they failed to obtain that which they wanted; though they coveted that which others possessed, they did not obtain; and (2) their lives were consequently barren and prayerless. It should be observed that each of the clauses of verse 2 is closely related in meaning: *They wish for that which they do not have; they seek to obtain it improperly and by force and this results in strife and war.* The desire to possess those things which they did not have led to sin, even as it does today. There are two reasons assigned why they did not have the things which they needed: (1) they sought for them in sinful fashion; (2) they did not ask God to give them needed blessing. Jesus has promised us such things as we need, when we ask for them in the right manner (Matt. 7: 7; 21: 22); and if these results do not follow our prayers, it is because (a) we do not pray properly; or (b) because, as in this case, we do not pray at all. Let us remember that some prayers are unanswered; others are unasked. We should, of course, want only the things God wants us to have, and to ask him for no others. In this manner alone may the heart's deepest needs be realized.

3 Ye ask, and receive not,—Some, among those of whom James wrote, did not receive, because they did not *ask;* others asked but did not *receive.* If we are disposed to be shocked by the suggestion that men may be lustful, covetous, murderers (at heart) and constant wranglers and, at the same time, be given to prayer, we need only to recall that it is not unusual for men to invoke the blessings of God upon them, though engaged in the most high-handed wickedness. In medieval times particularly, multitudes of people were slaughtered in the name of religion; and campaigns were launched on the pretense of doing God's will. "Woe unto you, scribes and Pharisees, hypocrites! for ye build the sepulchres of the prophets, and garnish the tombs of the righteous, and say, If we had been in the days of our fathers, we should not have been partakers with them in the blood of the prophets. Wherefore ye witness to yourselves, that ye are sons of them that slew the prophets. Fill ye up then the measure of your fathers. Ye serpents, ye offspring of vipers, how shall ye escape the judgment of hell? Therefore, behold, I send unto you prophets, and wise men, and scribes: some of them shall ye kill and crucify; and some of them shall ye scourge in your synagogues, and persecute from city to city: that upon you may come all the righteous blood shed on the earth, from the blood of Abel the righteous unto the blood of Zachariah the son of Barachiah, whom ye slew between the sanctuary and the altar." (Matt. 23:29-35.) "They shall put you out of the synagogues: *yea,* the hour cometh, *that whosoever killeth you shall think that he offereth service unto God."* (John 16: 2.)

Our Lord said, "For where thy treasure is, there will thy heart be also." (Matt 6: 21.) If our interests are largely centered in the things of the earth, we will be disposed chiefly to seek for such things; and, if we pray at all, to pray for them. These of whom James wrote were motivated by the desire for material things; and jealousy, envy and strife characterized them in the search. From this we learn that it is quite possible for those who have obeyed the gospel to give attention to the wrong things in their quest for happiness. Jesus said, "But seek ye first his kingdom, and his righteousness; and all these things shall be added unto you." (Matt. 6: 33.) The word "added," in this passage, is from the Greek word *prostithemi,* the meaning of which is very near our Southern provincialism, *to boot,* something thrown in extra to make the bargain more attractive. Jesus thus promises us that if we put his affairs first he will give us our material needs *to boot, in addition* to our salvation! We are assured that God will answer the prayers of his people. Jesus said, "Ask, and it shall be given you; seek, and ye shall find; knock, and it shall be opened unto you; for every one that asketh receiveth; and he that seeketh findeth; and to him that knocketh it shall be opened." (Matt. 7: 7, 8.) We must, however, understand that these promises are conditioned on (a) asking for the right things, (b) in the right way, and (c) from right motives. The verb *aiteite,* "ye ask," means to request, to beg; and is the usual word where one, consciously inferior, makes a petition to one regarded as superior. (Acts 12: 20; Matt. 7: 9; 1 John 3: 22.) It is of significance that our Lord never used this term in his petitions to the Father in behalf of the disciples; his approach was on the basis of a Son before his Father.

One may, however, ask for the right things, and the prayer still be improper because of wrong motives. These of whom James wrote asked, but in the wrong fashion.

because ye ask amiss,—*(dioti kakos aiteisthe,* because ye ask evilly.) Here, the verb *aiteo,* to ask, is in the middle voice, to ask for one's self. We thus learn that where selfishness is involved petitions to God are fruitless. God will not grant a request the purpose of which is to satisfy selfish desire. "Amiss" *(kakos)* designated that which is base or mean. To ask amiss is, therefore, to be influenced by low, mean, selfish considerations. This is a general statement explaining why those of whom James wrote did not receive that for which they prayed; in the statement which follows in the text the reason why their petitions were regarded as improper is indicated.

that ye may spend it in your pleasures.—*(Hina en tais hedonais humon dapanesete,* a purpose clause, introduced with *hina,* the verb of which is *dapanesete,* aorist subjunctive, signifying to consume wastefully, to squander.) Thus, that which is to be used by us for purely selfish gratification is, by our Lord, regarded as squandered, wasted; and, obviously, God is not going to give us that which is to be wasted! "Pleasures" here is the same word as that occurring in verse 1, and means desires of a fleshly, sensual nature, satisfied. Whether, therefore, God grants a petition for health, wealth, the ability to serve, depends on the motive which prompts such a petition. It is possible for one to pray for ability to serve others when the chief reason for the desire is not the welfare of man, but lust for power, fame, notoriety, etc. God will not answer such prayers, because they are evilly motivated. Those who thus ask, ask *amiss.*

It is vitally important that we be impressed with the realization that God will not hear and answer a prayer which has, as its chief motive, the gratification of fleshly desire. Such appears to have been the design of those to whom James refers in our text. This does not mean that God will never hear and answer a prayer involving material matters. The inspired writer does not rebuke his readers for asking God to prosper them materially. It is the motive which determines whether such a prayer is proper or not. If we ask in order that we may consume the blessings upon our lusts,

that ye may spend *it* in your pleasures. 4 Ye [11]adulteresses, know ye not that the friendship of the world is enmity with God? Whosoever therefore would be a friend of the world maketh himself an enemy of God. 5 Or think ye

[11]That is, *who break your marriage vow to God.*

---

he will not hear. If it is for our welfare, or the welfare of others and the cause of Christ it is in order for us so to pray. John prayed that his friend Gaius "in all things" would "prosper and be in health," even as his "soul prospereth." (3 John 2.) We are thus encouraged to bring our temporal needs to the Lord, with the assurance that if such are for our good he will bestow them freely and graciously.

We must, however, examine our motives with extreme care, for it is difficult for us to separate our needs from our desires, and to feel that the design is the former, when it is, in reality, the latter. Prayer is a marvelous privilege of every faithful child of God, and ought to be utilized regularly. We must always remember that there are well defined conditions with which we are to comply, if we may properly expect an answer. Those of whom James wrote did not obtain an answer to their petitions because they asked "amiss," (evilly, from wrong motives). When petitions are conceived in greed, and expressed hypocritically, God always turns a deaf ear. Only those prayers which have as their aim the glory of God, the advancement of his cause, and the genuine well being of his followers, ascend to the throne of grace, and bring a blessing. Our prayers reveal, in striking detail, and great accuracy, the character of our hearts to ourselves, to others, and to God.

GOD VERSUS THE WORLD
4: 4-6

4 **Ye adulteresses,**—(*Moichalides,* feminine form of *moichoi,* adulterers.) It would appear that the reference to "adulteresses" here is to be regarded as a figurative one, as the word "kill" is similarly used in verse 2. It is unaccountable that James would omit reference to the *men* involved and direct his condemnation to the *women* only, if the reference is to be taken literally. The figure of marriage, to indicate the relationship of men to God, is of frequent usage in the Scriptures; and the Old Testament abounds with references to Israel as the *wife* of Jehovah. (Psalm 73; Isa. 57; Ezek.

23; Hos. 3.)   In the New Testament, Christians are represented as married to the Lord. Or are ye ignorant, brethren, (for I speak to men who know the law), that the law hath dominion over a man for so long time as he liveth? For the woman that hath a husband is bound by law to the husband while he liveth; but if the husband die, she is discharged from the law of the husband. . . . Wherefore, my brethren, ye also were made dead to the law through the body of Christ; that ye should be joined to another, even to him who was raised from the dead, that we might bring forth fruit unto God." (Rom. 7: 1-4.)

Thayer, the Greek lexicographer, says of the word, "As the intimate alliance of God with the people of Israel was likened to a marriage, those who relapse into idolatry are said to commit adultery or play the harlot (Ezek. 15: 16; 23: 43); hence *moichalis* is figuratively equivalent to faithless to God, unclean, apostate. (James 4: 4.)" Paul uses this same figure in his reference to the *church* in its relationship to Christ: "Wives, be in subjection unto your own husbands, as unto the Lord. For the husband is the head of the wife, as Christ also is the head of the church, being himself the saviour of the body. But as the church is subject to Christ, so let the wives also be to their husbands in everything. Husbands, love your wives, even as Christ also loved the church, and gave himself up for it: that he might sanctify it, having cleansed it by the washing of water with the word, that he might present the church to himself a glorious church, not having spot or wrinkle or any such thing; but that it should be holy and without blemish. Even so ought husbands also to love their own wives as their own bodies. He that loveth his own wife loveth himself: for no man ever hated his own flesh; but nourisheth and cherisheth it, even as Christ also the church; because we are members of his body. For this cause shall a man leave his father and mother, and shall cleave to his wife; and the two shall become one flesh. This mystery is great: but I speak in regard of Christ and of the church." (Eph. 5: 22-32.)

A woman who is an adulteress is unfaithful to her husband; hence the disciples who exhibit friendship for the world demonstrate unfaithfulness to God and are, therefore, figuratively guilty of adultery. The writer evidently used the feminine form of the word in order to impress upon his readers the fact that Christians are espoused to the Lord, and thus are in the relationship of a wife to him. Such indeed Paul affirms in 2 Cor. 11 : 2: "For I am jealous over you with a godly jealously; for I espoused you to one husband, that I might present you as a pure virgin to Christ." That the American Standard translators regarded *moichalides* (adulteresses) to be figuratively used in this instance is evident from the marginal reading, "That is, *who break your marriage vow. to God."*

know ye not that the friendship of the world is enmity with God?—"Know ye not" *(ouk oidate)* is an appeal to their sense of reflection. The ordinary sense of perception should have led them logically and unerringly to the conclusion that one cannot be a friend of the world and of God at the same time. So foreign are the characteristics of the one to the other that there can never be harmony or concourse between them. Is one a friend of the world? He is then an enemy of God. Friendship with both is impossible. That this fact, so obvious to the discerning, is obscured in the minds of multitudes of people today, evidences the benumbing effect of sin, and demonstrates the fact that men, by their indulgence therein, lose their sense of values, and become unable to reason in that realm correctly. Proper discernment is essential to noble living, and is frequently enjoined in the sacred writings. "But solid food is for fullgrown men, even those who by reason of use have their senses exercised to discern good and evil." (Heb. 5: 14.) "And this I pray, that your love may abound yet more and more in knowledge and all discernment, *so that ye may approve the things that are excellent;* that ye may be sincere and void of offence unto the day of Christ." (Phil. 1: 9.) Individuals whose sense of sin is blunted frequently insist that they see no harm in participation in worldly matters; and, it is likely that they do not. But, neither does a blind man see the sun which, in all its brilliance, apparently moves along the vaulted sky; but, this does not mean that, because such a one is unable to see it, *the sun is not there!* It is sad when people persist in the practice of sin; more tragic still when they lose, through such participation, their ability to distinguish between right and wrong, and are without any sense of moral values.

There is significance in the fact that James uses the verb *oida* which means to know by reflection, instead of the common word *ginosko,* to know by observation. Proper discernment of sin does not require participation therein; one may know its character and fruit by reflection. It is not necessary to imbibe poison in order to know its devastating effect; nor does one have to take *potions* of human philosophy to know the deadly character thereof. We have only to reflect on the sad cases of those formerly among us who have succumbed to its fatal effects and are lost to the cause of Christ, to realize that the same tragic results may follow from our participation.

That which James would have his readers avoid is "the friendship of the world." The Greek phrase is *he philia tou kosmou;* and the love indicated here is warm, emotional, selfish. Those thus described are in love with the world; on it they have set their affections; and in it they find their chief delight. The word *philia* also denotes common interests. Two men, for example, find the same hobby interesting and exciting; this interest in a common matter creates between them a common interest, and they thus become fast friends. Thus, a friend of the world is one whose interests are worldly and who, therefore, loves the world. This disposition is straitly forbidden to all who would be acceptable to God. John warned: "Love not the world, neither the things that are in the world. If any man love the world, the love of the Father is not in him. For all that is in the world, the lust of the flesh and the lust of the eyes and the vainglory of life, is not of the Father, but is of the world. And the world passeth away, and the lust thereof: but he that doeth the will of God abideth for ever." (1 John 2: 15-17.) The world hates those who are not of it (1 John 3: 13), its domain is that of Satan (1 John 4: 4), and his spirit permeates it (1 John 5: 19).

The word "world" *(kosmos)* in our text is variously used in the New Testament to denote the material universe; the external framework in which we live; the earth and, in a moral and ethical way, those who are alienated from God because their hearts are centered in things below, and not in things above. (Col. 3: 1-4.) It is in this latter sense that it is used here, and repeatedly elsewhere in the Scriptures. Jesus used it in this sense when he said,

"The world cannot hate you; but me it hateth, because I testify of it, that its works are evil." (John 7: 7.) In this sense, the word appears in John's writings more than one hundred times. It is made to stand for, and to represent, all that is opposed to God in a spiritual and moral sense.

Obviously, the word "world" does not, as used here, embrace the visible creation which is the handiwork of God (Psalm 19: 1ff.) and which bears in its structure irresistible evidence of God's goodness, greatness and glory. We are not forbidden to appreciate, and entertain regard for those features of the earth which commend themselves to the eye, and which evoke appreciation such as forest, river, sea and mountain; the word indicates *an order* which has Satan as its chief ruler (John 14: 30), which lies in the power of that evil one (1 John 5: 19), and which, with all of its lust, must eventually pass away (1 John 2: 17). It is the order of evil, as opposed to the realm of good over which Christ reigns, that we are not to love, to have no fellowship with, but vigorously to oppose and expose! (Eph. 5: 19.)

The friendship of the world "is enmity with God," *(echthra tou theou),* is a *state* of enmity, hostility, war with God, inasmuch as those in love with the world have, by this very fact, arrayed themselves against God. But for the friendship which these to whom James wrote entertained for the world, there would not have been the strife, factions, and wars among them; it was because of their inordinate love of the material that they were in conflict with the spiritual. It is ever thus. Those whose chief delight is in the participation of things of the world, and who seek to obtain more and more of the material affairs of the world in order the more to indulge therein, find themselves in conflict with others similarly motivated with consequent strife and war. To live in such fashion is to be in violation of the marriage vow each takes with God in becoming a Christian; those who consort with the world thus evidence their unfaithfulness to God. To further the figure, it is impossible to be brides of Christ and of the world at the same time! Jesus said, "No man can serve two masters: for either he will hate the one, and love the other; or else he will hold to one, and despise the other. Ye cannot serve God and mammon." (Matt. 6: 24.) It is no credit to men that they have often sought to maintain friendly relations with God *and* the world; and, frequently in the past, and perhaps in the present, crimes of greed have been, and are being, committed, and a portion of the ill-gotten goods then piously tendered to God, as if this "gift" justified such action. "Nevertheless even of the rulers many believed on him: but because of the Pharisees they did not confess it, lest they should be put out of the synagogue: for they loved the glory that is of men more than the glory that is of God." (John 12: 41, 42.)

Whosoever therefore would be a friend of the world.—A conclusion drawn from the preceding premises. "Whosoever" is comprehensive of the whole. Anybody, everybody, all of us are embraced. To be a friend of the world, or to attempt such friendship, is to cast oneself in the role of an enemy of God. The phrase, "would be," is highly significant. It is translated from the word *boulethei,* first aorist passive subjunctive of *boulomai,* to purpose, to will. This evidences for us the fact that one need not actually participate in the things of the world in order to be worldly; the purpose, the will, the *desire* to do so (whether realized or not), constitutes worldliness in the eyes of God. It hence follows that worldliness is a state of mind as well as a manner of life, and is so regarded by the Lord. It is quite possible that people may, from various considerations, refrain from a life of worldly activity; but, if the desire, the will, the inclination is there, such are worldly. The aorist tense, point action, indicates that the will to be worldly is a definite act influencing the after life. How may we know when one is a friend of the world?

While it is impossible to probe the hearts of others and to know the innermost motives which influence them, it is nevertheless true that the friends of the world are easily recognized by their dispositions and acts. One is an obvious lover of the world who finds greater delight in the association of worldly people than with those who are followers of the Christ; who experiences greater pleasure in frequenting those places which are sinful and secular, rather than the assemblies of the saints; and, who promotes those things which are of the world in lavish fashion, while giving a bare pittance of his means into the service of the Lord. To be thus engrossed in the ways of the world, however pious such may at times appear, is to exhibit a worldly disposition, and to fall under the condemnation of the Lord. Those who take their stand *for* the world, in *this very act,* take their stand *against* God! When the world is permitted to come into the heart, God is thereby crowded out.

maketh himself an enemy of God.—The phrase, "maketh himself," in the American Standard Version, and simply "is" in the King James Version, is from the Greek *kathistatai,* likely the middle voice of the verb, present tense, indicative mood, thus signifying that such a one constitutes himself the enemy of God. That is, by his once-for-all decision to fix his affection on the things of the world, he makes himself an enemy *(echthros,* an adversary) of God. One does not have to declare war against God to make oneself an enemy of deity. To consort with God's enemies, to lend aid and comfort thereto, is sufficient to put oneself into a state of alienation from him. Thus is made clear James' teaching in this entire section of the Epistle. The people are styled "adulteresses," because they were consorting with the world—an act of unfaithfulness to God—and hence in violation of their marriage vow which they took when they became his followers. It is vitally important, in the light of these sobering facts, for all of us to search our hearts and properly evaluate our motives to determine whether we are disloyal to God by any undue affection for the things of the world. If there is any trace of such affection, we should speedily purge ourselves of every semblance thereof, and henceforth enthrone the Lord Jesus Christ there. We shall have no difficulty in ascertaining the status of our hearts. Every discerning person knows whether the church or the world claims his chief interest; and can, with ease, determine on which his heart is fixed. How horrible for one who professes to be a follower of Christ actually to be an enemy of God! For all such a day of destruction awaits. Not infrequently men deliberately abandon him for the evil one. "Demas forsook me, having loved this present world." (2 Tim. 4: 10.) How shall we avoid the destiny which shall inevitably come upon all such? "If then ye were raised together with Christ, seek the things that are above where Christ is, seated on the right hand of God. Set your affections on the things that are above, not on the things that are upon the earth. For ye died, and your life is hid with Christ in God. When Christ, who is our life, shall be mani-

that the scripture [12]speaketh in vain? [13]Doth the spirit which [14]he made to

[12]Or, *saith in vain.*
[13]Or, *The Spirit which he made to dwell in us he yearneth for even unto jealous envy.* Comp. Jer. 3. 14; Hos. 2. 19 f. Or, *That Spirit which he made to dwell in us yearneth* for us *even unto jealous envy.*
[14]Some ancient authorities read *dwelleth in us.*

fested, then shall ye also with him be manifested in glory!" We are "raised" with him when we come forth from the baptismal waters to walk "in newness of life." (Rom. 6: 1-4.) If we live faithfully the remnant of our days upon the earth, we shall indeed be manifested (made known) as his, and also be revealed with him "in glory." For such a marvelous anticipation we can indeed well afford to labor and to wait.

5 **Or think ye that the Scripture speaketh in vain?**—The phrase, "Or think ye," *(he dokeite),* means "does it seem to you. . .?" "Are you of the opinion of . . .?" "Do you suppose. . . ?" "Vain," in the text, from the Greek word *knos,* signifies that which is empty, valueless, void of significance; hence, the import of the passage is, "Do you suppose that what the Scripture says about friendship of the world being enmity toward God is meaningless and void of significance?" *What* scripture?

The word *graphe* (scripture), in the text, occurs more than fifty times in the New Testament; and, unless this is an exception, it always refers to the books of the Old Testament. (Matt. 21: 42; 22: 29; 26: 54, 56; John 2: 22; 5: 39; 7: 38, 42.) Yet, there is no *specific* passage in the Old Testament which *verbally* asserts that which James affirms. There are statements which *resemble* it, and which mean much the same things as his statement; and, it is highly probable that the writer refers to one of these; or, indeed, to all of them, in principle. In which case, the meaning would be: "Do you suppose that the general teaching of the scripture is without significance in this matter?" (Gen. 6: 3-7; Ex. 29: 5; Deut. 32: 1-21; Job 5: 12; Eccles. 4: 4; Prov. 27: 4.) Thus understood, and properly so, the difficulty which many expositors have seen in this passage vanishes. James' question, in effect, is: "Are you disposed to think lightly of the teaching of the word of God in this matter, and to regard it as an insignificant thing? Are you of the opinion that the words of scripture are idle threats and empty warnings? The sacred writers have straitly forbidden the worship of idols (Deut. 5: 20; 1 Sam. 7: 3), and have condemned all participation with those of the world who would, by their teaching and practice, seduce you. Do you imagine these warnings to be no more than empty utterances?" The Old Testament taught this principle by example also; and the history of the Israelite nation is an impressive lesson in the folly and tragedy of participation in things of the world.

Personality attributed to the Scripture is not unusual in the New Testament. "The scripture speaketh . . ." is a familiar phrase. Compare Gal. 3: 8; James 2: 23.

Among those to whom James wrote were many Jewish Christians. These people, raised to respect the law and the prophets from earliest childhood, would regard this appeal to the highest authority they had formerly recognized with great respect. It is significant that James, himself inspired, appealed to the Scripture in support of his affirmation. All truth is *one,* and always harmonizes. This was not an unusual practice of New Testament writers. (Gal. 3: 8; Rom. 8: 36; Heb. 8: 5.) The Holy Spirit, who directed the writing of both Old and New Testaments, did not contradict himself in either. We deplore the disposition current in some circles today to regard the Old Testament as an inferior document, and as containing sentiments which "sanctified common sense" cannot fully endorse. James did not need any particular passage to illustrate the doctrine he was led to teach by the Spirit which motivated his pen. The principle to which he alludes is taught repeatedly in both Testaments. The statement was by him doubtless put in question form for emphasis, signifying, "The scripture does not speak in vain when it declares that the friendship of the world is enmity with God." Some, among his readers, doubtless felt that this affirmation was a bit overdrawn; and were thus disposed to excuse some participation in the world and in worldly things on the ground that minor activity in this area was not spiritually unhealthy. James would have them know that his affirmation is in harmony with the tenor of teaching through Scripture.

Doth the spirit which he made to dwell in us long unto envying?—There is, perhaps, no more difficult passage in the Epistle. There are problems involving (a) the text; (b) the translation; (c) the punctuation; (d) the meaning. Those interested in a detailed discussion of the more critical aspects of the passage will need to consult a variety of sources, to obtain any real and substantial aid thereon; such is beyond the confines of a single volume commentary. We shall limit our efforts to the exposition of the meaning of the passage.

The statement is rhetorical, and in question form for emphasis. "Doth the Spirit which he made to dwell in us long unto envying," means, "The Spirit which he made to dwell in us longs unto envying." These questions arise, (1) What is the *Spirit* to which reference is made? (2) *What* is meant by the phrase, "Which he made to dwell in us?" *How* does the Spirit, "which he made to dwell" in us, "long unto envying?" *Why* does the Spirit thus long unto envying? Answers to these questions will enable us to gain a clear concept of the passage in its entirety.

What is the "spirit" to which James refers? The Holy Spirit, or the human spirit? The American Standard translators believed it to be the Holy Spirit, and thus capitalized the word in the text; the King James translators thought it referred to the human spirit, hence used the lower case "s." The Greek is *pneuma* (spirit), and inasmuch as there is no capitalization, as we follow today, in the Greek texts, this problem cannot be solved by an appeal thereto, and the answer must be sought in an examination of the passage itself. We shall, therefore, decide this question later.

What is meant by the phrase, "Which he made to dwell in us?" "He" is, of course, God; "us" refers to Christians in general; "to dwell" means to abide, live, have one's abode; thus, the significance of the statement is that God caused to live within us that which he earlier designates as the *pneuma*, the spirit.

How does the *pneuma* (spirit) which he made to dwell in us "long unto envying?" To answer his question, another must be raised and answered, what is meant by the statement "long unto envying?" The Greek is *pros phthonon epipothei,* literally, "to envy yearns." The King James translators rendered the phrase, "lusteth to envy," and, in the margin, for *envy* put "enviously." The American Standard Translation has these marginal readings: "The Spirit which he made to dwell in us he yearneth for even unto jealous envy." "That Spirit which he made to dwell in us yearneth for us even unto jealous envy." Whether the passage be rendered, "The spirit which dwells in us to envy yearns," or "The Spirit which he made to dwell in us to envy yearns," depends on a variation in manuscript reading, and sheds little light on the significance of the passage itself. Whatever the correct MMS reading, the passage alludes to a spirit, a spirit which dwells in us, a spirit which to envy yearns. How the spirit "to envy yearns" must be determined by the meaning of "to envy," and "yearns." The phrase, "to envy," signifies to be covetous, to be influenced by a selfish desire for what others have—a passion which drives men to the gravest of crimes in order to obtain that which they yearn for. "Yearns" means to look upon with desire. Thus, the phrase, "to envy yearns," means to covet with great desire.

Why does the spirit, which is in us, covet with great desire? Men in the flesh, and motivated by fleshly inclinations, are often prone to look with envious hearts upon those who enjoy greater prosperity than they possess; and covetously to desire the possessions of others. This disposition often leads them to hate their fellows, to attempt to obtain from them, by whatever means necessary, those things upon which they have fixed their hearts. Often people are exceedingly jealous of the possessions and attainments of others, and they desire to acquire that which others have, though they have no right thereto. Whether they are successful in this effort or not, their hearts are filled with envy, jealousy, covetousness. Such seems to have been the condition characteristic of many of those to whom James wrote. This disposition led to the commission of the crimes enumerated in the earlier part of the chapter. (Verses 1-4.) The writer had emphasized the sinfulness of all such; had shown that the general teaching of the Scripture forbids friendship with the world, and charged that the *spirit which God placed in them was exercising itself to envy.* We thus regard the passage to be declarative and not interrogative; the "spirit" (which to envy yearns) to be the human spirit, and not the Holy Spirit; the words, *envy* and *yearns,* to be taken in their ordinary sense, and thus believe the passage to teach: "The spirit which is in you is a covetous and envious one." We must reject the view of most denominational expositors that the spirit here designated is the Holy Spirit, the third person of the Godhead, and that God or the Holy Spirit is enviously jealous of us, for whatever reason, on the ground that it is incredible to us that the writer would affirm of *deity* that which he had earlier so severely condemned in *men!* If, as indeed it is, that envy and jealousy are wrong in man, we cannot believe that James intended to assert that such are characteristic of God.

It is to this passage that all advocates of the theory of a *personal* indwelling of the Holy Spirit (in the church and out of it) appeal in an effort to sustain the view that the Holy Spirit actually and literally dwells in Christians. We have seen (1) a more reasonable view of this passage in that the *pneuma* (spirit) is the human spirit, and not the divine one. (2) We shall now show that the conclusion deduced from it, and other passages, that there is a personal, actual, literal presence of the Spirit in man, is equally unsound. It is not surprising that such a view is advocated by those who believe in a direct operation of the Holy Spirit—independent of, and apart from the word of truth—upon the heart of the sinner; it is, however, amazing that there are those who, subscribing to the doctrine of the all-sufficiency of the Scripture in conversion and edification, would so do. Ten years ago, in our commentary on the Epistles of Peter, John and Jude, we penned the following comments on this matter, and we would not change one sentiment thereon today: " 'Hereby we know that we abide in him and he in us, because he hath given us of his Spirit. And we have beheld and bear witness that the Father hath sent the Son to be the Saviour of the world.' (1 John 4: 13, 14.) As a token by which we may know that we abide in him and he in us, he has given us 'his Spirit,'—the Holy Spirit. But how does the presence of the Spirit in us supply evidence of such an abiding presence? The first *fruit* of the Spirit is love: 'But the fruit of the Spirit is love, joy, peace, longsuffering, kindness, goodness, faithfulness, meekness, selfcontrol. . .' (Gal. 5: 22, 23.) How may we know that the Spirit dwells in our heart? Because we love God and one another! Why does this love dwell in us? 'And hope putteth not to shame; because the love of God hath been shed abroad in our hearts through the Holy Spirit which was given unto us.' (Rom. 5: 5.) . . . 'We thus learn that the Spirit has been given; that through this divine person love has been shed abroad in our hearts. But how is the Spirit given to us? Paul inquired of the Galatians:

'This only would I learn of you, Received ye the Spirit by the works of the law, or by the hearing of faith?' (Gal. 3: 2.) This is a rhetorical question, put in this manner for emphasis. The meaning is, 'Ye did not receive the Spirit by the works of the law; ye received the Spirit by the hearing (marginal reading, *message*) of faith.' How does faith come? 'So then belief (faith) cometh of hearing, and hearing by the word of Christ.' (Rom. 10: 17.) Paul's affirmation is, therefore, that the Galatians received the Spirit through hearing the word or message of faith—that is, the gospel. The word of truth—the gospel—is the instrument by which the Spirit exercises his influence on both saint and sinner. Thus, as one receives the truth into his heart *and allows it to motivate his life* he is, to this extent, motivated and influenced by the Spirit, and enjoys his abiding presence. This is, of course, not to be interpreted as meaning that the Holy Spirit *is* the word of truth; the Holy Spirit uses the word of truth as the medium by which he influences; and his influence is limited to this medium. The Spirit prompts love for others through the instruction which he has given in the Scriptures.

"The Epistles of John are filled with instruction touching the duty of children of God to love one another, as indeed, much of the New Testament. If it is the Spirit, independent of the word of truth, which produces such love, why was such instruction given? Why, indeed, *is* there teaching on *any* theme if all faithful children of God, then and now, possess a measure of the Spirit from which they derive (independently) such instruction? The question is not, Do children of God possess the Spirit? this, the verse before us and numerous others (e.g., Rom. 8: 9; Gal. 4: 6), affirm. Neither is it, Are children of God influenced by the Spirit today? This, too, the Scriptures abundantly assert. The question is the *manner* or *mode* of such indwelling, and not the fact of it, which we raise. This Paul settles in the rhetorical question alluded to above. The only impact of the Spirit on the heart of either alien or Christian is by means of the word of truth. Unfortunately, some brethren, while denying the direct operation of the Holy Spirit on the alien sinner, contend for just such an immediate and direct operation on the Christian following his baptism. The only difference between the positions is the *time when* the operation occurs. The denominational world contends for a direct operation on the sinner in order to his conversion; those who hold to the view of a *personal* and *immediate* indwelling of the Spirit in the Christian maintain that the operation of the Spirit is immediately following conversion. The one is as untenable as the other, and both wrong. The Spirit dwells in the heart of the Christian; the Father and Son, likewise; with reference to the latter, it would be absurd to contend that this indwelling is literal, actual, in their own persons. But, because the denominational idea of a mysterious, incomprehensible, intangible being as the Holy Spirit is alleged to be has been adopted in some circles, brethren have allowed themselves to fall into such an error respecting the Holy Spirit." (A Commentary On The Epistles of Peter, John and Jude, pp. 299-301, by Guy N. Woods, published by the Gospel Advocate Company, Nashville, Tennessee, 1954.)

"And hereby we know that he abideth in us, by the spirit which he gave us." This verse declares, (1) God abides in us; (2) we have knowledge of his abiding presence; (3) we possess this knowledge by the Spirit which he has given. It should be observed that it is not the *manner of entrance* nor the mode of the Spirit's dwelling which is here referred to, but the *fact* of it. The Spirit assures of approval by motivating its possessor to do those things which enable the Father and the Son to abide in us. If it be asked how the Spirit does this, the answer is, Through the word of God, the only motivating force in immediate contact with the individual. Neither here nor elsewhere do the Scriptures teach a direct operation of the Holy Spirit, either before or after conversion. It is as erroneous to assume an immediate impact of the Spirit on the Christian's heart as it is to argue similarly with reference to such impact on the sinner's heart. The fact of the Spirit's indwelling is often affirmed in the sacred writings. The manner or mode of such is an entirely different question. The two are not always distinguished; and the result is, a prepossession for some theory thereon creeps easily into our exegesis and colors our explanation, if we are not careful. The fact that the Scriptures assert that the Spirit dwells in the Christian does not justify the conclusion that this indwelling is personal, immediate, and apart from the word of God. Christ is in us (Col. 1: 25); from this we do not infer that

dwell in us long unto envying?　6 But he giveth [15]more grace.　Wherefore the scripture saith, [16]God resisteth the proud, but giveth grace to the hum-

[15]Gr. *a greater grace.*
[16]Prov. iii. 34.

in some mysterious, incomprehensible way he has, in his own person, taken up an abode in us.　Why should we fall into a similar error with reference to the third person of the Godhead—the Holy Spirit?　(Ibid., p. 286.)

6 **But he giveth more grace.**—(*Meidona de didosin charin,* "moreover, he gives greater grace.")　The antecedent of "he" is God, the one who makes the spirit (created it) to dwell within us. God gives greater grace.　Why does he give us grace, and why is it described as greater grace?　It is as if those to whom he penned the preceding passage had said, "You have correctly described our situation; and, it is very true that we are disposed to be lustful and envious, but this disposition is in our innermost parts, being exercised by our spirits.　Is not then our situation hopeless and helpless?"　James' answer is, "No.　Granting that such is your situation, there is no compelling reason for you to yield to such desires, because there is *grace* to assist you, sufficient grace to meet your needs, grace greater than the temptations which pull you down."　This statement is reminiscent of that in Rom. 5: 20: "And the law came in besides, that the trespass might abound: but where sin abounded, grace did abound much exceedingly: that, as sin reigned in death, even so might grace reign through righteousness unto eternal life, through Jesus Christ our Lord."　Or, as the King James translation has it, "Where sin abounded, grace did much more abound."　Grace always outdistances the need, and is sufficient for whatever situation it is supplied.　There is a contrast implied between envy and grace.　Envy possesses the heart of weak and vacillating men; God's grace is ever available to assist them in triumphing over their temptations.　It is not without much significance (and the thought should cheer our hearts) that the verb "giveth" *(didosin)* is in a construction in the Greek text which suggests continuous action.　God *keeps on* giving grace to help us resist the allurements of Satan all of our lives!　And, the verb itself etymologically denotes a gift that is freely bestowed.　God graciously, continuously and abundantly bestows upon us grace greater than any need we may possess.　If God requires of us com-

plete surrender of the world and its evil affairs, he rewards us with a superabundance of the riches of grace involving matters which the world could never possibly provide.

Wherefore the scripture saith,—*(Dio legei,* literally, "Wherefore it saith. . .") The subject of the Greek verb is understood, and must be supplied. The translators thought the pronoun refers to the Scripture, and thus rendered it; others have thought that the proper name, *God,* should be supplied, with the rendering, "Wherefore God said. . ." Whichever rendering is right, the meaning of the entire statement is the same. The conjunction *dio,* translated "wherefore," means "for the reason," "because of this," "on this account," and denotes the condition on which God will bestow the greater grace mentioned previously. Again, to support his own premise with a quotation regarded as entirely authoritative by his readers, James cites a passage from Old Testament Scripture.

God resisteth the proud, but giveth grace to the humble.— This is a quotation from Prov. 3: 34, and from the Septuagint Translation thereof, a rendering of the Old Testament Scripture from Hebrew into Greek, done about three hundred years before Christ came to the earth, and the Greek translation of Scripture which our Lord and the apostles and other sacred writers used. This passage, in our Old Testament today, reads, "Surely, he scoffeth at the scoffers; but he giveth grace unto the lowly." (Prov. 3: 34.) The clause, "God resisteth the proud," is, in the Greek text, *ho theos huperephanois antitassetai,* literally God against the proud sets himself in battle array. "Resisteth" is from *antitasso,* a military term which means to set in battle array; and, "proud," from the preposition *huper,* and the verb *phainomai,* literally to show oneself above others. God is said to fight against those who elevate themselves in this fashion. The humble have God on their side; the haughty are by him opposed. It will be noted that the word translated "resisteth" in this passage is *antitassetai,* from *anti,* against, and *tasso,* to place; "the proud" from *huper,* above, and *phainomai,* to show. The prepositions, *anti,* and *huper,* are quite significant here. God is *against* those who conceitedly show themselves *above* others. God accepts the challenge and arrays himself in battle against them.

ble. 7 Be subject therefore unto God; but resist the devil, and he will flee

God "giveth grace to the humble," *(tapeinois de didosin charin,* "Moreover, to the humble, God keeps on giving grace.") Thus, by additional scripture is the affirmation of the inspired writer in the preceding passage established. "The humble" *(tapeinois)* are those who are lowly in spirit; these are the recipients of the "grace" (favor) which God freely and continuously bestows. God is thus the giver and his children are the receivers of the grace (unmerited favor) which is given to meet our needs. We should be impressed with the fact, and deeply grateful that, even in this world, he *gives us* far more than we are required *to give up*, and then adds to this eternal life in the next world: "Peter began to say unto him, Lo, we have left all, and have followed thee. Jesus said, Verily I say unto you, There is no man that hath left house, or brethren, or sisters, or mother, or father, or children, or lands, for my sake, and for the gospel's sake, but he shall receive a hundredfold now in this time, houses, and brethren, and sisters, and mothers, and children, and lands, with persecutions; and in the world to come eternal life." (Mark 10: 30.)

SUBMISSION AND EXULTATION
4: 7-10

7 Be subject therefore unto God;—"Be subject" is translated from *hupotagete,* an ingressive aorist passive in the imperative mood, from *hupotasso,* derived from *hupo,* under, and *tasso,* to place oneself; thus to put oneself under (in this instance) God. It will be recalled that the verb "resisteth," in the second sentence of verse 6, above, is from *antitasso,* compounded from *anti,* against, and *tasso,* to place. The root has a military connotation, and means to array oneself; hence, "Those who are proud God arrays himself against; see to it that you array yourselves under God." The verb means to place yourselves in the position of those who are in the service of God; and, in the aorist imperative denotes immediate action, action influenced by a sense of urgency. It is significant that there are ten aorist imperatives in verses 7-10, all with a note of urgency, and requiring immediate and forthright action. Peter frequently refers to this obligation, an example of which is in 1 Pet. 5: 5, 6: " . . . God resisteth the proud, but gives grace to the humble. Humble yourselves therefore under the mighty hand of God, that he may exalt you in due time. . ." (See, also, 1 Pet. 2: 21-23.) The aorist tense suggests a once-for-all act in which we are forevermore to place ourselves in the rank of God's faithful soldiers, and *to remain* there. We cannot possibly please him by being a soldier today, and a citizen of the world tomorrow. Paul admonished Timothy to "suffer hardship with me as a good soldier of Christ Jesus," and reminded him that no soldier on service entangleth himself in the affairs of this life; that he may please him who enrolled him as a soldier." (2 Tim. 2: 3, 4.) And, John wrote, "Love not the world, neither the things that are in the world. If any man love the world, the love of the Father is not in him." (1 John 2: 15.) We must not overlook the fact that far more is involved here than in exercising a choice between submission to God and to the world. The verb *hupotagete* involves the matter of choosing between our own proud spirit's domination and the will of God. It requires that God be enthroned in our hearts, and be allowed to dominate our lives. Only as we yield ourselves wholly to his will do we discharge the duty set out in this passage. It was James' design to emphasize this obligation in order that those to whom he wrote might avail themselves of the grace which abounds to meet every need. And, more than mere mechanical obedience is involved. One may, from considerations of expediency, find it proper to conform to the will of another; but only those who allow God's will to become sovereign in their lives really submit themselves to him.

but resist the devil,—(*Antistete de toi diaboloi,* take your stand against the devil.) "Resist," from *antistete,* is an aorist active imperative verb from *antihistemi,* which in turn is from *anti* against, and *histemi,* to stand. This, too, has a military connotation, and was frequently used of those who placed themselves in battle array against an enemy and held their ground. We are, therefore, to face Satan in battle array; to recognize him as a formidable and dangerous enemy; and to fight off all of his advances. All is at stake in the effort; and the issues are life and death. Man must resist (stand against) Satan, or be taken captive by him. There can be no armistice, no terms of amnesty offered; it is a war of survival. Fortunately, the Christian is not without powerful aid and effective weapons of defense: "Finally, be strong in the Lord, and in the strength of his might. Put on the whole armor of God, that ye may be able to stand against the wiles of the devil. For our wrestling is not against flesh and blood, but against the principalities, against the powers, against the world-rulers of this darkness, against the spiritual hosts of wickedness in the heavenly places. Wherefore take up the whole armor of God, that ye may be able to withstand in the evil day, and have done all, to stand. Stand therefore having girded your loins with truth, and having put on the breastplate of righteousness, and having shod your feet with the preparation of the gospel of peace; withal taking up the shield of faith, wherewith ye shall be able to quench all the fiery darts of the evil one. And take the helmet of salvation, and the sword of the Spirit, which is the word of God: with all prayer and supplication praying at all seasons in the Spirit, and watching thereunto in all perseverance and supplication for all the saints. . . ." (Eph. 6: 10-18.)

He whom we are to resist is "the devil," *(toi diaboloi,* the accuser, the slanderer). He is, as his name indicates, a calumniator, a gossip-monger, one who slanders another for the purpose of injury. Other names assigned to this evil being in the Scripture are Satan (an opponent), the Dragon, the Evil One, the angel of the bottomless pit, the prince of this world, the prince of the powers of the air, the god of this World, Apollyon, Belial, and Beelzebub. The *devil* is the ruler of a band of evil spirits (Matt. 8: 28; 9: 34; 12: 26; Luke 11: 18, 19), the enemy of Christ and the Lord's people (Matt. 13: 19, 39; Mark 4: 15), a murderer from the beginning (John 8: 44), an enemy to, and a falsifier of, God's word (Matt. 13: 19, 39), whose destruction will be accomplished by, and in connection with, the return of Christ (2 Thess. 2: 3, 4), and whose destiny will be the burning lake which is the second death (Rev. 20: 10; 21: 8). For the difference between the *devil* and the *demons,* see the comments on James 2: 19.

We resist the devil by always refusing to yield to his allurements, and by repelling and opposing his temptations. He has many tricks (2 Cor. 2: 11), and we must not be ignorant of his devices. He is ever engaged in his insidious efforts to seduce the good; and, "as a roaring lion, walketh about, seeking whom he

from you. 8 Draw nigh to God, and he will draw nigh to you. Cleanse
your hands, ye sinners; and purify your hearts, ye doubleminded. 9 Be af-

may devour." (1 Pet. 4: 8.) It is necessary, therefore, as Peter admonished, to be "sober," and "watchful," with reference to this "adversary."

It would, however, be a fatal mistake to assume that Satan *always* identifies himself as such, or announces his intentions in advance. Often, he moves in and out among us quietly, politely, even piously, his influence as gentle as a summer zephyr until he has accomplished his evil designs. Not infrequently he is in the pulpit, affecting to be one of the Lord's ministers: "For such men are false apostles, deceitful workers, fashioning themselves into apostles of Christ. And no marvel; for even Satan fashioneth himself into an angel of light. It is no great thing therefore if his ministers also fashion themselves as ministers of righteousness, whose end shall be according to their works." (2 Cor. 11: 13-15.) The test of a teacher is not to be sought in the piety he affects, but in the loyalty to the word of God which he evidences in word and in life.

and he will flee from you.—The devil is by no means as brave as he would like to appear to be. In a confrontation by the saints of God, he takes to his heels in flight, and abandons his effort, at least, for the time. Christians therefore need have no fear of the outcome if they stedfastly resist the devil. We are assured that no temptation is sufficient to overcome us (1 Cor. 10: 12, 13), and the Lord left us an example in his effective use of the sword of the Spirit on the Mount of Temptation. (Matt. 4: 1-11.) Done in that fashion, the devil will flee from us, as he did in that historic encounter.

It is important to observe that we resist Satan only by a total rejection of his efforts. One who yields, even in the slightest degree, takes a step that may eventually lead to complete surrender. One who never tastes intoxicating liquors, for example, will never become a drunkard; one who yields to the temptation to try it "just once" may acquire a taste to him irresistible, being unable thenceforth to refrain from participation therein, and thus become an alcoholic. We are safe, where Satan is involved, only by following James' injunction, "Resist the devil. . ."

8 **Draw nigh to God,**—"Draw nigh," *(enggisate,* aorist active imperative of *enggus,* near), is an injunction to get close to God! The tense designates a decisive and once-for-all act, which brooks of no loitering or hesitancy. This statement appears in close connection with, and should be regarded as a part of, the overall admonition of James in this section. We are, (1) to resist the devil; (2) he will then flee from us; (3) we are to stay close to God; (4) God will then come close to us. In such a course alone is there safety. The edict of the writer here is a condition precedent to the favor of God which may be enjoyed only by those who thus do. David said to Solomon, "And you, Solomon my son, know thou the God of thy father, and serve him with a perfect heart and with a willing mind; for Jehovah searcheth all hearts and understandeth all the imaginations of the thoughts. If thou seek him, he will be found of thee; but if thou forsake him, he will cast thee off for ever." (1 Chron. 28: 9.)

One does not draw near to God by an attempt to get close to him physically. As a matter of fact he is not far away from any of us (Acts 17: 28; Deut. 4: 7; Jer. 23: 23); even sinners cannot escape his presence. "Whither shall I go from thy Spirit? Or whither shall I flee from thy presence? If I ascend up into heaven, thou art there: If I make my bed in Sheol, behold thou art there. If I take the wings of the morning, and dwell in the uttermost parts of the sea, even there shall thy hand lead me, and thy right hand shall hold me." (Psalm 139: 8-10.) We come near to God, when we study his word, worship him in spirit and in truth, and serve him faithfully. During one of Israel's periods of faithfulness to God, Moses said, "Behold, I have taught you statutes and ordinances, even as Jehovah my God commanded me, that ye should do so in the midst of the land whither ye go in to possess it. Keep therefore and do them: for this is your wisdom and your understanding in the sight of the people, that shall hear all these statutes, and say, Surely, this great nation is a wise and understanding people. For what great nation is there, *that hath a god so nigh unto them,* as Jehovah our God is whensoever we call upon him? And what great nation is there, that hath statutes and ordinances so righteous as all this law, which I set before you this day?" (Deut. 4: 5-8.)

The priests of the old order, when they came to the sanctuary, were said to draw nigh unto God (Ex. 19: 22); and, inasmuch as all Christians are priests today (1 Pet. 2: 9), and thus privileged to approach God in worship, they come near him in worship. We are not from thence to infer that only on such occasions do we draw near him; we have seen that the tense of the verb "draw nigh" suggests a once-for-all act, and refers to a definite and decisive action in which one puts sin and Satan away, and comes to God. The verb is intransitive; the action is, therefore, man's; while God draws by incentive, it is man's responsibility to come to God. Of some Jesus affirmed, "And ye will not come to me, that ye may have life." (John 5: 40.)

and he will draw nigh to you.—This follows when we draw nigh to God. He will come close to us, if we come close to him! The verb here is future; and, the promise conditional. Asariah, by the Spirit of God, testified to Asa, "Jehovah is with you, while ye were with him; and if ye seek him, he will be found of you; but if ye forsake him, he will forsake you." (2 Chron. 15: 2.) Paul reminded the Romans: "Behold then the goodness and severity of God: toward them that fell, severity; but toward thee, God's goodness: otherwise thou also shalt be cut off." (Rom. 11: 22.) And Isaiah, in a familiar passage, admonished: "Seek ye Jehovah while he may be found; call ye upon him while he is near; let the wicked forsake his way, and the unrighteous man his thoughts; and let him return unto Jehovah, and he will have mercy upon him; and to our God, for he will abundantly pardon." (Isa. 55: 7, 8.) We may, therefore, as the Hebrew writer declares, "Draw near with a true heart in fullness of faith" (Heb. 10: 22), with the assurance that the Lord will welcome and receive us, and be pleased with our devotions. "All that which the Father giveth me shall come unto me; and him that cometh to me I will in no wise cast out." (John 6: 37.) Those who choose to remain at a distance from deity need not expect to have showered upon them the blessings mankind needs.

Cleanse your hands, ye sinners;—"Cleanse," *katharisate,* second person plural of the aorist active imperative of *kathatizo,* to cleanse, and often in a ritual sense, reflects the Jewish practice of purification (Mark 7: 3, 19; Ex. 30: 19-21); is remindful of the

Levitical mode of worship in the temple and the tabernacle, and would, therefore, be most vivid in significance to the Jewish Christians among those to whom James wrote. Doubtless, the familiar phrase, "Draw nigh to God," which precedes it, and which was so often used of those who approached God in the worship of the older order (Jewish worship), led on to this ritualistic phrase, "Cleanse your hands. . ." Those who came to the tabernacle in the wilderness, and to the temple in Jerusalem, were said to "draw nigh to God," because his Holy Presence hovered there. And, as the priests were required to wash their hands and bodies before performing their duties in that worship, so worshippers today are "to cleanse" their "hands," as a prerequisite to acceptable worship in the new order, Christianity. (Ex. 30: 20; 2 Cor. 7: 1.) The *cleansing* is, of course, figurative: and has reference to purity of life and of heart in our approach to God. This conception is a common one in the Scripture, and the figurative usage is likewise frequently seen. "And when ye spread forth your hands, I will hide mine eyes from you; yea, when ye make many prayers I will not hear; your hands are full of blood. *Wash you, make you clean;* put away the evil of your doing from before mine eyes; cease to do evil; learn to do well; seek justice, relieve the oppressed, judge the fatherless, plead for the widow." (Isa. 1: 15-17.)

Here, it is the hands, *(cheiras)* which are to be cleansed. Soiled hands are, in the Scriptures, a symbol of guilt: "So when Pilate saw that he prevailed nothing, but rather that a tumult was arising, he took water, and washed his hands before the multitude, saying, I am innocent of the blood of this righteous man; see ye to it." (Matt. 37: 24.) In this instance, Pilate assumed that clean hands would suffice, without regard to the condition of his heart. In contrast with this common view, Jesus said, "For *out of the heart* come forth evil thoughts, murders, adulteries, fornications, thefts, false witness, railings, these are the things which defile the man; but to eat with unwashen hands defileth not the man." (Matt. 15: 19, 20.) The Pharisees erred in assuming that a ceremonial cleansing was sufficient; and, they placed little or no emphasis on purity of heart. Sinners cleanse their hands by putting away all guilt and all transgression; their hearts are purified in obedience to the truth: "Seeing ye have purified your souls in your obedience to the truth unto unfeigned love of the brethren, love one another from the heart fervently." (1 Pet. 1: 22.) There is no article before the word "hands," in the Greek text, and thus the noun is abstract in significance and stands for that which the hands do. Hands are the instruments by which deeds are done; to cleanse the hands is to cleanse our actions of wicked and unworthy deeds. David said, "I will wash my hands in innocency; so will I compass thine altar, O Jehovah; that I may make the voice of thanksgiving to be heard, and tell of all thy wondrous works." (Psalm 26: 6, 7.)

Those who are admonished to cleanse their hands are called "sinners," *(harmatoloi)* from the fact that their conduct was wholly reprehensible to God, even though they had obeyed the gospel and were, therefore, members of the church. It is noteworthy that the more common "brethren," by which James usually addressed his readers, gives way to this sharp term of reproach in this instance. This was doubtless done to impress them with the seriousness of the situation, and to shock them into action to remedy it. It was brought on by their friendship with the world; and it could be eliminated only by their immediate termination of this relationship. In a passage of similar import, Paul admonished the Corinthians: "Be not unequally yoked with unbelievers: for what fellowship have righteousness and iniquity? or what communion hath light with darkness? And what concord hath Christ with Belial? or what portion hath a believer with an unbeliever? And what agreement hath a temple of God with idols? for we are a temple of the living God; even as God said, I will dwell in them, and walk in them; and I will be their God, and they shall be my people. Wherefore,

> Come ye out from among them, and be ye separate saith
>   the Lord,
> And touch no unclean thing;
> And I will receive you,
> And will be to you a Father,
> And ye shall be to me sons and daughters, saith the
>   Lord Almighty.

Having therefore these promises, beloved, let us cleanse ourselves from all defilement of flesh and spirit, perfecting holiness in the fear of God." (2 Cor. 6: 14-18; 7: 1.)

and purify your hearts, ye doubleminded.—The word "purify" *(hagnisate,* aorist active imperative of *hagnizo,* often to make clean in a ceremonial manner) has reference here to moral cleansing. (1 John 3: 3; 1 Pet. 1: 22.) Here, too, the Jewish influence is to be seen, though the significance of the passage goes far beyond mere ceremonial purification, and requires the elimination of all sin from the heart and life insofar as it is possible for us so to do. To purify the heart has particular reference to the *seat* and *source* of sin in the individual; to cleanse the hands to the performance of the *acts* of sin. The heart is the spring of evil; the hands are (figuratively) the instruments by which the purposes of the sinful heart are accomplished. Thus, both the *source* and the *means* of sin are to be purged, if one is to receive the blessings of grace earlier promised by James. As the reference to *hands* is without the article, so also is the word "hearts" without it. Hence, cleanse hands, purify hearts.

For the significance of the word translated "double-minded," *(dipsuchoi),* in our text, see the comments thereon at James 1: 8. The world is ever about us, and its influences are often exceedingly strong. It is most difficult for the best of people always to avoid the defilements of the age; and, not infrequently Christians feel totally different influences tugging at them. Those who tolerate this situation, and suffer it to continue, find themselves vacillating in their loyalties, influenced by conflicting interests, and with a divided allegiance. Consequently, they lack that unity of thought and singleness of purpose which ought to characterize them; and are, therefore, double-minded (literally, two minded men.) Such are religious in part, but nonetheless, long for the things of the world. A man with two minds is one who prays to God, yet has such a regard for the world that he is disposed to divide his attentions. He would, if he could, *love* the world, and *live* with God hereafter. Such is, of course, impossible; but, alas, how very many of us often appear to be trying to accomplish just this! It will be remembered that Abraham said to the rich man of Luke 16, "Son, remember that thou, in thy lifetime, receivest *thy good things,* and Lazarus in like manner evil things: but now here he is comforted, and thou art in anguish." (Luke 16: 25.) We must choose where we will have our "good things," it may be *either* here or hereafter; we cannot have them *both* here and hereafter. Jesus

flicted, and mourn, and weep: let your laughter be turned to mourning, and

---

solemnly urged: "But seek ye first his kingdom and his righteousness." (Matt. 6: 33.) Paul warned: "And have no fellowship (joint-participation), with the unfruitful works of darkness, but rather reprove (expose, bring to light) them." (Eph. 5: 11.)

9 **be afflicted, and mourn, and weep:**—The verb "be afflicted," *(talaiporesate,* aorist active imperative), signifies to be wretched, to carry and to be conscious of heavy burdens. Thus, these to whom James wrote are urged to become aware of the heavy load of sin they were carrying—the first requisite to repentance. The writer is not instructing them to impose upon themselves acts of penance on the ground that the greater the hardship suffered the more worthy of salvation they are; but to acquire such a sense of the enormity of their sin, that they will speedily turn from all such in genuine penitence. Those possessed of a deep sense of sin are wretched; Paul, in the remarkable passage of Rom. 7, in contemplation of the man without the hope of the gospel, cried out, "Wretched man that I am! who shall deliver me out of the body of this death?" (Rom. 7: 24.) This is the hopeless cry of the individual without Christ; and is a vivid representation of the condition of every person conscious of the intolerable load of sin borne without the knowledge of Christ and his cause, and the glorious relief it affords. This, Paul clearly indicates in the statement following: "I thank God through Jesus Christ our Lord." (Rom. 7: 25.) Helpless and lost without him, there is hope and assurance in Christ.

This wretchedness, if properly felt, will result in mourning and weeping. People, deeply aware of their rebellion against God, will experience and exhibit grief for their sins. Peter wept bitterly over his tragic lapse; and the sinful woman of Luke 7: 27-50 cried unashamedly at the feet of Jesus. Thus, those in the mind of James, far from glorifying in their guilt, should have felt distress and shame at their condition, and to have shown this remorse in mourning and weeping, rather than in laughter and joy. This passage should impress us all with the realization that we must not regard lightly a sinful life, and should not attempt to brush off, as a trivial and inconsequent thing, our guilt; instead, we should be painfully conscious of, and feel the weight of, God's displeasure when we have sinned, and should experience and give evidence of grief therefor. Often, those most in need of repentance are least concerned about it; and those who ought to be exhibiting sorrow over sin are gay, frivolous and vain. Such a disposition is wholly opposed to that which should characterize individuals under the censure of God.

let your laughter be turned to mourning, and your joy to heaviness.—We are not from this to assume that the Holy Spirit frowns upon the lighthearted and those often given to laughter and joy. Christianity is a happy religion, and those who are truly good should be genuinely happy. Our Lord honored, with his presence, a marriage feast (John 2: 1ff.), traditionally one of the most joyous of occasions. Contemplated here are those who have been in sin; who ought, therefore, to feel deeply the guilt involved, and to exhibit evidence of penitence. Those whose hands are stained with sin, and whose lives are polluted by the corruption of the world, are in no position to laugh and experience joy. Instead, they ought to mourn over their waywardness, and fall at the feet of Jesus for mercy. "Laughter," *(gelos),* is not, of itself, sinful; it is indeed, one of God's gracious gifts to those who are faithful: "Behold, God will not cast away a perfect man, neither will he uphold the evil-doers. He will yet fill thy mouth with laughter, and thy lips with shouting." (Job 8: 20, 21.) There is, however, a kind of laughter which issues from a wicked heart and which demonstrates perverseness and rebellion. Those who indulge in such laughter must eventually weep, not because of genuine penitence, but from an overwhelming sense of loss, when their sins have brought them into judgment: "Woe unto you, ye that laugh now! for ye shall mourn and weep." (Luke 6: 25.) Those who weep from a sense of sin shall find comfort: "Blessed are they that mourn: for they shall be comforted." (Matt. 5: 4.)

The word for "mourning," a term often joined with "weeping" (Mark 16: 10; Rev. 18: 16), is *penthesate,* aorist active imperative of *pentheo,* a word which originally meant to lament over the dead, and then to designate any great grief, derives from the same root as that used by our Lord in the second of the Beatitudes. There was in the word a suggestion of exhibition of mourning; indeed, the ancient Greeks wore black tokens as evidence of it; and

your joy to heaviness. 10 Humble yourselves in the sight of the Lord, and he shall exalt you.

James emphasizes here that the light-hearted laughter (which all can *hear*) ought to be turned into mourning (which all can *see*). Moreover, the "joy" which some of those to whom James wrote were experiencing was to be turned into "heaviness." It should be noted that there are two pairs of contrasts drawn in this section: laughter and mourning, joy and heaviness. The laughter is to be turned into mourning, the joy into heaviness. The first pair is largely outward in character; the second pair is more nearly dispositions of heart. The word translated "heaviness," *katepheian,* is compounded from *kata,* down and *phae, eyes;* hence, one with downcast eyes, one whose appearance is that of sorrowful dejection. An instance of this disposition is to be seen in the case of the publican who would not so much as lift his eyes heavenward, "but smote his breast, saying, God, be thou merciful to me a sinner." (Luke 18: 13.) This attitude is not to be identified with moroseness of spirit and a gloomy disposition; it is a sobering consciousness of the weight and guilt of sin. Now, as then, there are many who ought to be penitent, sad and contrite over their sins, but who are vain, gay and frivolous, and for whom a day of terrible judgment awaits.

10 **Humble yourselves in the sight of the Lord,**—The spirit of humility is peculiarly characteristic of all faithful disciples and is enjoined again and again in the sacred writings. (Matt. 23: 12; 18: 3.) The phrase, "humble yourselves," is from the Greek *tapeinothete,* aorist passive imperative of *tapeino,* and literally means *be humbled,* rather than "humble yourselves." Occasionally, the passive has a middle or reflective sense, and this may well be its significance here. Whether one humbles oneself, or suffers oneself to be humbled, the result is the same; and is that which is here enjoined. Humility is the voluntary acceptance of a place of lowliness in order to be pleasing to God. While James had in mind humility in the act of repentance here, humility of life is repeatedly taught in the New Testament. Peter, for example, wrote: "Yea, all of you gird yourselves with humility, to serve one another; for God resisteth the proud but giveth grace to the humble." (1 Pet. 5: 5.) Earlier, Peter had set out duties applicable to different

groups and individuals; here, the effort to designate obligations of the separate classes is dropped and the duty of all declared. It is as if the apostle had said, "Why should I attempt to specify particular duties for each class when one injunction will cover them all? All of you gird yourselves with humility to serve one another." "Gird yourselves" is translated from the Greek verb *engkombomai,* a term of exceeding interest and significance. The noun from which it is derived *(Kombos)* signifies a knot; and the noun form means to tie with a knot. From this noun the verb of our text, denoting the garment thus tied on, is derived. It was used at the beginning of the Christian era of the white scarf or apron which slaves wore tightly fastened around the waist to distinguish them from freemen. Used figuratively here, the meaning, "Tie on humility like a slave's apron." The saints were thus to array themselves in humility; to tie it on securely like a garment so that it might never fall away. Peter probably had a vivid mental picture of the Lord's action when he tied a towel about him and washed the disciples' feet, as he penned these words. (John 13: 10-17.) The statements of Peter and James are almost identical here. (Cf. James 4: 10 with 1 Pet. 5: 5.)

It is possible for one to appear humble when the motive is not right; to be acceptable, it must be for the purpose of pleasing God, and not in order to obtain the plaudits of men. We have, in the story of the prodigal son, a splendid example of humility and contrition. Said he, when he had come to himself in the far country, "I will arise and go to my father, and will say unto him, Father, I have sinned against heaven, and in thy sight; I am no more worthy to be called thy son: make me as one of thy hired servants." (Luke 15: 18, 19.) And, as the father rejoiced to have his lost son return, so God will gladly receive and restore and exalt his returning prodigals.

and he shall exalt you.—"He" is God, the Father, against whom all sin is committed; though the reference may simply be to deity which, in this case is *one,* insofar as sin is concerned. When men sin, they sin against the entire Godhead,—the Father, the Son and the Holy Spirit. Peter said to the first detected liar and hypocrite in the early church, "Ananias, why hath Satan filled thy heart to lie to the Holy Spirit, and to keep back part of the price of the land? While it remained, did it not remain thine own? and after it was sold, was it not in thy power? How is it that thou hast conceived this thing in thy heart? Thou hast not lied unto men, but unto God." (Acts 5: 3-5.)

The way to true exaltation is through humility. Our Lord said, "And whosoever shall exalt himself shall be humbled; and whosoever shall humble himself shall be exalted." (Matt. 23: 12.) This teaches us that the *way up* is *first down;* the road to genuine greatness is along the way of complete surrender. Those who turn to God in penitence, however great their sin, are assured of full and complete pardon. David, keenly conscious of the enormity of his sin, humbly confessed it, and begged for mercy: "Have mercy upon me, O God, according to thy lovingkindness; according to the multitude of thy tender mercies blot out my transgressions. . . Create in me a clean heart, O God; and renew a right spirit within me." Assured that God would do this, he penned a statement that has brought hope and comfort to countless thousands who have also transgressed the law of God, and are burdened with a heavy load of sin: *"The sacrifices of God are a broken spirit; a broken and a contrite heart, O God, thou wilt not despise!"* (Psalm 51: 1-19.)

SECTION 9
4: 11, 12

EVIL SPEAKING CONDEMNED
4: 11

11 Speak not one against another, brethren. He that speaketh against a brother, or judgeth his brother, speaketh against the law, and judgeth the law: but if thou judgest the law, thou art not a doer of the law, but a judge.

11 **Speak not one against another, brethren.**—James reverts to a subject, *the improper use of the tongue,* which has claimed his attention again and again in the Epistle. To no other matter does he devote so much time and space. We must therefore conclude that those to whom he wrote were particularly prone to this sin and therefore needed special instruction and warnings touching the matter. If those of that day were prone to sin in this manner, they evidence the fact that they were much like us today; there is certainly no more common sin among "saints" and sinners today; and no more obvious and clear indication of the depravity of man than the disposition to engage in slander, calumny and detraction. It is not unlikely that the writer intended for this section to be construed in close connection with the preceding one; the haughty and proud disposition there discussed often leads those who allege their own superiority to speak disparagingly of those whom they regard as beneath them. Moreover, the writer had discussed, in detail, in the verses preceding, the sins which result from an absence of love for God; here, he gives attention to those sins which follow from a lack of love for the brethren. It is, of course, the want of love for each other that prompts us to express adverse judgments regarding others. We are all especially prone to make excuses for those whom we appreciate and love; to excuse, justify and forgive them for their weaknesses; and to criticize, condemn and flay those whom we dislike. Such a disposition is sinful, and vigorously condemned by James in this section. One may speak evil of another by unjustly criticizing his actions, words, life; by taking up evil reports originated by others against a brother and giving them further circulation. All such censorious activity is sinful and wrong.

"Speak not one against another," *(me katalaleite allelon),* is, literally, "Stop speaking against each other!" The imperative with the negative *me* (not) is significant, and condemns the habit or practice of thus engaging. This construction forbids not only the *act,* but also the *will* so to do. This would include and forbid not only the *expression* of harsh words regarding others but also the entertainment of such *thoughts* concerning them. Whether the rendering here should be "against each other," or "about one another," the meaning is, in this instance, much the same; condemned is censorious comment regarding others. That these to whom James wrote were engaging actively in that which he forbids is evident from the use of the present imperative with the negative; hence, "Stop speaking against each other." Those thus engaged are *styled brethren.* Members of the church are thus by no means immune from this sin.

It would be well for all of us to remember that if there is such a thing as *evil-speaking,* there is also *evil-hearing,* a necessary accompaniment of evil-speaking. Indeed, were it not for those who *listen* to calumnies regarding others, there would be no one to *speak* such. Because we *enjoy hearing* bad things about each other is a basic reason why slanderers *enjoy telling* bad things about others. We are disposed, as conversationalists, to relate matters which please our hearers; and, because many listeners delight in slander, we are tempted to satisfy this desire, and thus to tell that which we know pleases them. To "run another down" was a common sin in the ancient world, and is not less practiced today. The verb implies not only evil-speaking, but such speaking as is done in the absence of another, i.e., "behind his back." Those who indulge in such conversation greatly displease the Father, and effectively close the door of grace against them. David inquired, "Jehovah, who shall sojourn in thy tabernacle? Who shall dwell in thy holy hill?" The Psalmist answered his own questions in these words: "He that walketh uprightly, and worketh righteousness, and speaketh truth in his heart; *he that slandereth not with his tongue,* nor doeth evil to his friend, nor taketh up a reproach against his neighbor. . ." (Psalm 15: 1-3.)

He that speaketh against a brother, or judgeth his brother, speaketh against the law, and judgeth the law:—To judge a brother, in the sense here intended, is to form unfavorable opinions regarding him without being able or willing to know the real character of the act condemned, or the motives which led to its commission. It is to impute unworthy motives to others; to put the worst possible interpretation on their words and actions. One who thus does not only violates the injunction which forbids evil speaking against a brother, such a one also speaks against the law, and judges the law. This one does, by ignoring that precept of the law which bids us to love one another, and by acting in a fashion contrary to it. By refusing to do what the law commands,—to love one's neighbor as oneself—such a person passes judgment upon the law by declaring that it is not good nor worthy of being obeyed. Such a practice is, in effect, to say that the law of love is a bad one, or at best defective; and may, therefore, be disregarded. This attitude is highhanded and presumptuous; it is a wicked attempt to pass judgment upon the acts of God himself! To exercise the office of a censor is to play the part of a judge; and this one does who abandons the law of love and speaks evil of his brethren. The proper province of Christians is to be "doers of the law," not judges of it; and to be guilty of that which James here condemns—cataloging the faults of others—is to violate the very law for which such affect great respect.

but if thou judgest the law, thou art not a doer of the law, but a judge.—The "judging," which is condemned here, is censorious judgment, a type of ill-natured criticism resulting from hasty and imperfect conceptions, and based upon partial or incorrect information. There is, in the effort, an allegation of superiority, the implication that the one doing it is better, more intelligent, possessed of greater wisdom than others. The critic thus becomes a judge, not exercising his judgment in a specific realm, and with reference to detailed charges established by testimony from credible and competent witnesses, but from surmise, suspicion, and malice. This is a palpable and strict violation of the law of love. (Luke 19: 18.) It is the responsibility of us all to obey the law of God, and not violate it, or attempt to pass judgment as to its worth or validity. The law contemplated here is doubtless the law of Christ; but the principle is applicable to any law under which we live, and to which we are answerable, if it is not in violation of Scripture. It is absurd for one to affect great respect for law, and

12 One *only* is the lawgiver and judge, *even* he who is able to save and to destroy: but who art thou that judgest thy neighbor?

---

to condemn unjustly one's brother when the disposition is itself a violation of the law. The tense of the verbs here used indicates, not an occasional lapse into this sin, but a constant and habitual addiction thereto. Such appears to have been characteristic of those to whom James wrote; and is not surprising, because those who speak evil of others occasionally will eventually fall into the harmful habit of doing it continuously. We thus learn that it is impossible to be in a right relationship with God, without sustaining the proper relation with our brethren. "If a man say, I love God, and hateth his brother, he is a liar: for he that loveth not his brother whom he hath seen, cannot love God whom he hath not seen." (1 John 4: 20.) "He that loveth his brother abideth in the light, and there is no occasion of stumbling in him. But he that hateth his brother is in the darkness, and knoweth not whither he goeth, because the darkness hath blinded his eyes." (1 John 2: 10, 11.)

JUDGMENT BELONGS TO ANOTHER
4: 12

12 **One only is the lawgiver and judge,**—There is but one lawgiver and judge; this is Christ Jesus our Lord; hence, no other is empowered with the authority of *making* laws for his people or of passing judgment on the validity of the laws he has made. It is a remarkable fact that God has always looked with greater severity upon those who presume *to make laws* for him than upon those who *break the laws* which he made. The latter may result from weakness, ignorance and downright stupidity; the former is officious presumption of the most highhanded nature. From the beginning, it has been characteristic of brethren to legislate where God has not; and this hurtful and harmful tendency has been the occasion of much division and heartache in the church of Christ. (Col. 2: 20-22; Acts 20: 29; 1 Tim. 4: 1ff.; 2 Tim. 4: 1ff.; 1 John 4: 1.) Every effort on the part of men to enact legislation apart from, and independent of, the law of Christ, such as that done in councils, conferences, synods, and the like, and to urge such legislation upon the people of God, is sinful in nature and an act of rebellion against God. Nor must edicts be adopted by councils and

synods, or incorporated into creeds, confessions of faith, church manuals, etc., to be equally reprehensible. A creed, because it is unwritten, and though it is promulgated *by brethren*, is no less obnoxious. Instances of such legislation may be seen in *the unwritten laws* some have made in our own day forbidding systematic Bible study in classes, the use of individual containers for the fruit of the vine on the Lord's table, and the care of destitute and fatherless children in homes supported from the church treasury. It is basic to Christianity itself that no rule of faith and practice, save the New Testament, may be urged upon Christians; and all efforts the design of which is to bind upon the conscience of others matters which the Lord has not enjoined are to be regarded as an unwarranted invasion of the will and work of Christ himself.

This means that there is but one who has the right to serve in this capacity as lawgiver and judge—and this is, as we have seen, Christ the Lord. (Matt. 28: 18-20; Acts 17: 31.) He has all authority in heaven and earth in his hands (Mark 16: 15, 16), and is thus equipped to perform the functions of lawgiver and judge. While reference in the text is doubtless to the promulgation of laws of a spiritual nature, and such as are designed to govern us in this realm, it may be observed that the principle is one applicable in all realms. Civil powers, legislative bodies, and earthly tribunals derive their rights only by, and in subjection to, the will of Christ. Jesus said to Pilate, "Thou wouldest have no power against me, except it were given thee from above; therefore he that delivered me unto thee hath greater sin." (John 19: 11.) No body of men, however powerful, has the right to pass laws which interfere with the rights, privileges, and obligations of children of God. This principle may be violated in several ways: (1) By enacting laws which are in conflict with the law of God; (2) by attempting to nullify some of the laws of God; (3) by presuming to act for God in issuing rules, edicts and regulations of a religious nature for the people of God.

It is, of course, an unwarranted extension of the principle taught by James to apply it to the actions of legislators and legislative bodies concerned solely with the civil and legal affairs of the land. These, indeed, are ordained of God in the sphere of civil and moral activity and thus serve under him in this sphere. (Rom. 13: 1ff.)

Under the ban of the sacred writer are such efforts as would nullify the law of God, on the ground that it is not good, and to erect human standards in its stead. Of course, any legislative body, seeking to invade the realm of God and which opposes, weakens the law of God, or attempts to nullify it, must be resisted by all children of God. "But Peter and the apostles answered and said, *We must obey God rather than men."* (Acts 5: 29.)

even he who is able to save and to destroy:—This is the one lawgiver and judge. There is no other empowered to save the soul or to cast it down to hell. Our Lord himself said, "And be not afraid of them that kill the body, but are not able to kill the soul: but rather fear him who is able to destroy both soul and body in hell." (Matt. 19: 28.) Since he alone is thus empowered, it is presumptuous for another or others to attempt to usurp his prerogative of making laws and of serving as judges in his realm. In his hands alone has God placed such powers; and he alone has the right to legislate in matters affecting the weal and woe of human beings. From this we learn that, (1) our Lord is *able;* vouchsafed to him is sufficient power to accomplish fully the will of God concerning him and us (Matt. 28: 18-20) ; (2) he is able *to save (sozo),* to deliver us from the guilt, the power, the pollution, and eventually, from the presence of sin, and to enable us to enjoy the bliss of heaven throughout eternity; (3) he is able *to destroy (appolumi,* to render useless). The verb does not denote annihilation, as is sometimes argued by materialists; it is the Greek adjective for the condition of the prodigal son in Luke 15, when he was said to be *lost,* i.e., completely alienated from his father and his father's house. The word does not mean extinction or non-existence when affirmed of the wicked; the Scriptures plainly teach that such will exist in a conscious state, and be punished, throughout all eternity. (Mark 9: 42-50; Rev. 20: 10-15.)

but who art thou that judgest thy neighbor?—Withering scorn and great irony emanate from this statement. "Thou," *(su),* is emphatic. "You, frail and ignorant individual that you are, how dare you to presume to become God and to pronounce judgment upon another?" The statement is reminiscent of Paul's castigation of the Romans: "Who art thou that judgest the servant of another? to his own lord he standeth or falleth. . . But thou, why dost thou judge thy brother? or thou again, why dost thou set at nought thy brother? for ye shall all stand before the judgment seat of God. For it is written, As I live, saith the Lord, to me every knee shall bow, and every tongue shall confess to God. So then each one of us shall give account of himself to God. Let us not therefore judge one another any more: but judge ye this rather, that no man put a stumbling-block in his brother's way, or an occasion of falling." (Rom. 14: 4, 10-13.)

The rhetorical question, put in this form for emphasis, is designed to show (a) the absence of any right to engage in such judging; and (b) the inability of those who thus do, to do so properly. Being without either the right or the ability, the attempt is presumptuous. Thus, the final clause of the sentence is designed to show the absurdity of the effort on our part, and for the foregoing reasons. Admitting that there are matters which are not what they should be among brethren; granting that they should be examined, condemned and opposed by the proper authority, are *we the ones* best qualified to do it? Earlier, the writer had raised the question of the authority by which one presumes to judge another. He had emphasized that no such right exists. Here, this matter has been put aside, and the question of one's personal qualifications raised. Is there such moral rectitude, such sobriety of conduct, such blamelessness of life on our part that we are the proper persons for such action? Let us remember that in any matter involving the conduct of members of the church, it is the responsibility of *the elders of the church* to make investigation thereof, and from the facts uncovered to make a decision later to be made known to the church, and thence to be carried out by the church. (Rom. 16: 17; 1 Thess. 3: 6-15; 1 Cor. 5: 1-13.)

The *judging* forbidden is the running down of another *(katalalei,* to speak against, or down upon); those forbidden to do it are all disciples; the "neighbor" *(ton plesion)* is, literally, one near us, and then anybody, whether saint or sinner.

We are not from this to conclude that we are not at liberty to determine the tree from the fruit it produces, or that we sustain no obligation to exhort (Heb. 3: 12), admonish (1 Thess. 5: 14), and counsel (1 Tim. 6: 3, 17). Forbidden here, as also in the

Sermon on the Mount (Matt. 7: 1ff.), are all censorious judgments exercised without sufficient information, by people who are
without right to do so, and whose design is detraction, slander and
defamation of character.

SECTION 10
4: 13-17

PRESUMPTUOUS CONFIDENCE
4: 13, 14

13 Come now, ye that say, To-day or to-morrow we will go into this city,

---

13 **Come now, ye that say,**—There is an exceedingly close connection between this section, and the preceding one. As a matter of fact, the whole of chapter 4 is a penetrating analysis of the sins which were common to those of whom James wrote, the basic character of which was a presumptuous disregard for God and his way. Verses 1-10 show that those people chose the world in preference to God; verses 11, 12 indicate their contempt for the law of God; and here, verses 13, 14 introduce another sin of this category: presumptuous confidence with reference to the future—a future from which God was excluded, and where there was no recognition of the operations of divine providence. Jews have ever been a restive and restless people; and, this, plus the fact that they have often been persecuted and driven from their homes and lands, has made them a nomadic people. They have, in consequence, developed great skill in buying and selling and trading, and this has, through the centuries, required much travel. Those thus engaged are prone to formulate plans without regard for God, a disposition by no means limited to Jews, nor to the people and period of which James wrote. The attitude is a common one; and one doubtless characteristic of all of us, at one time or another. Dependence on God is the most fundamental premise of Christianity; the disposition to leave him out of our affairs is gross indifference; and, when to this is added the feeling that he is not *needed* in such plans, the attitude is godless in nature.

"Come now," *(age nun),* is an interjectional phrase, the design of which is to gain attention, and simply means (though not literally), "See!" "Behold!" "Listen!" The Greek word is often used in connection with the imperative for the purpose of gaining a hearing. It also occurs in James 5: 1. Here, the implication of it is that there is something seriously wrong and those thus addressed should give careful heed to what the writer is about to set forth. If there is a close relationship in thought between this and the rebukes of the preceding section, it is by no means unrelated to those earlier portions of the Epistle wherein censorious judgment is condemned. The presumptuous disregard of the law of love as evidenced in such unjust judgment also shows itself in plans for a future from which God has been excluded. James does not mean by the words, "Ye that say . . ." that he is actually quoting some man or group of men among them; it is an imaginary case in which a band of traveling merchants are freely expressing their plans for the future, a future which does not take account of God, or of his will. The noun *logos,* from which the verb, "say," in the passage, derives *(legontes),* which denotes reasoning and thought, shows that these men were not indulging in idle, meaningless, chatter; their plans were well laid, carefully thought out, and adopted only after much consideration. Their sin was not in such careful planning, but in planning without regard for God and the realization that all plans are dependent on his will for success.

To-day or to-morrow we will go into this city, and spend a year there, and trade, and get gain:—A simple analysis of this statement will reveal, in striking detail, the appalling presumption characteristic of these people; (1) the *time* when they will leave is of their own choosing; it may be today, *or* tomorrow; (2) the *city* to which they will go they also select; (3) they will *remain* there a year; (4) the business they will pursue there is *trading;* (5) from such activity they will derive gain. Their assumption is that the whole matter is in their hands; all is settled, and of course in their favor; God is completely disregarded. If we are disposed to be shocked by this callous presumption, let us take stock and inquire of ourselves how near to our own practice does this approach? Do not all of us assume that tomorrow, next week, next year are all ours, and are we not continually making plans which necessitate the assumption that we will be here and able fully to carry them all out? Solomon solemnly warned, "Boast not thyself of tomorrow; for thou knowest not what a day may bring forth." (Prov. 27: 1.) It was this common characteristic of humanity which prompted our Lord to deliver the parable of the rich fool who, in formulating his plans for the future, forgot the length of life is a matter over which man has no control; and discovered to his dismay, that just as he believed himself to be in position to enjoy the fruits of his plans he was called, by death, forevermore away from them. (Luke 12 : 16-21.)

Though the proposition, "All men are mortal," must by all be admitted as true, most of us reason regarding it as we do concerning an automobile accident; it will not happen to us; we are the exceptions. It is not that we think we shall never die; we feel that, in our cases, it is far distant and there is no occasion, at least for the moment, to give our attention to it. It is most difficult to impress those in youth and in early life with the realization that they *ought* to be making plans for the day when they must leave this world; that eventuality is, to them, so remote as to be of little interest. Those for whom the years have flown and who find themselves in middle age (a misnomer truly, because those of this classification have long since passed the mid-point of life in years, and may reasonably expect only a fraction of the time they have lived, at most), live and act as if there is ample time for preparation for the future. Even the aged, those who have definitely reached "the golden years," are frequently disposed to refuse to admit their status, and to reason as did Bernard Baruch that "Old Age is ten or fifteen years older than you are!" One seventy years old can look about him and see others living who are eighty, ninety, or more, and thence assume that such will be characteristic of himself as well. This disposition, in some measure, common to us all, is a delusive one; and fails to take into account two things: (1) The uncertainty of life; (2) divine providence.

We are without assurance that we shall be living the next minute, much less the next day, the next week or the next year. Death often comes with shocking suddenness—a sudden stroke, a fatal heart attack, the rending crash of an automobile, and it is over, in a moment, without an instant's warning. The writer of these comments preaches in approximately forty gospel meetings each year and it is not unusual for him to preach to people in the outset of a meeting and for some days thereafter, and yet, before the meeting ends, either to preach, or to attend, their *funerals*. A Jewish sage once said, "Care not for tomorrow, for you know not

and spend a year there, and trade, and get gain: 14 whereas ye know not
what shall be on the morrow. What is your life? For ye are a vapor that

what a day may bring forth. Perhaps he may not be alive on the
morrow, so have cared for a world that does not exist for him."

14 **whereas ye know not what shall be on the morrow.**—This
statement appears to contain considerable irony. Those to whom
James wrote were making plans that contained a year of tomor-
rows; whereas, they did not know what would occur on the first of
these morrows! The contingencies involved every aspect of the future, (a) whether they would be alive; (b) whether there would be
a tomorrow; (c) whether they would be physically able to make
the trip planned; (d) whether circumstances would allow them to
enter the city; (e) whether if they were able to enter, they would
be able to pursue their business; and (f) whether such activity
would prove to be profitable. What great folly there is in disre-
garding all of these uncertainties, each of which is in God's hand.
Though we are utterly unable to fathom the future and to ascertain
what it holds, and are powerless to determine the situation for a
single hour, yet all of us are disposed to act as if the future is in
our hands.

The sentence, "Whereas ye know not what shall be on the morrow," *(hoitines ouk epistasthe tes aurion),* means "You do not
know with certainty what shall occur on tomorrow." The verb
epistasthe means to be certain, to know assuredly. It is, therefore,
sheer folly for one to act as if the future is under one's control
when one is wholly ignorant of what even one day holds.

What is your life?—*(Poia he zoe humon,* literally "of what
character is your life?") It is as if James were saying, "Stop and
consider! Before making plans for the future, determine what sort
of life you have. Is it permanent, abiding, enduring, possessed of
those qualities which assure that you will be here tomorrow, next
week, the following year, over in the next century? Inasmuch as
your future plans depend on the maintenance of life, what is the
character of it?" Some have sought to place emphasis on the
pronoun "your," and to understand James to be pointing to the
emptiness, and ultimate destruction of an ungodly life. It is quite
true that his address here is to the people who have eliminated God

from their plans, and who presume on the permanence of life which is but a vapor; but the same is true of the physical life of all, whether good or bad. The sacred writers have, as we shall see below, frequently recognized the fleeting character of life and have mournfully chronicled its inevitable end as the grave. This characteristic of life James indicates in the statement following.

For ye are a vapor that appeareth for a little time, and then vanisheth away.—Life is "a vapor," *(atmis,* mist) which appears "for a little time," *(pros oligon),* "and then vanisheth," *(phaino-mene epeita kai aphanizomene),* a play on words in the original text, *"appears,* then in a moment, *disappears."* Such is life, a languid wisp of cloud that floats idly in the airy ether of the heavens, outlined momentarily in a setting of liquid turquoise, and then disappears to be seen no more. Nothing is more unsubstantial than a vapor, and it is an excellent representation of the brevity of life, and the fleeting and unstable existence characteristic of all of us here. It is the same idea as that expressed by Job when he said,

"My days are swifter than a weaver's shuttle,
And are spent without hope.
Oh remember that my life is a breath;
Mine eye shall no more see good.
The eye of him that seeth me shall behold me no more;
Thine eyes shall be upon me, but I shall not be.
As the cloud is consumed and vanisheth away,
So he that goeth down to Sheol shall come up no more.
He shall return no more to his house,
Neither shall the place know him any more." (Job 7: 6-10.)

The transitoriness of life and the inevitability of death are familiar themes to all Bible students. Again and again the writers thereof have commented on this fact and have sought to impress us, with vivid figures, to this end. Life is by them compared to water spilled on the ground, to a flying shadow which flits across the sky and in whose shade the toiler rests briefly and looks up only to find that it has flown away; to a frail and fragile flower; to sleep, to a dream, to a handbreadth, to a shepherd's tent which has been removed, to a tale that is told, to a long journey one is about to undertake. These are Inspiration's answers to the question, *What is your life?*

appeareth for a little time, and then vanisheth away. 15 [17]For that ye ought
to say, If the Lord will, we shall both live, and do this or that. 16 But now

[17]Gr. *Instead of your saying.*

RECOGNIZING GOD IN OUR AFFAIRS
4: 15, 16

15 **For that ye ought to say, if the Lord will, we shall both
live, and do this or that.**—That is, in contrast with what you are
saying, ("Today or tomorrow we shall go into this city and spend
a year there, and trade, and get gain") (verse 13,) "for that ye
ought to say," *(anti tou legein humas,* literally, *instead of saying as
to you,* i.e., Instead of your saying (margin) what you actually
say, you ought instead to say, "If the Lord will, we shall both live,
and do this or that." The phrase, "If the Lord will," *(ean ho ku-
rios thelesei)* is a condition of the third class with *ean,* and the
present indicative subjunctive. "This or that," *(touto e ekeino),*
includes our every act; and thus the proper attitude in all of our
planning for the future is to be mindful of the fact that "Man proposes, but God disposes," and that everything we purpose is dependent on his will. Our plans should, therefore, always be made
with the proviso that they will be carried out, "If God will. . ."
This does not mean that such words must always be on our lips
and that we must give utterance thereto in formulating or expressing these plans. It is not a formula, but an attitude of heart which
James enjoins; and which must characterize us if we are to have
the proper attitude toward God.

The faithful disciples of the Lord will always take God into consideration in all that he proposes to do; and to understand, if he
does not say, that God's will is always to take precedence over his
own. He who loves God, and who respects his will, wants to
please him; he desires always that God's will shall overrule his
own in all the affairs of life. Paul was keenly conscious of the
Lord's hand in his affairs, and frequently made mention thereof.
His return to Ephesus was dependent on "If God will" (Acts 18:
21); he purposed to visit Corinth, "If the Lord will" (1 Cor. 4:
19); and to spend some time there "If the Lord permit" (1 Cor.
16: 7). So common has this sentiment become with many it has
been stereotyped into a formula and stock phrase, expressed by the

ye glory in your vauntings: all such glorying is evil. 17 To him therefore that knoweth to do good, and doeth it not, to him it is sin.

Latin words, *Deo Volente,* often abbreviated to the letters D.V. It is evident that it was not James' design to urge the expression of this sentiment as a mere appendage to the expression of plans for the future; repeated in every assertion, it would soon become meaningless, and thus profane. It is then not a glib, formal phrase, but a sentiment that should *live* in our hearts, and govern in all of our purposes and plans. It is a recognition of God's hand in the affairs of men, and a consciousness of our complete dependence upon him. Moreover, we are all in constant need of his assistance; and our plans should be formulated with the idea that, if they are in harmony with his will, he will guarantee their success; and, if they are not, they deserve to fail. Thus motivated, the failures and disappointments of life will not dismay and defeat us; we may, in such cases, properly assume that it was not his will that such plans should be carried to completion, and in this realization, be content. No purpose can prevail without his permission; every purpose is certain of success when he favors it, and we do our part properly. "Trust in Jehovah with all thy heart, and lean not upon thine own understanding: in all thy ways acknowledge him, and he will direct thy paths." (Prov. 3: 6.)

16 **But now ye glory in your vauntings:**—"Vauntings," (from *alazon,* a boaster or braggart), denotes insolent, arrogant and empty assurance; the disposition to ignore God in life's affairs, and to live with the assumption that man alone is the architect of his fortunes. This description of the attitude characteristic of those to whom James wrote contrasts sharply with that which is proper and right, and which he urges in verse 15. Theirs was a boastful attitude; they not only felt sufficient, they sought to leave the impression upon all others that they were wholly so, and were thus without any need of God in their affairs! Such self-glorification was high-handed presumption; a deliberate effort to exclude God from their lives. The etymology of the word translated "vauntings" suggests a calculated effort on their part to claim sufficiency without God. It is significant that, in its only other occurrence in the New Testament, it appears in the phrase, "the vainglory of life." (1 John 2: 16.) It denotes the disposition to claim

cleverness, strength, skill; hence, sufficiency; and, of course, without God. They compounded their sin by not only entertaining this conception in their hearts, but by expressing it to others. Bad as it is to feel independent of God, it is worse to glory in it, and to boast of it to others. This is not surprising, however; and but indicates the normal course of sin. Men who *feel* no obligation to God will soon boastfully and insolently *express* to others their disregard of him.

all such glorying is evil.—That is, such glorying as the writer had just condemned. Some "glorying" *is* good. "For what is our hope, or joy, or crown of glorying? Are not even ye, before our Lord Jesus at his coming? for ye are our glory and our joy." (1 Thess. 2: 19.) Some "glorying" *is not* good: "Your glorying is not good. Know ye not that a little leaven leaveneth the whole lump?" (1 Cor. 5: 6.) In other matters we may, and properly, glory: "But far be it from me to glory, save in the cross of our Lord Jesus Christ, through which the world hath been crucified unto me, and I unto the world." (Gal. 6: 14.) But, those who make plans from which God has been excluded, and who glory in such, do that which is "evil," *(ponera,* an active form of wickedness). They engage actively in sin, in so doing. God wants us to use the talents he has placed at our disposal, and to do all we can while on the earth, but he expects us to do this in harmony with his will. We must ever remember that God is the superintendent of the universe; we are the creatures of his hand; and we should conduct ourselves accordingly.

THE SIN OF OMISSION

4: 17

17 **To him therefore that knoweth to do good, and doeth it not, to him it is sin.**—He who recognizes life's transient and fleeting character, but refuses to acknowledge the hand of God in the affairs of men, and who may even boast of his sufficiency and independence, but who will not do that which is right, is guilty of sin. Whether the whole of verse 17 is to be regarded as a comprehensive principle, a *maxim,* the truth of which is applicable to any situation where one *knows,* but *does not do* one's duty; or, is to be construed only in connection with the preceding section, it is clear that the statement was suggested by, and developed from, the mat-

ters there affirmed from the writer's use of the logical device, "therefore," *(oun,* in view of the foregoing premises). There is obviously some connection between the section preceding and this affirmation; but it is not to be restricted to the context or limited to the matters just discussed. It would appear that it was James' design to show that these who were given to insolent and arrogant expressions of self-sufficiency and who refused to acknowledge providence in their affairs were those who affected to be best informed in what is right and hence merely compounded their guilt in their refusal to "do good." The principle is one which often appears in the sacred writings, and in a variety of forms. Jesus said to the Pharisees, "If ye were blind, ye would have no sin: but now ye say, We see: your sin remaineth." (John 9: 41.) "And that servant, who *knew* his lord's will, and made not ready, nor did according to his will, shall be beaten with many stripes; but he that *knew not,* and did things worthy of stripes, shall be beaten with few stripes." (Luke 12: 47, 48.) "If I had not come and spoke unto them, they had not had sin: but now they have no excuse for their sin." (John 15: 22.) "If ye know these things blessed are ye if ye do them." (John 13: 17.) The implication is clear. To know what is right, and then not to do it, aggravates one's sin, and enhances one's guilt.

The principle is also applicable in matters involving wrongdoing. If it is our obligation to *do* that which is *good,* when we *know* what the good is, we must also avoid that which is wrong by the application of the knowledge we have, or may obtain, from God's word. Whether James' statement, "To him therefore that knoweth to do good, and doeth it not, to him it is sin," is to be regarded as an allusion to Paul's affirmation in Rom. 14: 13, "And whatsoever is not of faith is sin," it is very true that the statements, taken together, establish the fact that (a) a knowledge of what is right creates the obligation to discharge the duty involved in it; and (b) doubt regarding the propriety of an act necessitates abstinence from it. One sins in doing that which is of doubtful propriety; one sins in knowing an act is obligatory, yet does not perform it.

The error characteristic of those of whom James wrote is a common and persistent one. Many there are in the church today who take pride in a knowledge possessed which is largely, and oftentimes wholly, inactive in good works. Many *hear,* but seldom *heed.* They overlook or disregard the fact that there are sins of omission as well as commission. Those of this category are careful to observe the "Thou shalt nots," of the Scriptures, but are little concerned with the "Thou shalts." They assume they are good, simply because they are not bad! They forget that goodness is a positive quality; not merely the absence of the bad. The barren fig-tree (Matt. 21: 19) was not an evil growth. It was not harmful; it did not exude poison dangerous to men and beasts; it was simply an insignificant tree by the side of the road. Jesus, observing that it had leaves, made his way to it and, though it was not the season for figs, when he found no fruit on it, pronounced a curse upon it. Why? The order of the Palestinian fig is (1) fruit; (2) leaves. This tree had leaves; the assumption was that fruit was there also. On observing that the leaves were mere pretense, Jesus pronounced the curse upon it. Thus, to the situation of fruitlessness, this tree added that of pretense. This is not an unusual order. Those who are aware of the little they do for the Lord are disposed to pretend to be doing more than they really are. Their fruitlessness thus develops into pretense, and pretense into hypocrisy.

So wedded is man to the premise that it is possible for one to be saved on the basis of the things *not* done, there are those to be at the judgment who shall actually argue this point with the Lord! From the great tribunal the wicked are to be turned away into eternal punishment with the charge, "I was hungry and ye did not give me to eat; I was thirsty, and ye gave me no drink; I was a stranger, and ye took me not in; naked, and ye clothed me not; sick, and in prison and ye visited me not." (Matt. 25: 42, 43.) Why were these brought to such a horrible doom? By murder, adultery, robbery theft, etc.? Certainly such lead inevitably to such a destiny; but of these no such conduct is affirmed. They had known to do good, and had not done it. It was not something done that was wrong which earned for them this fearful destiny; it was *the good* they had failed to do. This evidences the fact that our Lord, who went about always doing good, looks with the greatest disfavor upon those who are inactive in his service, and who regards each moment not spent in useful employment, *an act of sin.*

Every judgment parable in the New Testament reveals that the punishment meted out was not for something *bad* the individual involved *did*, but something *good* he did *not* do. It is affirmed of the one-talent man that he was "wicked." It is quite obvious that this word is used in this parable in a sense wholly foreign to our usage today. A wicked person is, in our view, one who *does bad things.* Nothing of an evil character whatsoever is affirmed of him. We have often said that were we required to defend him in a legal action today, by obtaining a jury of brethren, we would most likely get a verdict in his favor! If one's fitness for eternal bliss is to be determined by the things one does not do, an excellent defense might be made for him: (1) He was not an embezzler; (2) he did not squander the money in riotous living: (3) he was not remiss in the trust, in that the talent was returned whole; (4) he was not dishonest; (5) he was not a drunkard, thief, murderer, immoral character, etc. Yet, he was a *wicked* man! Why? Because of *the good he did not do.* This fundamental premise each of us should take carefully to heart, and govern our lives accordingly. *To him . . . that knoweth to do good and doeth it not to him it is sin.*

SECTION 11
5: 1-6

THE RICH WARNED
5: 1-3

1 Come now, ye rich, weep and howl for your miseries that are coming

1 **Come now, ye rich,**—Though the rich are here directly addressed, it is not likely that they were Christians. (1) There is to them no exhortation to repentance; (2) they are not admonished to a better life; and (3) there is to them no promise of reconciliation to God. On the contrary, they are "to weep and howl," not in penitence, but in view of impending retribution and ruin. It would appear that the statement of the inspired writer is an *apostrophe,* wherein he turns aside, for the moment, to denounce the rich and to declare their ultimate doom, for the edification of the poor saints who were experiencing oppression at the hands of the rich. Though his readers are again and again called "brethren," (e.g., four times in the six verses from James 5: 7), in no instance are these so designated. In the section immediately preceding this (4: 13-17), and applicable both to saint and to sinner, the rebuke is addressed to those *who desired to be rich,* and here to those *already so,* and whose interests were wholly in material things. That the statement of the writer is a solemn pronouncement of woe, rather than a call to repentance, indicates the utter abandonment to the world which was characteristic of them. Of course, there may have been some who *had been* Christians among them. The retribution and judgment announced are those which await all who live as did these particularly in the mind of the author.

"Come now, ye rich," *(age nun hoi plousioi),* age nun "come now," second person singular; *hoi plousioi,* "the rich," plural. This is an exclamatory interjection. Those thus addressed are first singled out individually, and then addressed collectively as a class. The rich are often condemned in the sacred writings. (Jer. 4: 8; Isa. 5: 8; Amos 3: 10; Prov. 11: 28; 1 Tim. 6: 19; Luke 6: 24; 18: 24.) We are not from this to assume that there is merit in being poor, or sin in being rich. There is, *per se,* no virtue in poverty, nor vice in riches. A rich man may be, and often is, a good man, and a blessing to the world; and, contrariwise, some of the most corrupt characters on earth are poverty-stricken. The state of beggary to which Lazarus was reduced did not guarantee to him an entrance into Abraham's bosom, nor did the lovely linen garments and the richly laden table of the rich man provide the occasion for his descent into Hades. Riches and poverty are of outward circumstances and not *directly* related to the state of the soul—the determining factor in one's salvation. However, one's inner state is often affected by outward circumstances; and it is this which makes both poverty and riches important factors in one's salvation. Either may be the means to lift one's soul heavenward or drag it downward to destruction. All possessed of a considerable store of this world's goods should carefully and prayerfully ponder these questions: (a) By what means were these material things obtained? (b) How are they being enjoyed? (c) To what use are they being put? If the means by which the wealth was obtained were improper; or, if their mere possession is that in which one finds chief interest; or, if they are not being properly used, then the terrible denunciation about to be delivered by James would be equally applicable to those thus possessed today.

weep and howl for your miseries that are coming upon you. —It is by many believed that the reference here is to the terrible conditions to characterize the rich, unbelieving Jews (so vividly portrayed by the Jewish historian Josephus), at the destruction of Jerusalem, in A.D. 70, by the armies of Titus, the Roman General, when the rich suffered so greatly in the siege there maintained. But, the physical suffering of the poor (who, of course, greatly outnumbered the rich) was as intense in those terrible days as that of the rich; and it seems better to conclude that this is simply a picture of the retribution and judgment which shall come, at the end of the age, and following the general judgment, upon all those who have lived in the fashion here described.

The verbs "weep" and "howl" vividly denote the reaction which ought to characterize those whose doom is certain. Instead of the continual round of banqueting and revelry then characteristic of them, they should weep *(klausate,* ingressive aorist active of *klaio,* begin to cry out in grief), and "howl," *(ololuzontes,* present

upon you. 2 Your riches are corrupted, and your garments are moth-eaten.

active participle of *ololuzo,* an onomatopoetic term). *Onoma-topoeia* is "the formation of a word by imitating the natural sound associated with the object or action involved, for example, tinkle, buzz, chickadee." (Webster's New World Diction-ary.) The Holy Spirit, through James, thus reproduces the sounds which these idle and wicked rich should make over their ultimate destiny. The tenses are significant. They are *to begin* to weep and *to continue* to howl over the "miseries" to befall them in judgment. The word "miseries" (from *talaiporiais)* denotes hard-ship, sufferings, great distresses. This destiny was inevitable to them in their present condition. The phrase, "That are coming upon you," is from *tais eperchomenais* (present middle participle), indicating that in undeviating fashion the difficulties threatened were marching upon them, and these they could neither avoid nor evade. When the day of destruction dawned how ineffectual would their riches be! In less than ten years, a vengeance was visited upon Jerusalem and the Jews, scarcely paralleled in the world's history. When, at length, the besieged city fell before the conquering legions of Rome, the slaughter that followed was be-yond description. Rich and poor were sought out and mercilessly killed; and all, without regard to their material and financial condi-tion, suffered. And, if, as we believe, the writer describes the des-tiny of the rich in judgment, an even more terrible destruction awaits. In view of such a destiny, these ought even now to begin to weep and to howl continuously over their ultimate destiny.

2 Your riches are corrupted,—"Riches," from *ho ploutos,* de-notes that which is full, overflowing; and sums up the earthly pos-sessions of those described. It should be carefully noted that James specifies *whose* riches are corrupted. Emphasis is on the "your." We are not to conclude that *all* riches are corrupted. In Biblical parlance, a rich man, in the objectional sense, is not neces-sarily one possessed of large amounts of money or property, but one who has the wrong attitude toward what he has. It is not the number of dollars, *but the attitude one has toward them,* that de-termines whether one is rich in this sense or not. "And Jesus looked round about, and saith unto his disciples, How hardly shall they that have riches enter into the kingdom of God! And the disciples were amazed at his words. . . . But Jesus answered again, and saith unto them, Children, *how hard it is for them that trust in riches* to enter into the kingdom of God!" (Mark 10: 23, 24.) The apostle John, in his Letter to his esteemed friend Gaius, indicates how safely rich one may be: "Beloved, I pray that *in all things* thou mayest prosper, and be in health, *even* as thy soul prospereth." (3 John 2.) So long as one's soul prospers, the more of this world's goods one possesses the greater one's potentiality for good becomes. Riches are evil only when they impair the soul's health, and become thorns which choke out the wheat. (Luke 8: 14.)

The riches of those particularly described in our text were by the author of James regarded as already "corrupted," *(sesepen,* second person active indicative of *sepo,* rotten; hence, has rotted). Being material in character, such would inevitably become their condition; but, spiritually speaking, this was already true; they were, in the sight of the Lord, even now rotten. How very vivid is the remarkable contrast here drawn! Men (and women, too) may appear in public in the most dazzling garments, they may be arrayed in the most alluring and attractive fashion, in the eyes of men; but, in God's sight, these dashing symbols of wealth are, by the Lord, already regarded as rotten. We are to remember that in Oriental lands, riches, in addition to gold, silver and precious stones, consisted of highly perishable goods, such as grain, oil, food, and garments of many types and kinds. The destruction which all such perishable materials eventually suffer is a figure of the ultimate destruction which shall come upon their possessors from the improper use of wealth.

and your garments are moth-eaten.—*(Setobrota gegonen,* from *ses,* a moth, and *brotos,* to eat; and the perfect indicative of *ginomai,* to become; thus, literally, *have become* moth-eaten.) It is worthy of note that the word "garments," from *himatia,* usually described the *outer* garment, the expensive robe worn in public and thus easily shown off. These garments must inevitably suffer destruction *by moths,* and the body which they covered *by worms*: (Mark 9: 43-48.) How ironical is the fact that the desire of the heart of some thus improperly to adorn the body leads to its own

3 Your gold and your silver are rusted; and their rust shall be for a testimony [18]against you, and shall eat your flesh as fire. Ye have laid up your

[18]Or, *unto*

---

eternal destruction in the fire which is not quenched, and to the everlasting misery of the spirit which it clothes!

3 **Your gold and your silver are rusted;**—It will be observed that the general term for wealth (riches, *ho ploutos)* is used, and then the writer descends to particulars—garments, gold, and silver. To this day in the Arab world it is customary to accumulate such stores as one's financial condition will permit of garments, shawls, robes, rugs, and household furnishings. All such wealth is, of course, susceptible of destruction from the ravages of the years, the corrupting influence of moisture, dry rot, and, in the case of garments, especially the moth.

The verb "rusted," *(katiotai,* perfect passive indicative, from *kata,* and *ioo*), means to rust through, all the way to the bottom. The word thus used to denote the condition of gold and silver improperly held is more properly construed as figurative, inasmuch as gold and silver do not *literally* rust. Not all of the rich would allow their garments to be subjected to moths; not all of them would permit their wealth to rot, or their money to become cankered. Since such material possessions must eventually suffer destruction, it appears likely that James, in this section, figuratively describes the condition eventually to characterize all such, and typical of the end which must inevitably come upon those who hold their wealth improperly as did the rich particularly described in this section. Though silver and gold coins do not literally acquire rust, or deteriorate in this manner, and to the natural eye they may shine with dazzling brilliance, they may, through hoarding, become corroded in the sight of God and thus become a testimony against their possessors in the day of judgment. This, indeed, the writer next affirms:

and their rust shall be for a testimony against you,—The word "testimony" here means a witness *(marturion).* The ruin often characteristic of their hoarded possessions portrayed and testified to their own destruction. It was thus a witness to their own eventual end. They were to experience destruction by the fire of

God's judgment, just as rust, corruption, and decay were destroying their earthly goods. When, from long possession, their garments deteriorated, their money became tarnished, and their jewels discolored, such testified to the improper use to which they had put such possessions. Rust witnesses to disuse, or improper use; and its existence evidences in unmistakable fashion that those in possession thereof have not handled that which is thus affected aright.

and shall eat your flesh as fire.—It is, in this section, affirmed that (1) the riches of those who are particularly warned are corrupted (have become rotten); (2) their garments have been rendered useless by moths; (3) their gold and silver have rusted (become tarnished and corroded); (4) these obvious signs of disuse witness to the sin of mishandling; and (5) the "rust" which has spotted their silver and gold will eventually "eat the flesh" of those addressed "as fire." This latter statement must, of course, be regarded as figurative. It evidently means that as silver and gold must eventually suffer destruction when long hoarded, so *they* must suffer similar destruction in the punishment which awaited them, because of their miserliness and greed. This entire section is reminiscent of the familiar words of our Lord, when he said: "Lay not up for yourselves treasures upon the earth, where moth and rust consume, and where thieves break through and steal: but lay up for yourselves treasure in heaven, where neither moth nor rust doth consume, and where thieves do not break through nor steal: for where thy treasure is, there will thy heart be also." (Matt. 6: 19-21.) Thus, in our text, the gold and silver are, by James, visualized as glowing metal (hugged closely to the heart, perhaps), and ultimately to consume the flesh, i.e., the life. As rust eats through, and destroys metal, so the greed, avarice and love for money which characterized these people would destroy them. This figure is a common one in the Old Testament: "And I will set my face against them; they shall go forth from the fire, but the fire shall devour them; and ye shall know that I am Jehovah, when I set my face against them." (Ezek. 15: 17.) "Therefore will the Lord, Jehovah of hosts, send among his fat ones leanness; and under his glory there shall be kindled a burning like the burning of fire. And the light of Israel will be for a fire, and his Holy One for a flame; and it will burn and devour his thorns and his briers in one day." (Isa. 10: 16.)

It should be not overlooked that the word "flesh," in our text, is plural, literally, "your fleshes," *(tassarkas),* and the reference is to every part of them.   (Cf. Rev. 19: 18, 21.)   It is a solemn thought that the *bodies* on which the rich have lavished so much care, and which they have so richly laden with evidence of their material prosperity, shall suffer destruction in the fire of judgment to come. Here is indirect evidence of the resurrection of the body (of the wicked) which is denied by some materialistic sects.   The reference of James to the destruction of these wicked persons is the same as that of our Lord, when he speaks of "thy whole body be cast into hell," (Matt. 5: 29); "the hell of fire," (5: 22); and the destruction of "both soul and body in hell" (Matt. 10: 28).

Ye have laid up your treasure in the last days.—These of whom James wrote had (a) laid up treasure; (b) the time when it was "laid up" was "in the last days."   The phrase, "in the last days, "must undoubtedly refer to the period immediately preceding the coming of the Lord in judgment. We reject, without hesitation, the view that James (and other New Testament writers), labored under the erroneous impression that the coming of the Lord and the end of the world were about to occur in their day.   The "treasure" which these people had "laid up" for themselves was the condemnation which their conduct deserved. Paul, in a similar affirmation, wrote: "But after thy hardness and impenitent heart *treasurest up for thyself* wrath in the day of wrath and revelation of the righteous judgment of God."   (Rom. 2: 5.)   The bitter irony of this statement should not be lost upon us. Many there are in the world today who imagine themselves to be laying up a sizeable store of this world's goods so that, like the foolish man, they may take their ease and be merry; but, who are, in reality, simply storing up wrath "against the day of wrath," and the terrible retribution which must, because of their wickedness here, inevitably fall upon them. In the light of these solemn facts, all who are possessed of this world's goods, *whether little or much,* should carefully and prayerfully review how such were obtained, how they

treasure in the last days. 4 Behold, the hire of the laborers who mowed your fields, which is of you kept back by fraud, crieth out: and the cries of them that reaped have entered into the ears of the Lord of Sabaoth. 5 Ye

are regarded, and to what use they are being put, that those thus possessed may avoid the destiny here described.

SINS OF THE RICH
5: 4-6

4 **Behold, the hire of the laborers who mowed your fields,** —"Behold," *(idou,* see, consider, take notice of), is a term the design of which was to direct attention particularly to the matter James desired, at the moment, especially to discuss. The "hire" *(homisthos)* was wages; the "laborers" *(ergaton)* were those who worked; the kind of work that is described as mowing in the field *(ton amesanton),* a general term for reaping. The laborers were, therefore, farm workers who toiled in the fields for the rich and from whose labors the rich became even more affluent.

which is of you kept back by fraud, crieth out:—The "hire" (wages) of the poor who reaped their fields, little though it was, was not always paid; under one pretext or another, the rich managed to fleece the poor of their daily wages, thus obtaining not only their labor but the fruits thereof. The phrase, "Which is of you kept back by fraud," is from the Greek *ho aphusteremenos aph' humon,* and means "having been held out by you," a very common and vicious practice through the ages, and particularly characteristic of the land of Judaea in the period in which James wrote. The law of Moses straitly condemned those who retained the wages of a hired workman for even one night (Lev. 19: 13); and the prophet Jeremiah thundered against him who "useth his neighbor's service without wages; and giveth him not his hire." (Jer. 22: 13.) See Mal. 3: 5. The law of the Old Testament was especially jealous of the rights of the poor; and the foregoing rebukes of the prophets indicate gross neglect of the duty enjoined. One of the evidences of the decline of respect for the law, and allegiance to it, was this disregard of its provisions for the poor; and the avarice and greed characteristic of the rich Jews of the first century reveal how far removed from the "old paths" was Judaism in the period in which James wrote.

The relationship of *employer and employee* is one existing in every land and age; and the Scriptures abound with instructions to each. The exploitation of the worker by the employer and the disposition of the employee to shirk his duties to his employer are alike condemned in the sacred writings. Capital and labor both have their rights, and neither may properly encroach upon that of the other. Peace between these segments of our society will come only when each side respects and recognizes the rights of the other, and guarantees them. Both are obligated to each other; neither may exist without the other. Inasmuch as their interests are intertwined, it is to the best interests of both that they work to their common good and neither defraud the other. While, in this instance, James deals with the fraud of the employer, he would, under considerations, condemn the loafing employee as quickly. The employer is entitled to a reasonable return on his investment and the employee to a decent wage for his labors. Neither should steal from the other by withholding that which is due. This, the employer does, when he does not pay a fair wage; this, the employee does, when he loafs on the job and does not give a full measure of activity to his employer. Though the following quotation, from the Colossian Epistle, deals primarily with the relation of masters and servants, the principle is applicable to the employer-employee relationship: "Servants, obey in all things them that are your masters according to the flesh; not with eye-service, as men-pleasers, but in singleness of heart, fearing the Lord; whatsoever ye do, work heartily, as unto the Lord, and not unto men; knowing that from the Lord ye shall receive the recompense of the inheritance: ye serve the Lord Christ. For he that doeth wrong shall receive again for the wrong that he hath done: and there is no respect of persons. Masters, render unto your servants that which is just and equal; knowing that ye also have a master in heaven." (Col. 3: 22-25; 4: 1.)

The fraudulent dealings of the rich "crieth out," and the wrong done *is heard in heaven!* This is, of course, a highly figurative statement, the thought of which occurs more than once in the Old Testament. Abel's blood, shed by his brother Cain, cried out to God from the ground (Gen. 4: 9-13); and the sin of Sodom ascended up to the ears of Jehovah and cried out for punishment (Gen. 19: 13). The word "crieth," *(krazei),* means more than mere weeping. It means to "yell," and thus we learn that the wages which these covetous people improperly retained from their poor laborers *yelled to heaven for vengeance.* It is an interesting observation, often made, that the withholding of that which is due others is one of the four sins which are said to cry out to heaven. (Cf. Gen. 4: 9-13; Heb. 12: 18-29; Gen. 19: 13; Job 16: 18; 31: 38; Rev. 6: 6-9.) To these cries for vengeance God does not turn a deaf ear:

and the cries of them that reaped have entered into the ears of the Lord of Sabaoth.—Though the rich will not listen to the entreaties of the poor whom they are defrauding, *God will;* and he duly records the transaction from which judgment will be rendered in the last day. It will be observed that in this solemn scene, there is a preview of the judgment day. The court is convened, the judge is on the throne, the wages of the oppressed, held back by greedy and fraudulent employers, are present to testify, having already spoken loudly their depositions into the ears of the Great Jehovah, identified here as "the Lord of Sabaoth." The word "Sabaoth" means *hosts,* and thus God is identified here as the Lord of hosts, a term denoting might, power, and glory. Those who have no one *on earth* to secure their rights have one in heaven; he is the Lord of hosts, and is thus amply able to defend them and to guarantee to them justice in the end. Occurring only one other time in the New Testament (and in that instance in a quotation from the Old Testament, Rom. 9: 29), it appears frequently in the Hebrew Old Testament often, though not always, translated by the phrase, "Jehovah of hosts." Occasionally, it is rendered in the Greek Septuagint, by *pantokrator,* Almighty. See Rev. 4: 6, where this significance is found. The Lord of hosts is a familiar appellation for Jehovah in the Old Testament, occurring in Malachi nearly two dozen times. The meaning of our text is, therefore, that God is not unmindful of the oppression of the poor, his ears are ever open to their entreaties, and he will fully avenge them in the day of accounts. He who directs the winds, who holds the worlds in his hands, by whose orders the heavenly hierarchies act, will make available his mighty powers to those who are oppressed

have lived delicately on the earth, and taken your pleasure; ye have nour-

---

and who suffer for their faithfulness here. Those who defraud the poor will one day face the combined might of God. Of the outcome of that conflict there is no doubt. Those who are disposed to deprive others of their due should lay these matters to heart, and solemnly determine whether the pittance thus unfairly obtained is worth the ultimate cost.

5 Ye have lived delicately on the earth,—The word "delicately" describes the manner of living characteristic of those so severely condemned. The verb is from *etruphesate,* aorist indicative of *truphao,* to lead an indolent, fleshly indulgent life for the gratification of the flesh, and for the pleasure of a worldly mind. The word occurs nowhere else in the New Testament. The life described is one of luxury and extravagance, and made possible, in large measure, by depriving toilers in the field of their just wages. It is well to take note of the fact that the word here used does not denote a wicked and sinful life, *per se;* although the fraud they practiced was in this category; their manner of living, though not of itself sin, was useless, indolent, vain; it contributed nothing to the welfare of others, nor to the advancement of the persons thus engaging. One does not have to live a sinful life to fall under the censure of the Lord; a life the design of which is fleshly ease and personal gratification is everywhere condemned in the Scriptures. Of course those thus censured by James added active and vicious sin by the methods which they used to obtain money. We should be impressed with the fact that though the latter is not characteristic of us, if we live indolently, selfishly, uselessly, our lives are not pleasing in the sight of God. The fact that we possess life creates within us an obligation to perform useful duties and to add our share to the sum of useful activity in the world. "And he said unto them: Take heed, and keep yourselves from all covetousness; for a man's life consisteth not in the abundance of the things which he possesseth. And he spake a parable unto them, saying, The ground of a certain rich man brought forth plentifully: and he reasoned within himself, saying, What shall I do, because I have not where to bestow my fruits? And he said, This will I do: I will pull down my barns and build greater; and there will I bestow all my grain and my goods. And I will say to my soul, Soul, thou hast much goods laid up for many years; take thine ease, eat, drink, be merry. But God said unto him, Thou foolish one, this night is thy soul required of thee; and the things which thou hast prepared, whose shall they be? So is he that layeth up treasure for himself, and is not rich toward God." (Luke 12 : 15-21.)

and taken your pleasure;—The verb is *espatalesate,* aorist active indicative of *spatalao,* to live wastefully, wantonly. These people were thus living both *uselessly* and *wastefully;* they contributed nothing to the age in which they lived; and, they were consuming, in extravagant fashion, the material blessings of God, which they had obtained by deceptive and oppressive measures. This is a vivid picture of the idle rich, multiplied instances of which may be seen in almost every land, and throughout the ages. These have their treasure on earth, and make no provision for heaven; and they shall of course have none there. In addition, they must suffer for their sins in hell throughout eternity. Those who choose to have their "good things" (Luke 16 : 25) *here* will not be heard to complain when the good things of heaven are withheld from them *hereafter.* Those who live for pleasure alone soon eventually lose the ability to live for any other reason. A life of ease enervates the mind and body, renders the individual thus influenced unable to exercise himself in useful pursuits, makes honest toil highly disagreeable, and induces a state of mind that prompts one to use all of his faculties in worthless pursuits, rather than in gainful employment. Jesus warned of this disposition when he said to his disciples, "But take heed to yourselves, lest haply your hearts be overcharged with surfeiting, and drunkenness, and cares of this life, and that day come on you suddenly as a snare: for so shall it come upon all them that dwell on the face of the earth." (Luke 21 : 34, 35.)

ye have nourished your hearts in a day of slaughter.—To "nourish" here is *ethrepsate,* aorist active indicative of *trepho,* to fatten. The figure is of animals fed and fattened for butchering. Animals, in order to be fattened quickly, are provided *all the food they can consume;* here, the hearts of these indolent Jews are said to have been fattened; i.e., supplied with everything they desired. Though this was the design of these rich people, James does not let

ished your hearts in a day of slaughter. 6 Ye have condemned, ye have killed the righteous *one*; he doth not resist you.

---

the figure rest there; he pursues it to its obvious conclusion. True, they were engaged in the fattening business; and, that which they were fattening was their own hearts; but what they did not take into account was the fact that they were simply fattening themselves for a day of slaughter—*their own!* The day of slaughter is the judgment. This statement is reminiscent of one by Amos, in which that ancient prophet portrayed the idleness and ease which prevailed among the people of his day: "Woe unto them that are at ease in Zion . . . that lie upon beds of ivory, and stretch themselves upon their couches, and eat the lambs out of the flock, and the calves out of the midst of the stall; that sing idle songs to the sound of the viol; that invent for themselves instruments of music like David; that drink wine in bowls, and anoint themselves with the chief oils; but they are not grieved for the affliction of Joseph." (Amos 6: 1-6.)

Notwithstanding the fact that those who live in the manner described by James and Amos regard themselves as especially astute and wise, because of their ability to accumulate large stores of wordly goods, and thus to be able to live in luxurious and voluptuous style, the measure of such a man's life is simple stupidity. We do not regard as wise the stupid pig which follows a few grains of corn from the pen to the slaughterhouse; nor is a man either prudent or understanding who surfeits his heart with the things of this world at the expense of his soul; and who, in James' words, fattens his heart for the day of slaughter.

The *tenses* of the verbs of this sentence are significant. They are aorist active indicatives; and they represent the viewpoint of the inspired writer as at the day of judgment from which point he looks back upon the lives of those described, and portrays the condition which shall characterize them when they stand before the judgment seat of Christ. (2 Cor. 5: 10.) The tenses give vividness and emphasis to the statement, and they reveal in retrospect the lives of those thus condemned. It is as if James had said: "We are now at the judgment; this is the way you lived; therefore your destruction is inevitable, because you prepared yourselves for this destiny."

6 **Ye have condemned, ye have killed the righteous one;**—
The verbs of these clauses are aorist active indicatives; hence, a
better rendering is, "Ye condemned, ye killed the Righteous One."
The first verb is from *katadike,* condemnation; and denotes the
fact that the rich were able to influence even the courts of the land
and to secure sentences in keeping with their wishes.   To the
grievous sins of fraud and oppression, the rich, who were the objects of James' severe denunciations, added the crime of subordina-
tion, they controlled the courts and influenced the decisions of the
judges.   The verb *katedikasate* has the implication of a trial, le-
gally arranged to determine the innocence or guilt of an accused;
but, the accused had already been adjudged guilty by those who
arraigned him and the trial was, therefore, a mockery of justice.

"Ye have killed the Righteous One" denotes the carrying out of
the predetermined sentence of the court thus influenced. Thus in
addition to fraud, to oppression, to corruption of legal procedures,
the rich particularly condemned by James compounded their guilt
by becoming accessories before the fact to legal murder. This is
not an unusual order. So insidious is sin in its working that men
are led on from one crime to another until they do not shrink from
the capital crime of murder. Earlier James, in tracing the course
of sin, indicated its steps as follows: "Let no man say when he is
tempted, I am tempted of God; for God cannot be tempted with
evil, and he himself tempteth no man: but each man is tempted,
when he is drawn away by his own lust, and enticed. Then the
lust, when it hath conceived, beareth sin: and the sin, when it is
fullgrown, bringeth forth death."   (James 1: 13-15.)

Who is the "Righteous One," to whom reference is made in this
text?   There are two views widely advocated: (1) The (any)
righteous man, in contrast with the wicked man; (2) the Lord
Jesus Christ. Those who subscribe to the first view allege that
(a) it is not likely that James would blame the rich Jews to whom
he addressed his sharp denunciations for the death of Christ, which
crime was committed by others, and many years earlier; (b) the
"righteous one" is to be regarded as representative of a class, in
contrast with the wicked (Isa. 3: 10); (c) the reference is to any
good man who might be treated as these wicked Jews dealt with
the poor of James' day. These objections are exceedingly weak

and inconclusive. The allegation that the Jews of that day would not be blamed with the guilty of the death of our Lord because they did not personally participate in it is not relevant; that act was the culmination of a national sin in which all were participants and those who did not accept Christ persisted in the rebellion characteristic of the nation as a whole. Moreover, it was characteristic of the inspired writers and of the Lord himself to see in the wicked acts of those of their day the fruit and hence the guilt of sins committed in earlier days.

As an example of the foregoing, note that Zachariah, the son of Barachiah, was slain many centuries before our Lord came to the earth, yet Christ clearly indicated that the Jews of the final days of the Jewish age shared in the guilt: "Woe unto you, scribes and Pharisees, hypocrites! for ye build the sepulchres of the prophets, and garnish the tombs of the righteous, and say, If we had been in the days of our fathers, we should not have been partakers with them in the blood of the prophets. Wherefore ye witness to yourselves, that ye are sons of them that slew the prophets. Fill ye up then the measures of your fathers. Ye serpents, ye offspring of vipers, how shall ye escape the judgment of hell? Therefore, behold, I send unto you prophets, and wise men, and scribes: some of them shall ye kill and crucify; and some of them shall ye scourge in your synagogues, and persecute from city to city: that upon you may come all the righteous blood shed on the earth, from the blood of Abel the righteous unto the blood of Zachariah son of Barachiah, whom ye slew between the sanctuary and the altar." (Matt. 23 : 29-35.)

The phraseology, the context, and the facts all point impressively to Christ as the "Righteous One" intended. (a) The Greek phrase is *ton dikaion,* singular number; hence "the Just (righteous) one"; (b) by this phrase our Lord is repeatedly identified in the New Testament. (Acts 3 : 14.) "But ye denied the Holy and Righteous One, *(dikaion),* and asked for a murderer to be delivered unto you." (Acts 7 : 52.) "Which of the prophets did not your fathers persecute? and they killed them that showed before of the coming of the Righteous One *(tou dikaiou);* of whom ye have now become betrayers and murderers." "The God of our fathers hath appointed thee to know his will, and to see the Righteous

One, *(ton dikaion),* and to hear a voice from his mouth." (Acts 22: 14.) "My little children, these things write I unto you that ye may not sin. And if any man sin, we have an Advocate with the Father, Jesus Christ the righteous" *(dikaion).* (1 John 2: 1.) To what other victim condemned by a corrupt court, and murdered under legal pretense, might these words be more properly applied? The conclusion seems irresistible that the title, "The Righteous One," can be applied only to Christ, the antitype of all who have died unjustly for the cause of the Great Jehovah.

he doth not resist you.—The antecedent is "he" is the "Righteous One" of the preceding clause; the "you," the rich persecutors. Here is additional evidence of the correctness of the exegesis given above. Christ did not resist his antagonists, but submitted himself to their persecution uncomplainingly. "For hereunto were ye called; because Christ also suffered for you, leaving you an example, that ye should follow his steps: who when he was reviled, reviled not again; when he suffered, threatened not, but committed himself to him that judgeth righteously." (1 Pet. 2: 21-23.) And, in the great Messianic chapter of Isa. 53 (and quoted by Luke in his narrative of Philip and the eunuch, Acts 8: 32, 33), it is said of the Lord: "He was oppressed, yet when he was afflicted he opened not his mouth; as a lamb that is led to the slaughter, and as a sheep that before its shearers is dumb, so he opened not his mouth." (Isa. 53: 7.) Only those who follow his example in these matters are by him regarded as his faithful disciples: "Ye have heard that it was said, An eye for an eye, and a tooth for a tooth: but I say unto you, Resist not him that is evil: but whosoever smiteth thee on thy right cheek, turn to him the other also. . . Ye have heard that it was said, Thou shalt love thy neighbor, and hate thine enemy: but I say unto you, Love your enemies, and pray for them that persecute you; that ye may be sons of your Father who is in heaven." (Matt. 5: 38, 39, 43-45.)

SECTION 12
5: 7-12

PATIENCE AND THE LORD'S RETURN
5: 7-9

7 Be patient therefore, brethren, until the [1]coming of the Lord. Behold, the husbandman waiteth for the precious fruit of the earth, being patient

[1]Gr. *presence.*

---

7 **Be patient therefore, brethren,**—Here, the inspired writer returns to the main stream of thought in the Epistle, and again writes directly to the "brethren," from whom he had turned aside, beginning at 5: 1, to address the unbelieving rich whose oppressive measures and fraudulent practices were so burdensome to the poor disciples. The ultimate retribution and destruction which shall eventually fall upon all of those who thus do have been made crystal clear; they shall receive their just recompense of reward; those who suffer at their hands and are faithful to the end shall be blessed; *therefore,* (in view of these facts), "be patient!" These words translate the verb *makrothumesate,* aorist active imperative of *makrothumeo,* derived from *makros,* and *thumos,* literally, long of temper, that is, one not short of the will to persist; longsuffering. It is as if James had said, "Your trials are now exceedingly great, and the wrongs you are experiencing at the hands of the wicked are especially flagrant; but, this must eventually end; the Lord will see that justice is done to all, provided you follow his example of longsuffering and patience."

It is noteworthy that the word translated "patient" here *(makrothumeo)* is not the same as that thus rendered in the first chapter of the Epistle. (James 1: 3ff.) There, it is the word *hupomone,* to bear up under. The first of these words *(makrothumeo)* is used to denote patience with *persons,* the second *(hupomone)* with *things.* In James 1, the writer bids his readers to endure the trials of life knowing that the exercise of patience produces strength of character. In James 5, the suffering saints are to exhibit longsuffering toward their tormentors, knowing that God will certainly avenge them and see to it that full justice is done. Thus, the meaning is, "With unwavering determination bear up under the burdens which weigh so heavily upon you, knowing that a day of redress is coming." Implied is the assurance that the triumph of the faithful will be contemporary with the overthrow and destruction of the wicked. In similar vein, Paul wrote to the Thessalonians: "We are bound to give thanks to God always for you, brethren, even as it is meet, for that your faith groweth exceedingly, and the love of each one of you all toward one another aboundeth; so that we ourselves glory in you in the churches of God for your patience and faith in all your persecutions and in the afflictions which ye endure; which is a manifest token of the righteous judgment of God; to the end that ye may be counted worthy of the kingdom of God, for which ye also suffer: if so be that it is a righteous thing with God to recompense affliction to them that afflict you, and to you that are afflicted rest with us, at the revelation of the Lord Jesus from heaven with the angels of his power in flaming fire, rendering vengeance to them that know not God, and to them that obey not the gospel of our Lord Jesus: who shall suffer punishment, even eternal destruction from the face of the Lord and from the glory of his might, when he shall come to be glorified in his saints, and to be marvelled at in all them that believed (because our testimony unto you was believed) in that day." (2 Thess. 1: 3-10.)

James' design in emphasizing the eventual retribution to come upon the wicked oppressors of that day was to vindicate their sense of justice, and to remind those to whom he wrote *that right would eventually triumph.* The will to resist, to endure, to be faithful fades in unbelief; but, those whose faith remains steadfast know that ultimately those who do wrong will be properly punished, and those who do right will be richly rewarded. Supported by this realization, they suffer uncomplainingly life's hardships and difficulties.

until the coming of the Lord.—The "Lord" is, of course, Christ; "the coming," his return on the clouds. (Acts 1: 11; Heb. 9: 28.) The reference here is to his *second* coming at which time the consummation of all things will occur. This "coming" of our Lord is referred to repeatedly in the New Testament, there being more than three hundred references either directly or indirectly to this event. (Cf. Matt. 24: 3; 1 Thess. 2: 19; 2 Pet. 3: 4.) Believers throughout the Christian dispensation are taught to "watch" for (live in expectation of) the coming of the Lord, and thus be prepared for that event. (Mark 13: 33-37.) It is not correct to say that the apostles believed they would be living when the Lord returned; they knew no more of the *time* of his return than do we. *Because they did not know when he would come, they instructed people to live as if he would come at any moment.* This is all that this (and similar statements of Holy Writ) imply; and it is neither right nor necessary to imply that (a) the inspired writers erroneously thought the Lord would come in their day; or (b) that this has reference to the coming of the Lord for the saints at death. On the contrary, Peter in his second Epistle indicates that he would die before the event: "Wherefore I shall be ready always to put you in remembrance of these things though ye know them and are established in the truth which is in you. And I think it right, as long as I am in this tabernacle, to stir you up by putting you in remembrance: knowing that the putting off of my tabernacle cometh swiftly, even as our Lord Jesus Christ signified unto me. Yes, I will give diligence that at every time ye may be able after my decease to call these things to remembrance." (2 Pet. 1 : 12-15.)

It should be particularly noted that Peter, in the foregoing statement, penned shortly before his death, desired and expected the brethren to call to remembrance what he had written after his "decease," thus indicating that they would outlive him, that they would need the instruction he was giving them; and hence time would not terminate with his passing. That the early disciples *hoped* for the coming of the Lord, *prayed* for it, and lived daily *in expectation of it,* we do not doubt (2 Pet. 3: 9ff.) ; such should and must be characteristic of the saints today if we are to please God; but this is far from saying that from any intimation of the Lord or statement of the Holy Spirit a conclusion may be properly drawn that he would come at any *specific* time. It is for the very reason that we do not *know* when he is coming that the event is ever nigh and for which we must always be in complete readiness. The allegation that the inspired writers predicted the coming of the Lord in their day is to convict them of error. That some Bible expositors imply or affirm such indicates what low and unworthy views they entertain of the inspiration and inerrancy of the Scriptures.

The *fact* of the Lord's return is, to Bible believers, beyond controversy; the *time* of it is hidden in the inscrutable counsel of the divine will. Of the *certainty* of it we need entertain no doubt whatsoever; because we do not know *the time* we must live in a state of readiness. The *certainty* of his coming *and the uncertainty* of the time thereof taken together operate to keep our faith, our hope and our patience ever alive and alert. The suffering saints, oppressed by their rich and dishonest employers, were to endure patiently whatever life held for them, assured that the Lord would eventually come, end their oppression, punish their oppressors, and reward them for their faithfulness, longsuffering and fidelity to his cause.

Behold, the husbandman waiteth for the precious fruit of the earth,—"Behold," *idou,* See! Look! Take notice of! A device designed to focus attention particularly on the illustration of the "husbandman." The "husbandman" *(ho georgos,* from *ge,* earth; and *ergo,* to work; thus, literally, a worker in the earth) is a farmer, a tiller of the soil. With patience *(makrothumon,* longsuffering), he waits *(ekdechetai,* looks with expectation) for "the precious fruit of the earth," the harvest of grain. The farmer is well aware of the fact that if he is to receive the earth's precious fruit, he must exercise patience and wait out the normal season for the fruition and harvest. It was the design of James to show that it is the conviction that future good justifies present effort that makes all trial endurable. The harvest is at the end of the effort; not at its beginning. (Matt. 13: 39) One must sow in order to reap.

being patient over it, until it receive the early and latter rain.—All who farm, or are acquainted with the cultivation of the soil, know that there are frequent periods of uncertainty during the growing season; sometimes uncertainty whether there will be any harvest at all. The experienced tiller of the soil is aware of this, and does not lose faith in the natural laws and the promise of God. Having done his part, he trusts to God and to the agencies which God uses to supply "seed to the sower and bread for food" (2 Cor. 9: 10); and he knows that "while the earth remaineth, seedtime and harvest, and cold, and heat, and summer and winter, and day and night shall not cease" (Gen. 8: 22). He, therefore, exhibits pa-

over it, until [2]it receive the early and latter rain. 8 Be ye also patient;

²Or, *he*

tience (longsuffering), "until it receive the early and latter rain."
The early and latter rains are often mentioned in the Old Testament. (Deut. 11: 14; Jer. 5: 24; Hos. 6: 3; Joel 2: 23.) The
early rain was that which came about October, soon after or about
the time of the fall sowing, and which provided the necessary moisture for the grain to germinate; the *latter rain* fell about March,
and which caused the grain to fill out and ripen. Thus the patient
farmer implicitly trusted the Lord to provide him with the moisture to make his grain sprout, the rain to cause his grain to fill out
and be bountiful, always confident that God would not fail him.
The lesson is, therefore, one of patience; of waiting for the development of that which, like seedtime and harvest, works out for
man's ultimate good.

8 **Be ye also patient;**—The Greek word translated "patient" is
the same as that occurring in verse 7 *(makrothumeo),* a better
rendering of which is "longsuffering." The burdened disciple, in
imitation of the farmer, is to wait patiently for deliverance from his
trials, and for the certain triumph of justice in his case. Christians
should not fruitlessly fret against life's difficulties, nor wearily
wear their lives away on useless anxiety over the hardships which
press them in on every side; they are to realize, as does the farmer,
that the law of God is operative for them, and it will accomplish
the divine purpose in his own good time. The tiller of the soil is
aware that he cannot possibly speed the processes by which the
ground brings forth her fruit; but he also knows that under the
beneficent influences of sun and shower the earth will give bounti-
fully from her store of good things. In like fashion, though the
seed of truth may lie buried for long seasons, the law in the spiritual world is as immutable and sure as that in the natural world,
and it will ultimately operate to bless and deliver and save those
who conform thereto.

establish your hearts:—"Establish," *(sterixate,* to strengthen,
to make stable), means to make the purposes of the heart firm and
sure and unwavering in the face of the trials then besetting them.
The strength by which this was to be accomplished was the assurance that their cause was just, the Lord was coming, and would

vindicate them fully, and punish their oppressors. Because it is not easy to live the Christian life, all of us need the admonition given. The verb means literally to prop, brace, from *sterix,* a support; we are, therefore, to prop up our hearts by faith, and not let them sag into weary moodiness, weakening uncertainty, and eventual unbelief. The admonition to establish (strengthen) our hearts is one often occurring in the sacred writing. See 1 Thess. 3: 13, where, however, it is God who is said to establish them for us, which, of course, he does through the assurances he gives in his word. James was later to write: "Behold, we call them blessed that endured." (James 5: 11.) Hebrews 11, Inspiration's Hall of Fame for the gallant heroes of the faith of ages long passed, demonstrates the ultimate triumph of those who, despite great difficulty, trusted God implicitly for the fulfillment of his promises.

for the coming of the Lord is at hand.—The significance of this statement is the same as that in verse 7, where reference is made to "the coming of the Lord." See the comments there. The word translated "coming" is, in the Greek, *parousia,* which means presence. See margin. The return of Christ is so real, so certain, so sure of fulfillment, that he is always regarded as near at hand. This is as true for us today as it was of those of the apostolic age, in view of the fact that he *may* come at any moment. It is, however, quite certain that James did not mean that there was evidence that the Lord would appear in the lifetime of those living, inasmuch as Jesus himself taught that no one knows the time of his return except the Father: "But of that day and hour knoweth no one, not even the angels of heaven, neither the Son, but the Father only. And as were the days of Noah, so shall be the coming of the Son of man. For as in those days which were before the flood they were eating and drinking, marrying and giving in marriage, until the day that Noah entered into the ark, and they knew not until the flood came and took them all away; *so shall be the coming of the Son of man.*" (Matt. 24: 36-39.) It is incorrect to speak of "the delay" of the return of Christ. The word "delay" means: "to put off to a future time; postpone." It implies interference of something that causes a detainment or postponement. (See Webster's New World Dictionary of the English Language.) Thus, to speak of "the delay" of the return of Christ is to imply that the event is off schedule, postponed, not in keeping with the original arrangement. But, inasmuch as we are without any information whatsoever regarding any "original arrangement," how do we know that the Lord has delayed his coming? We may be sure that it is on schedule, and in exact harmony with his purpose and plan. We must carefully avoid the disposition characteristic of many today to assign to terms in the Scripture which refer to the acts of deity the limitations which are true of men. It is because of this practice that some are disposed to interpret the clause, "the coming of the Lord is at hand," to mean that it was then imminent. That such was not its significance is clear from the fact that nearly two thousand years have elapsed since these words were penned, and the Lord has not yet come. We must not overlook the fact also that with God, who inhabits eternity, matters may be "at hand," in his view, which are greatly distant in our human imperfect concept. (Compare Isa. 13: 6.) Peter points to some in his day who alleged that, because things continued in regular fashion and without variation from the uniformity which has characterized the world for ages, it was not likely that he would *ever* come:

"Knowing this first, that in the last days mockers shall come with mockery, walking after their own lusts, and saying, Where is the promise of his coming? for, from the day that the fathers fell asleep, all things continue as they were from the beginning of the creation. For this they wilfully forget, that there were heavens from of old, and an earth compacted out of water and amidst water, by the word of God; by which means the world that then was, being overflowed with water, perished: but the heavens that now are, and the earth, by the same word have been stored up for fire, being reserved against the day of judgment and destruction of ungodly men." (2 Pet. 3: 3-7.) In the light of these most solemn facts, Peter admonished his readers to give diligence to be "found in peace, without spot and blameless in his sight." (2 Pet. 3: 14.) We may, therefore, be certain that the Lord will come; he will come on schedule, he will come unexpectedly, "as a thief in the night," at which time the earth, "and the works that are therein shall be burned up." "Seeing that these things are thus all to be dissolved, what manner of persons ought ye to be in all holy living

establish your hearts: for the ¹coming of the Lord is at hand. 9 Murmur
not, brethren, one against another, that ye be not judged: behold, the judge

---

and godliness, looking for and earnestly desiring the coming of the
day of God, by reason of which the heavens being on fire shall be
dissolved, and the elements shall melt with fervent heat? But, according to his promise we look for new heavens and a new earth,
wherein dwelleth righteousness." (2 Pet. 3: 10-13.)

9 **Murmur not, brethren, one against another,**—The verb is a
present active imperative, with the negative, from *stenazo,* to
groan; thus, literally, "Do not keep on groaning against each
other. . ." The verb denotes fretfulness, impatience with others;
the disposition to blame others for one's distresses. The saints to
whom these words were addressed were sorely burdened, their lives
were exceedingly hard; and it was, therefore, not always easy for
them to bear up under their difficulties with patience and resignation. Often, they were fretful, morose, quarrelsome, disposed to
blame their brethren, easy to take offense, and quick to find fault
with others, all of which made their own lives miserable, and
created serious problems for others. Some, of course, are by nature disposed to be difficult to get along with; such exhibit a sour
and unpleasant temper; they never see anything good in others, or
anything improper in themselves; they are envious, jealous, and
critical of all others. Their attitude is wholly foreign to the spirit
of Christ, and is repeatedly condemned in the Scriptures. (Matt.
7: 1; Luke 3: 14; Phil. 4: 11; Heb. 13: 5.) Such a disposition of
heart and mind the saints were to strive always to avoid. The present imperative indicates that the situation was a continuing one,
and therefore ever necessary to watch. This admonition of James
we would all do well to consider earnestly. It is easy to become a
chronic grumbler. It requires but few brains, and but little intelligence. It is the surest way to lose any friends one may have.
Those who practice such are condemned.

that ye be not judged:—To murmur is to pass judgment of an
adverse character upon others; and those who thus do shall be
judged (condemned) themselves. Those who improperly assume
the office of judge will themselves suffer judgment (condemnation). There is an undoubted allusion to the words of the Lord in
the Sermon on the Mount: "Judge not, that ye be not judged.

For with what judgment ye judge, ye shall be judged: and with what measure ye mete, it shall be measured unto you. And why beholdest thou the mote that is in thy brother's eye, but considerest not the beam that is in thine own eye? Or how wilt thou say to thy brother, Let me cast out the mote out of thine eye; and lo, the beam is in thine own eye? Thou hypocrite, cast out first the beam out of thine own eye; and then shalt thou see clearly to cast out the mote out of thy brother's eye." (Matt. 7: 1-5.)

behold, the judge standeth before the doors.—Literally, ". . . is standing before the doors," *(pro ton thuron hesteken,* perfect active indicative), and thus ready to execute sentence. The "judge" is Christ; the phrase, "before the door," indicates his nearness. This statement corroborates our interpretation of the phrase, "the coming of the Lord is at hand," inasmuch as it indicates that the certainty of the judgment was such that Christ is represented as *even then* standing outside the door ready to enter and execute judgment. That it was not intended to mean that this would actually occur *in that day* is evident from the fact that twenty centuries have passed and the judgment is yet future. All that is meant is that the day of retribution for the evil is certain and sure and the one who shall administer punishment should be regarded as at the door, ready to enter at any time. An inspired commentary on this statement, "standeth before the doors," is to be seen in Rev. 3: 20, where Christ is represented as standing before the door of the church in Laodicea: "Behold, I stand at the door and knock: if any man hear my voice and open the door, I will come in to him, and will sup with him, and he with me." The figure, "before the door," represents Christ as (a) near; (b) in position to enter suddenly and unexpectedly; and (c) ready to accomplish his purpose without delay. It was therefore vitally important that those to whom James wrote should cease their murmuring and complaining lest the Lord should open the door without advance notice and discover that instead of waiting patiently and faithfully for him they were fretful, dissatisfied and morose, and engaged in quarrels among themselves. The author has assured his readers that they would be blessed for their patience and longsuffering; and here he points out that if murmuring and dissatisfaction have been substituted therefor, they must suffer judg-

standeth before the doors. 10 Take, brethren, for an example of suffering

ment themselves. God will not fail to avenge his faithful; but he will judge them if they fall short of his will. Compare Rom. 12: 19 with 1 Pet. 4: 19. See, especially, in this connection, the parable of the wicked servant. (Luke 12: 45-48.)

EXAMPLES OF PATIENCE
5: 10, 11

10 **Take, brethren, for an example of suffering and of patience, the prophets**—The order of the Greek is emphatic: "For an example of affliction and longsuffering, take, brethren, the prophets. . ." *(Hupodeigma labete, adelphoi, tes kakopathias, kai tes makrothumias, tous prophetas.)* The word translated "suffering" *(kakopathias)* denotes suffering from without and is thus objective in character; the word "patience" *(makrothumia)* is subjective and indicates the manner in which the suffering was accepted. The word "example," (from *hupodeigma),* means a copy to be imitated. Thus, the meaning is, "Brethren, for the proper way to endure affliction, follow the example of the prophets." The prophets were seldom far removed from persecution and trial; as a class, they were the most persecuted men in history. (Matt. 23: 34.) "Which of the prophets did not your fathers persecute? and they killed them that showed before of the coming of the Righteous One! of whom ye have now become betrayers and murderers." (Acts 7: 52.) Jesus said, "Blessed are ye when men shall reproach you, and persecute you, and say all manner of evil against you falsely, for my sake, Rejoice, and be exceeding glad: for great is your reward in heaven: *for so persecuted they the prophets* that were before you." (Matt. 5: 12.)

The disciples to whom James wrote, many of whom were of Jewish ancestry, would be familiar with the manifold instances of affliction and suffering experienced by Isaiah, Jeremiah, Daniel, Elijah and others. Those godly men did not escape persecution; we may, therefore, expect it; these men endured faithfully the trials of life; so should we. They suffered with patience; they thus serve as examples for all succeeding generations who would in such fashion please God. Suffering is, indeed, for the faithful disciple, and when experienced for righteousness sake, a token of divine approval. Peter said, "Beloved, think it not strange concerning the fiery trial among you, which cometh upon you to prove you, as though a strange thing happened unto you: but insomuch as ye are partakers of Christ's sufferings, rejoice; that at the revelation of the name of Christ blessed are ye, because the Spirit of glory and the Spirit of God resteth upon you. . . . But if a man suffer as a Christian, let him not be ashamed; but let him glorify God in this name." (1 Pet. 4: 12-16.)

who spake in the name of the Lord.—These were the prophets alluded to in the preceding clause; they "spake," (taught) in the "name of the Lord," i.e., by the Lord's authority. Theirs was thus a divine mission; and the message which they delivered to the people was authenticated by the Lord and inspired by the Spirit. Here is additional evidence of the validity and truth of the writings of the prophets of the Old Testament. The word "prophet," from *pro* and *phemi,* means to speak for, or on behalf of, another; and thus those of this classification in both the Old and the New Testament were mouthpieces for God, the instruments by which he delivered his message to the people. Often, the message was highly unpalatable to the wicked and rebellious people; and they showed their resentment by evilly treating the messengers. To reject the message was not only to reject the messenger, but also him Who originated the message—*God himself.* It will be recalled that when Samuel, in somewhat petulant fashion, informed God that he had been rejected by the people of Israel, when they demanded a king, God said to him, "Hearken unto the voice of the people in all that they say unto thee; for they have not rejected thee, they have rejected me that I should not be king over them." (1 Sam. 8: 4-9.) The statement is evidently elliptical. The meaning is, "They have not rejected thee *only,* they have *also* rejected me that I should not reign over them." The suffering saints, so cruelly mistreated by their rich and oppressive employers, might well look to the prophets as examples of those whose faith failed not, but who served Jehovah under the most trying circumstances. Patient endurance under great difficulty is an object lesson in faith to others. It serves to induce those of us who witness it to try a little harder on the ground that if others can succeed under trial, so can we. What great multitudes of the sorely tried must have gained great

and of patience, the prophets who spake in the name of the Lord. 11 Behold, we call them blessed that endured: ye have heard of the [3]patience of Job, and have seen the end of the Lord, how that the Lord is full of pity, and merciful.

---

[3]Or, *endurance*

---

strength and renewed faith from the noble examples of Heb. 11! How wonderful it is to know that we, like Abraham, may through the eye of faith see beyond the distant haze, "the city" which "hath the foundations, whose builder and maker is God!"

11 Behold, we call them blessed that endured:—For the significance of the word "behold," see the comments on this word at verse 7, above. The "we" includes not only James and the faithful disciples to whom he wrote, but all who honor and respect those who, through great trial and affliction, maintain their loyalty to God and their devotion to his will. "Blessed" is from *makarizomen,* present active indicative of *makarizo,* from *makarios* "happy." However, the word "happy" does not adequately convey the meaning of the term used here. Happiness, from *hap,* chance, denotes that which is accidental and which depends on outward circumstances; here, the blessedness which the word indicates is inward, and results from the peace which reigns in the hearts of those who faithfully serve the Lord. The form of the word occurring here appears in Luke 1: 48, its only other instance in the New Testament, although the word *makarios* (the word for the Beatitudes, Matt. 5: 3-11) occurs often. The faithful have, through the ages, often suffered great harrassment, endured much hardship and suffered agonizing pain. In one of the most vivid passages of the Bible, the Hebrew writer describes the trials of the saints in ages past in the following remarkable fashion:

"And what shall I more say? for the time will fail me if I tell of Gideon, Barak, Samson, Jephthah; of David and Samuel and the prophets: who through faith subdued kingdoms, wrought righteousness, obtained promises, stopped the mouths of lions, quenched the power of fire, escaped the edge of the sword, from weakness were made strong, waxed mighty in war, turned to flight armies of aliens. Women received their dead by a resurrection; and others were tortured, not accepting their deliverance; that they might obtain a better resurrection: and others had trial of mockings and scourgings, yea, moreover of bonds and imprisonment: they were stoned, they were sawn asunder, they were tempted, they were slain with the sword: they went about in sheepskins, in goatskins; being destitute, afflicted, ill-treated (of whom the world was not worthy), wandering in deserts and mountains and caves, and the holes of the earth." (Heb. 11: 32-38.)

If the good and great of past ages suffered so much for the Cause they loved, why should we hope to obtain the garland they wore if we shrink from the battles they fought so valiantly? We call them blessed. Why? Because they did not waver in faith. Had they thrown their weapons down and had forsaken the fray, no one would have honored their name or called them blessed. Only those who endure are regarded as blessed.

Those who "endured" were those who bore up uncomplainingly under the burdens which were theirs, and whose faith did not fail in the hours of trial. The verb "endured" is from the Greek *hupomeno* which, as a participle, means to exhibit patience in matters pertaining to things. For its significance, and the distinction which obtains between it and the word translated "patient" *(makrothumo)* occurring earlier in the chapter, see the comments on verse 5. The meaning here is that the faithful to whom James alludes here bore uncomplainingly the heavy loads of life which included galling persecution, intense suffering and bitter hardship of many kinds. It is the determination to serve God, whatever the odds, plus patient endurance, that prompts succeeding generations to call those who thus endure blessed. The inspired writer pointed his readers to these instances of faithfulness and devotion by great and good men to encourage them in the fiery trial through which they were then passing. It was not James' intention to leave the impression that the reward inherent in the term "blessed" would be received in this life: on the contrary, many evils persist, and are never corrected here; but it is a matter of faith that in God's own good time, he will redress the wrongs of the poor, and mete out to the wicked the punishment they deserve in the day of final accounts. The Psalmist once fretted greatly over this matter. He observed that the good are often in great difficulty and the wicked often prosper; and he penned the following words, to indicate his perplexity:

"Surely God is good to Israel, even to such as are pure in heart. But as for me, my feet were almost gone; my steps had well nigh slipped. For I was envious at the arrogant, when I saw the prosperity of the wicked. For there are no pangs in their death; but their strength is firm. *They are not in trouble as other men; neither are they plagued like other men.* Therefore pride is as a chain about their neck; violence covereth them as a garment. Their eyes stand out with fatness: they have more than heart could wish. They scoff, and in wickedness utter oppression: they speak loftily They have set their mouth in the heavens, and their tongue walketh through the earth. Therefore his people return hither; and waters of a full cup are drained by them. And they say, How doth God know? And is there knowledge in the Most High? Behold, these are the wicked; and being always at ease, they increase in riches. Surely in vain have I cleansed my heart, and washed my hands in innocency; for all the day long have I been plagued, and chastened every morning. If I had said, I will speak thus; Behold, I had dealt treacherously with the generation of thy children." (Psalm 73: 1-15.)

Why did the wicked prosper, the righteous suffer? These were matters which perplexed and disturbed David, as they have the good of every generation. On entering the "sanctuary," the solution of this vexing problem was at hand:

"When I thought how I might know this, it was too painful for me; until I went into the sanctuary of God, *and considered their latter end.* Surely thou settest them in slippery places; thou casteth them down to destruction. How are they become a desolation in a moment? They are utterly consumed with terrors." (Psalm 73: 16-18.) Not here, but in the judgment will the wicked answer for their misdeeds. An infidel once addressed the following note to the editor of a county paper: "Sir: I have a religious neighbor who, when he prays, I curse; when he goes to church, I go fishing; yet, in October my harvest is as bountiful as his. How do you explain it?" The editor answered: "Sir, you err in assuming God settles all of his accounts in October!" In a remarkable passage in 2 Thess. 1: 7-9, Paul solemnly warns of the ultimate destruction of the wicked: "And to you that are afflicted rest with us, at the revelation of the Lord Jesus from heaven with the angels of his power in flaming fire, rendering vengeance to them that know not God, and to them that obey not the gospel of our Lord Jesus: who shall suffer punishment, even eternal destruction from the face of the Lord and from the glory of his might, when he shall come to be glorified in his saints."

ye have heard of the patience of Job,—This intensely interesting story of that valiant and faithful Old Testament character was a familiar one to James' readers. All of their lives, the Jewish Christians had heard and read of the agonies Job experienced, the miseries inflicted upon him by his so-called friends, and the cries which were wrung in pain from his lips. Though he could not quench the wailing cry of pain which sprang up from the very depths of his soul, he remained true to his convictions and thus became the Bible's best example of patient endurance under great trial of the Old Testament age. (Job 1: 21; 2: 10; 16: 19; 19: 27.) He has, through the centuries, been honored for his faith, and all succeeding generations have called him blessed. His name, in the roll of the ancient heroes, occupies a niche of special honor, along with Noah and Daniel. (Ezek. 14: 14, 20.) The lesson for us is that though a saint, he suffered greatly, and we need not expect to escape that which was the lot of the great and good of all the centuries. Incidental lessons of great value emerge from this reference: (1) We learn that all suffering, however great and prolonged, must eventually end; and the saints will triumph; (2) the Old Testament narratives, including Job, were written to sustain us in our trials (1 Cor. 10: 1-13); and (3) the Holy Spirit, who inspired James to pen the words of our text, by this reference to Job, evidences the fact that the book is not, as modernists affirm, an allegory, or mythical composition, but a true and reliable history of a specific character caught up in a series of specific incidents there especially detailed and described. The book of Job demonstrates the fact that a faithful man will bear any form of trial rather than forsake God. It exhibits in clear and striking fashion the struggles of one who, while he cannot understand, at the moment, the occasion for his sore trials, *does not blame God with them,* and maintains his faith in Deity. Job and his experiences provide us with an object lesson in unwavering faith in the face of tremendous trial. Despite his physical afflictions, the loss of his earthly possessions, the scorn and false accusations of his friends, and the faithlessness of his wife, "Job sinned not, nor charged God foolishly." (Job 1 : 22.)

and have seen the end of the Lord,—The word translated "end" here, *telos,* often with the significance of termination, consummation, etc., also designates *purpose, aim, design,* its obvious meaning here. We, in our day, and from our vantage point (James is saying), can now see the purpose and design of God's plan in Job's case, which was not nearly so apparent *then.* The over-all lesson here indicated ought not to be lost on us today. There is "a divinity that shapes our ends," and though, for the moment, we are unable to discern the purpose or plan which God has, we should patiently wait for the unfolding thereof, knowing that eventually he will vindicate himself and all matters will turn out for our good. "And we know that to them that love God all things work together for good, even to them that are called according to his purpose. . . . What then shall we say to these things? If God is for us, who is against us? He that spared not his own Son, but delivered him up for us all, how shall he not also with him freely give us all things?. . . Nay, in all these things we are more than conquerors through him that loved us. For I am persuaded, that neither death, nor life, nor angels, nor principalities, nor things to come, nor powers, nor height, nor depth, nor any other creature, shall be able to separate us from the love of God, which is in Christ Jesus our Lord." (Rom. 8: 28, 31, 32, 37, 38.)

how that the Lord is full of pity, and merciful.—That is, "the end" (design, purpose, plan) of the Lord is to show great pity and much mercy for his suffering saints. In Job's case, the Lord exhibited the greatest pity and compassion; and, this will he also do for all who similarly endure. The phrase, "full of pity," denotes the fact that God is tender-hearted; he is not unmindful of the agonies of his people, nor does he turn a deaf ear to their cries. He abounds in pity *(polusplagchnos),* he is filled with it. Moreover, he is *"merciful," (oiktirmon),* i.e., full of compassion for those who suffer. This characteristic of God was especially evidenced in the case of the prophets and particularly in Job. Though that Old Testament character suffered as few men have, God richly blessed him in his last days: "And Jehovah turned the

12 But above all things, my brethren, swear not, neither by the heaven, nor by the earth, nor by any other oath: but [4]let your yea be yea, and your nay, nay; that ye fall not under judgment.

[4]Or, *let yours be the yea, yea, and the nay, nay* Ccmp. Mt. 5. 37.

captivity of Job, when he prayed for his friends: and Jehovah gave Job twice as much as he had before. Then came there unto him all his brethren, and all his sisters, and all they that had been of his acquaintance before, and did eat bread with him in his house: and they bemoaned him, and comforted him concerning all the evil that Jehovah had brought upon him: every man also gave him a piece of money, and every one a ring of gold. So Jehovah blessed the latter end of Job more than this beginning: and he had fourteen thousand sheep, and six thousand camels, and a thousand yoke of oxen, and a thousand she-asses. . . . And in all the land were no women found so fair as the daughters of Job: and their father gave them inheritance among their brethren. And after this Job lived a hundred and forty years, and saw his sons, and his sons' sons, even four generations. So Job died, being old and full of days." (Job 42: 10-17.)

Lessons in patience and resignation are many in the Old Testament, and all of them we should carefully and prayerfully take to heart today. The desire for wordly gain often possesses members of the body of Christ; and the disposition to be fretful, dissatisfied with our lot is a common one. We should learn the folly of worldly acquisition as a means to happiness; and that "patience in affliction" is the proper attitude for us, as Christians, to have all of our days.

SWEARING FORBIDDEN

5: 12

12 **But above all things, my brethren,**—The phrase, "Above all things," *(pro panton)* was designed to emphasize the importance of the injunction with reference to oaths. On this matter they were to be especially careful and to it give particular attention. It is not possible to determine whether the phrase is temporal ("Before doing anything else, give attention to this,") or designed to indicate priority ("Give particular attention to this matter"). In either event, the writer's words emphasize the importance of the

injunction, and his desire that the readers apply themselves to it at once.

swear not,—*(Me omnuete,* present active imperative with the negative), literally, "Do not keep on swearing." The prohibition forbids it of those practicing vice; and it charges those who have not started it to refrain from doing so. One cannot escape the conclusion that there is here a very obvious reference to the words of our Lord on this subject in the Sermon on the Mount. The following parallel will evidence this fact:

<table>
<tr><td align="center">Sermon On The Mount</td><td align="center">James 5 : 12</td></tr>
<tr><td>"*Swear not* at all; *neither by the heaven,* for it is the throne of God; *nor by the earth,* for it is the footstool of his feet; nor by Jerusalem, for it is the city of the great King. . . . But let your speech be *Yea, yea; Nay, nay;* and whatsoever is more than these *is of the evil one.*"</td><td>"Swear not, neither by the heaven, nor by the earth, nor by any other oath: but let your yea be yea, and your nay, nay; that ye fall not under judgment."</td></tr>
</table>

To swear is to invoke the name of God, or other sacred names and things; to utter an oath. The practice appears to have been an exceedingly common one in the first century. The Jews understood (from the third commandment), that they were to avoid any profane and flagrant use of the names of God, but they resorted to technicalities and illogical reasoning to justify oaths where there was no *specific* mention of the name of God. Some rabbis held that one was bound to tell the truth only when the names of Deity were mentioned, on the ground that God became a party to the agreement when thus involved; but that if his name were not included in the oath any promise made one did not have to keep. Thus by mental reservation, by trickery and evasive methods, by skillful use of words, many in that day callously broke their promises and violated their oaths. Others avoided the use of God's name in their oaths by swearing by the handiwork of God—the heavens, the earth, the sun, the moon and the stars. This, of course, did not excuse them because all of these objects are the works of God; and, to swear by them is still to involve God. Hence the following prohibition:

neither by the heaven, nor by the earth, nor by any other oath:—This statement forbids the use of all oaths under the circumstances *particularly before the writer*. All such swearing must be regarded as sinful. All oaths, whether pious or not, which fall into this classification, are wrong. Jehovah has ever regarded, with the greatest displeasure, any disposition on the part of man to use his name in flippant, frivolous and profane fashion. The first commandment of the decalogue was designed to protect the sanctity of God's being; the second forbade man to approach him through some human device; the third—"Thou shalt not take the name of Jehovah thy God in vain: for Jehovah will not hold him guiltless that taketh his name in vain"—was formulated to guarantee respect and reverence for his name. (Deut. 5: 7-11.)

One is profane who uses sacred things in an irreverent and blasphemous manner. The word *vain*, in the third commandment of the decalogue, is translated from a word in the Hebrew language which means in a light, flippant and contemptuous fashion. It is of serious consequence that many members of the church today have allowed to creep into their phraseology words and phrases the use of which amounts to profanity. Others, who would not dare use the holy names, God, Christ, Jesus, Jerusalem, Heaven, Hell, Hades, as interjections ("An ejaculatory word or form of speech, usually thrown in without grammatical connection," Webster) and for emphasis, will, nevertheless, use euphemisms (the substitution of a word or phrase less offensive or objectionable), the derivation of which goes back to one of the foregoing forms. Were those who thus do aware of the origin of many of these common bywords they would be shocked! It is therefore important that we obtain a clear conception of the significance of such words and phrases and avoid all which even indirectly border on the profane. Among them are such words as *Gee Whiz, Gosh, Gad, Egad, Golly, Good Gracious, Good Grief, My Goodness, Jeminy, Zounds, Jove, etc., etc.*

Gee is an euphemistic construction of the name of Jesus. It is slang, and has no proper use in our language. It is used as an interjection and to express surprise. It is, in effect, to say: "Jesus!" (Cf. Webster's Unabridged Dictionary which says that it is "a minced form of Jesus, used in mild oaths.") *Whiz* is slang for anything excellent, "a corker, sometimes applied to a clever person or thing of excellence. Something or some one of exceptional ability or quality." The words, *Gee Whiz!*, are, therefore, an oath in which Jesus and something extraordinary or unusual are joined. Whiz originally signified something of a humming or whirring sound, and then anything unusual or exceptional. A *Whizzer* in slang is that which is above and beyond the ordinary.

Gosh is an interjection and is used euphemistically for God. It is an exclamatory slang expression indicating surprise. The Century Dictionary says that it is "A minced form of God: often used interjectionally as a mild oath." Webster's Unabridged Dictionary says that it is "a softened form of God, used as a mild oath." It is occasionally used in hyphenated fashion such as *Gosh-awful*. In this form it is often used as an adjective, and euphemistically.

Gad, Egad, are interjections and are used euphemistically for the word "God," in mild oaths. They indicate surprise, disgust, dismay, and similar emotions, and are ejaculatory in character. Gee, Gosh, Gad, Egad, and similar forms are used synonymously. They are often joined with other terms for further emphasis, such as Gee Whilikins, Gad Bodkins, of which usage, the Unabridged Dictionary says, "A softened form of the word God as used in a mild oath or mild oaths in which the second element is often a corruption or made up word."

Golly, of extremely common use, is described by the New World Dictionary as "an exclamation of surprise, a euphemism for God. It is often used in conjunction with the word *by,* i.e., 'By Golly!' sometimes as an interjection for the word God."

Good Gracious! Good Grief! My Goodness!, etc., are all mild oaths, where the word good or goodness is used euphemistically for God. See Webster's New World Dictionary, College Edition. There are many forms of this usage, such as Goodness Sake! Goodness Knows! Thank Goodness!—all ejaculatory and exclamatory expressions in reference to the goodness of God, but used slangily and for emphasis. One who thus speaks calls God to witness to the statement with which the oath is associated. "In goodness knows who it could have been, it means God only knows and I do not; in goodness knows it wasn't I, it means God knows it and could confirm my statement." (American English Usage, Nicholson.)

Heavens! Good Heavens! For Heaven's Sake! and similar

expressions are statements of exclamatory character in which the heavens are called to witness to the truth of the statement made, or to support the affirmation. All such expressions when used as by-words, as slang, and in flippant, frivolous fashion, violate our Lord's injunction: "Swear not at all: neither by the heaven, for it is the throne of God; nor by the earth, for it is the footstool of his feet; nor by Jerusalem, for it is the city of the great King." (Matt. 5 : 34.)

We are not from this to conclude that it is wrong to use the various names of God in our conversation when such usage is reverent, respectful and sober. We have, indeed, numerous instances of such usage in the Scriptures. (Cf. "God forbid," "If God wills," "The Lord grant mercy," etc.) The Jews regarded the name of Jehovah as ineffable and to this day refuse to pronounce it in Hebrew. It is the profane use of sacred things and names against which the Bible inveighs, and all such expressions as these we have above analyzed which should be rigidly excluded from our vocabularies.

but let your yea be yea, and your nay, nay; that ye fall not under judgment.—Be certain always that when you say, "Yes," *yes* is the true answer; when you say, "No," *no* is the correct answer. See to it that your statements are true, without the necessity of reenforcing them with an oath. Here, it would appear, is the key to this passage. That it was not the design of James (and our Lord, in Matt. 5 : 34-37) to forbid *all* oaths, including those of a judicial nature, seems evident from the following considerations: (1) Jesus, before Caiaphas, testified under oath. (Matt. 26 : 63, 64.) (2) Paul often solemnly asserted things in the form of an oath, e.g., "For God is my witness, whom I serve in my spirit in the gospel of his Son, how unceasingly I make mention of you, always in my prayers. . ." (Rom. 1 : 9; cf. 2 Cor. 1 : 23; Phil. 1 : 8; Gal. 1 : 20.) (3) God swore by himself when he could swear by no greater. (Heb. 6 : 13.) (4) The prophets often involved the names of God in their solemn affirmations. (Isa. 65 : 16.) Thus, the sin forbidden in this section is that of *profanity;* the frivolous, flippant use of the names of God and sacred things. The Jews of that day were especially addicted to the vice of constant and continuous profanity; of calling God to witness the most common and frivolous matters, the practice of which prostituted the names of God to the level of the most insignificant things. A judicial oath, a legal oath, statements before notaries public, and the like, are not within the classification intended by the writer.

There are those who seek to avoid an oath on the witness stand by resorting to an *affirmation* that what they are about to testify to is the truth, the whole truth, and nothing but the truth. Most legal tribunals allow one to affirm in lieu of swearing to the truth of that about which one speaks. Those who thus do, though they do not follow the form of oaths usually administered, nevertheless bind themselves to tell the truth; and can be convicted of perjury for failing so to do.

But, did not James include, among the prohibitions, "any other oath"? Would not this embrace not only those specifically prohibited, but oaths of every type and kind, *including those required by law?* It is most significant that an oath, *by the name of God,* is not mentioned; surely, if he had intended to forbid all swearing (oaths), this would have been the first designated; as a matter of fact, this type of oath, in contrast with others, was commanded under the law. (See Deut. 6: 13; 10: 20.) It would appear that the failure to designate such an oath indicates what has been emphasized above, that the type of oaths mentioned is such as was characteristic of the Jews of that day of asserting with an oath the most commonplace matters of life. Instead of doing this, to establish the truth of what they said, they should let their yeas be yeas, their nays, nays; that is, they were to tell the truth always, and without the necessity of resorting to such devices. Further evidence of the correctness of this conclusion is to be seen in the word the Holy Spirit used to designate any other oath. Had James intended to assert that any oath, all oaths, every oath, must be eschewed, he would have used for the word *other* the Greek *heteros,* which means another of a *different* kind; instead of *allos* (which he did use), another of the *same* kind. It is, therefore, clear that the sacred writer intended to include only such oaths as were of the type specifically under consideration, and to which the people of that day were especially addicted. There is no exegetical reason to extend his remarks to oaths not embraced in his own classification. We must, from all the facts in the case, conclude that both the

Lord and James had in mind the habit of using sacred names in ordinary statements rather than in the solemn appeals which are made to God by all faithful people on occasion of serious moment.

To "fall" under "judgment" is to be put in a position where one will be judged. The word translated judgment *(krisis)*, denotes the process of judging, rather than the sentence rendered. It means that those guilty of that which James writes in this section will stand in judgment for their actions. Jesus, in the parallel statement, declares that what is more than this "is of the evil one," i.e., it originates with him. Thus to engage in useless, vain oath-taking (profanity) is to be influenced by the devil; and it puts one in a situation where judgment must ultimately be experienced.

SECTION 13

5 : 13-20

PRAYER AND PRAISE
5 : 13

13 Is any among you suffering? let him pray. Is any cheerful? let him

---

13 **Is any among you suffering?**—It was the opinion of our translators that the Greek phrase *kakopathei tis* ("Is any among you suffering?") is an interrogative, and should, therefore, be rendered as it appears in our text, rather than as an indicative statement ("Some one among you is afflicted,") and, perhaps, rightly so, although there are no punctuation marks in the oldest Greek manuscripts and such must, in every instance, be supplied. There is but little difference, whether the statement be regarded as a question, or as an affirmation of fact. Often, in cases of this kind, statements are couched in rhetorical form for emphasis. Some among those to whom James wrote were indeed suffering at the hands of their oppressors, suffering persecution from those who opposed Christianity, suffering from affliction, hardship and much difficulty.

The verb *kakopathei* (occurring elsewhere in 2 Tim. 2 : 3, 9 ; 4 : 5 and in noun form in James 5 : 10) is compounded from the adjective *kakos,* evil and *pascho*, to suffer ; hence, literally, to suffer evil. It is, therefore, sufficiently comprehensive to embrace every type of affliction, whether of outward bodily character or of inner mental anguish. There was much affliction among the saints of that day, as there is in ours ; indeed, in every congregation there are those who experience sickness, bereavement, and loss of one kind or other. Sorrow, suffering, pain, indeed, all of the burdens of life at one time or another fall upon the shoulders of the Lord's people ; and the instruction which this verse contains for those of the first century is equally applicable to this. Here it is made clear that the proper attitude of the suffering saint is exhibited in worship, and not in oaths and vain swearing of any type.

let him pray.—*(Proseuchestho,* present middle imperative of *proseuchomai,* to pray, thus literally, *let him keep on praying.)* In view of the fact that affliction and suffering, both physical and mental, are ever with us, men may blame God *for* it, or go to God for relief *from* it. Some are guilty of the former; Christians rejoice to be able to do the latter. When the troubles of the world fall upon our shoulders, instead of morbid, fretful complaining, we should ask God for wisdom to cope with our problems, and the requisite strength to overcome them. This was Paul's method, and he found it eminently successful. Beset by his "thorn in the flesh," he besought the Lord, on three different occasions, to remove it. The Lord said to him, "My grace is sufficient for thee: for my power is made perfect in weakness." Paul thenceforth reasoned, "Most gladly therefore will I rather glory in my weaknesses, that the power of Christ may rest upon me. Wherefore I take pleasure in weaknesses, in injuries, in necessities, in persecutions, in distresses, for Christ's sake: for when I am weak, then am I strong." (2 Cor. 12: 7-10.) We may be certain that God will support us in our trials; and we should, therefore, turn to him for the help he so freely proffers when clouds, ominous and heavy, appear on our horizon, and obstacles apparently insurmountable are in our path. Whatever the nature or character of our affliction, it is always right, proper and beneficial to pray. There is, indeed, a natural inclination on the part of man to turn to God in prayer when human supports fall away. Abraham Lincoln once said that in the dark hours which faced him, he turned to God for help, from the realization that he had no other to whom to turn. Of course, we should remember our obligations to the Lord *at all times,* and not fall back upon him as a final recourse. It is encouraging to know that when all others fail us, he will not; but he will lend a sympathetic ear to our entreaties, and invite us to turn to him in the hours of our extremity. (2 Chron. 33: 12; Psalm 34: 4; 50: 5; Matt. 7: 7.) How reassuring it is to know that God is our refuge, our very present help in time of trouble! It is truly a wonderfully consoling thought that through prayer we may not only find relief from the afflictions of life, but the cause that produced them may likewise be removed. Are some of us afflicted? Then, let us pray! This is heaven's message to all of the Lord's saints.

Is any cheerful?—*(Euthumei.)* The word thus translated does not convey the notion of fun or frivolity, but describes a disposition that is friendly, joyful, pleasant and agreeable. One "cheerful," in the original sense of the term, is one in good spirits, one possessed of a frame of mind that is free of anxiety and disturbing problems. The verb also occurs in Acts 27: 22, 25, where Paul besought his traveling companions to "be of good cheer." The word used by James describes an attitude exactly opposite to that indicated in the word "suffering," in the earlier portion of the verse. It is not improbable that the "suffering" one and the "cheerful" one of this passage are the same person. That is, he who is suffering is to pray to the Father to lift his burden; and, when it is gone, to be cheerful, and to express such in praise and worship. Praise has been called "the highest form of prayer," and it is the natural expression of a contented and thankful heart. If, in affliction, we are to pray; it is surely proper, in contentment, to express praise; and in either to feel and to demonstrate our innermost needs to God.

let him sing praise.—*(Psalleto,* present active imperative of *psallo,* "in the New Testament to sing a hymn, to celebrate the praises of God in song," (Thayer, Greek English Lexicon of the New Testament). Literally, "Let him keep on singing." The word occurs in 1 Cor. 14: 15; Rom. 15: 9; Eph. 5: 19.) It has had a varied meaning through the years. It has signified the act of plucking out the hair, snapping a carpenter's string, twanging the strings of an instrument; and, in the New Testament, *to sing.* Its basic meaning, to pluck or twang, is thus metaphorically seen in its New Testament usage, in that the chords of the heart are to be "twanged" or played upon: "And be not drunken with wine, wherein is riot, but be filled with the Spirit; speaking one to another in psalms and hymns and spiritual songs, singing and making melody *(psallo) in your heart* to the Lord." (Eph. 5: 19.) There are those who, in an effort to justify the use of mechanical instruments of music in Christian worship today, point to *earlier* meanings of the word, and urge that such significance should be assigned to it today. But those who thus do are unable to follow their own argument to its conclusion. It is conceded by the most avid defender of instrumental music in worship that one may acceptably approach God in public religious devotion without it; that its use is a matter of personal choice; and is, therefore, in the realm of expediency. But, if the instrument inheres in the word and to *psallete* is to use a stringed instrument, it follows that one cannot *psallete* without it. The instrument is either in the word, or it is not. If it is in it, one cannot worship God without an instrument of music; if it is not in it, then the argument fails. If it be urged that the instrument inheres in the word, the following conclusions irresistibly follow: (1) It is impossible *to psallete* without an instrument of music; (2) since each individual is commanded to *psallete,* each must personally twang the strings of a mechanical instrument in worship to be acceptable; (3) to prepare people to worship acceptably would necessitate assisting them in such use; (4) only stringed instruments might properly be used, inasmuch as these are the only type which may be twanged or plucked. This would eliminate all *wind* instruments such as organs, horns, etc. In view of the fact that not one of the advocates of instrumental music in worship is willing to accept these obvious conclusions, it follows that they have little respect for the argument they make.

Dozens of the world's most profound Greek scholars, including all of those which have produced the major English translations, have borne witness to the fact that the New Testament meaning of the word does not include the use of a mechanical instrument; and that its meaning today is simply to sing. An interesting and significant sidelight on this is the fact that the Greek Orthodox Churches—whose members are, for the most part, *Greek*-speaking people—have never used instrumental music in their worship. Those desiring to pursue the meaning of the word further will find a wealth of exceedingly valuable material in "Instrumental Music In Christian Worship," by M. C. Kurfees, published by the Gospel Advocate Company, Nashville, Tennessee

The use of such instruments in the *Jewish* order characteristic of the Old Testament period falls far short of justifying their use in *Christian* worship today. The burning of incense, the offering of animal sacrifices were a part of the worship in the former dispensation; we do not thence conclude that the burning of incense in Jewish devotions justifies an incense burner in the church today. Advocates of the doctrine of infant church membership attempt to sustain their position in precisely the same fashion. Were not infants a part of the Jewish economy? Ought they not therefore to

sing praise. 14 Is any among you sick? let him call for the elders of the church; and let them pray over him, [5]anointing him with oil in the name of

[5]Or, *having anointed*

be in the church today? Those who so contend make out a case for church membership for babies as successfully as do those who seek to justify instrumental music in the church today in the same fashion. The truth is, God has ordained neither infant membership nor instrumental music in the church today, and those who practice either go beyond that which is written. (Deut. 4: 2; Prov. 30: 6; Rev. 22: 18, 19.)

It is a well established historic fact which may be confirmed by consulting any reliable encyclopedia that instrumental music in so-called Christian worship was first used, in this dispensation, in A.D. 670, when introduced into the Church of the Great Apostasy; and, it created such a furor therein that it was speedily removed to avert a split; and, it was not until about A.D. 800 that it came to be common in that ecclesiasticism. *Our Lord never authorized it, no apostle ever sanctioned it, no New Testament writer ever commanded it, no New Testament church ever practiced it.* It was born in the bosom of the apostasy, and is used with no greater sanction than the burning of incense, the counting of beads, the sprinkling of babies.

We walk by faith and not by sight (1 Cor. 5: 7); and, faith comes by hearing God's word (Rom. 10: 17). It follows, therefore, that we are at liberty to do, in Christian worship, only those things specifically commanded; and, inasmuch as the New Testament is silent regarding the use of instrumental music in worship, we dare not use it. We are, however, commanded to *sing* and to make melody in our heart (not on an instrument!) and we are assured that such practice is acceptable to him who commanded it. Authorized items of worship, to be performed on the Lord's day, —the first day of the week—are, teaching, singing, the contribution, the Lord's Supper, and prayer. (Acts 2: 42; Eph. 5: 19; 1 Cor. 16: 2; Acts 20: 7.)

ELDERS AND THE SICK
5: 14, 15

14 **Is any among you sick?**—The word translated "sick," *(as-*

theneo, literally, to be weak, without strength), is a term often used for illness, in the New Testament. (Matt. 10: 8; John 5: 7; Acts 9: 37; Phil. 2: 27.) The author, in verse 13, designates "suffering" in general; here, one particular type of suffering—physical illness—is specifically mentioned. Sickness, of one kind or other, is a universal affection of man; and, James, having just admonished those to whom he wrote to pray when suffering, sing when cheerful, passes to the subject of physical illness, perhaps because it is the most common kind of affliction to which human beings are subjected. We are not informed of the nature or extent of the illness here contemplated; nor is there anything, in this instance, to indicate whether the term is used literally, or figuratively. The context would suggest that it is literal sickness inasmuch as it is mentioned in connection with literal suffering, praying, cheerfulness, and singing. In verse 15, below, it is clearly shown that the illness contemplated here is physical in character, in view of the fact that it is mentioned in connection with, *and in addition to,* spiritual illness. These conclusions follow: (1) It is possible for children of God to get sick. (2) Sickness is a physical ailment which eventually comes to all, whether good or bad. (3) The fact that one is sick does not mean that such a one has been or is guilty of specific sin. Often, the most devout suffer from prolonged illness; frequently those who live in open sin enjoy robust health. Paul was possessed of great physical weakness; there were infirmities of the flesh which bore heavily upon him and he ever lived with the painful reminder of the thorn in his flesh. (2 Cor. 12: 1ff.) (4) There were sick people in the early church even as there are many in this category among us today. Sickness is a burden all must, at one time or another, bear.

let him call for the elders of the church;—*(Proskalesasthe,* aorist middle imperative, "Let *him* call (at once) for the elders of the church.") The "church" referred to here is, obviously, the local congregation, inasmuch as it has "elders." The word church is used in the New Testament to designate the Lord's people as a whole (Matt. 16: 18); the people within a geographical area (1 Cor. 1: 2); the assembly of the saints (1 Cor. 14: 28). Elders supervise the local congregation (Acts 20: 28), not the church in the aggregate. The church, as a whole, is an organism with Christ as its head (Eph. 1: 19-23), and children of God the members of the body (1 Cor. 12: 12-28).   All New Testament churches, *when fully organized,* had a plurality of elders, whose duty it was to feed the flock of God, and to oversee the work of the congregation.   (Acts 14: 23; 15: 2; 16: 4; 21: 18; 20: 28; 1 Pet. 5: 1-4.)   To these the congregation is taught to submit, because they watch for the souls of those committed to their care.   (Heb. 13: 7, 17.)   The "elders" are also designated *bishops* (Acts 20: 28), *pastors* (Eph. 4: 11), *presbyters* (1 Tim. 4: 14).   Cf. the Greek of Acts 11: 30.   Their qualifications are set out in detail in 1 Tim. 3: 1-7; Tit. 1: 5-9.

and let them pray over him,—*(Proseuzasthosam ep' auton.)* The verb is an aorist middle imperative.   "Them" are the elders; "him" the sick man.   The prayer the elders are to pray is to be "over" him, not literally, of course, but figuratively; *they are to pray in his behalf.*   It seems absurd to assume, with some commentators, that the instructions necessitated standing with bowed heads over his prostrate body.   There is an additional requirement, mentioned in the next clause.

anointing him with oil in the name of the Lord:—The verb here is an *aorist* participle, indicating that the act of anointing was to be performed either before the prayer, or in connection with it. (See margin.)   Thus, the sick man is to be anointed; anointed with oil; anointed with oil in the name of the Lord.   Olive oil was used both medicinally and symbolically in Biblical times.   It was used symbolically in the appointment and coronation of prophets, priests and kings of the Old Testament period implying an anointing of the Holy Spirit.   (1 Sam. 10: 1, 9.)   Our Lord sometimes used outward symbols in connection with his healing.   (John 9: 6, 11.)   Olive oil also has therapeutic value, instances of which may be seen in Luke 10: 34, where oil was poured into the wounds of the man who fell among thieves.   It appears quite clear here that the use of the oil was *symbolic,* and not medicinal; and thus served as a token of the power of God by which the healing was accomplished.   *Elders,* not doctors, were to be sent for.   Had the healing art *through means* been intended, the instruction would have been "Call for the doctors and let them diagnose his case and prescribe the proper treatment. . . ."   It was, as we shall see, the "prayer of

the Lord: 15 and the prayer of faith shall save him that is sick, and the
Lord shall raise him up; and if he have committed sins, it shall be forgiven

---

faith" which accomplished the purpose, not the administration of
oil. While olive oil is beneficial for some ailments, it is useless in
others. Obviously, the application of olive oil to the head or body
of one suffering from a heart condition is of little avail.

The act,—anointing with oil—was to be performed "in the name
of the Lord"; i.e., by the Lord's authority. The meaning is that
the Lord ordained that such should be done and the blessing which
accompanied it would be accomplished by him. This corroborates
the view already indicated in these notes, and to be emphasized
below, that the healing of this passage was miraculous. The
phrase, "in the name of the Lord," is to be construed with the
anointing, and not with the verb "pray." Thus, the anointing with
oil was symbolic of the power which Christ himself would exercise
in behalf of the sick man.

15 **and the prayer of faith shall save him that is sick,**—The
prayer of faith *(he euche tes pisteos)* is a prayer which results
from faith; a prayer prayed because of the faith of those praying.
Of this prayer it is affirmed that it "shall save," *(sosei,* future active of *sozo,* to make one well), "him that is sick." It should be
observed that James declares that it is *the prayer of faith* which
accomplishes this; not prayer *and oil;* not prayer and medicinal
treatment; not prayer and the laying on of hands. The prayer of
faith was that prayed by the elders in which, of course, the interested one, who called for the elders, joined. This prayer is said to
save (in the original and primary import of the word, to make
well) the sick. This word must therefore, in this instance, be regarded as limited in its significance to the physical, temporal healing of the affliction which possessed the man, inasmuch as the additional fact of the forgiveness of his sins is later affirmed.

and the Lord shall raise him up;—Observe that it is *the Lord*
who will do this; and, that from which the sick is to be raised is
his bed of pain and illness. The verb here occurs in this same connection in Mark 1: 31; Matt. 8: 15, and often elsewhere in the
Greek Testament. Here is positive proof of the falsity of the
Roman Catholic interpretation of this passage. That ecclesiasti-

cism affects to see in this verse support for their doctrine of Extreme Unction in which they anoint one *about to die*. Here, however, the anointing was to be done in an action the design of which was to enable the sick *to live!* Moreover, the "elders of the church" were those to be called in such instances, not Roman Catholic priests. This affirmation of James bears not the remotest resemblance to the monstrous doctrine advocated by the Church of Rome which they style Extreme Unction.

and if he have committed sins, it shall be forgiven him.— This is promised in addition to the healing of his body. Inasmuch as the Lord forgives the sins of his people only when they repent and turn away from them, this fact must be implied in this passage. (1 John 1: 7-9; 2: 1.) From the foregoing considerations, it must be quite obvious to the discerning student that this passage was applicable to the period of miraculous gifts in the church and limited to it. On the assumption that it is today applicable, if the sick called for the elders as directed here, and the elders did their duty, *no one in the church would ever die!* Yet, the Hebrew writer solemnly affirmed, "It is appointed unto men once to die. . ." (Heb. 9: 27.)

Evidently, for a limited time, and for special purposes, God ordained that the foregoing instructions should be followed; and in every case the promise was realized. That it was not widely followed, or intended to be a universal practice during the apostolic age, follows from the fact that not infrequently saints were sick and often died. (Acts 9: 32-43; Phil. 2: 19-30; 1 Tim. 5: 23; 2 Tim. 4: 1-8.) While those to whom this passage particularly applied received, without exception, the blessing of healing and forgiveness, others of the apostolic age were often afflicted without relief. Paul had a thorn in the flesh; Timothy had a stomach disorder, and Trophimus was by Paul left in Miletus sick.

It seems quite clear from all the facts in the case that the elders contemplated here were miraculously endowed—through the laying on of an apostle's hands—and were thus able to participate in miraculous acts of healing in the manner described. In the apostolic age, and in a day of special gifts, conferred through the laying on of the apostles' hands, acts of healing were done independently of means; today God still heals, *but by means,* and through the vari-

him. 16 Confess therefore your sins one to another, and pray one for another, that ye may be healed. The supplication of a righteous man availeth

ous techniques of healing with which the world is today blessed. God once fed people miraculously, and independently of means; he still feeds us, but the seed, the sower, the soil, the sunshine, the harvest, the mill, the baker are all means to that end. It is as foreign to God's plan today to expect miraculous healing independently of means as it is to expect him to feed us as Jesus did when he multiplied the loaves and fishes. It is, of course, proper and right for us to pray for the sick; to pray that they may be healed; to pray that the Lord will raise them up and restore them to their usual places in life; but, we must recognize that he works *through means* today, and that he has chosen to accomplish his purposes in this manner. One who *rejects* these means today—such as medicine, surgery, and all other approved techniques—and alleges dependence upon God alone, actually *rejects God* who chooses to work in this manner now. He who is raised up from death's door by modern miracle drugs is *assuredly healed by the power of God* as were those in the first century who were the recipients of Christ's healing ministry in that day. Let us be thankful for, and use without hesitation, these marvelous means from the hand of God.

EXAMPLE OF PRAYER
5: 16-18

16 **Confess therefore your sins one to another,**—This injunction, by James, is associated logically and grammatically with the section immediately preceding it. It is affirmed of "him that is sick," (verse 15), that "if he have committed sins, it shall be forgiven him." Inasmuch as the Lord forgives the sins of his people only when they confess, and turn away from them, there is a confession *implied* in the instance cited. Moreover, the word "therefore" *(oun)* indicates a close connection with the statement preceding it, and is a conclusion drawn from premises in it. Confession and prayer are enjoined in this section. The verbs are present imperatives, and mean: "Keep on confessing your sins one to another, and keep on praying one for another. . . ." It is significant that this passage does not deal with confession *to God (that* is implied in verse 15), to the elders or preacher exclusively, but to *one*

another. It thus becomes the duty of elders and preachers to confess their sins to other members of the one body as for others to confess sins to them.

This passage is often cited by the Catholics to support their doctrine of Auricular Confession (confession in the ear), the practice of regularly confessing to a priest; but the words "one to another" constitute a fatal addition, insofar as that doctrine is concerned! If this teaches that one is to confess to the priest, it teaches as clearly that the priest must then immediately confess his sins *to the confessee!* (A practice, we may add, not characteristic of them.) Nor are the sins here contemplated such as are against men *only*, on the assumption that because they are to be confessed to men, they must be against men. The noun designates transgressions against God's law, whether such involves the relationship of God or man. The word "confess," from *exomologeisthe* (present middle imperative), means to agree to; to acknowledge; to confess, is therefore, to acknowledge wrong. Taught here is the simple obligation of all Christians both to confess their sins to each other and to pray for each other.

There is nothing in the word "confess" itself which indicates whether the confession is *public* or *private;* but the context in which it appears does, inasmuch as it is to one another; and this, by implication, means that the confession is to be as public as the sins committed. The reason for this is obvious. We are to pray one for another. We may, however, effectively do so, only when a brother confesses his sins and turns away from them. (1 John 5: 16.) (See the comments on this in *A Commentary on The Epistles of Peter, John and Jude,* published by the Gospel Advocate Company, Nashville, Tennessee.) It is necessary in the nature of the case that those who have known of the sins should have equal knowledge of the penitence. But, this we can know only through a confession of the brother involved. *It is, therefore, a practical rule that the confession should be as public as the sin.* It should be carefully observed that this passage is not limited in its application to those instances where one commits grievous sin against God and confesses to him. In this instance, the confession is to the brethren. Nor, is the sin contemplated necessarily against those to whom confession is made. The tenses of the verbs indicate a continual confession and regular prayer by us all. This passage does not therefore deal exclusively with the "formal confession" made by one who has committed public, open sin and is making confession before the church for it, though it includes such. It is a daily obligation, applicable to all of us.

and pray one for another, that ye may be healed.—Prayer for one another, enjoined by this passage, was much more common in the apostolic age than now. Paul often prayed for the brethren; and he exhibited great interest in the prayers of others in his behalf: "I thank my God upon all my remembrance of you, always in every supplication of mine on behalf of you all making my supplication with joy. . ." (Phil. 1: 3); "Finally, brethren, pray for us. . ." (2 Thess. 3: 1). When Peter was imprisoned, prayer was made for him by the whole church. (Acts 12: 5.) Here, of course, the purpose of the prayer is specifically for the bestowal of blessing from God in the matter of forgiveness and healing.

The phrase, "that ye may be healed," has reference to the subject introduced in verses 14, 15, and is a natural conclusion from what is there affirmed. Obviously, only those who were willing to confess their sins could claim the promise there set out. An impenitent person would not likely call for the elders of the church; if he did, the elders could not consistently pray for his forgiveness and healing; and if they did, the Lord would not forgive him and heal him in his impenitence. God will not bestow his blessings upon those who insist on maintaining a barrier between themselves and him.

The supplication of a righteous man availeth much in its working.—A "supplication" *(deesis,* entreaty, petition) is an approach to God in prayer, where the emphasis is on the sense of need characteristic of the one who supplicates. In the ordinary Greek of the New Testament period it was the usual word for petition from an inferior to a superior. Though it points up the aspects of entreaty, it is a general term involving petition, thanksgiving, praise, devotion, etc. A "righteous man" *(dikaios),* literally a *just* man, is one who keeps the commandments of the Lord. A "righteous" man is one who *does right.* But, only those who keep the commandments do right; therefore, a righteous man is one who keeps the commandments. "If ye know that he is righteous,

much in its working. 17 Elijah was a man of like ⁶passions with us, and he
prayed ⁷fervently that it might not rain; and it rained not on the earth for

⁶Or, *nature*
⁷Gr. *with prayer.*

ye know that every one also that doeth righteousness is begotten of
him." (1 John 2: 29.) "My little children, let no man lead you
astray: he that doeth righteousness is righteous, even as he is righteous." (1 John 3: 7.)

The prayer of a man who keeps the commandments "availeth
much" *(polu ischuei,* has great force). Here, too, the verb is in
the present tense and means that the prayer of a man who keeps
the commandments keeps on having great force. Here is clear and
convincing testimony to the effectiveness and efficiency of prayer
by good men. Such prayers avail *much.* How much is much?
"Much" is a comparative term; it is, however, *more than a little;*
and it is therefore safe for us to affirm that prayer avails more than
a little in its working when engaged in by a man who keeps the
commandments of the Lord. Thus, when one denies the efficacy
of prayer the effort is an exhibition of skepticism.

The phrase, "in its working," means in the manner in which it
accomplishes its purpose. It is a type or kind of prayer which is
wrought out effectively. Examples of such supplications which
readily come to mind, of the truth of this affirmation, will include
the insistent widow and the unwilling judge (Luke 18: 1-8), and
the Syro-Phoenician woman whose daughter was ill (Matt. 15:
21-28). Thus, the passage emphasizes the power of prayer when
engaged in by one spiritually endowed with the right to pray. We
may summarize the statement in this fashion: *"The effect of a
prayer by a good man is great."* From this we learn that (1)
prayer is effectual; (2) it is right to pray, and we may entertain
the expectation that our prayers, when properly uttered, will be
heard; and (3) we must keep the commandments of the Lord if
we are to expect answers to our prayers.

17 Elijah was a man of like passions with us,—The great
prophet of the Old Testament period, Elijah, is brought forward
by James to illustrate the effectiveness of prayer by a "righteous
man." The activities of this remarkable man of God are set out in
great detail in First Kings. He was possessed of a faith in God

which apparently knew no bounds, and his moral courage and zeal for Jehovah were unequalled by any. It seemed that no duty was too difficult or dangerous for him to perform, if it involved the work of the Lord. He himself said, "I have been very jealous for Jehovah the God of hosts." (1 Kings 19: 10.) Though stern and unbending in principle, he was as tender hearted as a child and could and did weep over the death of the widow's child and over the waywardness of the people of Israel.

He was a man of "like passions" *(homoiopathes,* suffering like another), with us. By this it is meant that Elijah was possessed of the same human frame with its sorrows, emotion, joys, that we have. These words were penned by James to allay any feeling that the remarkable exploits of this marvelous man of God set him apart from the rest of his fellows, and he could not be regarded as an example of an ordinary person. James would have his readers to know that in spite of his great faith and tireless efforts in behalf of the cause of the Lord, he was like all the rest of us in his feelings, sorrows, temptations, weaknesses, etc. The word translated "of like passions" occurs only here and in Acts 14: 15, where Paul and Barnabas assured the people of Lycaonia, who were trying to make gods of them, that they were "men of like passions" (margin, *nature)* with them. Thus Elijah in nature was just like other men.

and he prayed fervently that it might not rain;—*(proseuchei proseuxato,* literally, he "prayed with prayer," an emphatic statement indicating the intensity of it.) The meaning is, He prayed with great earnestness that it might not rain. Some commentators have made much of the fact that it is not expressly stated, in the Old Testament narrative, that Elijah actually prayed. It is, as we shall note later, implied; and James, an inspired man, *said* he did; and this settles it. The Old Testament does *not* say that he did *not* pray; the New Testament says he *did* pray.

and it rained not on the earth for three years and six months.—The phrase, "on the earth," is likely limited by the context to the land of Israel; and the meaning, therefore, is, "It did not rain in all of the land of Israel for the period designated." For an instance of this usage of "the earth," see Luke 2: 1. The phrase, "the earth," is often used as a synonym for the land of Is-

three years and six months. 18 And he prayed again; and the heaven gave rain, and the earth brought forth her fruit.

rael. There is no definite statement in the Old Testament record of this incident of the time involved, but we have the testimony of both James and Jesus that it was for "three years and six months." "But of a truth I say unto you, There were many widows in Israel in the days of Elijah, when the heaven was shut up three years and six months, when there came a great famine over the land. . ." (Luke 4: 25.)

18 **And he prayed again; and the heaven gave rain, and the earth brought forth her fruit.**—This appears to be a reference to 1 Kings 18: 42, 45, though it is not there stated in so many words that Elijah prayed. But that extraordinary narrative shows that he was in the position of prayer; and it is merely captious cavalling to deny that prayer is implied: "And Elijah said unto Ahab, Get thee up, eat and drink; for there is the sound of abundance of rain. And Ahab went up to eat and to drink. And Elijah went up to the top of Carmel; *and he bowed himself down upon the earth, and he put his face between his knees.* And he said to his servant, Go up now, look toward the sea. And he went up, and looked, and said, There is nothing. And he said, Go again seven times. And it came to pass at the seventh time, that he said, Behold, there ariseth a cloud out of the sea, as small as a man's hand. And he said, Go up, say unto Ahab, Make ready thy chariot, and get thee down, that the rain stop thee not. And it came to pass in a little while that the heavens grew black with clouds and wind, and there was a great rain." (1 Kings 18: 41-45.)

In a land where droughts are frequent and people's lives are directly dependent upon rain, rainfall is vitally important, and the blessings involved in the coming of the rain exceedingly great. When the heaven gives rain, the earth, particularly in Palestine, brings forth her fruit abundantly. This incident was cited by James to show us the power of prayer. If one of like passions with us (possessed of the same human nature) as Elijah could accomplish so much in prayer, then we should not deny its efficacy today. If we are disposed to wonder if a similar prayer prayed today—that is for rain or for its cessation—would be answered, we may be sure that if the same circumstances existed and the will of

19 My brethren, if any among you err from the truth, and one convert

---

the Lord was the same, the result would likewise be the same. However, where the circumstances differ so greatly, and we are not sure what the will of the Lord is in such matters, our prayers should always be conditioned by the desire that the will of the Lord be done.

It is by no means necessary to assume that the incident to which James refers was a miracle—above and beyond the ordinary laws of nature. A cloud appeared in the sky and from it rain fell. Is not this the usual way in which it rains? If it be alleged that the cloud was miraculously provided; does not the Lord, in the final analysis, provide us with *all the clouds* from which rain falls? However, it was not James' intention to affirm that God answers prayer in the same way that Elijah's prayers, on that occasion, were answered. The purpose for which it was introduced was to show that God *answers prayer* and not to demonstrate how he does it. It is enough for us to know that he does; we may properly leave to him the providential operations by which it is accomplished. The lesson is simply this: *Elijah was a mere man; God answered his prayer; he will, therefore answer ours as well.*

19 **My brethren, if any among you err from the truth,—** *(Ean tis en humin planethei* aorist passive subjunctive, a third class condition, "In case one of you is led away from the truth. . . .") It follows from this statement that (a) a brother may sin; (b) a brother may err; (c) a brother may err from the truth. Not indicated is whether the truth here is to be regarded as practical or "doctrinal"; i.e., whether it is a lapse from what is right, the espousal of false doctrine and hence the abandonment of the truth, or both. Either instance may, and often does, occur: "Brethren, even if a man be overtaken in any trespass, ye who are spiritual restore such a one in the spirit of gentleness; looking to thyself, lest thou also be tempted." (Gal. 6: 1.) As a matter of fact, it is not easy to separate the two concepts. Those who yield to temptation do so from a failure to exercise caution regarding the sin which so easily besets them (Heb. 12: 2); and those who forsake the truth intellectually repudiate it in practical fashion, also. This is simply to say that it is not possible to separate *doctrine* and

practice, in their practical aspects, in one's life. Doctrine, without practice, is worthless (James 2 : 14-26) ; and practice without doctrine is aimless and will not long persist.

We have observed from the numerous warnings which the Epistle contains that those to whom James wrote were ever in danger of forsaking the truth, and of falling into the sins which were peculiar to, and characteristic of, their time and situation. The warning which this passage contains was, therefore, especially opportune. Moreover, the statement is a rebuke to all who would minimize "doctrine." Why do men sin and fall? Because they err from the truth. What is the only really effective way by which men may be restrained from falling? By inducing them to accept, and abide by, the truth. Jesus said "to those Jews that believed on him, If ye abide in my word, then are ye truly my disciples: and ye shall know the truth, and the truth shall make you free." (John 8 : 31, 32.) A man's life, in its outward aspects, is a true reflection of his character ; and his character is a mirror of what he believes. *Of course it makes a difference what one believes!* He who believes that his ancestral tree contained apes will live like an ape if the temptation to is sufficiently strong: he who is impressed with the realization that he has the stamp of divinity on him will strive to reach up to God.

Men are begotten by the word of truth (James 1 : 18) ; their souls are purified by it (1 Pet. 1 : 22, 23) ; by it they are saved (1 Cor. 15 : 1-3) ; and in it they are made free (John 8 : 31, 32). It follows, therefore, that any lapse from what is right is simply *an abandonment of the truth* which elevated them to the point from which they fell. In the light of these facts, it is amazing that men who affect to believe the Bible would nevertheless insist that it is impossible for a child of God to sin and fall away so as to be finally lost in hell. In an uncopyrighted tract written many years ago, a Mr. Morris, under the title DO A CHRISTIAN'S SINS DAMN HIS SOUL, said:

> "We take the position that a Christian's sins do not
> damn his soul. The way a Christian lives, what he says,
> his character, his conduct, or his attitude toward other
> people have nothing whatever to do with the salvation
> of his soul. . . . All the prayers a man may pray, all the
> Bibles he may read, all the churches he may belong to,

> all the services he may attend, all the sermons he may
> practice, all the debts he may pay, all the ordinances he
> may observe, all the laws he may keep, all the benevolent
> acts he may perform will not make his soul one whit
> safer; and all the sins he may commit from idolatry to
> murder will not make his soul in any more danger. . . .
> The way a man lives has nothing whatever to do with
> the salvation of his Soul. . . ."

This sentiment, repugnant to reason and revelation alike, is refuted hundreds of times in both Testaments. The following illustrations, one from each, will suffice to demonstrate the fact: "And thou Solomon, my son, know thou the God of thy father, and serve him with a perfect heart and a willing mind; for Jehovah searcheth all hearts, and understandeth all the imaginations of the thoughts. If thou seek him, he will be found of thee; but if thou forsake him, he will cast thee off for ever." (1 Chron. 28:9.) "Behold, I Paul say unto you, that if ye receive circumcision, Christ will profit you nothing. Yea, I testify again to every man that receiveth circumcision, that he is a debtor to do the whole law. Ye are severed from Christ, ye who would be justified by the law; *ye are fallen away from grace.*" (Gal. 5: 2-4.) The Scriptures not only assert the possibility of apostasy, they cite us to numerous instances of it, one of which is the following: "But shun profane babblings: for they will proceed further in ungodliness, and their word will eat as doth a gangrene: of whom is Hymaneaeus and Philetus; men who concerning the truth have erred, saying that the resurrection is past already, and overthrow the faith of some." (2 Tim. 2: 16-18.)

and one convert him;—*(Ho epistrepsas,* aorist active participle of *epistrepho,* to turn.) Thus, to convert one is to turn one away from the course being followed. This is not to be construed as meaning that one man can literally save another; what is meant is that by teaching, encouragement, and assistance, one may turn another back from the fatal course being followed, reestablish his confidence in the truth and thus set him in the right way again. While here the statement has particular reference to the erring disciple, the principle is equally applicable to any sinner, alien or otherwise. In either instance, such a one must be "converted"; i.e., turned from the disastrous course he is pursuing, and brought back

him; 20 [8]let him know, that he who converteth a sinner from the error of his way shall save a soul from death, and shall cover a multitude of sins.

[8]Some ancient authorities read *know ye.*

to the right way. The word of God—the truth of the gospel—is, of course, the instrument; but an instrument which must be wielded by men, inasmuch as "it pleased God *by the foolishness of preaching* to save them that believe." (1 Cor. 1 : 21.)

20 let him know, that he who converteth a sinner from the error of his way—The "him" is the "one" of verse 19, and is further identified as "he who converteth a sinner from the error of his way," in verse 20. The phrase, "Let him know," *(ginosketo,* present active imperative), is literally, "Let him keep on knowing. . . ." The word "converteth" has the same significance as in verse 19, and means "to turn." The "sinner," *(hamartolon,* from *hamartia,* to miss the mark), is any one who does wrong; though here, by the context, it is evidently limited to erring brethren. "The error of his way" is the course followed after forsaking the truth. The word rendered "error," *(plane),* means not only sin, but sin induced by deception. (1 John 4: 6; 2 Pet. 2: 18; 3: 17.) There is, of course, always an element of deception involved in apostasy, inasmuch as one follows such a course only because of deception regarding what is preferable or desirable.

shall save a soul from death,—The "soul" to be saved from death in this fashion is, of course, the soul of the one turned back from error. It is absurd to say, as do some commentators, that the soul saved is that of the person who turns the sinner from the error of his way. For a discussion of the words, "soul" and "spirit," see notes under James 2: 26. The "death" contemplated is spiritual—not physical. All, except those living when the Lord returns, must eventually die, both good and bad; none, in the normal run of events, can escape physical death. The word *death* denotes "separation." Thus, to "save a soul from death" is to enable such a one to escape eternal separation from God and all that is good.

and shall cover a multitude of sins.—Not only is an erring brother, through the ministrations of another, thus saved from spiritual death, the action involved covers "a multitude of sins."

To cover is to hide, put out of sight. Thus, by enabling a brother to obtain forgiveness, we bring him back from a situation which must, if permitted to proceed, result in eternal separation from God; and his sins are put away, hidden, covered. There appears to be in the statement, "and shall hide a multitude of sins," a clear allusion to a common Hebrew concept associated with the cover of the ark or, as it is sometimes called, "the mercy seat." "Blessed is he whose transgression is forgiven, whose sin is covered. Blessed is the man unto whom Jehovah imputeth not iniquity." (Psalm 32: 1, 2.) "Even as David also pronounceth blessing upon the man, unto whom God reckoneth righteousness apart from works, saying, Blessed are they whose iniquities are forgiven, and whose sins are covered." (Rom. 4: 6-8.) To "cover" sins is, therefore, to put them away, cancel them out, forgive them. The Hebrew usage clearly establishes this significance of the term; and this is accomplished when a brother is made to see the error of his way, and is prompted to turn to God for the forgiveness which he alone can provide.

Emphasized here is an obligation repeatedly taught in the Scriptures. We neither live nor die unto ourselves; and we thus sustain a tremendous responsibility to those about us—whether saints or sinners—to help them to heaven. "And they that are wise shall shine as the brightness of the firmament; and they that turn many to righteousness as the stars for ever and ever." (Dan. 12: 3.) "The fruit of the righteous is as a tree of life; and he that is wise winneth souls." (Prov. 11: 30.) To be assured of going to heaven ourselves we must serve the Lord faithfully, and seek to take as many people with us as possible. Tragic indeed will the situation be if in judgment some friend or associate should say, "I lived with you in yonder's world; I was associated with you for many years; and notwithstanding the fact that you assisted me in many *material* matters, you exhibited no interest in my soul's welfare, nor sought to turn me to the Lord. In fact, you never mentioned Him to me!" Someone has well said:

> "I think I should mourn o'er my sorrowful fate,
>   If sorrow in heaven can be;
> If no one should be at the Beautiful Gate,
>   There watching and waiting for me."

And thus ends the Epistle of James, one of the truly great documents of the New Testament. There is no formal conclusion; the Letter ends on the high and fraternal plane on which it begins: an earnest and impressive appeal to "my brethren."   (1 : 2; 5 : 19.) Here, indeed, is the apex of Christian service; the only way, in truth, to genuine greatness in this life—to that place where love finds its fullest, richest realization.

ᶜΙΑΚΩΒΟΥ   ΕΠΙΣΤΟΛΗ ΚΑΘΟΛΙΚΗ.ᵇ
⁴OF ⁵JAMES [¹THE]   ³EPISTLE   ²GENERAL.

JAMES, a servant of God and of the Lord Jesus Christ, to the twelve tribes which are scattered abroad, greeting.

ΙΑΚΩΒΟΣ θεοῦ καὶ κυρίου ᶜΙησοῦ χριστοῦ δοῦλος, ταῖς δώδεκα φυλαῖς ταῖς ἐν τῇ διασπορᾷ χαίρειν.

James ²of ³God ⁴and ⁵of [⁶the] ⁷Lord ⁸Jesus ⁹Christ ¹bondman, to the twelve tribes which [are] in the dispersion, greeting.

ᵗ πειθόμεθα we persuade ourselves LTTrAW.   ᵛ — ἔργῳ T.   ʷ + αὐτῷ to himself L.
ˣ ἡμῖν us T.   ʸ ἀνέχεσθαι to bear L.   ᶻ + ἡμῶν (read our brother) LTTrAW.   ᵃ — ἀμήν T.
ᵇ — the subscription GLTW; Πρὸς Ἑβραίους TrA.

ᶜ + τοῦ ἀποστόλου the Apostle E ; Ἐπιστολαὶ (— Ἐπιστ. L) καθολικαί. Ἰακώβου ἐπιστολή General Epistles. Epistle of James GLW; Ἰακώβου ἐπιστολή TTrA.

2 Πᾶσαν χαρὰν ἡγήσασθε, ἀδελφοί.μου, ὅταν πειρασμοῖς
All   joy   esteem [it], my brethren, when ⁴temptations

περιπέσητε ποικίλοις, 3 γινώσκοντες ὅτι τὸ δοκίμιον ὑμῶν
³ye ²may ²fall ⁴into ⁵various,   knowing   that the proving of your

τῆς πίστεως κατεργάζεται ὑπομονήν· 4 ἡ.δὲ.ὑπομονὴ ἔργον
faith   works out   endurance.   But ²endurance [⁴its] ⁵work

τέλειον ἐχέτω, ἵνα ἦτε τέλειοι καὶ ὁλόκληροι, ἐν μηδενὶ λει-
⁶perfect ¹let ²have, that ye may be perfect and complete, in nothing lack-

πόμενοι. 5 εἰ.δέ τις ὑμῶν λείπεται σοφίας, αἰτείτω παρὰ τοῦ
ing.   But if anyone of you lack wisdom, let him ask from ⁸who

διδόντος θεοῦ πᾶσιν ἁπλῶς, καὶ μὴ.ὀνειδίζοντος, καὶ δοθήσε-
⁹gives ¹God to all   freely, and   reproaches not, and it shall be

ται αὐτῷ. 6 αἰτείτω.δὲ ἐν πίστει, μηδὲν διακρινόμενος· ὁ.γὰρ
given to him: but let him ask in faith, nothing doubting. For he that

διακρινόμενος ἔοικεν κλύδωνι θαλάσσης ἀνεμιζομένῳ καὶ
doubts   is like a wave of [the] sea being driven by the wind and

ῥιπιζομένῳ. 7 μὴ.γὰρ οἰέσθω ὁ.ἄνθρωπος.ἐκεῖνος, ὅτι ᵈλή-
being tossed; for ²not ¹let ³suppose ⁴that ⁵man   that he

ψεταιᵈ τι παρὰ τοῦ κυρίου· 8 ἀνὴρ δίψυχος,
shall receive anything from the Lord; [he is] a ²man ¹double-minded,

ἀκατάστατος ἐν πάσαις ταῖς.ὁδοῖς.αὐτοῦ. 9 Καυχάσθω.δὲ
unstable in   all   his ways.   But let ⁶boast

ὁ ἀδελφὸς ὁ ταπεινὸς ἐν τῷ.ὕψει.αὐτοῦ· 10 ὁ.δὲ πλούσιος
¹the ²brother ³of ⁴low ⁵degree in his elevation, and the rich

ἐν τῇ.ταπεινώσει.αὐτοῦ, ὅτι ὡς ἄνθος χόρτου παρελεύ-
in   his humiliation, because as ³flower [¹the] ²grass's he will pass

σεται. 11 ἀνέτειλεν.γὰρ ὁ ἥλιος σὺν τῷ.καύσωνι, καὶ ἐξή-
away.   For ²rose ¹the ²sun with [its] burning heat, and dried

ρανεν τὸν χόρτον, καὶ τὸ ἄνθος αὐτοῦ ἐξέπεσεν, καὶ ἡ εὐ-
up the grass, and the flower of it   fell,   and the

πρεπεια τοῦ.προσώπου.αὐτοῦ ἀπώλετο· οὕτως καὶ ὁ πλούσιος
comeliness of its appearance perished: thus also the rich

ἐν ταῖς.πορείαις.αὐτοῦ μαρανθήσεται. 12 Μακάριος ἀνὴρ
in his goings   shall wither.   Blessed [is the] man

ὃς ὑπομένει πειρασμόν· ὅτι δόκιμος γενόμενος ᵉλήψεταιᵉ
who endures temptation; because ³proved ¹having ²been he shall receive

τὸν στέφανον τῆς ζωῆς, ὃν ἐπηγγείλατο ᶠὁ κύριοςᶠ τοῖς
the   crown   of life, which ²promised ¹the ⁴Lord to those that

ἀγαπῶσιν αὐτόν.
love   him.

13 Μηδεὶς πειραζόμενος λεγέτω, Ὅτι ἀπὸ ᵍτοῦᵍ θεοῦ πειρά-
²No ³one ⁴being ⁵tempted ¹let say,   From   God I am

ζομαι· ὁ.γὰρ.θεὸς ἀπείραστός ἐστιν κακῶν, πειράζει.δὲ αὐτὸς
tempted. For God ²not ³to ⁴be ⁵tempted ¹is by evils, and ²tempts ¹himself

οὐδένα. 14 ἕκαστος.δὲ πειράζεται, ʰὑπὸʰ τῆς.ἰδίας ἐπιθυμίας
no one.   But each one is tempted, by   his own   lust

ἐξελκόμενος καὶ δελεαζόμενος· 15 εἶτα ἡ ἐπιθυμία συλλαβοῦσα
being drawn away and being allured; then lust having conceived

τίκτει ἁμαρτίαν· ἡ.δὲ.ἁμαρτία ἀποτελεσθεῖσα ἀποκύει
gives birth to sin; but sin having been completed brings forth

θάνατον. 16 Μὴ.πλανᾶσθε, ἀδελφοί μου ἀγαπητοί· 17 πᾶσα
death.   Be not misled, ³brethren ¹my ²beloved.   Every

δόσις ἀγαθὴ καὶ πᾶν δώρημα τέλειον ἄνωθέν ἐστιν
³act ³of ⁴giving ¹good and every ²gift ¹perfect ⁶from ⁷above   ²is

2 My brethren, count it all joy when ye fall into divers temptations; 3 knowing this, that the trying of your faith worketh patience. 4 But let patience have her perfect work, that ye may be perfect and entire, wanting nothing. 5 If any of you lack wisdom, let him ask of God, that giveth to all men liberally, and upbraideth not; and it shall be given him. 6 But let him ask in faith, nothing wavering. For he that wavereth is like a wave of the sea driven with the wind and tossed. 7 For let not that man think that he shall receive any thing of the Lord. 8 A double minded man is unstable in all his ways. 9 Let the brother of low degree rejoice in that he is exalted: 10 but the rich, in that he is made low: because as the flower of the grass he shall pass away. 11 For the sun is no sooner risen with a burning heat, but it withereth the grass, and the flower thereof falleth, and the grace of the fashion of it perisheth: so also shall the rich man fade away in his ways. 12 Blessed is the man that endureth temptation: for when he is tried, he shall receive the crown of life, which the Lord hath promised to them that love him.

13 Let no man say when he is tempted, I am tempted of God: for God cannot be tempted with evil, neither tempteth he any man: 14 but every man is tempted, when he is drawn away of his own lust, and enticed. 15 Then when lust hath conceived, it bringeth forth sin: and sin, when it is finished, bringeth forth death. 16 Do not err, my beloved brethren. 17 Every good gift and every perfect gift is from above, and cometh down from the Father of lights, with

---

ᵈ λήμψεταί LTTrA.   ᵉ λήμψεται LTTrA.   ᶠ — ὁ κύριος (read ἐπηγ. he promised) LTTrA.
ᵍ — τοῦ GLTTrAW.   ʰ ἀπὸ A.

whom is no variableness, neither shadow of turning. 18 Of his own will begat he us with the word of truth, that we should be a kind of firstfruits of his creatures.

καταβαῖνον ἀπὸ τοῦ πατρὸς τῶν φώτων, παρ' ᾧ οὐκ.ἔνι
⁴coming ⁵down from the Father of lights, with whom there is not
παραλλαγή, ἢ τροπῆς ἀποσκίασμα. 18 βουληθεὶς ἀπε-
variation, or ²of ³turning ¹shadow. Having willed [it] he be-
κύησεν ἡμᾶς λόγῳ ἀληθείας, εἰς τὸ εἶναι ἡμᾶς ἀπαρχήν
gat us by [the] word of truth, for ⁴to ³be ⁵us ⁷first-fruits
τινα τῶν.αὐτοῦ.κτισμάτων.
⁶a ⁸sort ⁹of of his creatures.

19 Wherefore, my beloved brethren, let every man be swift to hear, slow to speak, slow to wrath: 20 for the wrath of man worketh not the righteousness of God. 21 Wherefore lay apart all filthiness and superfluity of naughtiness, and receive with meekness the engrafted word, which is able to save your souls. 22 But be ye doers of the word, and not hearers only, deceiving your own selves. 23 For if any be a hearer of the word, and not a doer, he is like unto a man beholding his natural face in a glass: 24 for he beholdeth himself, and goeth his way, and straightway forgetteth what manner of man he was. 25 But whoso looketh into the perfect law of liberty, and continueth therein, he being not a forgetful hearer, but a doer of the work, this man shall be blessed in his deed. 26 If any man among you seem to be religious, and bridleth not his tongue, but deceiveth his own heart, this man's religion is vain. 27 Pure religion and undefiled before God and the Father is this, To visit the fatherless and widows in their affliction, and to keep himself unspotted from the world.

19 ᵢ"Ὥστε," ἀδελφοί μου ἀγαπητοί, ἔστω ᵏ πᾶς ἄνθρωπος
So that, ³brethren ¹my ²beloved, let ³be ¹every ²man
ταχὺς εἰς τὸ ἀκοῦσαι, βραδὺς εἰς τὸ λαλῆσαι, βραδὺς εἰς ὀργήν.
swift to hear, slow to speak, slow to wrath;
20 ὀργὴ.γὰρ ἀνδρὸς δικαιοσύνην θεοῦ ᵗοὐ.κατεργάζεται."
for ²wrath ¹man's ⁷righteousness ⁶God's ³works ⁴not ⁵out.
21 Διὸ ἀποθέμενοι πᾶσαν ῥυπαρίαν καὶ περισσείαν κα-
Wherefore, having laid aside all filthiness and abounding of wick-
κίας, ἐν πραΰτητι δέξασθε τὸν ἔμφυτον λόγον, τὸν δυνά-
edness, in meekness accept the implanted word, which [is]
μενον σῶσαι τὰς.ψυχὰς.ὑμῶν. 22 γίνεσθε.δὲ ποιηταὶ λόγου,
able to save your souls. But be ye doers of [the] word,
καὶ μὴ ᵐμόνον ἀκροαταί," παραλογιζόμενοι ἑαυτούς. 23 ὅτι
and not only hearers, beguiling yourselves. Because
εἰ τις ἀκροατὴς λόγου ἐστὶν καὶ οὐ ποιητής, οὗτος
if any man a hearer of [the] word is and not a doer, this one
ἔοικεν.ἀνδρὶ κατανοοῦντι τὸ πρόσωπον τῆς γενέσεως αὐτοῦ
is like to a man considering ³face ²natural ¹his
ἐν ἐσόπτρῳ· 24 κατενόησεν.γὰρ ἑαυτὸν καὶ ἀπελήλυθεν, καὶ
in a mirror: for he considered himself and has gone away, and
εὐθέως ἐπελάθετο ὁποῖος ἦν. 25 ὁ.δὲ παρακύψας εἰς
immediately forgot what ²like ¹he ⁸was. But he that looked into
νόμον τέλειον τὸν τῆς ἐλευθερίας, καὶ παραμείνας,
[the] ²law ¹perfect, that of freedom, and continued in [it],
ⁿ"οὗτος" οὐκ ἀκροατὴς ἐπιλησμονῆς γενόμενος, ἀλλὰ ποιητὴς
this one not a ²hearer ¹forgetful having been, but a doer
ἔργου, οὗτος μακάριος ἐν τῇ.ποιήσει.αὐτοῦ ἔσται. 26 Εἰ
of [the] work, this one blessed in his doing shall be. If
ᵒτις δοκεῖ θρῆσκος εἶναι ᴾἐν ὑμῖν," μὴ χαλιναγωγῶν
anyone ³seems ⁶religious ⁴to ⁵be ¹among ²you, not bridling
γλῶσσαν.αὐτοῦ, ᵠ"ἀλλ'" ἀπατῶν καρδίαν.ʳαὐτοῦ," τούτου
his tongue, but deceiving his heart, of this one
μάταιος ἡ ˢθρησκεία." 27 ˢθρησκεία" καθαρὰ καὶ ἀμίαντος
vain [is] the religion. Religion pure and undefiled
παρὰ ᵗ"τῷ" θεῷ καὶ πατρὶ αὕτη ἐστίν, ἐπισκέπτεσθαι ὀρ-
before God and [the] Father ²this ¹is: to visit or-
φανοὺς καὶ χήρας ἐν τῇ.θλίψει.αὐτῶν, ἄσπιλον ἑαυτὸν τηρεῖν
phans and widows in their tribulation, unspotted ⁸oneself ¹to ²keep
ἀπὸ τοῦ κόσμου.
from the world.

II. My brethren, have not the faith of our Lord Jesus Christ, the Lord of glory, with respect of persons. 2 For if there come un-

2 Ἀδελφοί.μου, μὴ ἐν ᵛ"προσωποληψίαις" ἔχετε τὴν πίστιν
My brethren, ³not ⁴with ⁵respect ⁶of ⁷persons ¹do ²have the faith
τοῦ.κυρίου.ἡμῶν Ἰησοῦ χριστοῦ τῆς δόξης· 2 ἐάν.γὰρ
of our Lord Jesus Christ, [Lord] of glory; for if

εἰσέλθῃ εἰς ᵂτὴνˡσυναγωγὴν ὑμῶν ἀνὴρ χρυσοδακτύλιος
may have come into   your synagogue   a man   with gold rings

ἐν ἐσθῆτι λαμπρᾷ, εἰσέλθῃ δὲ καὶ πτωχὸς ἐν ῥυπαρᾷ
in ²apparel ¹splendid, and may have come in also a poor [man] in vile

ἐσθῆτι, 3 ˣκαὶ ἐπιβλέψητε ἐπὶ τὸν φοροῦντα τὴν ἐσθῆτα
apparel,   and ye may have looked upon him who wears   the ²apparel

τὴν λαμπράν, καὶ εἴπητε ʸαὐτῷ,ˮ Σὺ κάθου ὧδε καλῶς, καὶ
¹splendid,   and may have said to him, Thou sit thou here well,   and

τῷ πτωχῷ εἴπητε, Σὺ στῆθι ἐκεῖ, ἢ κάθου ᶻὧδεˮ ὑπὸ
to the poor   may have said, Thou stand thou there, or sit thou here under

τὸ ὑποπόδιόν μου· 4 ᵃκαὶ οὐ   διεκρίθητε   ἐν ἑαυτοῖς,
my footstool: ⁴also ³not ¹did ²ye make a difference among yourselves,

καὶ ἐγένεσθε κριταὶ διαλογισμῶν πονηρῶν; 5 Ἀκούσατε,
and became   judges [having] ²reasonings ¹evil?   Hear,

ἀδελφοί μου ἀγαπητοί, οὐχ ὁ θεὸς ἐξελέξατο τοὺς πτωχοὺς
³brethren ¹my ²beloved: ⁵not ⁶God ⁴did choose the   poor

ᵇτοῦ κόσμου,ˮ ᶜτούτου,ˮ πλουσίους ἐν πίστει, καὶ κληρονόμους
³world   ¹of ²this,   rich   in faith, and   heirs

τῆς βασιλείας ἧς ἐπηγγείλατο τοῖς ἀγαπῶσιν αὐτόν;
of the kingdom which he promised to those that love   him?

6 ὑμεῖς δὲ ἠτιμάσατε τὸν πτωχόν.   ᵈοὐχˮ οἱ πλούσιοι
But ye dishonoured the poor [man]. ²Not ³the ⁴rich

καταδυναστεύουσιν ᵉὑμῶν,ˮ καὶ αὐτοὶ ἕλκουσιν ὑμᾶς
¹do oppress   you,   and [²not] ³they ¹do drag you

εἰς κριτήρια; 7 οὐκ αὐτοὶ βλασφημοῦσιν τὸ καλὸν
before [the] tribunals? ²not ³they ¹do blaspheme the good

ὄνομα τὸ ἐπικληθὲν ἐφ' ὑμᾶς; 8 Εἰ μέντοι νόμον τελεῖτε
name which was called upon you? If indeed [the] ²law ³ye ⁴keep

βασιλικόν, κατὰ τὴν γραφήν, Ἀγαπήσεις τὸν πλησίον σου
¹royal   according to the scripture, Thou shalt love thy neighbour

ὡς σεαυτόν, καλῶς ποιεῖτε· 9 εἰ δὲ ᶠπροσωπολημπτεῖτε,ˮ ἁμαρ-
as thyself, ·³well ¹ye ²do. But if ye have respect of persons, ⁵sin

τίαν ἐργάζεσθε, ἐλεγχόμενοι ὑπὸ τοῦ νόμου ὡς παραβάται.
¹ye ²work, being convicted by the law as transgressors.

10 ὅστις γὰρ ὅλον τὸν νόμον ᵍτηρήσει, πταίσειˮ δὲ ἐν ἑνί,
For whosoever ²whole ¹the law shall keep, ²shall ³stumble ¹but in one

γέγονεν πάντων ἔνοχος. 11 ὁ γὰρ εἰπών, Μὴ μοι-
[point], he has become ²of ³all ¹guilty. For he who said, ³not ¹Thou

χεύσῃς, εἶπεν καί, Μὴ φονεύσῃς· εἰ δὲ
²mayest commit adultery, said also, Thou mayest not commit murder. Now if

οὐ ʰμοιχεύσεις, φονεύσειςˮ δέ, γέγονας
thou shalt not commit adultery, ²shalt ³commit ⁴murder ¹but, thou hast become

παραβάτης νόμου. 12 Οὕτως λαλεῖτε καὶ οὕτως ποιεῖτε, ὡς
a transgressor of [the] law. So   speak ye and so   do,   as

διὰ νόμου ἐλευθερίας μέλλοντες κρίνεσθαι· 13 ἡ γὰρ κρίσις
by [the] law of freedom being about to be judged;   for judgment

ⁱἀνίλεως,ˮ τῷ μὴ ποιήσαντι ἔλεος· ᵏκαὶ κατα-
[will be] without mercy to him that wrought not mercy. And ²boasts

καυχᾶται ἔλεος κρίσεως.
³over ¹mercy judgment.

14 Τί ˡτὸ ὄφελος, ἀδελφοί μου, ἐὰν πίστιν ᵐλέγῃ τις,ˮ
What [is] the profit, my brethren, if ⁵faith ²say ¹anyone

to your assembly a
man with a gold ring,
in goodly apparel, and
there come in also a
poor man in vile rai-
ment; 3 and ye have
respect to him that
weareth the gay cloth-
ing, and say unto him,
Sit thou here in a good
place; and say to the
poor, Stand thou there,
or sit here under my
footstool: 4 are ye not
then partial in your-
selves, and are be-
come judges of evil
thoughts? 5 Hearken,
my beloved brethren,
Hath not God chosen
the poor of this
world rich in faith,
and heirs of the king-
dom which he hath
promised to them that
love him? 6 But ye
have despised the poor.
Do not rich men op-
press you, and draw
you before the judg-
ment seats? 7 Do not
they blaspheme that
worthy name by the
which ye are call-
ed? 8 If ye fulfil the
royal law according to
the scripture, Thou
shalt love thy neigh-
bour as thyself, ye do
well: 9 but if ye have
respect to persons, ye
commit sin, and are
convinced of the law
as transgressors. 10 For
whosoever shall keep
the whole law, and yet
offend in one point, he
is guilty of all. 11 For
he that said, Do not
commit adultery, said
also, Do not kill. Now
if thou commit no
adultery, yet if thou
kill, thou art become a
transgressor of the law.
12 So speak ye, and so
do, as they that shall
be judged by the law
of liberty. 13 For he
shall have judgment
without mercy, that
hath shewed no mercy;
and mercy rejoiceth
against judgment.

14 What doth it
profit, my brethren,

though a man say he hath faith, and have not works? can faith save him? 15 If a brother or sister be naked, and destitute of daily food, 16 and one of you say unto them, Depart in peace, be ye warmed and filled; notwithstanding ye give them not those things which are needful to the body; what *doth it* profit? 17 Even so faith, if it hath not works, is dead, being alone. 18 Yea, a man may say, Thou hast faith, and I have works: shew me thy faith without thy works, and I will shew thee my faith by my works. 19 Thou believest that there is one God; thou doest well: the devils also believe, and tremble. 20 But wilt thou know, O vain man, that faith without works is dead? 21 Was not Abraham our father justified by works, when he had offered Isaac his son upon the altar? 22 Seest thou how faith wrought with his works, and by works was faith made perfect? 23 And the scripture was fulfilled which saith, Abraham believed God, and it was imputed unto him for righteousness: and he was called the Friend of God. 24 Ye see then how that by works a man is justified, and not by faith only. 25 Likewise also was not Rahab the harlot justified by works, when she had received the messengers, and had sent *them* out another way? 26 For as the body without the spirit is dead, so faith without works is dead also.

III. My brethren, be not many masters, knowing that we shall receive the greater condemnation. 2 For in many things we offend all. If any man

---

ἔχειν, ἔργα.δὲ μὴ.ἔχῃ; μὴ δύναται ἡ πίστις σῶσαι αὐτόν;
[³he] ⁴has, but works have not? is ²able ¹faith to save him?

15 ἐὰν.ⁿδὲ‖ ἀδελφὸς ἢ ἀδελφὴ γυμνοὶ ὑπάρχωσιν, καὶ λειπό-
Now if a brother or a sister ²naked ¹be, and desti-

μενοι °ὦσιν‖ τῆς ἐφημέρου τροφῆς, 16 εἴπῃ.δέ τις αὐτοῖς
tute may be of daily food, and ⁸say ¹anyone ⁶to ⁷them

ἐξ ὑμῶν, Ὑπάγετε ἐν εἰρήνῃ, θερμαίνεσθε καὶ χορτά-
²from ³amongst ⁴you, Go in peace; be warmed and be fill-

ζεσθε, μὴ.δῶτε.δὲ αὐτοῖς τὰ ἐπιτήδεια τοῦ σώματος, τί
ed; but give not to them the needful things for the body, what [is]

ᴾτὸ‖ ὄφελος; 17 οὕτως καὶ ἡ πίστις ἐὰν μὴ ᵠἔργα ἔχῃ‖ νεκρά
the profit? So also faith, if ³not ⁴works ⁵it ²have, ⁶dead

ἐστιν καθ' ἑαυτήν. 18 ἀλλ' ἐρεῖ τις Σὺ πίστιν ἔχεις,
¹is by itself. But ³will ⁴say ¹some ²one, Thou ²faith ¹hast

κἀγὼ ἔργα ἔχω· δεῖξόν μοι τὴν.πίστιν.σου ʳἐκ‖ τῶν ἔργων
and I ²works ¹have. Shew me thy faith from ²works

ˢσου,‖ κἀγὼ ᵗδείξω σοι‖ ἐκ τῶν.ἔργων.μου τὴν πίστιν ᵘμου.
¹thy, and I will shew thee from my works ²faith ¹my.

19 σὺ πιστεύεις ὅτι ᵛὁ θεὸς εἷς ἐστιν.‖ καλῶς ποιεῖς· καὶ τὰ
Thou believest that God ²one ¹is. ⁵Well ³thou ⁴doest; even the

δαιμόνια πιστεύουσιν, καὶ φρίσσουσιν. 20 θέλεις.δὲ γνῶναι,
demons believe, and shudder. But wilt thou know,

ὦ ἄνθρωπε κενέ, ὅτι ἡ πίστις χωρὶς τῶν ἔργων ʷνεκρά‖ ἐστιν;
O ²man ¹empty, that faith apart from works dead is?

21 Ἀβραὰμ ὁ.πατὴρ.ἡμῶν οὐκ ἐξ ἔργων ἐδικαιώθη, ἀνε-
³Abraham ⁴our ⁵father ²not ⁷by ⁸works ¹was ⁶justified, having

νέγκας Ἰσαὰκ τὸν.υἱὸν.αὐτοῦ ἐπὶ τὸ θυσιαστήριον; 22 βλέ-
offered Isaac his son upon the altar? Thou

πεις ὅτι ἡ πίστις ˣσυνήργει‖ τοῖς.ἔργοις.αὐτοῦ, καὶ ἐκ τῶν
seest that faith was working with his works, and by

ἔργων ἡ πίστις ἐτελειώθη;ʸ 23 καὶ ἐπληρώθη ἡ γραφὴ ἡ
works faith was perfected. And was fulfilled the scripture which

λέγουσα, Ἐπίστευσεν.δὲ Ἀβραὰμ τῷ θεῷ, καὶ ἐλογίσθη·
says, Now ²believed ¹Abraham God, and it was reckoned

αὐτῷ εἰς δικαιοσύνην, καὶ φίλος θεοῦ ἐκλήθη. 24 Ὁρᾶτε
to him for righteousness, and friend of God he was called. Ye see

ᶻτοίνυν‖ ὅτι ἐξ ἔργων δικαιοῦται ἄνθρωπος, καὶ οὐκ ἐκ πίστεως
then that by works is justified a man, and not by faith

μόνον.ᵃ 25 ὁμοίως.δὲ καὶ Ῥαὰβ ἡ πόρνη οὐκ ἐξ ἔργων
only. But in like manner also ³Rahab ⁴the ⁵harlot ²not ⁷by ⁸works

ἐδικαιώθη, ὑποδεξαμένη τοὺς ἀγγέλους, καὶ ἑτέρᾳ ὁδῷ
¹was ⁶justified, having received the messengers, and by another way

ἐκβαλοῦσα; 26 ὥσπερ.γὰρ τὸ σῶμα χωρὶς ᵇπνεύματος
having put [them] forth? For as the body apart from spirit

νεκρόν ἐστιν, οὕτως καὶ ἡ πίστις χωρὶς ᵇτῶν‖ ἔργων νεκρά
²dead ¹is. so also faith apart from works ²dead

ἐστιν.
¹is.

3 Μὴ πολλοὶ διδάσκαλοι γίνεσθε, ἀδελφοί.μου, εἰδότες ὅτι
²Not ³many ⁴teachers ¹be, my brethren, knowing that

μεῖζον κρίμα ᶜληψόμεθα·ᵃ 2 πολλὰ.γὰρ πταίομεν ἅπαντες.
greater judgment we shall receive. For ³often ¹we ⁴stumble ⁵all.

ᵃ — δὲ now TTr. ° — ὦσιν TTrA. ᴾ — τὸ L. ᵠ ἔχῃ ἔργα GLTTrAW. ʳ χωρὶς apart from GLTTrAW. ˢ — σου LTTrAW. ᵗ σοι δείξω TTr. ᵘ — μου TTrAW. ᵛ εἷς ἐστιν ὁ θεός LTTr; εἷς ὁ θεός ἐστιν AW. ʷ ἀργή idle LTTrA. ˣ συνεργεῖ works with TTr. ʸ *Read verse 22 interrogatively, as pointed in the Greek.* EGLTTrW. ᶻ — τοίνυν GLTTrAW. ᵃ *Read verse 24 as a question* GI.Tr. ᵇ — τῶν T[Tr]. ᶜ ληψόμεθα LTTrA.

εἴ τις ἐν λόγῳ οὐ.πταίει, οὗτος τέλειος ἀνήρ, δυνατὸς
If anyone in word stumble not, this one [is] a perfect man, able
χαλιναγωγῆσαι καὶ ὅλον τὸ σῶμα. 3 [d]Ἰδοὺ‖ τῶν ἵππων
to bridle also [3]whole [1]the body. Lo, [6]of [7]the [8]horses
τοὺς χαλινοὺς εἰς τὰ στόματα βάλλομεν [e]πρὸς‖ τὸ πείθεσθαι
[1]the [2]bits [3]in [4]the [5]mouths we put, for [2]to [3]obey
αὐτοὺς [f]ἡμῖν,‖ καὶ ὅλον τὸ.σῶμα.αὐτῶν μετάγομεν. 4 Ἰδοὺ
[1]them us, and [2]whole [1]their body we turn about. Lo,
καὶ τὰ πλοῖα τηλικαῦτα ὄντα, καὶ ὑπὸ [g]σκληρῶν ἀνέμων‖
also the ships, [2]so [3]great [1]being, and by violent winds
ἐλαυνόμενα, μετάγεται ὑπὸ ἐλαχίστου πηδαλίου, ὅπου
being driven, are turned about by a very small rudder, wherever
[h]ἂν‖ ἡ ὁρμὴ τοῦ εὐθύνοντος [i]βούληται.‖ 5 οὕτως καὶ
the impulse of him who steers may will. Thus also
ἡ γλῶσσα μικρὸν μέλος ἐστίν, καὶ [k]μεγαλαυχεῖ.‖ Ἰδού,
the tongue a little member is, and boasts great things. Lo,
[l]ὀλίγον‖ πῦρ ἡλίκην ὕλην ἀνάπτει· 6 [m]καὶ‖ ἡ γλῶσσα
a little fire how large a wood it kindles; and the tongue [is]
πῦρ, ὁ κόσμος τῆς ἀδικίας. [n]οὕτως‖ ἡ γλῶσσα καθίσταται
fire, the world of unrighteousness. Thus the tongue is set
ἐν τοῖς.μέλεσιν.ἡμῶν, [o]ἡ‖ σπιλοῦσα ὅλον τὸ σῶμα, καὶ φλο-
in our members, the defiler [of] [2]whole [1]the body, and setting
γίζουσα τὸν τροχὸν τῆς γενέσεως, καὶ φλογιζομένη ὑπὸ τῆς
on fire the course of nature, and being set on fire by
γεέννης· 7 πᾶσα.γὰρ φύσις θηρίων.τε καὶ πετεινῶν, ἑρπε-
gehenna. For every species both of beasts and of birds, [2]of [3]creeping
τῶν τε καὶ ἐναλίων, δαμάζεται καὶ δεδάμασται τῇ
[4]things [1]both and things of the sea, is subdued and has been subdued by
φύσει τῇ ἀνθρωπίνῃ· 8 τὴν.δὲ γλῶσσαν οὐδεὶς [p]δύναται
[3]species [1]the [2]human; but the tongue no one [3]is [4]able
ἀνθρώπων δαμάσαι·‖ [q]ἀκατάσχετον‖ κακόν, μεστὴ ἰοῦ
[1]of [2]men to subdue; [it is] an unrestrainable evil, full of [2]poison
θανατηφόρου. 9 ἐν.αὐτῇ εὐλογοῦμεν [r]τὸν θεὸν‖ καὶ πατέρα,
[1]death-bringing. Therewith we bless God and [the] Father,
καὶ ἐν.αὐτῇ καταρώμεθα τοὺς ἀνθρώπους τοὺς καθ'
and therewith we curse men who according to [the]
ὁμοίωσιν θεοῦ γεγονότας· 10 ἐκ τοῦ αὐτοῦ στόματος ἐξέρ-
likeness of God are made. Out of the same mouth goes
χεται εὐλογία καὶ κατάρα. οὐ χρή, ἀδελφοί.μου, ταῦτα
forth blessing and cursing. [5]Not [6]ought, [1]my [2]brethren, [3]these [4]things
οὕτως γίνεσθαι. 11 μήτι ἡ.πηγὴ ἐκ τῆς αὐτῆς ὀπῆς
thus to be. [3]The [4]fountain [5]out [6]of [7]the [8]same [9]opening
βρύει τὸ γλυκὺ καὶ τὸ πικρόν; 12 μὴ δύναται, ἀδελφοί
[1]pours [2]forth sweet and bitter? Is able, [2]brethren
μου, συκῆ ἐλαίας ποιῆσαι, ἢ ἄμπελος σῦκα; [s]οὕτως‖ [t]οὐδεμία
[1]my, a fig-tree olives to produce, or a vine figs? Thus no
πηγὴ ἁλυκὸν καὶ‖ γλυκὺ ποιῆσαι ὕδωρ.
fountain [is able] salt and sweet [2]to [3]produce [1]water.

offend not in word, the same *is* a perfect man, *and* able also to bridle the whole body. 3 Behold, we put bits in the horses' mouths, that they may obey us; and we turn about their whole body. 4 Behold also the ships, which though *they be* so great, and *are* driven of fierce winds, yet are they turned about with a very small helm, whithersoever the governor listeth. 5 Even so the tongue is a little member, and boasteth great things. Behold, how great a matter a little fire kindleth! 6 And the tongue *is* a fire, a world of iniquity: so is the tongue among our members, that it defileth the whole body, and setteth on fire the course of nature; and it is set on fire of hell. 7 For every kind of beasts, and of birds, and of serpents, and of things in the sea, is tamed, and hath been tamed of mankind: 8 but the tongue can no man tame; *it is* an unruly evil, full of deadly poison. 9 Therewith bless we God, even the Father; and therewith curse we men, which are made after the similitude of God. 10 Out of the same mouth proceedeth blessing and cursing. My brethren, these things ought not so to be. 11 Doth a fountain send forth at the same place sweet *water* and bitter? 12 Can the fig tree, my brethren, bear olive berries? either a vine, figs? so *can* no fountain both yield salt water and fresh.

13 Τίς σοφὸς καὶ ἐπιστήμων ἐν ὑμῖν; δειξάτω ἐκ τῆς
Who [is] wise and understanding among you; let him shew out of

13 Who *is* a wise man and endued with knowledge among you?

---

[d] ἴδε G; εἰ δὲ but if (*read* καὶ also) LTTrAW. [e] εἰς LTTrA. [f] ἡμῖν αὐτούς A. [g] ἀνέμων σκληρῶν LTTrAW. [h] — ἂν (*read* where) TTr. [i] βούλεται wills TTr. [k] μεγάλα αὐχεῖ LTTrA. [l] ἡλίκον *literally* how great (*some translate* how small) LTTrAW. [m] — καὶ (*read* the tongue kindles. A fire, &c.) T. [n] — οὕτως LTTrAW. [o] καὶ (*read* both defiling) T. [p] δαμάσαι δύναται ἀνθρώπων LTrA. [q] ἀκατάστατον an unsettled LTTrAW. [r] τὸν κύριον the Lord LTTrA. [s] — οὕτως LTTrAW. [t] οὔτε ἁλυκὸν neither salt [water is able] GLTTrAW.

let him shew out of a good conversation his works with meekness of wisdom. 14 But if ye have bitter envying and strife in your hearts, glory not, and lie not against the truth. 15 This wisdom descendeth not from above, but is earthly, sensual, devilish. 16 For where envying and strife is, there is confusion and every evil work. 17 But the wisdom that is from above is first pure, then peaceable, gentle, and easy to be intreated, full of mercy and good fruits, without partiality, and without hypocrisy. 18 And the fruit of righteousness is sown in peace of them that make peace. IV. From whence come wars and fightings among you? come they not hence, even of your lusts that war in your members? 2 Ye lust, and have not: ye kill and desire to have, and cannot obtain: ye fight and war, yet ye have not, because ye ask not. 3 Ye ask, and receive not, because ye ask amiss, that ye may consume it upon your lusts. 4 Ye adulterers and adulteresses, know ye not that the friendship of the world is enmity with God? Whosoever therefore will be a friend of the world is the enemy of God. 5 Do ye think that the scripture saith in vain, The spirit that dwelleth in us lusteth to envy? 6 But he giveth more grace. Wherefore he saith, God resisteth the proud, but giveth grace unto the humble. 7 Submit yourselves therefore to God. Resist the devil, and he will flee from you. 8 Draw nigh to God, and he will draw nigh to you. Cleanse your hands, ye sinners; and purify your hearts, ye double minded. 9 Be afflicted, and mourn, and weep: let your

καλῆς ἀναστροφῆς τὰ ἔργα αὐτοῦ ἐν πραΰτητι σοφίας. 14 εἰ δὲ
good conduct his works in meekness of wisdom; but if

ζῆλον πικρὸν ἔχετε καὶ ἐριθείαν ἐν τῇ καρδίᾳ ὑμῶν, μὴ κατα-
"emulation ¹bitter ye have and contention in your heart, ᵃnot ¹do

καυχᾶσθε ᵘκαὶ ψεύδεσθε κατὰ τῆς ἀληθείας.ᵘ 15 Οὐκ ἔστιν
boast against and lie against the truth. ²Not ²is

αὕτη ἡ σοφία ἄνωθεν κατερχομένη, ᵛἀλλ'ᵘ ἐπίγειος, ψυ-
¹this the wisdom from above coming down, but earthly, na-

χική, δαιμονιώδης. 16 ὅπου γὰρ ζῆλος καὶ ἐριθεία, ἐκεῖ
tural, devilish. For where emulation and contention [are]; there

ἀκαταστασία καὶ πᾶν φαῦλον πρᾶγμα. 17 ἡ δὲ ἄνωθεν
[is] commotion and every evil thing. But the ²from ³above

σοφία πρῶτον μὲν ἁγνή ἐστιν, ἔπειτα εἰρηνική, ἐπιεικής,
¹wisdom ⁵first ⁶pure ⁴is, then peaceful, gentle,

εὐπειθής, μεστὴ ἐλέους καὶ καρπῶν ἀγαθῶν, ἀδιάκριτος ᵂκαὶᵘ
yielding, full of mercy and of ⁶fruits ⁷good, impartial and

ἀνυπόκριτος. 18 καρπὸς δὲ ˣτῆςᵘ δικαιοσύνης ἐν εἰρήνῃ σπεί-
unfeigned. But [the] fruit of righteousness in peace is

ρεται τοῖς ποιοῦσιν εἰρήνην. 4 Πόθεν πόλεμοι καὶ ʸ
sown for those that make peace. Whence [come] wars and

μάχαι ἐν ὑμῖν; οὐκ ἐντεῦθεν, ἐκ τῶν ἡδονῶν ὑμῶν
fightings among you? [Is it] not thence, from your pleasures,

τῶν στρατευομένων ἐν τοῖς μέλεσιν ὑμῶν; 2 ἐπιθυμεῖτε, καὶ
which war in your members? Ye desire, and

οὐκ ἔχετε· φονεύετε καὶ ζηλοῦτε, καὶ οὐ δύνασθε ἐπιτυχεῖν.
have not; ye kill and are emulous, and are not able to obtain;

μάχεσθε καὶ πολεμεῖτε, ᶻοὐκ ἔχετε ᵃδέ,ᵘ διὰ τὸ μὴ αἰτεῖσθαι
ye fight and war, ²ye ³have ⁴not ¹but because ¹not ²ask

ὑμᾶς· 3 αἰτεῖτε, καὶ οὐ λαμβάνετε, διότι κακῶς αἰτεῖσθε ἵνα
¹you. Ye ask, and receive not, because evilly ye ask, that

ἐν ταῖς ἡδοναῖς ὑμῶν δαπανήσητε. 4 ᵇΜοιχοὶ καὶᵘ μοιχα-
in your pleasures ye may spend [it]. Adulterers and adulte-

λίδες, οὐκ οἴδατε ὅτι ἡ φιλία τοῦ κόσμου, ἔχθρα ᶜτοῦ
resses, know ye not that the friendship of the world enmity [with]

θεοῦ ἐστιν;ᵘ ὃς ᵈἂνᵘ οὖν βουληθῇ φίλος εἶναι τοῦ κόσμου,
God is? Whosoever therefore be minded a friend to be of the world,

ἐχθρὸς τοῦ θεοῦ καθίσταται. 5 ἢ δοκεῖτε ὅτι κενῶς ἡ γρα-
an enemy of God is constituted. Or think ye that in vain the scrip-

φὴ λέγει;ᵉ πρὸς φθόνον ἐπιποθεῖ τὸ πνεῦμα ὃ ᶠκατῴκησενᵘ
ture speaks? with envy does ³long ¹the ²Spirit which took up [his] abode

ἐν ἡμῖν;ᵍ 6 μείζονα δὲ δίδωσιν χάριν· διὸ λέγει, Ὁ θεὸς
in us? But ³greater ¹he ²gives grace. Wherefore he says, God

ὑπερηφάνοις ἀντιτάσσεται, ταπεινοῖς δὲ δίδωσιν χάριν.
[⁴the] ⁵proud ¹sets ²himself ³against, but to [the] lowly he gives grace.

7 Ὑποτάγητε οὖν τῷ θεῷ· ἀντίστητε ʰ τῷ διαβόλῳ, καὶ
Subject yourselves therefore to God. Resist the devil, and

φεύξεται ἀφ' ὑμῶν· 8 ἐγγίσατε τῷ θεῷ, καὶ ἐγγιεῖ ὑμῖν.
he will flee from you. Draw near to God, and he will draw near to you.

καθαρίσατε χεῖρας, ἁμαρτωλοί, καὶ ἁγνίσατε καρδίας,
Have cleansed [your] hands, sinners, and have purified [your] hearts,

δίψυχοι. 9 ταλαιπωρήσατε καὶ πενθήσατε ⁱκαὶᵘ κλαύσατε.
ye double minded. Be wretched, and mourn, and weep.

ᵘ τῆς ἀληθείας καὶ ψεύδεσθε T.   ᵛ ἀλλὰ TTr.   ᵂ — καὶ LTTrA.   ˣ — τῆς GLTTrAW.
ʸ + πόθεν whence LTTrAW.   ᶻ + καὶ and T.   ᵃ — δέ GLTTrA.   ᵇ — Μοιχοὶ καὶ
LTTrAW; join adulteresses to what precedes T.   ᶜ ἐστὶν τῷ θεῷ is with God T.   ᵈ ἐάν LT.
ᵉ — ; Text. Rec. and LA.   ᶠ κατῴκισεν he made to dwell LTTrA.   ᵍ — ; T.   ʰ + δὲ but
(resist) LTTrA.   ⁱ — καὶ T.

ὁ.γέλως.ὑμῶν εἰς πένθος μεταστραφήτω, καὶ ἡ.χαρὰ εἰς
*Your ³laughter ⁴to ⁵mourning ¹let be turned, and [your] joy to
κατήφειαν. 10 ταπεινώθητε ἐνώπιον ᵏτοῦ‖ κυρίου, καὶ ὑψώ-
heaviness. Humble yourselves before the Lord, and he will
σει ὑμᾶς.
exalt you.

11 Μὴ.καταλαλεῖτε ἀλλήλων, ἀδελφοί· ὁ καταλαλῶν
Speak not against one another, brethren. He that speaks against
ἀδελφοῦ, ¹καὶ‖ κρίνων τὸν.ἀδελφὸν.αὐτοῦ, καταλαλεῖ
[his] brother, and judges his brother, speaks against [the]
νόμου, καὶ κρίνει νόμον· εἰ.δὲ νόμον κρίνεις, οὐκ
law, and judges [the] law. But if [the] law thou judgest, ²not
εἶ ποιητὴς νόμου, ἀλλὰ κριτής. 12 εἷς ἐστιν ὁ νομο-
¹thou ²art a doer of [the] law, but a judge. One is the law-
θέτηςᵐ, ὁ δυνάμενος σῶσαι καὶ ἀπολέσαι· σὺ ⁿ τίς εἶ ᵒὃς
giver, who is able to save and to destroy: ³thou ¹who ²art that
κρίνεις‖ τὸν ᴾἕτερον‖·;
judgest the other?

13 Ἄγε νῦν οἱ λέγοντες, Σήμερον ᑫκαὶ‖ αὔριον ʳπορευ-
Go to now, ye who say, To-day and to-morrow we may
σώμεθα‖ εἰς τήνδε.τὴν.πόλιν, καὶ ˢποιήσωμεν‖ ἐκεῖ ἐνιαυτὸν
go into such a city · and may spend there ²year
ᵗἕνα‖ καὶ ᵛἐμπορευσώμεθα,‖ καὶ ʷκερδήσωμεν·‖ 14 οἵτινες οὐκ
¹one and may traffic, and may make gain, ye who ²not
ἐπίστασθε ˣτὸ‖ τῆς αὔριον· ποία.ʸγὰρ‖ ἡ.ζωὴ.ὑμῶν;
¹know what on the morrow [will be], (for what [is] your life?
ἀτμὶς ᶻγὰρ‖ ᵃἐστιν‖ ἡ πρὸς ὀλίγον φαινομένη, ἔπειτα
A vapour even it is, which for a little [while] appears, ²then
ᵇδὲ‖ ἀφανιζομένη· 15 ἀντὶ τοῦ λέγειν.ὑμᾶς, Ἐὰν ὁ κύριος
¹and disappears,) instead of your saying, If the Lord
θελήσῃ, καὶ ᶜζήσωμεν,‖ καὶ ᵈποιήσωμεν‖ τοῦτο ἢ ἐκεῖνο.
should will and we should live, also we may do this or that.
16 νῦν.δὲ καυχᾶσθε ἐν ταῖς.ᵉἀλαζονείαις‖.ὑμῶν· πᾶσα καύχη-
But now ye boast in your vauntings: all ²boasting
σις τοιαύτη πονηρά ἐστιν. 17 εἰδότι οὖν καλὸν ποιεῖν,
¹such evil is. To [him] knowing therefore good to do,
καὶ μὴ ποιοῦντι, ἁμαρτία αὐτῷ ἐστιν.
and not doing [it], sin to him it is.

5 Ἄγε νῦν οἱ.πλούσιοι, κλαύσατε ὀλολύζοντες ἐπὶ ταῖς
Go to now, [ye] rich, weep, howling over
ταλαιπωρίαις ὑμῶν ταῖς ἐπερχομέναις. 2 ὁ πλοῦτος
²miseries ¹your that [are] coming upon [you]. ²Riches
ὑμῶν σέσηπεν, καὶ τὰ.ἱμάτια.ὑμῶν σητόβρωτα γέγονεν·
¹your have rotted, and your garments moth-eaten have become.
3 ὁ.χρυσὸς.ὑμῶν καὶ ὁ ἄργυρος κατίωται, καὶ ὁ.ἰὸς.αὐτῶν
Your gold and silver has been eaten away, and their canker
εἰς μαρτύριον ὑμῖν ἔσται, καὶ φάγεται τὰς.σάρκας.ὑμῶν ὡς
for a testimony against you shall be, and shall eat your flesh as
πῦρ· ἐθησαυρίσατε ἐν ἐσχάταις ἡμέραις. 4 ἰδού, ὁ μισθὸς
fire. Ye treasured up in [the] last days. Lo, the hire

laughter be turned to mourning, and your joy to heaviness. 10 Humble yourselves in the sight of the Lord, and he shall lift you up.

11 Speak not evil one of another, brethren. He that speaketh evil of his brother, and judgeth his brother, speaketh evil of the law, and judgeth the law: but if thou judge the law, thou art not a doer of the law, but a judge. 12 There is one lawgiver, who is able to save and to destroy: who art thou that judgest another?

13 Go to now, ye that say, To day or to morrow we will go into such a city, and continue there a year, and buy and sell, and get gain: 14 whereas ye know not what shall be on the morrow. For what is your life? It is even a vapour, that appeareth for a little time, and then vanisheth away. 15 For that ye ought to say, If the Lord will, we shall live, and do this, or that. 16 But now ye rejoice in your boastings: all such rejoicing is evil. 17 Therefore to him that knoweth to do good, and doeth it not, to him it is sin.

V. Go to now, ye rich men, weep and howl for your miseries that shall come upon you. 2 Your riches are corrupted, and your garments are moth-eaten. 3 Your gold and silver is cankered; and the rust of them shall be a witness against you, and shall eat your flesh as it were fire. Ye have heaped treasure together for the last days. 4 Behold, the

---

ᵏ — τοῦ (*read* [the]) LTTrA.   ¹ ἢ or LTTrA.   ᵐ + καὶ κριτής and judge, GLTTrA.
ⁿ + δὲ but (who) GLTTrA.   ᵒ ὁ κρίνων LTTrA.   ᴾ πλησίον (*read* [thy] neighbour) LTTrA.
ᑫ ἢ or ELTTr.   ʳ πορευσόμεθα we will go ELTTrAW.   ˢ ποιήσομεν will spend ELTAW.
ᵗ — ἕνα (*read* a year) LTTr.   ᵛ ἐμπορευσόμεθα will traffic ELTTrAW.   ʷ κερδήσομεν will
make gain ELTTrAW.   ˣ τὰ L.   ʸ [γὰρ] Tr.   ᶻ — γάρ L.   ᵃ ἐστε ye are LTTrAW.
ᵇ καὶ LTTrA; — δὲ W.   ᶜ ζήσομεν we shall live LTTrAW.   ᵈ ποιήσομεν we shall do
ELTTrAW.   ᵉ ἀλαζονίαις T.

hire of the labourers
who have reaped down
your fields, which is
of you kept back by
fraud, crieth: and the
cries of them which
have reaped are en-
tered into the ears of
the Lord of sabaoth.
5 Ye have lived in
pleasure on the earth,
and been wanton; ye
have nourished your
hearts, as in a day of
slaughter. 6 Ye have
condemned *and* killed
the just; *and* he doth
not resist you.

7 Be patient there-
fore, brethren, unto
the coming of the Lord.
Behold, the husband-
man waiteth for the
precious fruit of the
earth, and hath long
patience for it, until
he receive the early
and latter rain. 8 Be
ye also patient; sta-
blish your hearts: for
the coming of the
Lord draweth nigh.
9 Grudge not one a-
gainst another, bre-
thren, lest ye be con-
demned: behold, the
judge standeth before
the door. 10 Take, my
brethren, the prophets,
who have spoken in
the name of the Lord,
for an example of suf-
fering affliction, and
of patience. 11 Be-
hold, we count them
happy which endure.
Ye have heard of the
patience of Job, and
have seen the end of
the Lord; that the
Lord is very pitiful,
and of tender mercy.
12 But above all things,
my brethren, swear
not, neither by hea-
ven, neither by the
earth, neither by any
other oath: but let
your yea be yea;
and *your* nay, nay;
lest ye fall into con-
demnation. 13 Is any
among you afflicted?
let him pray. Is any
merry? let him sing
psalms. 14 Is any sick
among you? let him
call for the elders of
the church; and let
them pray over him,
anointing him with
oil in the name of the

τῶν ἐργατῶν τῶν ἀμησάντων τὰς.χώρας.ὑμῶν, ὁ [f]ἀπεστερη-
of the workmen who harvested your fields, which has been
μένος[‖] ἀφ' ὑμῶν κράζει, καὶ αἱ βοαὶ τῶν θερισάντων εἰς
kept back by you, cries out, and the cries of those who reaped, into
τὰ ὦτα κυρίου Σαβαὼθ [g]εἰσεληλύθασιν.[‖] 5 ἐτρυφήσατε
the ears of [the] Lord of Hosts have entered. Ye lived in indulgence
ἐπὶ τῆς γῆς, καὶ ἐσπαταλήσατε. ἐθρέψατε τὰς.καρδίας.ὑμῶν
upon the earth, and lived in self-gratification; ye nourished your hearts
[h]ὡς[‖] ἐν ἡμέρᾳ σφαγῆς. 6 κατεδικάσατε, ἐφονεύσατε τὸν δί-
as in a day of slaughter; ye condemned, ye killed, the
καιον· οὐκ.ἀντιτάσσεται ὑμῖν.
just; he does not resist you.

7 Μακροθυμήσατε οὖν, ἀδελφοί, ἕως τῆς παρουσίας τοῦ
Be patient therefore, brethren, till the coming of the
κυρίου. ἰδού, ὁ γεωργὸς ἐκδέχεται τὸν τίμιον καρπὸν τῆς
Lord. Lo, the husbandman awaits the precious fruit of the
γῆς, μακροθυμῶν ἐπ' αὐτῷ ἕως [i]ἂν[‖] λάβῃ [j]ὑετὸν[‖] [k]πρώ-
earth, being patient for it until it receive [the] [4]rain [1]ear-
ϊμον[‖] καὶ ὄψιμον· 8 μακροθυμήσατε καὶ ὑμεῖς, στηρίξατε
ly [2]and [3]latter. Be patient also ye: establish
τὰς.καρδίας.ὑμῶν, ὅτι ἡ παρουσία τοῦ κυρίου ἤγγικεν.
your hearts, because the coming of the Lord has drawn near.
9 Μὴ.στενάζετε [l]κατ' ἀλλήλων, ἀδελφοί,[‖] ἵνα μὴ [m]κατακρι-
Groan not against one another, brethren, that [2]not [1]ye [3]be con-
θῆτε·[‖] ἰδού, [n] κριτὴς πρὸ τῶν θυρῶν ἕστηκεν. 10 Ὑπό-
demned. Lo, [the] judge before the door stands. [As] an ex-
δειγμα λάβετε [o]τῆς κακοπαθείας, ἀδελφοί.μου,[‖] καὶ τῆς
ample [5]take [1]of [2]suffering [3]evils, [7]my [8]brethren, [4]and
μακροθυμίας, τοὺς προφήτας οἳ ἐλάλησαν [p] τῷ ὀνόματι κυ-
[6]of [6]patience, the prophets who spoke in the name of [the]
ρίου. 11 ἰδού, μακαρίζομεν τοὺς [q]ὑπομένοντας.[‖] τὴν ὑπο-
Lord. Lo, we call blessed those who endure. The en-
μονὴν Ἰὼβ ἠκούσατε, καὶ τὸ τέλος κυρίου [r]εἴδετε,[‖] ὅτι
durance of Job ye have heard of, and the end of [the] Lord ye saw; that
πολύσπλαγχνός ἐστιν ὁ κύριος καὶ οἰκτίρμων. 12 Πρὸ
full of tender pity is the Lord and compassionate. [2]Before
πάντων δέ, ἀδελφοί.μου, μὴ.ὀμνύετε, μήτε τὸν οὐρανόν,
[3]all [4]things [1]but my brethren, swear not, neither [by] heaven,
μήτε τὴν γῆν, μήτε ἄλλον.τινὰ ὅρκον· ἤτω.δὲ ὑμῶν τὸ ναί,
nor the earth, nor any other oath; but let be of you the yea,
ναί, καὶ τὸ οὔ, οὔ· ἵνα μὴ [s]εἰς ὑπόκρισιν[‖] πέσητε. 13 κακο-
yea, and the nay, nay, that not into hypocrisy ye may fall. Does [4]suf-
παθεῖ τις ἐν ὑμῖν; προσευχέσθω· εὐθυμεῖ τις;
fer [5]hardships [1]anyone [2]among [3]you? let him pray: is [2]cheerful [1]anyone?
ψαλλέτω. 14 ἀσθενεῖ τις ἐν ὑμῖν; προσκαλεσάσθω
let him praise; is [2]sick [1]anyone among you? let him call to [him]
τοὺς πρεσβυτέρους τῆς ἐκκλησίας, καὶ προσευξάσθωσαν ἐπ'
the elders of the assembly, and let them pray over
αὐτόν, ἀλείψαντες [t]αὐτὸν[‖] ἐλαίῳ ἐν τῷ ὀνόματι [v]τοῦ[‖] κυρίου·
him, having anointed him with oil in the name of the Lord;

---

[f] ἀφυστερημένος TTr. [g] εἰσελήλυθαν LTTrAW. [h] — ὡς LTTrAW. [i] — ἂν TTrA.
[j] — ὑετὸν (*read* [rain]) LTTrA. [k] πρόϊμον TTr. [l] ἀδελφοί, κατ' ἀλλήλων LTrA. [m] κρι-
θῆτε [1]ye [2]be judged GLTTrAW. [n] + ὁ the GLTTrAW. [o] , ἀδελφοί μου, τῆς κακοπαθείας
(— μου my LTTrAW) GLTTrAW. [p] + ἐν in (the) LTTr. [q] ὑπομείναντας endured LTTrA.
[r] ἴδετε see ye A. [s] ὑπὸ κρίσιν under judgment EGLTTrAW. [t] — αὐτὸν (*read* [him]) T.
[v] — τοῦ (*read* of [the]) L[Tr]A.

15 καὶ ἡ εὐχὴ τῆς πίστεως σώσει τὸν κάμνοντα, καὶ ἐγε-
and the prayer · of faith shall save the exhausted one, and ⁵will
ρεῖ αὐτὸν ὁ κύριος· κἂν ἁμαρτίας ᾖ.πεποιηκώς,
⁶raise ⁷up ⁴him ¹the ²Lord; and if ⁷sins ¹he ²be[³one ⁴who] ⁵has ⁶committed,
ἀφεθήσεται αὐτῷ. 16 ἐξομολογεῖσθε ʷ ἀλλήλοις
it shall be forgiven him. Confess to one another [your]
ˣτὰ παραπτώματα,‖ καὶ ʸεὔχεσθε‖ ὑπὲρ ἀλλήλων, ὅπως ἰαθῆ-
offences, and pray for one another, that ye may be
τε. πολὺ ἰσχύει δέησις δικαίου ἐνεργουμένη.
healed. ⁹Much ⁸prevails [¹the] ³supplication ⁴of ⁵a ⁶righteous[⁷man] ²operative.
17 ᶻʹΗλίας‖ ἄνθρωπος ·ἦν ὁμοιοπαθὴς ἡμῖν, καὶ προσευχῇ
Elias ²a ³man ¹was of like feelings to us, and with prayer
προσηύξατο τοῦ μὴ βρέξαι· καὶ οὐκ.ἔβρεξεν ἐπὶ τῆς γῆς
he prayed [for it] not to rain; and it did not rain upon the earth
ἐνιαυτοὺς τρεῖς καὶ μῆνας ἕξ. 18 καὶ πάλιν προσηύξατο, καὶ
²years ¹three and ²months ³six; and again he prayed, and
ὁ οὐρανὸς ᵃὑετὸν ἔδωκεν,‖ καὶ ἡ γῆ ἐβλάστησεν τὸν
the heaven ²rain ¹gave, and the earth caused ³to ⁴sprout
καρπὸν αὐτῆς.
²fruit ¹its.

19. ʾΑδελφοί, ᵇ ἐάν τις ἐν ὑμῖν πλανηθῇ ἀπὸ τῆς ἀλη-
Brethren, if anyone among you err from the truth,
θείας, καὶ ἐπιστρέψῃ τις αὐτόν, 20 ᶜγινωσκέτω‖ ὅτι ὁ
and ²bring ³back ¹anyone him, let him know that he who
ἐπιστρέψας ἁμαρτωλὸν ἐκ πλάνης ὁδοῦ.αὐτοῦ, σώσει
brings back a sinner from [the] error of his way, shall save
ψυχὴν ᵈ ἐκ θανάτου, καὶ καλύψει πλῆθος ἁμαρτιῶν.
a soul from death, and shall cover a multitude of sins.
ᵉʾΙακώβου ἐπιστολή.‖
³Of ²James ¹epistle.